FACTS ABOUT
ALASKA

THE ALASKA ALMANAC®
16TH EDITION

FACTS ABOUT ALASKA

THE ALASKA ALMANAC®
16TH EDITION

Alaska Northwest Books™
Anchorage • Seattle

Sixteenth edition
Previously published as *The ALASKA ALMANAC®: Facts About Alaska*

ISBN 0-88240-249-8
ISSN 1051-5623
Key title: Facts About Alaska

From the editors of *The MILEPOST®, The ALASKA WILDERNESS MILEPOST®*
and *NORTHWEST MILEPOSTS®*

Compiled by Barbara Brynko
Edited by Carolyn Smith
Editorial Assistance by Fay L. Bartels
Designed by Cameron Mason
Illustrations by Val Paul Taylor and David Berger
Cover illustration by David Berger

Alaska Northwest Books™
A division of GTE Discovery Publications, Inc.
22026 20th Avenue S.E.
Bothell, Washington 98021

Contents

Miscellaneous Facts

Motto: "North to the Future."
State capital: Juneau.
Organized as a territory: 1912.
Entered the Union: Jan. 3, 1959; 49th state.
Number of boroughs: 14.
Governor: Walter J. Hickel.
Land area: 586,412 square miles, or about 365,000,000 acres—largest state in the union; one-fifth the size of the Lower 48.
State population: 570,000 from 1991 census.
Largest city in population: Anchorage, population 226,338 from 1990 census.
Largest city in area: Juneau with 3,108 square miles (also largest city in square miles in North America).
Typical Alaskan: According to 1990 census figures, 28.9 years old and male. This compares to 32.3 years for the United States. About 51 percent of Alaskans are male, the highest percentage of any state.
Average household income: $60,853, in 1989, fifth highest in the nation (latest available figures).
Per capita personal income: $21,932 in 1991, sixth highest in the nation.
Area per person: There are approximately 1.02 square miles for each person in Alaska. New York State has .003 square miles per person.
Highest/Lowest temperatures: Highest 100°F at Fort Yukon, 1915. Lowest −80°F at Prospect Creek Camp, 1971.
Heaviest annual snowfall: 974.5 inches at Thompson Pass

near Valdez, during the winter of 1952–53.
Tallest mountain: Mount McKinley, 20,320 feet.
Largest natural freshwater lake: Iliamna, 1,150 square miles.
Longest river: Yukon, 1,400 miles in Alaska; 1,875 total.
Largest glacier: Bering Glacier complex, 2,250 square miles, which includes the Bagley Icefield.
Oldest building: Erskine House in Kodiak, built by the Russians, probably between 1793 and 1796.
Farthest north supermarket: In Barrow; constructed on stilts to prevent snow build-up, at a cost of $4 million.
World's largest and busiest seaplane base: Lake Hood, in Anchorage, accommodating more than 800 takeoffs and landings on a peak summer day.
Largest state park in the nation: Wood–Tikchik State Park with 1.6 million acres of wilderness.
World's largest concentration of bald eagles: Along the Chilkat River, just north of Haines. More than 3,500 bald eagles gather here in fall and winter months for late salmon runs.
America's biggest earthquake: Occurred March 27, 1964, Good Friday. Measuring 8.6 on the Richter Scale (has since been revised upward to 9.2—the strongest ever recorded in North America), the earthquake devasted much of Southcentral Alaska.
Second greatest tide range in North America: 38.9 feet near Anchorage in Upper Cook Inlet.

Agriculture

Agriculture in Alaska ranges from backyard gardens to 2,000-acre barley farms. Volatile weather and a short growing season challenge cultivation in the state, but certain crops—notably potatoes and carrots—thrive in the cool soil temperatures. Overall, climatic conditions are not the greatest impediments to Alaska farming. More significant hurdles are the lack of access to major metropolitan markets, high production costs and competition from the Lower 48.

Alaska's commercial farming is concentrated in two major regions: the Matanuska Valley, northeast of Anchorage, which in 1991 contributed 61 percent of the state's farm market receipts; and the Tanana Valley, outside of Fairbanks, which was responsible for 32 percent.

An estimated 15 to 18 million acres in Alaska are believed to be arable, but only 1.4 million acres—less than one-half of 1 percent of the state—are currently considered land in farms. In 1991, crops covered 25,653 acres; the balance was in pasture or uncleared land.

Total of Alaska's agricultural products in 1991 were $26,620,000—$174,000 less than in 1990. Feed crops accounted for $2.47 million of the total; and vegetables, including potatoes, were $2.43 million of the total. The annual production of eggs remains unchanged from 1990 at 58,000, and the value of egg production was $86,000 in 1991.

Greenhouse and nursery industries—an ever-increasing portion of the state's agricultural picture—amounted to $15.3 million, or 57 percent of total receipts for 1991.

The annual milk production in 1991 totaled 13,300,000 pounds, a decrease of 3.5 million pounds from 1990. Dairy products brought in $2.58

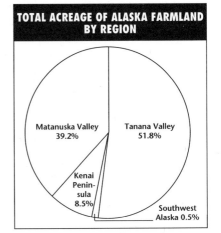

TOTAL ACREAGE OF ALASKA FARMLAND BY REGION

Matanuska Valley 39.2%

Tanana Valley 51.8%

Kenai Peninsula 8.5%

Southwest Alaska 0.5%

million in 1991, down from $3.25 million in 1990.

Almost 90 percent of the barley grown in 1991 was harvested in the Tanana Valley. Total production netted 250,000 bushels, yielding 50 bushels per acre. Production value for the 1991 barley crop was roughly $838,000, almost double the value of the 1990 crop of $455,000. Harvest of oats yielded 54 bushels per acre for a total of 59,400 bushels at an estimated value of $143,000. This reflects a sizable increase from 1990 with 23,700 bushels valued at $56,000.

Another agricultural enterprise showing continued success is the raising of reindeer. Officials estimate there are 16 herds in western Alaska, or a total population of approximately 37,000. Most of the reindeer are located on the Seward Peninsula and Nunivak Island, where they contribute heavily to the local economies. Among the byproducts of reindeer is the powder made from clipped antlers, much of which is exported to the Far East. Sales related to reindeer were valued at $2,168,000 in 1991, up $226,000 from 1990.

Products*	Acres Harvested	1991 Crop Value
Hay (19.5 tons)*	16,700	$3,413,000
Potatoes (140 cwt.)*	650	1,547,000
Vegetables (except potatoes)	248	883,000
Barley (250 bu.) (for grain)*	5,000	838,000
Silage (6.7 tons)*	1,700	320,000
Oats (54.9 bu.) (for grain)*	1,100	143,000

*Volume in thousands

9

Less encouraging is the state of dairy farming in Alaska. Economic stresses continue to reduce the number of farmers involved in this capital-intensive industry. In 1989, 1,500 cows produced nearly one million gallons of milk. By 1991, the number of cows decreased to 1,100, causing milk production to plummet. Fewer than 10 dairies are now operating in the state.

According to the state Division of Agriculture, the value and volume of the principal agricultural products in 1991 were quoted as shown on page 9.

The small vegetable gardens of the Russian fur traders are believed to constitute the first Alaskan agriculture. Gold rush days saw growing interest in local farming possibilities, but it wasn't until 1935 that there was a concerted effort to introduce commercial growing. President Franklin Roosevelt's New Deal resettlement plan transplanted 200 farm families from the Midwest to the Matanuska Valley, hoping to create a food source for the territory. Valley farmers still supply Anchorage and nearby military installations; dairy farming, including feed crops for cows, is the dominant income source. The growing season is 120 days, and there are up to 19 hours of sunlight in the summer (occasionally producing giant-sized vegetables).

The Tanana Valley growing season is shorter than that of the Matanuska Valley, consisting of 90 frost-free days. Because growing season temperatures are warmer in the Tanana Valley, many experts consider the area to have greater agricultural potential. Barley, oats and wheat are raised for grain and hay. Most Alaska-grown grain is used for domestic livestock feed. Almost all are spring varieties, since few winter types survive the cold.

Beef, hay, eggs and potatoes are produced on the Kenai Peninsula. Umnak and Unalaska islands provide grazing area for 2,000 sheep, down from 27,000 in 1970.

Across Alaska, the pressure of urban development is reducing the number of acres available for farming. At the same time, the state is attempting to increase the number of farms through sales of smaller tracts. Farming is also used by some individuals as a supplement to other income. In 1989, there were 600 farms with annual sales of $1,000 or more.

Since 1978, state land sales have placed more than 165,000 acres of potential agricultural land into private ownership. Most of this acreage is in the Delta Junction area, where tracts of up to 3,200 acres were sold by lottery for grain farming. The Nenana area is among those under consideration for future agricultural development.

More information is available from the Alaska Department of Natural Resources, Division of Agriculture, P.O. Box 949, Palmer 99645.

Air Travel

Alaska is the "flyingest" state in the Union; the only practical way to reach many areas of rural Alaska is by airplane. According to the Federal Aviation Administration, Alaska Region, by October 1991, there were close to 9,600 registered pilots, 1 out of every 58 Alaskans, and 9,408 registered aircraft, 1 for every 58 Alaskans. Alaska has approximately 6 times as many pilots per capita and 16 times as many airplanes per capita as the rest of the United States.

According to the FAA, Alaska has about 700 airports, including seaplane landing sites and heliports. That puts Alaska seventh, behind Texas, Illinois, California, Pennsylvania, Ohio and Florida, in the number of airports in the state. Of the seaplane bases, Lake Hood in Anchorage is the largest and busiest in the world. On a yearly basis, an average of 234 takeoffs and landings occur daily, and more than 800 on a peak

summer day. Merrill Field in Anchorage records more than 230,000 takeoffs and landings each year, making it one of the nation's busiest general aviation airports. Anchorage International Airport saw more than 4.5 million passengers pass through in 1991.

Flying in Alaska, as elsewhere, is not without its hazards. In 1991, there were 165 airplane accidents in which 36 persons lost their lives.

Pilots who wish to fly their own planes to Alaska should have the latest United States government flight information publication, *Alaska Supplement*, and a booklet titled *Flight Tips for Pilots in Alaska* available from the Federal Aviation Administration, 222 W. Seventh Ave., #14, Anchorage 99513-7587.

Scheduled passenger service is available to dozens of Alaskan communities (*see* Intrastate Service, this section). Contact the airlines for current schedules and fares.

Air taxi operators are found in most Alaskan communities, and aircraft can be chartered to fly you to a wilderness spot and pick you up later at a prearranged time and location. (Many charter services charge an hourly standby fee if the customer is not on time at the pickup point.) Most charter operators charge an hourly rate either per plane load or per passenger (sometimes with a minimum passenger requirement); others may charge on a per-mile basis. Flightseeing trips to area attractions are often available at a fixed price per passenger. Charter fares range from $140 to $175 per person (four-person and up minimum) for a short flightseeing trip, to $350 an hour for an eight-passenger Cessna 404 (multiengine planes are generally more expensive to charter than single-engine planes).

A wide range of aircraft is used for charter and scheduled passenger service in Alaska. The larger interstate airlines—Alaska, Continental, Northwest, United and Delta—use jets (Douglas DC-8, DC-10, Boeing 727, 737, 757, 767); Reeve Aleutian flies Electra and YS-11. MarkAir uses 737 and de Havilland Dash-7. Prop jets and single- or twin-engine prop planes on wheels, skis and floats are used for most intrastate travel. Here are a few of the types of aircraft flown in Alaska: DC-3, 19-passenger de Havilland Twin Otter, 10-passenger Britten-Norman Islander, 7-passenger Grumman Goose (amphibious), 5-passenger Cessna 185, 9-passenger twin-engine Piper Navajo Chieftain, 5- to 8-passenger de Havilland Beaver, 3- to 4-passenger Cessna 180, 5- to 6-passenger Cessna 206 and single-passenger Piper Super Cub.

INTERSTATE SERVICE

U.S. carriers providing interstate passenger service: Alaska Airlines, Continental Airlines, Delta Air Lines, MarkAir, Morris Air, Northwest Airlines, Reeve Aleutian Airways and United Airlines. These carriers also provide freight service between Anchorage and Seattle. Reeve Aleutian Airways provides freight and passenger service between Cold Bay and Seattle.

International carriers servicing Alaska through the Anchorage gateway: Aeroflot, AOM Minerve SA, British Airways, China Airlines, Iberia Airlines, Japan Airlines, KLM Royal Dutch Airlines, Korean Airlines, SAS Scandinavian Airlines and Swiss Air.

INTRASTATE SERVICE
From Anchorage

Alaska Airlines, 4750 International Road, Anchorage 99502. Serves Cordova, Fairbanks, Gustavus/Glacier Bay, Juneau, Ketchikan, Kotzebue, Nome, Petersburg, Prudhoe Bay, Sitka, Wrangell and Yakutat. Additional routes served on a contract basis by local carriers.

Alaska Island Air, P.O. Box 220374, Anchorage 99522. Serves Willow.

Delta Air Lines. Serves Fairbanks.

Era Aviation, 6160 S. Airpark Drive, Anchorage 99502. Serves Homer, Kenai and Valdez.

MarkAir, P.O. Box 196769, Anchorage 99519. Serves Aniak, Barrow, Bethel, Dillingham, Dutch Harbor, Fairbanks, Galena, King Salmon, Kodiak, St. Marys and Unalakleet, with connections into 17 other cities.

Peninsula Airways, 6231 Collins Way, Anchorage 99502. Serves Cold Bay, Dillingham, King Salmon and Kodiak.

Reeve Aleutian Airways, P.O. Box 559, Anchorage 99510. Serves the

Alaska Peninsula, Aleutian Islands and Pribilof Islands.

Ryan Air, 1205 E. International Airport Road, Suite 201, Anchorage 99518. Serves Bethel, Kotzebue, McGrath, Nome and many other bush communities in Alaska.

Southcentral Air, 135 Granite Point Court, Kenai 99611. Serves Homer, Kenai and Soldotna.

United Airlines. Serves Fairbanks.

Wilbur's Inc., 1740 E. Fifth Ave., Anchorage 99501. Serves Anchorage, Aniak, Cordova, Holy Cross, McGrath, Nikolai, Red Devil and Valdez.

From Barrow

Barrow Air, P.O. Box 184, Barrow 99723. Serves Atkasuk, Nuiqsut and Wainwright.

Cape Smythe Air, P.O. Box 549, Barrow 99723. Serves Brevig Mission, Elim, Golovin, Shishmaref, Teller, Wales and White Mountain.

From Fairbanks

Frontier Flying Service, 3820 University Ave., Fairbanks 99709. Serves Allakaket, Anaktuvuk Pass and Bettles.

Larry's Flying Service, P.O. Box 2348, Fairbanks 99707. Serves Denali National Park and Preserve (McKinley Park airstrip).

From Glennallen

Gulkana Air Service, P.O. Box 31, Glennallen 99588. Serves Anchorage.

From Gustavus

Glacier Bay Airways, P.O. Box 1, Gustavus 99826. Serves Excursion Inlet, Hoonah and Juneau.

From Haines

L.A.B. Flying Service, P.O. Box 272, Haines 99827. Serves Hoonah, Juneau and Skagway.

From Juneau

Wings of Alaska, 1873 Shell Simmons Drive, Suite 119, Juneau 99801. Serves Angoon, Elfin Cove, Gustavus/Glacier Bay, Haines, Hoonah, Kake, Pelican, Skagway and Tenakee.

From Kenai

Southcentral Air, 135 Granite Point Court, Kenai 99611. Serves Anchorage, Homer, Seward and Soldotna.

From Ketchikan

Ketchikan Air Service, P.O. Box 6900, Ketchikan 99901. Serves Stewart, British Columbia, and Hyder.

Temsco Airlines, P.O. Box 5057, Ketchikan 99901. Serves Craig, Hydaburg, Klawock, Metlakatla and other Southeast points.

From Nome

Bering Air Inc., P.O. Box 1650, Nome 99762. Serves Kotzebue and points in western Alaska.

From Tanana

Tanana Air Service, P.O. Box 60713, Fairbanks 99706. Serves Eagle, Fairbanks, Huslia, Manley Hot Springs, Nenana, New Minto and Rampart.

From Tok

40-Mile Air Ltd., P.O. Box 539, Tok 99780. Serves Boundary, Chicken, Delta Junction, Eagle, Fairbanks and Tetlin.

Related reading: *In the Shadows of Eagles,* by Rudy Billberg as told to Jim Rearden. An aviation pioneer shares his adventures of flying in the Last Frontier. *Heroes of the Horizon,* by Gerry Bruder. Profiles of daring bush pilots who flew during the "golden age" of Alaska aviation. *See* ALASKA NORTHWEST LIBRARY in the back of the book.

Alaska-Canada Boundary

In 1825, Russia, in possession of Alaska, and Great Britain, in possession of Canada, established the original boundary between Alaska and Canada. The demarcation was to begin at 54°40′ north latitude, just north of the mouth of Portland Canal, follow the canal to 56° north latitude, then traverse the mountain summits parallel to the coast as far as 141° west longitude. From there it would conform with that meridian north to the Arctic Ocean. The boundary line along the mountain summits in southeastern Alaska was never to be farther inland than 10 leagues—about 30 miles.

After purchasing Alaska, the United States found that the wording about the boundary line was interpreted differently by the Canadians. They felt the measurements should be made inland from the mouths of bays, while Americans argued the measurements should be made from the heads of the bays. In 1903, however, an international tribunal upheld the American interpretation of the treaty, providing Alaska the 1,538-mile-long border it has with Canada today. The southeastern Alaska border is 891 miles long, and 181 miles of that border is over water. If the Canadians had won their argument they would have had access to the sea, and Haines, Dyea and Skagway now would be in Canada.

The 20-foot-wide vista—a swath of land cleared 10 feet on each side of the boundary between southeastern Alaska, British Columbia and Yukon Territory—was surveyed and cleared between 1904 and 1914. Portions of the 710-mile-long boundary were again cleared in 1925, 1948, 1978 and 1982 by the International Boundary Commission. Monument and vista maintenance of 1978 and 1982 was conducted by the Canadian section of the commission and by the U.S. section in 1983, 1984 and 1985.

The Alaska–Canada border along the 141st meridian was surveyed and cleared between 1904 and 1920. Astronomical observations were made to find the meridian's intersection with the Yukon River, then, under the direction of the International Boundary Commission, engineers and surveyors of the U.S. Coast and Geodetic Survey and the Canadian Department of the Interior worked together north and south from the Yukon. The vista extends from Demarcation Point on the Arctic Ocean south to Mount St. Elias in the Wrangell Mountains (from there the border cuts east to encompass southeastern Alaska). This 647-mile stretch is one of the longest straight lines on record, varying less than 50 feet along its entire length.

Monuments are the actual markers of the boundary and are located so they tie in with survey networks of both the United States and Canada. Along the Alaska boundary most monuments are two-and-a-half-foot-high cones of aluminum-bronze set in concrete bases or occasionally cemented into rock. A large pair of concrete monuments with a pebbled finish mark major boundary road crossings. Because the boundary is not just a line but in fact a vertical plane dividing land and sky between the two nations, bronze plates mark tunnel and bridge crossings. Along the meridian, 191 monuments are placed, beginning 200 feet from the Arctic Ocean and ending at the south side of Logan Glacier.

Alaska Highway

(*See also* Highways)

This highway runs 1,520 miles through Canada and Alaska from Milepost 0 at Dawson Creek, British Columbia, through Yukon Territory to Fairbanks, Alaska. This well-traveled link between Alaska and the Lower 48 celebrated its 50th anniversary in 1992, with a year-long calendar of events and attractions. A special celebration, called Alaska Highway Rendezvous '92, hosted activities at local and international levels, including formal opening ceremonies on Feb. 16, 1992, at Dawson Creek, BC, and rededication of the highway in Solders Summit, YT, on Nov. 20, 1992. Tourism officials expected about 30,000 more visitors than usual to turn out for the events. For more information, contact: Great Alaska Highway Society, P.O. Box 74250, Fairbanks, AK 99707; Alaska Highway Rendezvous '92, #14, 9223 100 St., Fort St. John, BC V1J 3X3; Yukon Anniversaries Commission, Bag 1992, Whitehorse, YT Y1A 5L9.

History

The highway was built to relieve Alaska from the wartime hazards of shipping and to supply a land route for wartime equipment.

By agreement between the governments of Canada and the United States, the highway was built in eight months by the U.S. Army Corps of Engineers and was dedicated in November 1942. Crews worked south from Delta Junction, Alaska, north and south from Whitehorse, Yukon Territory, and north from Dawson Creek, British Columbia.

The building of the highway was recognized as one of the greatest engineering feats of the 20th century. Two major sections of the highway were connected on Sept. 23, 1942, at Contact Creek, Milepost 588.1, where the 35th Engineer Combat Regiment working west from Fort Nelson met the 340th Engineer General Service Regiment working east from Whitehorse. The last link in the highway was completed on November 20, when the 97th Engineer General Service Regiment, heading east from Tanacross, met the 18th Engineer Combat Regiment, coming northwest from Kluane Lake, at Milepost 1200.9. A ceremony commemorating the event was held at Soldiers Summit on Kluane Lake, and the first truck to negotiate the entire highway left that day from Soldiers Summit and arrived in Fairbanks the next day.

After WWII, the Alaska Highway was turned over to civilian contractors for widening and graveling, replacing log bridges with steel and rerouting at many points. Construction continues on the Alaska Highway today.

Road Conditions

The Alaska Highway is a two-lane road that winds and rolls across the wilderness. Some sections of road have no centerline, and some stretches of narrow road have little or no shoulder. The best driving advice on these sections is to take your time, drive with your headlights on at all times, keep to the right on hills and corners and drive defensively.

There are relatively few steep grades on the Alaska Highway. The most mountainous section of highway is between Fort Nelson and Watson Lake, where the highway crosses the Rocky Mountains.

Almost the entire length of the Alaska Highway is asphalt-surfaced, ranging from poor to excellent condition. Some rugged stretches exist with many chuckholes, gravel breaks, hardtop with loose gravel, deteriorated shoulders and bumps.

On the Alaska portion of the highway, watch for frost heaves. This rippling effect in the pavement is caused by the alternate freezing and thawing of the ground. Drive slowly in sections of frost heaves to avoid breaking an axle or trailer hitch.

Travelers should keep in mind that road conditions are subject to change. Be alert for bumps and holes in the road; some are signed or flagged, but many are not.

Watch for construction crews along the Alaska Highway. Extensive road construction may require a detour, or travelers may be delayed while waiting for a pilot car to guide them through the construction. Motorists may also encounter some muddy roadways at construction areas if there were heavy rains while the roadbed was torn up.

Dust and mud are generally not a problem anymore, except in construction areas and on a few stretches of the highway.

Don't drive too fast on gravel. Gravel acts just like many little ball bearings, and you could lose control of your vehicle. Driving fast on gravel is also hard on your tires, raises dust and throws rocks at oncoming cars. Heavy rain on a gravel road generally means mud. Considerable clay in the road surface means it is very slippery when wet.

Gas, food and lodging are found along the Alaska Highway on an average of every 20 to 50 miles. The longest stretch without services is about 100 miles. Not all businesses are open year-round, nor are most services available 24 hours a day. Regular, unleaded and diesel gasoline, and propane fuel are available along the highway. Both government campgrounds and commercial campgrounds are located along the Alaska Highway.

Preparation for Driving the Alaska Highway

Make sure your vehicle and tires are in good condition before starting out. An inexpensive and widely available item to include is clear plastic headlight covers to protect your headlights from flying rocks and gravel.

You might also consider a wire-mesh screen across the front of your vehicle to protect paint, grill and radiator from flying rocks. These may be purchased ready-made, or you may manufacture your own.

For those hauling trailers, a piece of 1/4-inch plywood fitted over the front of your trailer offers protection from rocks and gravel.

You'll find well-stocked auto shops in the North, but may wish to carry the following for emergencies: flares; first-aid kit; trailer bearings; good bumper jack with lug wrench; a simple set of tools, such as crescent wrenches, socket and/or open-end wrenches, hammer, screwdrivers, pliers, wire, pry bar; electrician's tape; small assortment of nuts and bolts; fan belt; one or two spare tires (two spares for traveling any remote road); and any parts for your vehicle that might not be available along the way. Include an extra few gallons of gas and also water, especially for remote roads. You may also wish to carry a can of fluid for brakes, power steering and automatic transmissions. You do not, however, want to overload your vehicle with too many spare parts.

Along the Alaska Highway, dust is at its worst during dry spells, following heavy rain (which disturbs the road surface), and in construction areas. If you encounter much dust, check your air filter frequently. To help keep dust out of your vehicle, try to keep air pressure in the car by closing all windows and turning on the fan. Filtered heating and air-conditioning ducts in a vehicle bring in much less dust than open windows or vents. Mosquito netting placed over the heater/fresh air intake and flow-through ventilation will also help eliminate dust.

Related reading: *Along the Alaska Highway,* photography by Alissa Crandall, text by Gloria J. Maschmeyer. Stunning color photographs and engaging text reveal the people and landscape of this epic highway. *See* ALASKA NORTHWEST LIBRARY in the back of the book.

Alcoholic Beverages

The legal age for possession, purchase and consumption of alcoholic beverages is 21 in Alaska.

Any business that serves or distributes alcoholic beverages must be licensed by the state. The number of different types of licenses issued is limited by the population in a geographic area. Generally one license of each type may be issued for each 3,000 persons or fraction thereof. Licensed premises include bars, some restaurants and clubs. Packaged liquor, beer and wine are sold by licensed package stores. Recreational site licenses, caterer's permits and special events permits allow the holder of a permit or license to sell at special events, and allow nonprofit fraternal, civic or patriotic organizations to serve beer and wine at certain activities.

State law allows liquor outlets to operate from 8 A.M. to 5 A.M., but provides that local governments can impose tighter restrictions.

Local governments may also ban the sale of or otherwise restrict alcoholic beverages. Barrow, Bethel, Kotzebue, Huslia, Iliamna and Nondalton have banned the sale of alcoholic beverages. Communities that have banned possession and/or the sale and importation of alcoholic beverages (knowingly bringing, sending or transporting alcoholic beverages into the community) are:

Akiak	Mekoryuk
Alakanuk	Minto
Allakaket	Mountain Village
Ambler	Napakiak
Anaktuvuk Pass	Napaskiak
Angoon	Newtok
Atka	Noatak
Atmautluak	Noorvik
Birch Creek	Nuiqsut
Brevig Mission	Nunapitchuk
Buckland	Pilot Station
Chalkyitsik	Platinum
Chefornak	Point Hope
Chevak	Point Lay
Deering	Quinhagak
Diomede	Russian Mission
Eek	St. Marys
Elim	St. Michael
Emmonak	Savoonga
Gambell	Scammon Bay
Golovin	Selawik
Goodnews Bay	Shaktoolik
Hooper Bay	Sheldon Point
Kaktovik	Shishmaref
Kasigluk	Shungnak
Kiana	Stebbins
Kipnuk	Stevens Village
Kivalina	Tanacross
Kobuk	Tatitlek
Kokhanok	Teller
Kongiganak	Tetlin
Kotlik	Togiak
Koyuk	Toksook Bay
Kwethluk	Tuluksak
Kwigillingok	Tuntutuliak
Lower Kalskag	Tununak
Manokotak	Wainwright
Marshall	Wales

Alyeska

Pronounced Al-YES-ka, this Aleut word means "the great land" and was one of the original names of Alaska. Mount Alyeska, a 3,939-foot peak in the Chugach Mountains, is the site of the state's largest ski resort.

Amphibians

In Alaska, there are three species of salamander, two species of frog and one species of toad. In the salamander order, there are the rough-skinned newt, long-toed salamander and northwestern salamander. In the frog and toad order, there are the boreal toad, wood frog and spotted frog. The northern limit of each species may be the latitude at which the larvae fail to complete their development in one summer. While some species of salamander can overwinter as larvae in temperate southeastern Alaska, the shallow ponds of central Alaska freeze solid during the winter. All but the wood frog, *Rana sylvatica,* which with its shortened larval period is found widespread throughout the state and north of the Brooks Range, are found primarily in southeastern Alaska.

Antiquities Laws

State and federal laws prohibit excavation or removal of historic and prehistoric cultural materials without a permit. Nearly all 50 states have historic preservation laws; Alaska's extends even to tidal lands, thereby making it illegal to pick up artifacts on the beach.

It sometimes is difficult to distinguish between historic sites and abandoned property. Old gold-mining towns and cabins, plus areas such as the Chilkoot and Iditarod trails, should always be considered historic sites or private property. Also, cabins that appear to be abandoned may in fact be seasonally used trapping cabins where the structure and possessions are vital to the owner.

Alaska law prohibits the disturbance of fossils, including prehistoric animals such as mammoths.

Archaeology

(*See also* Bering Land Bridge)

Alaska has a long and rich archaeological history. The first human migrants to North and South America some 20,000 to 12,000 years ago came first to Alaska, crossing over the now-submerged ice age Bering Land Bridge that connected Siberia to Alaska.

The oldest archaeological materials that demonstrate human occupation of

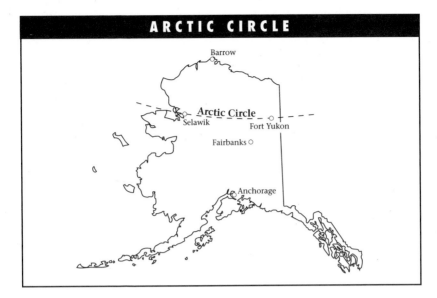

Alaska come from Trail Creeks Cave north of Nome, where a 15,000-year-old cracked bison leg bone and bone point were found. Better evidence can be found for human occupation from 11,000 years ago. Small hunting tools have been found throughout Alaska, except Prince William Sound, probably belonging to nomadic hunting and gathering peoples. The archaeological record becomes more complicated about 4,000 years ago, and reveals cultural patterns characteristic of Alaska Native groups at the time of contact with the white man.

There is still much to discover about Alaska's prehistory. Many archaeological sites are small, representing the camps of wandering hunters and gatherers; some sites, especially along the coast where rich natural resources allowed people to become more sedentary and established, are large and deep. Where permafrost occurs, preservation of even the most perishable organic materials offers a wealth of information on life in the past. While no exact count has been made, there are several thousand known archaeological sites in the state.

Archaeological excavations, or digs, are almost always confined to the summer months. The University of Alaska in both Fairbanks and

Anchorage frequently sponsors digs, as do several state and federal agencies. Recent excavations have taken place near Unalaska, Tok, Kodiak, Fairbanks and on the Kenai Peninsula.

Volunteers and visitors are frequently welcome, but check first with the anthropology departments at the University of Alaska for active sites and more information.

One of Alaska's archaeological treasures, "Blue Babe," a 36,000-year-old fully preserved Pleistocene bison, was discovered in 1979 in the permafrost near Fairbanks during a mining operation. "Blue Babe" is on display at the Alaska Museum in Fairbanks.

Arctic Circle

The Arctic Circle is the latitude at which the sun does not set for one day at summer solstice and does not rise for one day at winter solstice. The latitude, which varies slightly from year to year, is approximately 66°34′ north from the equator and circumscribes the northern frigid zone.

A solstice occurs when the sun is at its greatest distance from the celestial equator. On the day of summer solstice, June 20 or 21, the sun does not set at the Arctic Circle and because of refraction of sunlight, it appears not to set for four days. Farther north, at Barrow (the northernmost community in the United States), the sun does not set from May 10 to August 2.

At winter solstice, December 21 or 22, the sun does not rise for one day at the Arctic Circle. At Barrow, it does not rise for 67 days.

Arctic Winter Games

The Arctic Winter Games are a biennial event held in mid-March for northern athletes from Alaska, northern Alberta, Yukon Territory and Northwest Territories. The first games were held in 1970 in Yellowknife, NWT, and have since been held in Fairbanks and Whitehorse, YT. The 1994 games will take place March 6–13, in Slane Lake, Alberta. Alaska will host the games in 1996.

In 1992, 53 athletes from Russia and about 40 athletes from Greenland participated in the games. Speed skating and a speed skating-skiing-snowshoeing triathlon were dropped from the games, and dog mushing and Arctic Sports (Dene and Inuit) Games were added. Other competition includes badminton, cross-country skiing, curling, figure skating, basketball, broomball, gymnastics, silhouette shooting, ski biathlon, snowshoeing and volleyball. Participation by people of all ages is encouraged.

Aurora Borealis

The Phenomenon

The aurora borealis is produced by charged electrons and protons striking gas particles in the earth's upper atmosphere. The electrons and protons are released through sunspot activity on the sun and emanate into space. A few drift the one- to two-day course to Earth, where they are pulled to the most northern and southern latitudes by the planet's magnetic forces.

The color of the aurora borealis varies, depending on how hard the gas particles are being struck. Auroras can range from simple arcs to draperylike forms in green, red, blue and purple.

The lights occur in a pattern rather than as a solid glow, because electric current sheets flowing through gases create V-shaped potential double layers. Electrons near the center of the current sheet move faster, hit the atmosphere harder and cause the different intensities of light observed in the aurora.

Displays take place as low as 40 miles above the Earth's surface, but usually begin about 68 miles above and extend hundreds of miles into space. They concentrate in two bands roughly centered above the Arctic Circle and Antarctic Circle (the latter known as aurora australis) that are about 2,500 miles in diameter. In northern latitudes the greatest occurrence of auroral displays is in the spring and fall months, owing to the tilt of the planet in relationship to the sun's plane, but displays may occur on dark nights throughout the winter. If sunspot activity is particularly intense and the denser-than-usual solar wind heads to Earth, the resulting auroras can be so great that they cover all but the tropical latitudes. However, the cycle of sunspot activity is such that it will be many years before the numerous, brilliant displays of the late 1950s are regularly seen again.

Some observers claim that the northern lights make a noise similar to the rustle of taffeta, but scientists say the displays cannot be heard in the audible frequency range.

Residents of Fairbanks, which is located on the 65th parallel, see the aurora borealis an average of 240 nights a year.

Photographing the Aurora Borealis

To capture the northern lights on film, you will need a sturdy tripod, a locking-type cable release (some 35mm cameras have both *time* and *bulb* settings, but most have *bulb only,* which

f-stop	ASA 200	ASA 400
f1.2	3 sec.	2 sec.
f1.4	5	3
f1.8	7	4
f2	20	10
f2.8	40	20
f3.5	60	30

calls for use of the locking-type cable release) and a camera with an f/3.5 lens (or faster).

It is best to photograph the lights on a night when they are not moving too rapidly. And, as a general rule, photos improve if you manage to include recognizable subjects in the foreground—trees and lighted cabins being favorites of many photographers. Set your camera up at least 75 feet back from the foreground objects to make sure that both the foreground and aurora are in sharp focus.

Normal and wide-angle lenses are best. Try to keep your exposures under a minute—a 10- to 30-second exposure is generally best. The lens openings and exposure times are only a starting point, since the amount of light generated by the aurora is inconsistent. (For best results, bracket widely.)

Ektachrome 200 and 400 color film can be push-processed in the home darkroom or by some custom-color labs, allowing use of higher ASA ratings (800, 1200 or even 1600 on the 400 ASA film, for example). Kodak will push-process film if you include an ESP-1 envelope with your standard film-processing mailer. (Consult your local camera store for details.)

A few notes of caution: Protect the camera from low temperatures until you are ready to make your exposures. Some newer cameras, in particular, have electrically controlled shutters that will not function properly at low temperatures. Wind the film slowly to reduce the possibility of static electricity, which can lead to streaks on the film. Grounding the camera when rewinding can help prevent the static-electricity problem. (To ground the camera, hold it against a water pipe, drain pipe, metal fence post or other grounded object.) Follow the basic rules and experiment with exposures.

The first photographs to show the aurora borealis in its entirety were published in early 1982. These historic photographs were taken from satellite-mounted cameras specially adapted to filter unwanted light from the sunlit portion of the earth, which is a million times brighter than the aurora. From space, the aurora has the appearance of a nearly perfect circle.

Baleen

(*See also* Baskets *and* Whales and Whaling)

Baleen lines the mouths of baleen whales in long, fringed, bonelike strips. It strains out small fish and plankton, and the tiny, shrimplike creatures called krill from the water. Humpback whales are the largest of the baleen whales, having a coarse baleen similar in thickness to human fingernails. The inside edges of the baleen plates end in coarse bristles that are similar in appearance to matted goat hair. The color of the plates varies from gray to almost black and the bristles from white to grayish white. The number of plates in an adult humpback mouth varies from 600 to 800 (300 to 400 per side); the roof of the mouth is empty of plates. The bowhead whale has 600 plates, the longest of any whale species—some reach 12 feet or more in length. The sei whale has finely textured baleen, and the minkes are the smallest of the baleen whales. Other baleen whales are the right, blue, fin and gray. Baleen was once used for corset stays and buggy whips. It is no longer of significant commercial use, although Alaska Natives use brownish black bowhead baleen to make fine baskets and model ships to sell.

Barabara

Pronounced buh-rah-buh-ruh, this traditional Aleut or Eskimo shelter is built of sod supported by driftwood or whalebone.

Baseball

There are seven teams playing baseball in Alaska, making up two leagues. The Alaska Baseball League consists of the Fairbanks Goldpanners, Anchorage Bucs, Hawaiian Island Movers and Mendocino Blue Jays. The Alaska Central Baseball League includes the Anchorage Glacier Pilots, Mat–Su Miners and Kenai Peninsula Oilers.

Baseball season opens in June and runs through the end of July. Each team plays a round-robin schedule with the other Alaska teams, in addition to scheduling games with visiting Lower 48 teams. In 1991, the Anchorage Bucs celebrated a three-peat by winning the Hawaiian International Tournament. Competition was tough and included teams from Seoul, Korea, and Toyko, Japan. The highlight of the 1991 season, however, was the visit by the U.S. Olympic team. The Bucs hosted TEAM USA in a two-game series. The Bucs won the second game in the series, only the second time an amateur team has defeated TEAM USA. *Baseball Weekly* called it "an unprecedented win."

The 1992 season also included the second annual Miller Lite Invitational Tournament scheduled July 7–11. The Russian team from Moscow was hosted by the Bucs for a three-game series at the end of July.

The caliber of play in Alaska is some of the best nationwide at the amateur level. Since 1968, Alaska teams have won 10 National Baseball Congress championships, and are a great draw when they travel outside the state. Major league scouts rate Alaska baseball at A to AA, visiting each season to check out the talent for possible recruitment.

Alaska league teams are comprised primarily of college players, including both walk-on and recruited players.

Since 1969, Alaska baseball has sent more than 150 players on to careers in major league baseball. However, any college senior drafted by a major league team cannot play in the Alaska league.

The list of those now playing in the major leagues who were once in Alaskan teams is impressive, and includes such stars as Tom Seaver, Chris Chambliss, and Dave Winfield. In 1992, Bobby Jones, one of the Anchorage Bucs 1990 season pitchers, was drafted by the New York Mets.

Baskets

(*See also* Baleen *and* Native Arts and Crafts)

Native basketry varies greatly according to materials locally available. Athabascan Indians of the Interior, for example, weave baskets from willow root gathered in late spring. The roots are steamed and roasted over a fire to loosen the outer bark. Weavers then separate the bark into fine strips by pulling the roots through their teeth.

Eskimo grass baskets are made in river delta areas of southwestern Alaska from Bristol Bay north to Norton Sound and from Nunivak Island east to interior Eskimo river villages. The weavers use very fine grass harvested in fall. A coil basketry technique is followed, using coils from one-eighth to three-fourths inch wide. Seal gut, traditionally dyed with berries (today with commercial dyes), is often interwoven into the baskets.

Baleen, a glossy, hard material that hangs in slats from the upper jaw of some types of whales, is also used for baskets. Baleen basketry originated

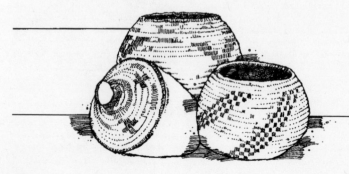

about 1905 when Charles D. Brower, trader for a whaling company at Point Barrow, suggested, after the decline of the whalebone (baleen) industry for women's corsets, that local Eskimos make the baskets as a source of income. The baskets were not produced in any number until 1916. The weave and shape of the baskets were copied from the split-willow Athabascan baskets acquired in trade. Men, rather than women, became the basket makers. Later, baleen baskets were also made in Point Hope and Wainwright.

Most birch-bark baskets are made by Athabascan Indians, although a few Eskimos also produce them. Commonly, they are shaped as simple cylinders and are held together with root bindings. Sometimes the birch bark is cut into thin strips and woven into diamond or checkerboard patterns. Birch bark is usually collected in spring and early summer; large pieces free of knots are preferred. Birch-bark baskets traditionally were used as cooking vessels; food was placed in them and hot stones added. Birch-bark baby carriers also are still made.

Among the finest of Alaskan baskets are the tiny, intricately woven Aleut baskets made of rye grass, which in the Aleutians is abundant, pliable and very tough. The three main styles of Aleut baskets—Attu, Atka and Unalaska—are named after the islands where the styles originated. Although the small baskets are the best known, Aleuts also traditionally made large, coarsely woven baskets for utilitarian purposes.

Tlingit, Haida and Tsimshian Indians make baskets of spruce roots and cedar bark. South of Frederick Sound, basket material usually consists of strands split from the inner bark of red cedar. To the north of the sound, spruce roots are used. Maidenhair ferns are sometimes interwoven into spruce root baskets in a technique that looks like embroidery. A large spruce root basket may take months to complete.

Examples of Alaska Native basketry may be viewed in many museums within the state, including the University of Alaska Museum, Fairbanks; the Anchorage Museum of History and Art, Anchorage; the Sheldon Jackson Museum, Sitka; and the Alaska State Museum, Juneau.

Prices for Native baskets vary greatly. A fine-weave, coiled beach grass basket may cost from $60 to $450; birch-bark baskets, which look like trays, may range from $30 to $100; willow root trays may cost $800; finely woven Aleut baskets may cost $200 to $600; cedar-bark baskets may range from $30 to $80; and baleen baskets range in price from $450 to more than $1,100 for medium-sized baskets. These prices are approximate and are based on the weave, material used, size, and decoration added, such as beadwork or ivory.

Beadwork

(*See also* Native Arts and Crafts)

Eskimo and Indian women create a variety of handsomely beaded items. Before contact with Europeans, Indian women sometimes carved beads of willow wood or made them from seeds of certain shrubs and trees. Glass seed beads became available to Alaskan Athabascan Indians in the mid-nineteenth century, although some types of larger trade beads were in use earlier. Beads quickly became a coveted trade item. The *Cornaline d'aleppo,* an opaque red bead with a white center, and the faceted Russian blue beads were among the most popular types.

The introduction of small glass beads sparked changes in beadwork style and design. More colors were available, and the smaller, more easily maneuvered beads made it possible to work out delicate floral patterns impossible with larger trade beads.

Historically, beads were sewn directly onto leather garments or other items with the overlay stitch. Contemporary beadwork is often done on a separate piece of felt that is not visible once the beads are stitched in place.

Alaskan Athabascan beadworkers sometimes use paper patterns, often combining several motifs and tracing their outline on the surface to be worked. The most common designs include flowers, leaves and berries, some in very stylized form. Many patterns are drawn simply from the sewer's environment. Recently, magazines, graphic art, advertising, and patriotic motifs have inspired Athabascan beadworkers, although stylized floral designs are still the most popular.

Designs vary regionally, as do the ways in which they are applied to garments or footgear. Women from some areas do beadwork so distinctive it can be recognized at a glance.

Bears

(*See also* Mammals)

Three species of bear inhabit Alaska: the black, the brown/grizzly and the polar bear. Most of Alaska can be considered bear country, and for those wishing to spend time in Alaska's great outdoors, bear country becomes "beware" country. It's good to remember that sows are extremely aggressive if their young are around and bear behavior should always be considered unpredictable. The Alaska Department of Fish and Game publishes *The Bears and You,* recommended reading for hikers and campers. The pamphlet is available from Fish and Game offices and government information centers.

Black Bears. Black bears are usually jet black or brown with a brown-yellow muzzle, and weigh from 100 to 200 pounds as adults. The brown color phase can sometimes be confused with grizzlies, but black bears are generally smaller and lack the grizzly's distinct shoulder hump. Black bear habitat covers three-fourths of Alaska, with high concentrations found in Southeast, Prince William Sound, and in the coastal mountains and lowlands of southcentral Alaska. Low to moderate densities are found in interior and western Alaska. Their range coincides with that of semi-open forests, and though carnivorous, their diet consists mainly of vegetation due to the difficulty of getting meat or fish. Black bears often spend their lives within five miles of their birthplace and will frequently return to their home range if transplanted. They easily climb trees, with both cubs and adults using trees as a place of escape. Cubs are generally born in late January or February weighing 8 to 10 ounces, and while average litter size is two cubs, three or four is not unusual. Black bears den up in winter for up to six months, but are not true hibernators. Their body temperature remains high, and they awaken easily—even in midwinter.

Brown/Grizzly Bears. Brown/grizzly bear fur color varies from blond to black with shades of brown and gray in between. As adults, they can weigh over 1,000 pounds, but are usually smaller; size depends on sex, age, time of year and geographic location. Coastal bears, referred to as "browns" or "brownies," are the largest living carnivorous land mammals in the world and grow larger than Interior "grizzlies." Habitat for browns or grizzlies is most of Alaska, with the exception of islands in the extreme southeastern part of the state. The lowest populations are found in the northern Interior and the Arctic. Their range is wherever food is abundant, but they prefer open tundra and grasslands. Diet consists of a wide variety of plants and animals, including their own kind, and humans under some circumstances. In their realm, grizzlies are king and fear no other animal except man with a firearm. While attacks on humans are the exception, when they occur the results are tragic. These bears are also tremendously strong and have been seen carrying—off the ground—an 800-pound moose. One to two hairless cubs are usually born in late January or February weighing 8 to 10 ounces, and sows have been known to adopt orphaned cubs. Time of year and duration of denning varies with the location and physical condition of the bear, and can be up to six months of the year. Dens are frequently on hillsides or on mountain slopes.

Polar Bears. The only areas on a polar bear not covered with heavy, white fur are its eyes and large, black nose. The bears, seemingly aware that their noses give them away to prey, will hold a paw up to hide it when hunting. An adult polar bear weighs 1,500 pounds or more and has a long neck with a proportionately small head. Their habitat is the Canadian–eastern Alaska Arctic and the western Alaska–eastern Soviet Union, the latter being home to the world's largest polar bears. Their range is

wherever the arctic ice cap floes, and they are more numerous toward the southern edge of the ice pack. Occasionally they will come ashore, but generally stay near the coast. While ashore they eat some vegetation, but their diet consists primarily of ringed seal, walrus, stranded whales, birds and fish. Cannibalism of cubs and young bears by older males is not unusual. Polar bears are natural swimmers, and reports exist of swimming bears seen 50 miles from the nearest land or ice. When swimming, they use their front paws for propulsion and trail their rear paws. Mother bears have been seen with a cub hanging onto their tail getting a tow through the water. Cubs are born in December with two being the common litter size. They weigh about a pound at birth and remain with their mother for about 28 months. Usually only pregnant sows den up, for an average of six months in the winter. Polar bears need stable, cold areas for denning, and dens in Alaska have been found 30 miles inland, along the coast, on offshore islands, on shorefast ice and on drifting sea ice.

Related reading: *The Great Bear: Contemporary Writings on the Grizzly,* edited by John A. Murray. *More Alaska Bear Tales,* by Larry Kaniut. *Grizzly Cub: Five Years in the Life of a Bear,* by Rick McIntyre. *See* ALASKA NORTHWEST LIBRARY in the back of the book.

Bering Land Bridge

The Bering Land Bridge, which joined eastern Siberia and western Alaska, is thought by most archaeologists to be the route by which the New World came to be occupied between 40,000 and 15,000 years ago. The land bridge rose as the formation of massive glaciers during the ice ages caused the sea levels to fall, creating an arctic grassland up to 900 miles wide called Beringia. Early migrants crossed Beringia in pursuit of prey such as the woolly mammoth and mastadon. While the two continents were connected, plants, animals and man migrated into Alaska, and probably down ice-free corridors to populate other parts of the western hemisphere. Even after the glaciers melted and the sea level rose, many of the indigenous peoples on both sides of the Bering Strait remained united by family ties, common traditions and common environments, and into this century used skin boats to cross the 55 miles of ocean separating the two continents.

Recognizing the need to preserve the unique archaeological record, both discovered and undiscovered, that the area holds, the National Park Service created Bering Land Bridge National Preserve. Located just below the Arctic Circle on the Seward Peninsula, the 2.8-million-acre preserve features ecological, geological, anthropological and historical processes rather than places. The low profile of the preserve's landscape gives a sense of unobstructed vastness and exposure to the elements.

The Soviet Union also plans to establish a park or preserve on the Chukotka Peninsula west of the Bering Strait. At the June 1990 summit conference, Presidents Gorbachev and Bush endorsed a Beringian Heritage International Park, leading the way for joint research, conservation and management of the region's unique resources.

Berries

Wild berries abound in Alaska with the circumboreal lingonberry/lowbush cranberry (*Vaccinium vitis-idaea*) being the most widespread. Blueberries of one species or another grow in most of the state. Some 50 other

Lingonberry/Lowbush Cranberry, *Vaccinium vitis-idaea* (Reprinted from *Alaska Wild Berry Guide and Cookbook*)

species of wild fruit are found in Alaska, including strawberries, raspberries, cloudberries, salmonberries, crowberries, nagoonberries and crabapples. Highbush cranberries (which are not really cranberries) can be found on bushes even in the dead of winter, and the frozen berries provide a refreshing treat to the hiker.

The fruit of the wild rose, or rose hip, is not strictly a berry but is an ideal source of vitamin C for bush dweller and city resident alike. A few hips will provide as much of the vitamin as a medium-sized orange. The farther north the hips are found, the richer they are in vitamin C.

Alaska does have one poisonous berry, the baneberry. Sometimes called doll's eyes or chinaberries, baneberries are extremely bitter to the taste. As few as six berries can induce violent symptoms of poisoning in an adult.

Related reading: *Alaska Wild Berry Guide and Cookbook*. Where to find the berries, what they are, how to recognize them, and the best recipes for cooking berries. *See* ALASKA NORTHWEST LIBRARY in the back of the book.

Billiken

This smiling ivory figure with a pointed head, though long a popular Northland souvenir, is not an Eskimo invention. The billiken was patented in 1908 by Florence Pretz of Kansas City. A small, seated, Buddhalike figure, the original billiken was manufactured by the Billiken Company of Chicago and sold as a good luck charm. Thousands of these figurines were sold during the 1909 Alaska–Yukon–Pacific Exposition in Seattle. Billikens vanished soon

afterward from most Lower 48 shops; however, someone had brought them to Nome, and the Eskimos of King Island, Little Diomede and Wales began carving ivory replicas of the billikins.

Billikens are still being made elsewhere in the world in such materials as wood, concrete and glass.

A popular notion contends that rubbing a billiken's tummy brings good fortune.

Birds

Authorities at the Anchorage Audubon Society acknowledge 430 bird species in Alaska. If unsubstantiated sightings are included, the species total increases.

Thousands of ducks, geese and swans come north to breeding grounds each spring. Millions of seabirds congregate in nesting colonies on exposed cliffs along Alaska's coastline, particularly on the Aleutian Islands, and on islands in the Bering Sea.

Migratory birds reach Alaska from many corners of the world. Arctic terns travel up to 22,000 miles on their round trip each year from Antarctica. Others come from South America, the South Pacific islands and Asia.

Each May one of the world's largest concentrations of shorebirds funnels through the Copper River Delta near Cordova. Waterfowl such as trumpeter swans and the world's entire flock of dusky Canada geese breed there.

Other key waterfowl habitats include the Yukon–Kuskokwim Delta, Yukon Flats, Innoko Flats and Minto Lakes. During migration, huge flocks gather at Egegik, Port Heiden, Port Moller, Izembek Bay, Chickaloon Flats, Susitna Flats and Stikine Flats.

Raptors, led by the bald eagle, range throughout the state. The largest gathering of eagles in the world takes place in Alaska every winter between October and February. In 1972, the Chilkat Bald Eagle Preserve was set aside to protect the 3,500 eagles that assemble at the site along the Chilkat River near Haines.

Alaska has three subspecies of peregrine falcon: Arctic, American and Peale's. Arctic and American peregrine falcons join the Eskimo curlew, Aleutian Canada goose and short-tailed albatross on the endangered or threatened species list for the state. The Steller's eider and the spectacled eider are now being considered as additions to the endangered or threatened species list by the U.S. Fish and Wildlife Service.

Following is a list of some geographically restricted birds whose origins are in Siberia or Asia, as well as a few of the state's more well-known species:

Aleutian Tern—Breeds in coastal areas, marshes, islands, lagoons, rivers and inshore marine waters. Nests only in Alaska on ground in matted, dry grass. Casual sightings in southeastern Alaska in spring and summer, and in northern Alaska in summer.

Arctic Tern—Breeds in tidal flats, beaches, glacial moraines, rivers, lakes and marshes. Nests in colonies or scattered pairs on sand, gravel, moss or in rocks. The arctic tern winters in Antarctica, bypassing the Lower 48 in its 20,000-mile round-trip migration. Common sightings in southeastern, southcoastal and western Alaska in spring, summer and fall, and in southwestern Alaska in spring and fall.

Arctic Warbler—Found in willow thickets. Nests on the ground in grass or moss in willow thickets. Common sightings in the Alaska Range, the Seward Peninsula and the Brooks Range in spring, summer and fall.

Bald Eagle—Found in coniferous forests, deciduous woodlands, rivers and streams, beaches and tidal flats, rocky shores and reefs. Nests in old-growth timber along the coast and larger mainland rivers. In treeless areas, nests on cliffs or on the ground. There are more bald eagles in Alaska than in all the other states combined, and common sightings occur in southeastern, southcoastal and southwestern Alaska year-round.

Bluethroat—Nests on the ground in shrub thickets in the uplands and the foothills of western and northern Alaska. Casual sightings in southwestern Alaska in spring and fall.

Emperor Goose—Nests near water in grassy marsh habitat on islands, banks or in large tussocks. The bulk of the world's population nests in the Yukon–Kuskokwim Delta, with a few others nesting farther north to Kotzebue Sound and a few more in eastern Siberia. Rarely is an Emperor Goose seen east or south of Kodiak. Common sightings in southwestern Alaska in spring, fall and winter, and in western Alaska in spring, summer and fall.

Horned Puffin—Nests on sea islands in rock crevices or in burrows among boulders, on sea cliffs and on grassy slopes. Breeds inshore, in marine waters and on islands. Common sightings in southwestern and western Alaska in spring, summer and fall.

Pacific Loon—Breeds in coniferous forests or in lakes on tundra, and nests on projecting points or small islands. Folklore credits the loon with magical powers, and several legends abound. Common sightings in southeastern and southcentral Alaska in spring, fall and winter, and in southwestern, central, western and northern Alaska in spring, summer and fall.

Red-faced Cormorant—Habitat includes inshore marine waters. Nests in colonies on ledges of sea cliffs, small piles of rocks and shelves on volcanic cinder cones. In North America this bird appears only in Alaska. Common sightings in southcoastal and southwestern Alaska year-round.

Red-legged Kittiwake—Breeds in the Pribilof Islands, and on Buldir and Bogoslof islands in the Aleutians. Nests on cliff ledges and cliff points. Common sightings near breeding areas in southwestern Alaska in summer.

White Wagtail—Found in open areas with short vegetation usually along the Seward Peninsula coast. Nests near or on the ground in crevices or niches in old buildings. Casual sightings in central Alaska in spring, and in southwestern Alaska in spring and summer.

Yellow Wagtail—Habitat is willow thickets on the tundra. Nests on open tundra under grass or overhanging banks. Common sightings in western Alaska in spring, summer and fall.

About 10 million swans, geese and ducks also nest in Alaska each year, making the state "critical" habitat for North America's waterfowl. In North America some species and subspecies use Alaska as their exclusive nesting grounds, while over half the North American population of other species nests in the state.

Five chapters of the National Audubon Society are based in Alaska: the Anchorage Audubon Society, Inc. (P.O. Box 101161, Anchorage 99510), the Juneau Audubon Society (P.O. Box 021725, Juneau 99802), the Arctic Audubon Society (P.O. Box 82098, Fairbanks 99708), the Kenai Audubon Society (P.O. Box 3371, Soldotna 99669) and the Kodiak Audubon Society (Box 1756, Kodiak 99615). In addition to trying to help people increase their knowledge of birds, the groups (except for Fairbanks) coordinate over 20 annual Christmas bird counts around the state. The Fairbanks Bird Club (P.O. Box 81791, Fairbanks 99708) conducts the annual Christmas count for that area.

Related reading: *Guide to the Birds of Alaska*. Revised Edition, by Robert H. Armstrong. Detailed information on all 437 species of birds found in Alaska. Fully illustrated with color photos, and drawings by wildlife artist John C.

Pitcher. *See* ALASKA NORTHWEST LIBRARY in the back of the book.

Blanket Toss

As effective as a trampoline, the blanket toss (or *nalukataq*) features a walrus hide blanket grasped by a number of people in a circle. They toss a person on the blanket as high as possible for as long as that person can remain upright. Every true Eskimo festival and many non-Native occasions

include the blanket toss, which was originally used to allow Eskimo hunters to spot game, such as walrus and seal, in the distance. Depending on the skill of the person being tossed and the number of tossers, a medium-weight person might typically go 20 feet in the air.

Boating

Travel by boat is an important means of transportation in Alaska, where highways cover only about one-third of the state. Until the advent of the airplane, boats were often the only way to reach many parts of Alaska. Most of Alaska's supplies still arrive by water and in Southeast—where precipitous terrain and numerous islands make road building impossible—water travel is essential. (*See also* Cruises *and* Ferries)

According to the U.S. Coast Guard, there are 44,488 vessels registered in Alaska. Of these, approximately 3,258 are longer than 30 feet (many are commercial fishing vessels) and 16,219 are longer than 20 feet.

Moorage

To accommodate the needs of this fleet, there are approximately 8,000 slips available at public small-boat harbors in Alaska. According to the state, actual service capacity is somewhat greater because of the transient nature of many boats and certain management practices allowing "double parking." There are also harbors at various remote locations; no services other than moorage are provided at these harbors.

Local governments have the major responsibility for operating public floats, grids, docks, launching ramps and associated small-boat harbor facilities throughout the coastal areas of the state. Moorage facilities constructed by the state are intended for boats up to a maximum of 100 feet, with a limited number of facilities for larger vessels where large boats are common. With the exception of Ketchikan, Sitka, Homer and Juneau, there are no private marine facilities.

Recreational Boating

Recreational boating opportunities in Alaska are too numerous and varied to list here; Alaska has thousands of miles of lakes, rivers and sheltered seaways. For information about boating within national forests, parks, monuments, preserves and wildlife refuges, contact the appropriate federal agency. For travel by boat in southeastern Alaska's Inside Passage and the sheltered seaways of southcentral Alaska's Prince William Sound—or elsewhere in Alaska's coastal waters—NOAA nautical charts, pilot guides and tidal current tables are available. (*See also* Information Sources)

Sea kayakers from around the world are drawn to Alaska to paddle its sheltered waterways and challenge its open coast. Kayakers in Alaska can visit tidewater glaciers and natural hot springs, meeting whales and sea otters along the way.

Inland boaters will find hundreds of river and lake systems suitable for traveling by boat, raft, kayak or canoe. Canoe routes have been established on the Kenai Peninsula (contact Kenai National Wildlife Refuge, 2139 Ski Hill Road, Soldotna 99669); in Nancy Lake State Recreation Area (contact Superintendent, Mat–Su District, HC32, Box 6706, Wasilla 99687); and on rivers in the Fairbanks and Anchorage areas (contact Bureau of Land Management, 1150 University Ave., Fairbanks 99709 and 222 W. Seventh Ave., #13, Anchorage 99513). Travel by water in Alaska requires extra caution. Weather changes rapidly and is often unpredictable; it's important to be prepared for the worst. Alaska waters, even in midsummer, are cold. A person falling overboard may become immobilized by the cold water in only a few minutes. And since many of Alaska's water routes are far from civilization, help may be a long way off.

Persons inexperienced in traveling Alaska's waterways might consider hiring a charter boat operator or outfitter. Guides offer local knowledge and provide all necessary equipment. The Division of Tourism (Pouch E, Juneau 99811) maintains current lists of such services. Recreation information on both state and federal lands is available at the three Alaska Public Lands Information Centers: 605 W. Fourth Ave., Suite 105, Anchorage 99501; 250 Cushman St., Suite 1A, Fairbanks 99701; and P.O. Box 359, Tok 99780.

Bore Tide

(*See also* Tides)

A bore tide is a steep, foaming wall of water formed by a flood tide surging into a constricted inlet. In Cook Inlet, where maximum tidal range approaches 40 feet, incoming tides are further compressed in Knik and Turnagain arms and tidal bores may sometimes be seen. Though one- to two-foot-high bores are more common, spring tides in Turnagain Arm may produce bore tides up to six feet high, running at speeds of up to 10 knots, and even higher bores have been reported when unusually high tides come in against a strong southeast wind. Good spots to view bore tides in Turnagain Arm are along the Seward Highway, between 26 and 37 miles south of Anchorage; they can be expected to arrive there approximately 2 hours and 15 minutes later than the tide book prediction for low tide at Anchorage.

Breakup

(*See also* Nenana Ice Classic)

Breakup occurs when melting snows raise the level of ice-covered streams and rivers sufficiently to cause the ice to break apart and float downstream. Breakup is one of two factors determining the open-water season for river navigation, the second being the depth of the river. Peak water conditions occur just after breakup.

The navigable season for the Kuskokwim and Yukon rivers is June 1 through September 30; the Nushagak

River, June 1 through August 31; and the Noatak River, late May through mid-June.

Breakup is a spectacular sight-and-sound show. Massive pieces of ice crunch and pound against each other as they push their way downriver racing for the sea, creating noises not unlike many huge engines straining and grating. The spine-tingling sound can be heard for miles. It marks the finale of winter and the arrival of spring in Alaska.

Sometimes great ice jams occur, causing the water to back up and flood inhabited areas. This natural phenomenon occurred at Fort Yukon in spring 1982 and at McGrath in 1990.

Bunny Boots

Bunny boots, also called vapor barrier boots, are large, insulated rubber boots that protect feet from frostbite. Black bunny boots are generally rated to –20°F, while the more common white bunny boots are even warmer and used in the most extreme conditions, including the heights of Mount McKinley. (The cumbersome boots are adequate for easy climbing but unsuitable for technical mountain climbing.) Prices for bunny boots range from about $50 for used boots to about $175 for new ones.

Bus Lines

Scheduled bus service is available in summer to and within Alaska, although buses don't run as frequently as in the Lower 48. (Local transit service is also available in some major communities.) Services may be infrequent; consult current schedules.

Alaska–Denali Transit, P.O. Box 4557, Anchorage 99510. Provides service between Anchorage, Talkeetna, Denali National Park, Fairbanks, Tok, Haines, Kenai and Homer.

Alaska Intercity Tours, 700 W. Sixth Ave., Anchorage 99501. Provides service between Mount McKinley, Kenai Peninsula, Valdez and Fairbanks.

Alaska Sightseeing Tours, 543 W. Fourth Ave., Anchorage 99501. Provides service between Anchorage, Denali

National Park, Columbia Glacier, Fairbanks, Golden Circle, Haines and Valdez.

Alaska–Yukon Motorcoaches, 543 W. Fourth Ave., Anchorage 99501. Provides service between Anchorage, Haines/Skagway, Valdez, Denali National Park and Preserve, and Fairbanks.

Alaskon Express, 300 Elliott Ave. W., Seattle, WA 98119. Provides service between Anchorage, Fairbanks, Haines, Skagway and Whitehorse.

Atlas Tours Ltd., P.O. Box 4340, Whitehorse, YT, Canada Y1A 3T5. Provides service between Whitehorse and Skagway.

Caribou Express Bus, 501 L St., Anchorage 99501. Provides service between Anchorage, Denali National Park, Fairbanks, Tok Junction, Alyeska, Portage Glacier, Homer and Seward.

Denali Express, 405 L St., Anchorage 99501. Provides service between Anchorage, Denali and Fairbanks.

Eagle Custom Tours, 329 F St., Anchorage 99501. Provides service between Anchorage, Portage Glacier, the Matanuska Valley, Mount McKinley, Seward and Talkeetna.

Gray Line of Alaska, 745 W. Fourth Ave., Anchorage 99501. Provides local city sightseeing tours, travel between Anchorage, Fairbanks, Denali National Park, Dawson, Prudhoe Bay, Skagway and Whitehorse.

Norline Coaches (Yukon) Ltd., 2191 Second Ave., Whitehorse, YT, Canada Y1A 4T8. Provides service between Whitehorse and Tok via Dawson City and Fairbanks.

Princess Tours, 519 W. Fourth Ave., Anchorage 99501. Provides sightseeing excursions and tours throughout Alaska.

Seward Bus Lines, P.O. Box 1338, Seward 99664. Provides service between Anchorage and Seward.

Valdez/Anchorage Bus Lines, P.O. Box 101388, Anchorage 99510. Provides service between Valdez and Anchorage via Glennallen.

Westours Motorcoaches, 547 W. Fourth Ave., Anchorage 99501. Provides service throughout Alaska and the Yukon.

White Pass and Yukon Motorcoaches, 300 Elliott Ave. W., Seattle, WA 98119. Provides service between Skagway, Haines, Valdez, Glennallen, Whitehorse and Anchorage.

Bush

Originally used to describe large expanses of wilderness beyond the fringes of civilization, inhabited only by trappers and miners, "bush" has come to stand for any part of Alaska not accessible by road. A community accessible only by air, water, sled or snow machine is considered a bush village, and anyone living there is someone from the bush.

The bush is home to most of Alaska's Native people and to many individuals who live on homesteads, operate mines or work as guides, pilots, trappers or fishermen.

The term "bush" has been adapted to the small planes and their pilots who service areas lacking roads. Bush planes are commonly equipped with floats and skis to match terrain and season. For their oftentimes courageous air service, bush pilots have become the modern frontier hero.

Related reading: *The ALASKA WILDERNESS MILEPOST*®. A complete guide to 250 remote towns and villages. *Skystruck: True Tales of an Alaskan Bush Pilot,* by Herman Lerdahl with Cliff Cernick. *See* ALASKA NORTHWEST LIBRARY in the back of book.

Cabin Fever

Cabin fever is a state of mind blamed on cold, dark winter weather when people are often housebound. It is characterized by depression, preoccupation, discontent and occasionally violence and has been described as "a 12-foot stare in a 10-foot room." Cabin fever is commonly thought to afflict miners and trappers spending a lonely winter in the wilderness, but, in truth, these people are active and outdoors enough to remain content. It is more likely to strike the snowbound or disabled. The arrival of spring or a change of scene usually relieves the symptoms.

Related reading: *Winter Watch,* by James Ramsey. For 266 days, the author tested himself against an Arctic winter in a remote cabin in the Brooks Range. *See* ALASKA NORTHWEST LIBRARY in the back of the book.

Cabins

(*See also* National Forests *and* State Park System)

Rustic cabins in remote Alaskan places can be rented from the Forest Service, the Bureau of Land Management (BLM), the Alaska State Parks and the Fish and Wildlife Service. The modest price ($15 to $25 per night per cabin) makes this one of the best vacation bargains in Alaska. It offers visitors a chance to try living "in the bush."

Almost 200 Forest Service cabins are scattered through the Tongass and Chugach national forests in southeast and southcentral Alaska. Some are located on salt water; others on freshwater rivers, streams or lakes. Some of the cabins can be reached by boat or trail, but because of the remote locations, visitors frequently come by chartered aircraft.

The average cabin is 12 by 14 feet and is usually equipped with a table, an oil or wood stove and wooden bunks without mattresses. Most will accommodate a group of four to six. There is no electricity. Outhouses are down the trail a little way. Visitors need to bring their own food, bedding, cooking utensils and (usually) stove fuel. In addition, it's advisable to have a gas or propane stove for cooking, a lantern and insect repellent. Splitting mauls are provided on site for cutting firewood.

Reservations may be made in person or by mail. Payment must accompany the reservation. Permits for use are issued on a first-come, first-served basis, up to 179 days in advance. Length of stay for some cabins is limited.

For reservations and information on **Chugach National Forest** cabins, contact: Alaska Public Lands Information Center (APLIC), 605 W. Fourth Ave., Anchorage 99501; phone (907) 271-2737.

For reservations and information on **Tongass National Forest** cabins, contact: USDA Forest Service Information Center, 101 Egan Drive, Juneau 99801.

The **Forest Service** recommends that visitors contact the Information Center and request a copy of the Recreation Cabins booklet. It's a good idea to do this at least six months before the date of desired occupancy. The booklet contains the applications for cabin use plus tips on planning a stay.

The **Bureau of Land Management** has eight public-use cabins in the White Mountains National Recreation area east of Fairbanks. These are used primarily by winter recreationists. Cabins must be reserved prior to use and a fee is required. Contact the Fairbanks Support Center Public Room, 1150 University Ave., Fairbanks 99709, phone (907) 474-2250.

The **U.S. Fish and Wildlife Service** maintains public-use cabins within Kodiak National Wildlife Refuge. Contact the Refuge Manager, 1390 Buskin River Road, Kodiak 99615.

The **Alaska Division of Parks and Outdoor Recreation** maintains 21 public-use cabins throughout the state. For reservations and information contact the following regional offices: *Southcentral,* P.O. Box 107001, Anchorage 99510-7001, phone (907) 762-2617; *Southeast,* 400 Willoughby Center, Juneau 99801, phone (907) 465-4563; *Northern Region,* 3700 Airport Way, Fairbanks 99709, phone (907) 451-2695; and *Kodiak State Park,* SR Box 3800, Kodiak 99615, phone (907) 486-6339.

Cache

Pronounced *cash,* this small storage unit is built to be inaccessible to

marauding animals. A cache resembles a miniature log cabin mounted on stilts. It is reached by a ladder that bears, dogs, foxes and other hungry or curious animals can't climb. Extra precautions include wrapping tin around the poles to prevent climbing by clawed animals and extending the floor a few feet in all directions from the top of the poles to discourage those clever enough to get that high.

Squirrels are the most notorious of Alaska's cache-marauding critters. To be truly animal-proof, a cache should be built in a clearing well beyond the 30-foot leaping distance a squirrel can manage from a treetop.

Bush residents use the cache as a primitive food freezer in winter. A cache may also contain extra fuel and bedding. Size is determined by need. Sometimes a cache will be built between three or four straight trees growing close together.

Calendar of Events

JANUARY

Anchorage—Nastar Ski Races, Alyeska Ski Resort; Sled Dog Races; Hatcher Cup Series, Hatcher Pass Lodge; All Alaska Juried Art Show. *Anchor Point*—Snow Rondi Fest. *Bethel*—Sled Dog Races. *Fairbanks*—Ski Joring and Sled Dog Races. *Haines*—Snow Machine Rally; Dalton Trail 30 Sled Dog Race. *Homer*—Snow Machine Races. *Juneau*—Rainier Downhill Challenge

Cup; Alascom Ski Challenge; State legislature convenes. *Kodiak*—Russian Orthodox Starring Ceremony; Russian Orthodox Masquerade Ball. *Seward*—Polar Bear Jump-off. *Sitka*—Russian Christmas and Starring; Alaska Airlines Basketball Tournament. *Soldotna*—Winter Games; Sled Dog Races. *Willow*—Winter Carnival.

FEBRUARY

Anchorage—Fur Rendezvous; Iron Dog Iditarod; Sled Dog Races; Northern Lights Women's Invitational; Ice Carving Competition; World Masters Cross Country Ski Championships. *Big Lake*—Winter Carnival. *Cordova*—Iceworm Festival. *Fairbanks*—Ski Joring and Sled Dog Races; Festival of Native Arts; Yukon Quest Sled Dog Race. *Homer*—Winter Carnival. *Juneau*—Taku Rendezvous; Alascom Divisional Championships. *Ketchikan*—Festival of the North. *Knik*—Iditabike; Iditaski Nordic Ski Race. *Nenana*—Ice Classic Tripod Raising Festival. *Nome*—Dexter Creek Sled Dog Race; Heart Throb Biathlon; Gold Rush Classic Snow Machine Race. *Palmer*—Sled Dog Races. *Petersburg*—Devil's Thumb Days Festival. *Sitka*—Basketball Tournament. *Soldotna*—Winter Games; Ski Joring; Sled Dog Races. *Tok*—Sled Dog Races. *Valdez*—Winter Carnival; Ice Climbing Festival. *Wasilla*—Iditarod Days. *Whitehorse*—Sourdough Rendezvous; Yukon Quest Sled Dog Race. *Wrangell*—Tent City Days.

MARCH

Anchorage—Iditarod Sled Dog Race begins; Native Youth Olympics. *Chatanika*—Chatanika Days. *Fairbanks*—Arctic Winter Games; Festival of Native Arts; Winter Carnival; Ice Festival; Sled Dog Races; Athabascan

Old-Time Fiddling Festival. *Juneau*—Sourdough Pro/Am Ski Race; Southeast Championships; Rainier Downhill Challenge Cup. *Kodiak*—Pillar Mountain Golf Classic; Comfish Alaska. *Nome*—Ice Golf Classic on the Bering Sea; Month of Iditarod; Sled Dog Races; Snow Machine Race; Dog Weight Pull; Basketball Tournament. *North Pole*—Winter Carnival. *Skagway*—Windfest Winter Festival; Buckwheat Ski Classic. *Tok*—Race of Champions Sled Dog Race. *Valdez*—Winter Carnival. *Wasilla*—Iditarod Days.

APRIL

Anchorage—Alyeska Spring Carnival; Native Youth Olympics. *Barrow*—Spring Festival. *Cordova*—Copper Day Celebrations. *Fairbanks*—Curling Bonspiel. *Juneau*—Folk Festival; Ski to Sea Race. *Kotzebue*—Arctic Circle Sunshine Festival. *Unalaska*—Tanner Crab Roundup Festival. *Valdez*—World Extreme Ski Championships. *Whittier*—Crab Festival.

MAY

Delta Junction—Buffalo Wallow Square Dance Jamboree. *Homer*—Halibut Derby. *Juneau*—Jazz and Classics Festival; Ski to Sea Relay Race. *Kodiak*—Crab Festival and Fishing Derby; Chad Ogden Ultramarathon. *Nome*—Annual Polar Bear Swim in the Bering Sea; Firemen's Ball. *Palmer*—Colony Days. *Petersburg*—Little Norway Festival; Salmon Derby. *Savoonga*—Walrus Festival, St. Lawrence Island. *Seldovia*—Fishing Derby. *Seward*—Exit Glacier Run. *Sitka*—Salmon Derby. *Talkeetna*—Miners' Day Festival. *Valdez*—Salmon Derby. *Whittier*—Prince William Sound Regatta of Ships.

JUNE

Anchorage—Renaissance Faire; Tent

City Festival; Mayor's Midnight Sun Marathon; Basically Bach Festival; Festival of Music. *Barrow*—Nalukataq Whaling Festival. *Fairbanks*—Tanana River Raft Classic; Yukon 800 Marathon River Boat Race; Midnight Sun Run; Midnight Sun Baseball Game; Air Show. *Homer*—Halibut Derby. *Kodiak*—Freedom Days. *Nenana*—River Daze. *Nome*—Midnight Sun Softball Tournament, Festival and Raft Race; ARCO–Jesse Owens Games. *Palmer*—Colony Days. *Sitka*—Salmon Derby; All Alaska Logging Championships; Writer's Symposium; Summer Music Festival. *Skagway*—Summer Solstice. *Valdez*—Halibut Derby; Whitewater Weekend. *Whitehorse*—Dog Show.

JULY

Fourth of July celebrations take place in most towns and villages. *Anchorage*—Freedom Days Festival; Tent City Festival; Bluegrass and Folk Festival. *Big Lake*—Regatta Water Festival; Fishing Derby. *Chugiak*—Bear Paw Festival. *Dawson City*—Yukon Gold Panning Championship. *Delta Junction*—Softball Tournament. *Fairbanks*—World Eskimo-Indian Olympics; Renaissance Faire; Golden Days; Summer Arts Festival. *Homer*—Halibut Derby. *Hope*—EMS 5-K Run and Crafts Bazaar. *Kodiak*—Freedom Days. *Kotzebue*—Northwest Native Trade Fair. *Nome*—Anvil Mountain Run. *North Pole*—Summer Festival. *Seward*—Mount Marathon Race; Softball Tournaments; Halibut Tournament; Silver Salmon Derby. *Sitka*—Fourth of July Celebration (four days). *Skagway*—Soapy Smith's Wake. *Soldotna*—Progress Days. *Talkeetna*—Salmon Derby; Moose Dropping Festival. *Valdez*—Pink Salmon Derby; Gold Rush Days. *Wasilla*—Water Festival. *Wrangell*—Logging Show.

AUGUST

Anchorage—Air Show. *Anchor Point*—Salmon Derby. *Cordova*—Silver Salmon Derby. *Dawson City*—Discovery Days. *Eagle River*—Alaskan Scottish Highland Games. *Fairbanks*—Tanana Valley Fair; Iditafoot Race; Summer Arts Festival. *Haines*—Southeast Alaska State Fair. *Juneau*—Golden North Salmon Derby. *Ketchikan*—Alaska Seafest;

Silver Salmon Derby; Blueberry Festival. **Kodiak**—*Cry of the Wild Ram* (outdoor historical pageant); Rodeo and State Fair; Pilgrimage to St. Herman's Monks Lagoon. **Ninilchik**—Kenai Peninsula State Fair. **Palmer**—Alaska State Fair. **Seward**—Silver Salmon Derby; Tok Run; Softball Tournament. **Skagway**—Dyea Dash. **Talkeetna**—Bluegrass Festival. **Tanana**—Valley Fair. **Unalaska**—Pink Salmon Derby. **Valdez**—Gold Rush Days; Silver Salmon Derby. **Wrangell**—Coho Derby. **Yukon**—Fireweed Festival.

SEPTEMBER

Anchorage—Oktoberfest; UAA Crafts Fair. **Cordova**—Salmon Derby. **Dillingham**—Fall Fair. **Fairbanks**—Tanana–Rampart Labor Day Race; Equinox Marathon. **Kenai**—Silver Salmon Derby. **Ketchikan**—Salmon Derby. **Kodiak**—Silver Salmon Derby; State Fair and Rodeo. **Nome**—Great Bathtub Race. **Petersburg**—Salmon Derby. **Skagway**—Klondike Trail of '98 Road Relay. **Valdez**—Silver Salmon Derby. **Whittier**—Silver Salmon Derby. **Wrangell**—Silver Salmon Derby.

OCTOBER

Anchorage—Quiana Alaska. **Fairbanks**—Oktoberfest. **Haines**—Alaska Day Fest. **Petersburg**—October Arts Festival. **Sitka**—Alaska Day Festival.

NOVEMBER

Anchorage—Great Alaska Shootout; Symphony of Trees. **Delta Junction**—Winter Carnival. **Fairbanks**—Northern Invitational Curling Spiel; Athabascan Old-Time Fiddling Festival; Sled Dog Races. **Juneau**—Public Market. **Kenai**—Christmas Comes to Kenai Celebration. **Ketchikan**—Christmas Festival of Lights; Singing in the Rain Festival.

DECEMBER

Anchorage—Seawolf Hockey Classic; Christmas Tree Lighting Ceremony. **Barrow**—Christmas Festival. **Cordova**—North Country Faire. **Fairbanks**—Ski Joring and Sled Dog Races. **Ketchikan**—Festival of Lights. **Nome**—Firemen's Carnival. **North Pole**—Candle Lighting Ceremony. **Palmer**—Colony Christmas. **Sitka**—Christmas Boat Parade. **Talkeetna**—Christmas Lighting; Bachelor Society Ball and Wilderness Women Contest. **Whittier**—Animals' Christmas.

Camping

(*See also* Cabins; Hiking; National Forests; National Parks, Preserves and Monuments; National Wildlife Refuges; *and* State Park System)

Numerous public and privately operated campgrounds are found along Alaska's highways. Electrical hookups and dump stations are scarce. The dump station at Russian River campground is available for Chugach National Forest visitors. Alaska's backcountry offers virtually limitless possibilities for wilderness camping. Get permission before camping on private land. If the land is publicly owned, it's worthwhile to contact the agency that manages the land regarding regulations and hiking/camping conditions.

Additional details about camping are found in *The MILEPOST®* and *The ALASKA WILDERNESS MILEPOST®*. See ALASKA NORTHWEST LIBRARY at the back of the book.

The U.S. Forest Service (Alaska Regional Office, U.S. Forest Service, P.O. Box 21628-RN, Juneau 99802) maintains 25 campgrounds in the Tongass and Chugach national forests, most with tent and trailer sites and minimum facilities. All campgrounds are available on a first-come, first-served basis, and stays are limited to 14 days.

Campground fees vary, from $5 to $8 per night depending upon facilities, which can include firegrates, pit toilets, garbage pickup, picnic tables and water. Most campgrounds are open from Memorial Day through Labor Day, or until snow conditions cause closing.

The National Park Service (Alaska Regional Office, 2525 Gambell St., Anchorage 99503) at Denali National Park offers one walk-in campground and six campgrounds accessible by road; most are available on a first-come, first-served basis. All of them require a $12 fee per night. Most campsite permits and shuttle bus coupons are issued at the Visitor Access Center located at the entrance to Denali National Park. These are issued in person, up to two days in advance. Allow two to three days during peak season (late June through August) to obtain campground permits or bus coupons.

The Alaska Public Lands Information Centers in Fairbanks and Anchorage reserve a limited number of campground permits and shuttle bus coupons for Denali. Reservations must be made in person; no reservations will be accepted by telephone. Campground reservations can be made 7 to 21 days in advance; shuttle bus reservations can be made 1 to 21 days in advance. All fees are collected in advance when making reservations, and there are no refunds.

Situated near the park entrance and open year-round are Riley Creek, for tents and trailers, and Morino, for walk-in tent campers. The other campgrounds are open between May and September, depending on weather. Brochures may be obtained from Denali National Park, P.O. Box 9, Denali Park 99755.

Glacier Bay and Katmai national parks each offer one campground for walk-in campers, and Katmai now requires reservations. Backcountry camping is permitted in Denali, Glacier Bay, Katmai and Klondike Gold Rush parks, as well as other national parks and monuments.

Alaska Division of Parks (P.O. Box 107001, Anchorage 99510) maintains the most extensive system of roadside campgrounds and waysides in Alaska.

All are available on a first-come, first-served basis. Fees are charged and a yearly pass is offered.

U.S. Fish and Wildlife Service (State Office, 1011 E. Tudor, Anchorage 99503) has several wildlife refuges open to campers, although most are not accessible by highway. The Kenai National Wildlife Refuge, P.O. Box 2139, Soldotna 99669, however, has several campgrounds accessible from the Sterling Highway linking Homer and Anchorage.

The Bureau of Land Management (222 W. Seventh Ave., #13, Anchorage 99513) maintains 10 campgrounds in interior Alaska; these campgrounds are free. Brochures describing BLM campgrounds are also available.

The Alaska Public Lands Information Centers provide information on all state and federal campgrounds in Alaska, along with state and national park passes and details on wilderness camping. Visit or contact one of the following centers: 605 W. Fourth Ave., Anchorage 99501; P.O. Box 359, Tok 99780; 250 Cushman, Suite 1A, Fairbanks 99701.

Chambers of Commerce

(See also Convention and Visitors Bureaus and Information Centers)

Alaska State Chamber, 217 Second St., Suite 201, Juneau 99801; phone (907) 586-2323; 415 E St., Suite 201, Anchorage 99501; phone (907) 278-2722.

Anchorage Chamber, 437 E St., Suite 300, Anchorage 99501; phone (907) 272-2401.

City of Barrow, P.O. Box 629, Barrow 99723; phone (907) 852-5222.

Bethel Chamber, P.O. Box 329, Bethel 99559; phone (907) 543-2911.

Big Lake Chamber, P.O. Box 520067, Big Lake 99652; phone (907) 892-6109.

Chugiak-Eagle River Chamber, P.O. Box 770353, Eagle River 99577-0353; phone (907) 694-4701.

Greater Copper Valley Chamber, P.O. Box 469, Glennallen 99588; phone (907) 822-3375.

Cordova Chamber, P.O. Box 99, Cordova 99574; phone (907) 424-7260.

Delta Junction Chamber, P.O. Box 987, Delta Junction 99737; phone (907) 895-4210.

Dillingham Chamber, P.O. Box 348, Dillingham 99576; phone (907) 842-5115.

Dutch Harbor Chamber, P.O. Box 833, Dutch Harbor 99692; phone (907) 581-2190.

Greater Fairbanks Chamber, P.O. Box 74446, Fairbanks 99707; phone (907) 452-1105.

Funny River Chamber, HC 1, Box 1424, Soldotna 99669; phone (907) 262-7711.

Haines Chamber, P.O. Box 518, Haines 99827; phone (907) 766-2202.

Homer Chamber, P.O. Box 531, Homer 99603; phone (907) 235-7740.

Greater Juneau Chamber, 124 W. Fifth St., Juneau 99801; phone (907) 586-6420.

Kenai Chamber, P.O. Box 497, Kenai 99611; phone (907) 283-7989.

Greater Ketchikan Chamber, P.O. Box 5957, Ketchikan 99901; phone (907) 225-3184.

Kodiak Chamber, P.O. Box 1485, Kodiak 99615; phone (907) 486-5557.

City of Kotzebue, P.O. Box 46, Kotzebue 99752; phone (907) 442-3401.

City of Nenana, P.O. Box 00070, Nenana 99760; phone (907) 832-5441.

Nome Chamber, P.O. Box 251, Nome 99762; phone (907) 443-5535.

North Peninsula Chamber, P.O. Box 8053, Nikiski 99635; phone (907) 776-8369.

North Pole Chamber, P.O. Box 55071, North Pole 99705; phone (907) 488-2242.

Greater Palmer Chamber, P.O. Box 45, Palmer 99645; phone (907) 745-2880.

Petersburg Chamber, P.O. Box 649, Petersburg 99833; phone (907) 772-3646.

Greater Prince of Wales Chamber, P.O. Box 89, Craig 99921; phone (907) 826-2927.

Seldovia Chamber, Drawer F, Seldovia 99663; phone (907) 234-7625.

Seward Chamber, P.O. Box 749, Seward 99664; phone (907) 224-3046.

Greater Sitka Chamber, P.O. Box 638, Sitka 99835; phone (907) 747-8604.

Skagway Chamber, P.O. Box 194, Skagway 99840; phone (907) 983-2214.

Soldotna Chamber, P.O. Box 236, Soldotna 99669; phone (907) 262-9814.

Sutton Chamber, P.O. Box 24, Sutton 99674; phone (907) 745-4527.

Talkeetna Chamber, P.O. Box 334, Talkeetna 99676; phone (907) 733-2330.

Tok Chamber, P.O. Box 389, Tok 99780; phone (907) 883-5887.

Valdez Chamber, P.O. Box 512, Valdez 99686; phone (907) 835-2330.

Greater Wasilla Chamber, 1801 Parks Highway, Wasilla 99687; phone (907) 376-1299.

Wrangell Chamber, P.O. Box 49, Wrangell 99929; phone (907) 874-2010.

Cheechako

Pronounced chee-CHA-ko, or chee-CHA-ker by some old-time Alaskans, the word means tenderfoot or greenhorn. According to *The Chinook Jargon,* a 1909 dictionary of the old trading language used by traders from the Hudson's Bay Company in the early 1800s, the word cheechako comes from combining the Chinook Indian word *chee,* meaning new, fresh, or "just now," with the Nootka Indian word *chako,* which means to come, to approach, or to become.

Chilkat Blankets

Dramatic, bilaterally symmetrical patterns, usually in black, white, yellow and blue, adorn these heavily fringed ceremonial blankets.

The origin of the Chilkat dancing blanket is Tsimshian. Knowledge of the

weaving techniques apparently diffused north to the Tlingit, where blanket-making reached its highest form among the Chilkat group. Visiting traders coined the blanket's name during the late nineteenth century.

Time, technical skill and inherited privileges were required to weave Chilkat blankets and other ceremonial garments. Both men and women wore the blankets and heavily decorated aprons and tunics.

Yarn for Chilkat dancing blankets was spun primarily from the wool of the mountain goat. The designs woven into Chilkat blankets consist of geometric totemic shapes that can be reproduced by the method known as twining. (Early blankets are unadorned or display geometric patterns lacking curvilinear elements.) Often, totemic crests on painted house posts and the designs woven into garments were quite similar. Weavers reused pattern boards of wood painted with a design.

A few weavers are producing the blankets today.

Chilkoot Trail

The Chilkoot Trail, from Skagway over Chilkoot Pass to Lake Bennett, British Columbia, was one of the established routes to Yukon Territory goldfields during the Klondike gold rush of 1897–98. Thousands of gold stampeders climbed the tortuous trail over Chilkoot Pass that winter. Those who reached Lake Bennett built boats to float down the Yukon River to Dawson City.

Today, the 33-mile Chilkoot Trail is part of Klondike Gold Rush National Historical Park and is climbed each year by hundreds of backpackers. The Chilkoot Trail begins about 8 miles from Skagway on Dyea Road. There are a dozen campgrounds along the trail and ranger stations on both the Alaska and British Columbia portions of the trail (the trail crosses the international border at 3,739-foot Chilkoot Pass, 16.5 miles from the trailhead). The trail ends at Bennett, site of a White Pass and Yukon Route railway station. For more information, contact Klondike Gold

Rush National Historical Park, Box 517, Skagway 99840.

Related reading: *Chilkoot Pass: The Most Famous Trail in the North,* by Archie Satterfield. This revised and expanded edition is a historical guide to the hiking trail and includes photos. *See* ALASKA NORTHWEST LIBRARY in the back of the book.

Chill Factor

The wind's chill factor can lower the effective temperature many degrees. While Alaska's regions of lowest temperatures also generally have little wind, activities such as riding a snowmobile or even walking can produce the same effect on exposed skin.

Temperature (Fahrenheit)	Wind Chill Temp. at Selected mph			
	10	20	30	45
40	28	18	13	10
30	16	4	–2	–6
20	4	–10	–18	–22
10	–9	–25	–33	–38
0	–21	–39	–48	–54
–10	–33	–53	–63	–70
–20	–46	–67	–79	–85
–30	–58	–82	–94	–102
–40	–70	–96	–109	–117

The wind's chill factor, when severe, can lead to frostnip (the body's early-warning signal of potential damage from cold—a "nipping" feeling in the extremities), frostbite (formation of small ice crystals in the body tissues) or hypothermia (dangerous lowering of the body's general temperature). Other factors that combine with wind chill and bring on these potentially damaging or fatal effects are exposure to wetness, exhaustion and lack of adequate clothing.

Chitons

Chitons are oval creatures with shells made up of eight overlapping plates. The gumboot and the Chinese slipper chiton are favorite Alaskan edible delicacies. The gumboot, named

for the tough, leathery, reddish-brown covering that hides its plates, is the largest chiton in the world. It has long been traditional food for southeastern Alaska Natives.

Climate

(*See also* Winds)

Alaska's climate zones are maritime, transition, continental and arctic. With the exception of the transition zone along western Alaska, the zones are divided by mountain ranges that form barriers to shallow air masses and modify those deep enough to cross the ranges. The Brooks Range inhibits the southward movement of air from the Arctic Ocean, thus separating the arctic climate zone from the Interior. The Chugach, Wrangell, Aleutian and Alaska mountain ranges often limit northward air movement and dry the air before it reaches the Interior's continental zone.

Other meteorologic/oceanographic factors affecting Alaska's climate zones are air temperature, water temperature, cloud coverage, and wind and air pressure. The amount of moisture that air can hold in a gaseous state is highly dependent on its temperature. Warm air can contain more water vapor than cold air. Therefore, precipitation, as rain or snow or in other forms, is likely to be heavier from warm than from cold air. Water temperatures change more slowly and much less than land temperatures. For this reason, coastal area temperatures vary less than those farther inland.

Climate Zones

The maritime climate zone includes Southeast, the Northern Gulf Coast and the Aleutian Chain. Temperatures are mild—relatively warm in the winter and cool in summer. Precipitation is heavy, 50 to 200 inches annually along the coast and up to 400 inches on mountain slopes. Storms are frequently from the west and southwest, resulting in strong winds along the Aleutian Islands and the Alaska Peninsula. Amchitka Island's weather station has recorded the windiest weather in the state, followed by Cold Bay. Frequent storms with accompanying high winds account for rough seas with occasional waves to 50 feet in the Gulf of Alaska, particularly in fall and winter.

The transition zone is, in effect, two separate zones. One is the area between the coastal mountains and the Alaska Range, which includes Anchorage and the Matanuska Valley. Summer temperatures are higher than those of the maritime climate zone, with colder winter temperatures and less precipitation. Temperatures, however, are not as extreme as in the continental zone.

Another transition zone includes the west coast from Bristol Bay to Point Hope. This area has cool summer temperatures that are somewhat colder than those of the maritime zone, and cold winter temperatures similar to the continental zone. Cold winter temperatures are partly due to the sea ice in the Chukchi and Bering seas.

The continental climate zone covers the majority of Alaska except the coastal fringes and the Arctic Slope. It has extreme temperatures and low precipitation. There are fewer clouds in the continental zone than elsewhere, so there is more warming by the sun during the long days of summer and more cooling during the long nights of winter. Precipitation is light because air masses affecting the area lose most of their moisture crossing the mountains to the south.

The Arctic, north of the Brooks Range, has cold winters, cool summers and desertlike precipitation. Prevailing winds are from the northeast off the arctic ice pack, which never moves far offshore. Summers are generally cloudy and winters are clear and cold. The cold air allows little precipitation and inhibits evaporation. Because continuous permafrost prevents the percolation

(Continued on page 40)

AVERAGE TEMPERATURES (FAHRENHEIT) AND PRECIPITATION (INCHES)							
	ANCHORAGE	BARROW	BETHEL	COLD BAY	FAIRBANKS	HOMER	JUNEAU
January							
Temperature	14.8	–13.7	6.6	28.4	–10.3	22.7	23.1
Precipitation	0.80	0.20	0.81	2.71	0.55	2.23	3.98
February							
Temperature	18.5	–19.2	7.3	27.5	–4.1	25.3	28.2
Precipitation	0.86	0.18	0.71	2.30	0.41	1.78	3.66
March							
Temperature	24.7	–15.4	12.3	29.5	10.0	28.3	32.0
Precipitation	0.65	0.15	0.80	2.19	0.37	1.57	3.24
April							
Temperature	35.2	–2.2	24.7	33.0	30.0	35.3	39.2
Precipitation	0.63	0.20	0.65	1.90	0.28	1.27	2.83
May							
Temperature	46.5	18.9	40.2	39.5	48.3	42.6	46.7
Precipitation	0.63	0.16	0.83	2.40	0.57	1.07	3.46
June							
Temperature	54.4	33.7	51.5	45.5	59.5	49.1	53.0
Precipitation	1.02	0.36	1.29	2.13	1.29	1.00	3.02
July							
Temperature	58.1	39.0	54.7	50.3	61.7	53.0	55.9
Precipitation	1.96	0.87	2.18	2.50	1.84	1.63	4.09
August							
Temperature	56.1	37.9	52.7	51.4	56.3	52.8	54.8
Precipitation	2.31	0.97	3.65	3.71	1.82	2.56	5.10
September							
Temperature	48.0	30.6	45.1	47.5	45.0	47.2	49.3
Precipitation	2.51	0.64	2.58	4.06	1.02	2.96	6.25
October							
Temperature	34.7	14.5	30.5	39.7	25.2	37.8	41.9
Precipitation	1.86	0.51	1.48	4.45	0.81	3.41	7.64
November							
Temperature	21.8	–0.7	17.4	34.4	3.8	28.8	32.8
Precipitation	1.08	0.27	0.98	4.33	0.67	2.74	5.13
December							
Temperature	15.2	–11.8	6.9	30.1	–8.1	23.3	27.2
Precipitation	1.06	0.17	0.95	3.16	0.73	2.71	4.48
Snowfall (mean)	14.0	2.1	9.0	10.2	12.5	11.7	23.2
Annual							
Temperature	35.7	9.3	29.1	38.1	26.5	37.2	40.3
Precipitation	15.37	4.67	16.90	35.84	10.37	24.93	52.86

KETCHIKAN	KING SALMON	KODIAK	MCGRATH	NOME	PETERSBURG	VALDEZ	
							January
34.2	15.0	32.3	−8.3	6.5	27.6	22.6	Temperature
14.01	1.11	9.52	0.81	0.88	9.31	5.63	Precipitation
							February
36.4	15.1	30.5	−1.7	3.5	31.1	24.3	Temperature
12.36	0.82	5.67	0.74	0.56	7.85	5.08	Precipitation
							March
38.6	21.7	34.4	9.1	8.3	34.7	30.3	Temperature
12.22	1.06	5.16	0.75	0.63	7.19	4.06	Precipitation
							April
43.0	30.8	37.6	26.0	17.3	40.4	37.0	Temperature
11.93	1.07	4.47	0.73	0.67	6.94	2.89	Precipitation
							May
49.2	42.3	43.6	44.3	35.5	47.2	45.3	Temperature
9.06	1.25	6.65	0.84	0.58	5.92	2.74	Precipitation
							June
54.7	50.0	49.6	55.4	45.7	53.0	52.0	Temperature
7.36	1.54	5.72	1.56	1.14	5.00	2.64	Precipitation
							July
58.0	54.5	54.5	58.4	50.8	55.8	55.0	Temperature
7.80	2.10	3.80	2.16	2.18	5.36	3.77	Precipitation
							August
58.7	53.8	55.2	53.9	49.8	55.0	53.6	Temperature
10.60	2.96	4.03	2.87	3.20	7.57	5.73	Precipitation
							September
54.0	47.0	50.2	43.9	42.3	50.3	47.3	Temperature
13.61	2.75	7.18	2.19	2.59	11.15	7.99	Precipitation
							October
47.0	32.6	41.2	25.4	28.3	43.5	38.1	Temperature
22.55	1.98	7.85	1.24	1.38	16.83	8.23	Precipitation
							November
40.4	22.9	35.0	5.0	16.6	35.6	27.8	Temperature
17.90	1.45	6.89	1.18	1.02	11.99	6.09	Precipitation
							December
36.0	14.7	32.1	−7.6	6.2	30.5	22.5	Temperature
15.82	1.19	7.39	1.12	0.82	10.66	6.65	Precipitation
							Snowfall
9.2	7.8	9.9	17.1	8.7	23.9	62.9	(mean)
							Annual
45.9	33.4	41.3	25.3	25.9	42.1	38.0	Temperature
155.22	19.28	74.33	16.18	15.64	105.77	61.50	Precipitation

(Continued from page 37)
of water into the soil, the area is generally marshy with numerous lakes. (*See also* Permafrost)

The chart on pages 38–39 shows normal monthly temperatures and precipitation for 14 communities in Alaska. Included are mean monthly snowfall for December and annual average temperatures and precipitation. The chart is based on data from NOAA and the Alaska state climatologist.

Climate Records

Highest temperature: 100°F, at Fort Yukon, June 27, 1915.

Lowest temperature: –80°F, at Prospect Creek Camp, Jan. 23, 1971.

Most precipitation in one year: 332.29 inches, at MacLeod Harbor (Montague Island), 1976.

Most monthly precipitation: 70.99 inches at MacLeod Harbor, November 1976.

Most precipitation in 24 hours: 15.2 inches, in Angoon, Oct. 12, 1982.

Least precipitation in a year: 1.61 inches, at Barrow, 1935.

Most snowfall in a season: 974.5 inches, at Thompson Pass, 1952–53.

Most monthly snowfall: 297.9 inches, at Thompson Pass, February 1953.

Most snowfall in 24 hours: 62 inches, at Thompson Pass, December 1955.

Least snowfall in a season: 3 inches, at Barrow, 1935–36.

Highest recorded snow pack (also highest ever recorded in North America): 356 inches on Wolverine Glacier, Kenai Peninsula, after the winter of 1976–77.

Highest recorded wind speed: 139 mph, at Shemya Island, December 1959.

Coal

(*See also* Minerals and Mining)

About half of the coal resource of the United States is believed to be in Alaska. The demonstrated coal reserve base of the state is over 6 billion short tons, identified coal resources are about 160 billion short tons, and hypothetical and speculative resource estimates range upward to 6 trillion short tons. The provinces containing the most coal are northwestern Alaska, Cook Inlet–Susitna Lowland and the Nenana Trend. Geologists estimate that perhaps 80 percent of Alaska's coal underlies the 23-million-acre National Petroleum Reserve on the North Slope. Although the majority of the coals are of bituminous and subbituminous ranks, anthracite coal does occur in the Bering River and Matanuska fields. In addition to the vast resource base and wide distribution, the important selling points for Alaska coal are its extremely low sulfur content and access to the coast for shipping.

Exploration, technology and economics will ultimately determine the marketability of Alaska's coal resources. Large-scale exploration programs have been conducted in most of Alaska's coal fields by private industry and state and federal governments. Maxus Energy, Inc., and Placer–Dome U.S. are working to develop the Beluga coal field west of Anchorage on Cook Inlet. Wishbone Hill Mine is in the permit phase and is scheduled to produce 1 million metric tons of clean coal per year. Exploration continues in the Nenana coal field. The Arctic Slope Regional Corporation is working to develop its coal reserves in northwestern Alaska.

Alaska's production of coal in 1991 was 1.52 million tons and came exclusively from the Usibelli Coal Mine near Healy. Of that estimate, one half was burned in interior Alaska power plants, and the remainder was shipped to Korea.

Coal production in Alaska was over $45 million in 1991, which was the same as in 1990.

Conk

Alaskans apply this term to a type of bracket fungus. The platelike conks

grow on dead trees. When dry and hard, conks are snapped off and used to paint on.

Constitution of Alaska

One of the most remarkable achievements in the long battle for Alaskan statehood was the creation of the constitution of the state of Alaska in the mid-1950s. Statehood supporters believed that creation of a constitution would demonstrate Alaska's maturity and readiness for statehood, so in 1955 the territorial legislature appropriated $300,000 for the cost of holding a Constitutional Convention in Fairbanks.

For 73 days in 1955–1956, a total of 55 elected delegates from all across the territory of Alaska met in the new Student Union Building (now called Constitution Hall) on the University of Alaska campus. William A. Egan, a territorial legislator and former mayor of Valdez, who later became the first governor of the state of Alaska, was president of the convention. Under his leadership, the disparate group of Alaskans hammered out a document that is considered a model for a state constitution.

The National Municipal League said that the brief 14,000-word document drafted by the convention delegates was "one of the best, if not the best, state constitutions ever written." By an overwhelming margin the people of Alaska approved the new constitution at the polls in 1956, paving the way for the creation of the 49th state in 1959.

Continental Divide

(*See also* Mountains)
The Continental Divide extends into Alaska. Unlike its portions in the Lower 48, which divide the country into east-west watersheds, the Continental Divide in Alaska trends through the Brooks Range, separating watersheds that drain north into the Arctic Ocean and west and south into the Bering Sea.

According to *Alaska Science Nuggets*, geologists used to regard the Brooks Range as a structural extension of the Rocky Mountains. Recent thinking, however, assumes the range to be 35 million to 200 million years older than the Rockies. The Alaska Range is comparatively young, only about 5 million years old.

Convention and Visitors Bureaus and Information Centers

Anchorage Convention and Visitors Bureau, 1600 A St., Suite 200, Anchorage 99501; phone (907) 276-4118.

Begich-Boggs Visitors Center, P.O. Box 129, Girdwood 99587; phone (907) 783-2326.

Bethel Visitor Center, P.O. Box 388, Bethel 99559; phone (907) 543-2798.

Big Lake Visitor Information Center, P.O. Box 520067, Big Lake 99652; phone (907) 892-9030.

Greater Copper Valley Visitor Information Center, P.O. Box 469, Glennallen 99588; phone (907) 822-5555.

Cordova Visitors Center, P.O. Box 391, Cordova 99574; phone (907) 424-7443.

Delta Junction Visitor Information Center, P.O. Box 987, Delta Junction 99737; phone (907) 895-5068.

Eagle River Visitor Center, P.O. Box 7001, Anchorage 99510; phone (907) 694-2108.

Fairbanks Convention and Visitors Bureau, 550 First Ave., Fairbanks 99701; phone (907) 456-5774.

Haines Visitor Information Center, City of Haines, P.O. Box 518, Haines 99827; phone (907) 766-2234.

Juneau Convention and Visitors Bureau, 369 S. Franklin St., Juneau 99801; phone (907) 586-1737.

Kenai Visitor Information Center, P.O. Box 497, Kenai 99611; phone (907) 283-7989.

Ketchikan Convention and Visitors Bureau, 131 Front St., Ketchikan 99901; phone (907) 225-6166.

Kodiak Island Convention and Visitors Bureau, 100 Marine Way, Kodiak 99615; phone (907) 486-4782.

Matanuska-Susitna Convention and Visitors Bureau, HCO-1, Box

6616J21, Palmer 99645; phone (907) 746-5000.

Nome Convention and Visitors Bureau, P.O. Box 251, Nome 99762; phone (907) 443-5535.

Petersburg Visitor Information, P.O. Box 649, Petersburg 99833; phone (907) 772-3975.

Seward Visitor Information Cache, P.O. Box 749, Seward 99664; phone (907) 224-3094.

Sitka Convention and Visitors Bureau, P.O. Box 1226, Sitka 99835; phone (907) 747-5940.

Skagway Convention and Visitors Bureau, P.O. Box 415, Skagway 99840; phone (907) 983-2854.

Valdez Convention and Visitors Bureau, P. O. Box 1603, Valdez 99686; phone (907) 835-2984.

Wrangell Convention and Visitors Bureau, P.O. Box 1078, Wrangell 99929; phone (907) 874-3800.

Coppers

(*See also* Potlatch)

Coppers (*tinnehs*) are beaten copper plaques that were important symbols of wealth among the Pacific Northwest Coast Natives. Coppers are shaped something like a keyhole or a shield, are usually two or three feet long and weigh approximately 40 pounds. Coppers varied in value from tribe to tribe.

Early coppers were made of ore from the Copper River area, although western traders quickly made sheet copper available. Some scholars believe that Tlingit craftsmen shaped placer copper into the desired form themselves, while others maintain that coppers were formed by Athabascans. The impressive plaques were engraved or carved in relief with totemic crests.

The value of coppers increased as they were traded or sold, and their transfer implied that a potlatch would be given by the new owner. Coppers were given names such as "Cloud," "Point of Island" or "Killer Whale," and were spoken of in respectful terms. They were thought of as powerful, and their histories were as well-known as those of the noblest families.

Coppers were often broken and destroyed during public displays and distribution of wealth. Some parts of the coppers were valued nearly as much as the whole.

To this day, certain coppers that have been part of museum collections for years are still valued highly by some tribes, and are used as symbols of wealth and prestige during marriage ceremonies and potlatches.

Cost of Living

(*See also* Income)

Alaska is an expensive place to live for a variety of reasons. The main mode of transportation in the state is by air travel or by sea. Alaska's sheer size, lack of a comprehensive road network and distance from the contiguous 48 states make personal and business transportation costly. Air travel, which may be a luxury for residents in other states, becomes a necessity for Alaskans living in places such as Barrow, Sitka or Nome. A typical living cost for these residents usually includes the high cost of transportation just to leave town.

Likewise, shipping goods as well as providing services and medical care to more remote areas in Alaska is expensive, especially when there is little or no competition to keep prices down. And because agriculture and industry in Alaska is limited, most consumption items are shipped in from Outside, adding to their cost.

Food: In a June 1991 Cost of Food study conducted by the University of Alaska Cooperative Extension Study, the U.S. Department of Agriculture and SEA Grant Cooperating, food prices fluctuated greatly among cities and towns within the state. Prices on the average were less expensive in the larger cities, such as Anchorage, and very expensive in rural communities. Food costs for the more isolated communities of Bethel and Dillingham can range between 50 percent and 70 percent more than Anchorage. For example, a week's worth of groceries for a family of four (with elementary schoolchildren) in June 1991 cost $102.84 in Anchorage, $152.49 in Bethel and $127.96 in Kodiak.

Housing: Though housing costs are

considered high in Alaska, other states nationwide reflect comparable prices. According to the Cost of Living Index for the first quarter of 1991 compiled by the American Chamber of Commerce Researchers Association, the sample purchase price of a house in Anchorage was $155,600; Fairbanks, $112,900; Juneau, $140,400; Ketchikan, $158,100; Kodiak $158,800; San Diego, CA, $211,700; Minneapolis, MN, $99,700; and Springfield, MA, $149,000.

Gasoline: The average cost for one gallon of gasoline (compiled March 1989) was: Juneau, $1.30; Anchorage, 97¢; Fairbanks, $1.12; Ketchikan, $1.30; Kodiak, $1.26.

Heating oil: The average cost for a 55-gallon drum of heating oil (compiled September 1988) was: Juneau, $67.19; Anchorage, $49.98; Fairbanks, $49.20; Nome, $76.18; Dillingham, $84.54.

Taxes: City and borough taxes (compiled in September 1988) were: Juneau, 4 percent sales; Anchorage, none; Fairbanks, none; Nome, 4 percent sales; Dillingham, 3 percent sales. There is no state income tax in Alaska.

Personal income: The cost of living in Alaska is high, and so is personal income. In 1991, the annual per capita personal income for Alaska was $21,932, which positioned Alaska as the sixth highest in the nation in income standings.

Courts

The Alaska court system operates at four levels: the supreme court, court of appeals, superior court and district court. The Alaska judiciary is funded by the state and administered by the supreme court.

The five-member supreme court, established by the Alaska Constitution in 1959, has final appellate jurisdiction of all actions and proceedings in lower courts. It sits monthly in Anchorage and Fairbanks, quarterly in Juneau and occasionally in other court locations.

The three-member court of appeals was established in 1980 to relieve the supreme court of some of its ever-increasing caseload. The supreme court retained its ultimate authority in all cases, but concentrated its attention on civil appellate matters, giving authority in criminal and quasi-criminal matters to the court of appeals. The court of appeals has appellate jurisdiction in certain superior court proceedings and jurisdiction to review district court decisions. It meets regularly in Anchorage and travels occasionally to other locations.

The superior court is the trial court, with original jurisdiction in all civil and criminal matters and appellate jurisdiction over all matters appealed by the district court. The superior court has exclusive jurisdiction in probate and in cases concerning minors. There are 30 superior court judges.

The district court has jurisdiction over misdemeanor violations and violations of ordinances of political subdivisions. In civil matters, the district court may hear cases for recovery of money, damages or specific personal property if the amount does not exceed $50,000. The district court may also inquire into the cause and manner of death, as well as issue marriage licenses, summons, writs of habeas corpus and search and arrest warrants. District court criminal decisions may be appealed directly to the court of appeals or the superior court. There are 17 district court judges.

Administration of the superior and district courts is divided by region into four judicial districts: First Judicial District, Southeast; Second Judicial District, Nome–Kotzebue; Third Judicial District, Anchorage–Kodiak–Kenai; and Fourth Judicial District, Fairbanks.

District magistrates serve rural areas and help ease the work load of district courts in metropolitan areas. In criminal matters, magistrates may enter judgment of conviction upon a plea of guilty to any state misdemeanor and may try state misdemeanor cases if the defendant waives his right to a district court judge. Magistrates may also hear municipal ordinance violations and state traffic infractions without the consent of the accused. In civil matters, magistrates may hear cases for recovery of money, damages or specific personal property if the amount does not exceed $5,000.

Selection of Justices, Judges and Magistrates

Supreme court justices and judges of the court of appeals, superior court and district court are appointed by the governor from candidates submitted by the Alaska Judicial Council. All justices and judges must be citizens of the United States and have been residents of Alaska for at least five years. A justice must be licensed to practice law in Alaska at the time of appointment and have engaged in active law practice for eight years. A court of appeals judge must be a state resident for five years immediately preceding appointment, have been engaged in the active practice of law not less than eight years immediately preceding appointment and be licensed to practice law in Alaska. Qualifications of a superior court judge are the same as for supreme court justices, except that only five years of active practice are necessary. A district court judge must be 21 years of age, a resident for at least five years, and (1) be licensed to practice law in Alaska and have engaged in active practice of law for not less than three years immediately preceding appointment, or (2) have served for at least seven years as a magistrate in the state and have graduated from an accredited law school.

The chief justice of the supreme court is selected by majority vote of the justices, serves a three-year term and cannot succeed him or herself.

Each supreme court justice and each judge of the court of appeals is subject to approval or rejection by a majority of the voters of the state on a nonpartisan ballot at the first general election held more than three years after appointment. Thereafter, each justice must participate in a retention election every 10 years. A court of appeals judge must participate every eight years.

Superior court judges are subject to approval or rejection by voters of their judicial district at the first general election held more than three years after appointment. Thereafter, it is every sixth year. District court judges must run for retention in their judicial districts in the first general election held more than two years after appointment and every fourth year thereafter.

District magistrates are appointed for an indefinite period by the presiding superior court judge of the judicial district in which they will serve.

The Alaska State Supreme Court, 1959–1992: Justices and Tenure

Jay A. Rabinowitz , 1965–
  Chief Justice, 1972–1975; 1978–1981;
  1984–1987; 1990–
Edmond W. Burke, 1975–
  Chief Justice, 1981–1984
Allen T. Compton, 1980–
Warren W. Mathews, 1977–
  Chief Justice, 1987–1990
Daniel A. Moore, Jr., 1983–
John H. Dimond, 1959–1971
Walter H. Hodge, 1959–1960
Buell A. Nesbett, 1959–1970
  Chief Justice, 1959–1970
Harry O. Arend, 1960–1965
George F. Boney, 1968–1972
  Chief Justice, 1970–1972
Roger G. Connor, 1968–1983
Robert C. Erwin, 1970–1977
Robert Boochever, 1972–1980
  Chief Justice, 1975–1978
James M. Fitzgerald, 1972–1975

The Alaska State Court of Appeals, 1980–1992: Judges and Tenure

Alexander O. Bryner, 1980–
  Chief Judge, 1980–
Robert G. Coats, 1980–
David Mannheimer, 1990–
James K. Singleton, Jr., 1980–1990

Cruises

(*See also* Boating *and* Ferries)

There are many opportunities for cruising Alaska waters, aboard either charter boats, scheduled boat excursions or luxury cruise ships.

Charter boats are readily available in southeastern and southcentral Alaska. Charter boat trips range from day-long fishing and sightseeing trips to overnight and longer customized trips or package tours. There is a wide range of charter boats, from simple fishing boats to sailboats, yachts and mini-class cruise ships.

In summer, scheduled boat excursions—from day trips to overnight cruises—are available at the following locations: Ketchikan (Misty Fiords); Sitka (harbor and area tours); Bartlett

Cove and Gustavus (Glacier Bay); Valdez and Whittier (Columbia Glacier, Prince William Sound); Seward (Resurrection Bay, Kenai Fjords); Homer (Kachemak Bay); and Fairbanks (Chena and Tanana rivers).

For details and additional information on charter boat operators and scheduled boat excursions, contact the Alaska Division of Tourism, P.O. Box E, Juneau 99811.

From May through September, luxury cruise ships carry visitors to Alaska via the Inside Passage. There are 24 ships to choose from and almost as many itineraries. There's also a bewildering array of travel options. Both round-trip and one-way cruises are available, or a cruise may be sold as part of a packaged tour that includes air, rail and/or motorcoach transportation.

Various shore excursions may be included in the cruise price or available for added cost. Ports of call may depend on length of cruise or time of sailing.

Because of the wide variety of cruise trip options, it is wise to work with your travel agent.

Following is a partial list of cruise ships serving Alaska in the 1992–93 season:

Alaska Sightseeing Tours, Suite 700, Fourth & Battery Bldg., Seattle, WA 98121; phone (206) 441-8687. *Glacier Seas, Sheltered Seas* (35 passengers); 4-day daylight cruise between Ketchikan and Juneau. *Spirit of Glacier Bay* (49 passengers); 3-day cruise between Juneau and Glacier Bay.

Clipper Cruise Lines, 7711 Bonhomme Ave., St. Louis, MO 63105-1965; phone 1-800-326-0010. *Yorktown Clipper* (138 passengers); 7-day round-trip cruise between Juneau and Ketchikan.

Costa Cruises, Inc., World Trade Center, 80 SW Eighth St., Miami, FL 33130; phone (305) 358-7325. MTS *Daphne* (420 passengers); 7-night round-trip cruises from Vancouver, British Columbia.

Cunard/NAC Lines, 555 Fifth Ave., New York, NY 10017; phone (212) 880-7500. *Sagafjord* (618 passengers); 11-day cruise between Vancouver, British Columbia, and Anchorage.

Holland America Line, 300 Elliott Ave. W., Seattle, WA 98119; phone (206) 281-3535. MS *Nieuw Amsterdam* (1,214 passengers); MS *Noordam* (1,214 passengers); SS *Rotterdam* (1,114 passengers) and the *Westerdam*; all ships offer 3-, 4- and 7-night round-trip cruises from Vancouver, British Columbia. The *Rotterdam* also offers 7- and 14-night cruises between Vancouver, British Columbia, and Seward.

Princess Cruises, 10100 Santa Monica Blvd., Suite 1800, Los Angeles, CA 90067; phone (213) 553-1770. *Dawn Princess* (925 passengers), *Island* and *Pacific Princess* (626 passengers) and *Fair Princess* (890 passengers); 7-day cruises between Vancouver, British Columbia, and Anchorage. *Star Princess* (1,470 passengers); 7-day round-trip Inside Passage cruise from Vancouver, British Columbia. *Sea Princess* (730 passengers); 10-day round-trip sailings from San Francisco.

Regency Cruises, 260 Madison Ave., New York, NY 10016; phone (212) 972-4499. MV *Regent Sea* (729 passengers); and *Regent Sun* (836 passengers); 7 days between Vancouver, British Columbia, and Whittier.

Royal Caribbean Cruise Line, 903 South America Way, Miami, FL 33132. *Sun Viking* (726 passengers); 7 days between Vancouver, British Columbia, and Skagway.

Royal Viking Line, 95 Merrick Way, Coral Gables, FL 33134; phone 1-800-422-8000. *Royal Viking Sea* (710 passengers); 11- and 13-day cruises from Vancouver, British Columbia.

Special Expeditions, 720 Fifth Ave., New York, NY 10019. *Sea Bird* (70 passengers) and *Sea Lion* (70 passengers); 11-day wilderness cruises between Prince Rupert, British Columbia, and Sitka.

World Explorer Cruises, 555 Montgomery St., San Francisco, CA 94111; phone 1-800-854-3835. SS *Universe* (554 passengers); 14-day round-trip cruises between Vancouver, British Columbia, and Seward.

YachtShip CruiseLine, Sixth & Pine Bldg., 523 Pine St., Seattle, WA 98101; phone (206) 623-4245. *Executive Explorer* (49 passengers); 7-day cruise between Ketchikan and Glacier Bay.

Dalton Highway

(*See also* Highways)

This all-weather gravel road bridges the Yukon River, crosses the Arctic Circle, climbs the Brooks Range and passes through tundra plains before reaching the Prudhoe Bay oil fields on the coast of the Arctic Ocean.

The highway was named for James Dalton, a post–World War II explorer who played a large role in the development of North Slope oil and gas industries. It was built as a haul road for supplies and to provide access to the northern half of the 800-mile trans-Alaska oil pipeline during construction. Originally called the North Slope Haul Road, it is still referred to as the "Haul Road."

The Dalton Highway has been partially opened by the state for public use. The public may drive the road's first 215.4 miles to Disaster Creek at Dietrich. North of Dietrich, the highway is closed to the public. Permits to travel north of Disaster Creek are issued only for commercial or industrial purposes. Permits may be obtained from the Alaska Department of Transportation and Public Facilities.

Fuel, limited food services and tire repairs, as well as wrecker service at $5 per mile, are available (for cash) at the Yukon Bridge and at Coldfoot. Travelers are advised that dust clouds, large trucks traveling fast and sometimes narrow, rough road surfaces may make stopping along the roadway dangerous. Also, because safe drinking water is not available along the road, travelers should carry their own.

The 414-mile-long Dalton Highway begins at Milepost 73.1 on the Elliott Highway.

Daylight Hours

(*See also* Arctic Circle)

Maximum (At Summer Solstice, June 20 or 21)

	Sunrise	Sunset	Hours of Daylight
Barrow	May 10	August 2	84 days continuous
Fairbanks	1:59 a.m.	11:48 p.m.	21:49 hours
Anchorage	3:21 a.m.	10:42 p.m.	19:21 hours
Juneau	3:51 a.m.	10:09 p.m.	18:18 hours
Ketchikan	4:04 a.m.	9:33 p.m.	17:29 hours
Adak	6:27 a.m.	11:10 p.m.	16:43 hours

Minimum (At Winter Solstice, December 21 or 22)

	Sunrise	Sunset	Hours of Daylight
Barrow	*	*	0:00 hours
Fairbanks	10:59 a.m.	2:41 p.m.	3:42 hours
Anchorage	10:14 a.m.	3:42 p.m.	5:28 hours
Juneau	9:46 a.m.	4:07 p.m.	6:21 hours
Ketchikan	9:12 a.m.	4:18 p.m.	7:06 hours
Adak	10:52 a.m.	6:38 p.m.	7:46 hours

*For the period November 18 through January 24—67 days—there is no daylight in Barrow.

Diamond Willow

Fungi, particularly *Valsa sordida Nitschke,* are generally thought to be the cause of diamond-shaped patterns in the wood grain of some willow trees. There are 33 varieties of willow in Alaska, of which at least five can develop diamonds. They are found throughout the state, but are most plentiful in river valleys. Diamond willow, stripped of bark, is used to make lamps, walking sticks and novelty items.

Dog Mushing

(*See also* Iditarod Trail Sled Dog Race *and* Yukon Quest International Sled Dog Race)

In many areas of the state where snow machines had just about replaced the working dog team, the sled dog has made a comeback, due in part to a rekindled appreciation of the reliability of nonmechanical transportation. In addition to working and racing dog teams, many people keep 2 to 10 sled dogs for recreational mushing.

Sled dog racing is Alaska's official state sport. Races ranging from local club meets to world championships are held throughout the winter.

The speed, or championship, races are usually run over two or three days, with the cumulative time for the heats deciding the winner. Distances for the heats vary from about 12 to 30 miles. The size of dog teams also varies, with mushers using anywhere from 7 to 16 dogs in their teams. Since racers are not allowed to replace dogs in the team, most finish with fewer than they started with (attrition may be caused by anything from tender feet to sore muscles).

Sprint mushing is divided into limited and open classes. Limited class ranges from 3 to 10 dogs and from 3 to 12 miles. Open class racing has no limit on the number of dogs and ranges from 10 to 30 miles.

Long-distance racing (the Yukon Quest, the Iditarod) pits racers not only against each other, but also against the elements. Sheer survival can quickly take precedence over winning when a winter storm catches a dog team in an exposed area. Stories abound of racers giving up their chance to finish "in the money" to help out a fellow musher who has gotten into trouble. Besides the weather, long-distance racers also have to contend with moose attacks on the dogs, sudden illness, straying off the trail and sheer exhaustion. With these and other threats to overcome, those who finish have truly persevered against the odds.

Purses range from trophies for the club races to $70,000 (including heat money) for the championships. A purse is split between the finishers. The richest purse in sled dog racing is the Iditarod, with a $387,000 purse in 1992.

Statistics for two of the biggest championship races follow on page 48. Other major races around the state include:

Alaska State Championship Race, Kenai to Soldotna. Two heats in two days, 15.4 miles each day. Held in February.

All-Alaska Sweepstakes, Nome to Candle, round-trip. The Nome Kennel Club sponsors this 408-mile race. Held in March, not an annual event.

Clark Memorial Sled Dog Race, Soldotna to Hope, 100 miles. Held in January.

Iditarod Trail Sled Dog Race. (*See* Iditarod Trail Sled Dog Race)

Junior World Championship Race, Anchorage. Three heats in three days. Held in February.

Kusko 300, Bethel to Aniak. Held in January.

Tok Race of Champions, Tok. Two heats in two days, 20.5 miles a day. Held in March.

Willow Winter Carnival Race, Willow. Two heats in two days, 18 miles each day. Held in January.

Women's World Championship Race, Anchorage. Three heats in three days, 12 miles each day. Held in February.

Yukon Quest International Sled Dog Race. (*See* Yukon Quest International Sled Dog Race)

Related reading: *Iditarod: The Great Race to Nome.* Photography by Jeff Schultz, text by Bill Sherwonit. A powerful visual record of the animal and human participants of the race, accompanied by compelling narrative that chronicles the grueling 1,100-mile journey from Anchorage to Nome. *Travelers of the Cold: Sled Dogs of the Far North,* by Dominique Cellura. A comprehensive text, illustrations and full-color photographs portray the strength and courage of these animals. *See* the ALASKA NORTHWEST LIBRARY at the back of the book.

WORLD CHAMPIONSHIP SLED DOG RACE, ANCHORAGE

Held in February. Best elapsed time in three heats over three days, 25 miles each day.

	Day 1	Day 2	Day 3	Total	Purse
		Elapsed Time (minutes:seconds)			
1974 Roland Lombard	105:32	108:34	101:36	310:10	$10,000
1975 George Attla	98:09	107:01	104:18	309:28	12,000
1976 George Attla	98:39	102:64	102:32	303:35	12,000
1977 Carl Huntington	97:42	105:29	*	201:11	12,000
1978 George Attla	102:59	108:38	107:11	318:48	15,000
1979 George Attla	99:51	97:23	99:07	296:21	15,000
1980 Dick Brunk	83:25	82:35	*	166:00	15,000
1981 George Attla	90:04	85:43	91:34	267:21	20,000
1982 George Attla	73:19	75:36	76:56	225:51	20,000
1983 Harris Dunlap	82:29	88:58	89:05	260:32	25,000
1984 Charlie Champaine	82:55	84:06	85:03	254:04	26,000
1985 Eddy Streeper	83:08	85:32	88:36	251:16	30,000
1986—Race canceled for the first time due to lack of snow					
1987 Eddy Streeper	87:07	88:36	86:05	261:48	30,000
1988 Charlie Champaine	103:53	92:00	89:33	285:26	30,000
1989 Roxy Wright-Champaine	87:30	90:32	89:22	266.84	50,000
1990 Charlie Champaine	89:00	96:13	94:01	279:14	50,000
1991 Charlie Champaine	89:10	94:49	95:43	279:42	70,000
1992 Roxy Wright-Champaine	87:30	89:50	92:22	269:42	70,000

*Trail conditions shortened race

OPEN NORTH AMERICAN SLED DOG CHAMPIONSHIP, FAIRBANKS

Held in March. Best elapsed time in three heats over three days; 20 miles on Days 1 and 2; 30 miles on Day 3.*

	Day 1	Day 2	Day 3	Total	Purse
		Elapsed Time (minutes:seconds)			
1974 Alfred Attla	72:00	74:25	108:29	254:54	$ 9,000
1975 George Attla	69:56	70:16	104:05	244:17	9,000
1976 Harvey Drake	72:00	73:43	116:00	261:43	10,000
1977 Carl Huntington	71:20	71:40	109:00	252:00	12,000
1978 George Attla	71:07	68:05	106:53	246:07	15,000
1979 George Attla	68:41	70:07	104:44	243:32	15,000
1980 Harvey Drake	63:48	66:49	94:30	225:07	15,000
1981 Peter Norberg	73:01	70:55	109:07	253:03	15,000
1982 Harris Dunlap	69:17	72:14	105:43	247:14	15,000
1983 Gareth Wright**	65:43	68:31	99:36	233:50	15,000
1984 Doug McRae	68:35	67:80	98:89	235:04	17,500
1985 Eddy Streeper	61:88	64:16	98:52	224:56	25,000
1986 George Attla	63:95	65:99	103:07	233:01	25,000
1987 George Attla	63:50	68:10	97:21	229:03	25,000
1988 Marvin Kokrine	63:52	66:16	95:42	225:49	30,000
1989 Roxy Wright-Champaine	62:10	62:42	92:07	216:59	44,000
1990 Charlie Champaine	62:47	67:38	95:40	226:05	45,000
1991 Ross Saunderson	60:12	63:53	97:44	221:50	46,000
1992 Roxy Wright-Champaine	66:17	65:59	94:29	226:46	52,000

*Until 1987, racing times were measured in minutes and hundredths of minutes. Times have been rounded off.
**This was Wright's second win of this race. He took his first championship in 1950.

Earthquakes

(*See also* Waves)

Between 1899 and early 1992, 10 Alaska earthquakes occurred that equaled or exceeded a magnitude of 8 on the Richter scale. During the same period, more than 70 earthquakes took place that were of magnitude 7 or greater, the most recent occurring in the Gulf of Alaska on March 6, 1988, and registering 7.6 on the Richter scale.

According to the Alaska Tsunami Warning Center, earthquake activity in Alaska typically follows the same pattern from month to month, interspersed with sporadic swarms, or groups of small earthquakes, and punctuated every decade or so by a great earthquake and its aftershocks. Alaska is the most seismic of all the 50 states, and the most seismically active part of the state is the Aleutian Islands arc system. Seismicity related to this system extends into the Gulf of Alaska and northward into interior Alaska to a point near Mount McKinley. These earthquakes are largely the result of underthrusting of the North Pacific plate, with most seismic activity taking place along the Aleutian Island chain. Many earthquakes resulting from this underthrusting occur in Cook Inlet—particularly near Mount Illiamna and Mount Redoubt—and near Mount McKinley. North of the Alaska Range, in the central interior, most earthquakes are of shallow origin.

An earthquake created the highest seiche, or splash wave, ever recorded on the evening of July 9, 1958, when a quake with a magnitude of 7.9 on the Richter scale rocked the Yakutat area. A landslide containing approximately 40 million cubic yards of rock plunged into Gilbert Inlet at the head of Lituya Bay. The gigantic splash resulting from the slide sent a wave 1,740 feet up the opposite mountain side, denuding it of trees and soil down to bedrock. It then fell back and swept through the length of the bay and out to sea. One fishing boat anchored in Lituya Bay at the time was lost with its crew of two; another was carried over a spit of land by the wave and soon after foundered, but its crew was saved. A third boat anchored in the bay miraculously survived intact. A total of four square miles of coniferous forest was destroyed.

The most destructive earthquake to strike Alaska occurred at 5:36 p.m. on Good Friday, March 27, 1964—a day now referred to as Black Friday. Registering between 8.4 and 8.6 on the Richter scale in use at the time, its equivalent moment magnitude has since been revised upward to 9.2, making it the strongest earthquake ever recorded in North America. With its primary epicenter deep beneath Miners Lake in northern Prince William Sound, the earthquake spread shock waves that were felt 700 miles away. The earthquake and seismic waves that followed killed 131 persons, 103 of them Alaskans. The death tally was: Chenega, 23; Kodiak 12; Point Nowell, 1; Point Whitshed, 1; Port Ashton, 1; Port Nellie Juan, 3; Seward, 11; Valdez, 31; Whittier, 12; Kalsin Bay, 6; Cape St. Elias, 1; Spruce Cape, 1. Of the 131 deaths, 119 were caused by the tsunami that resulted from the earthquake.

The 1964 earthquake released 10 million times more energy than the atomic bomb that devastated Hiroshima in World War II, and 80 times the energy of the San Francisco earthquake of 1906. It also moved more earth farther, both horizontally and vertically, than any other earthquake ever recorded except the 1960 Chilean earthquake. In the 69-day period after the main quake, there were 12,000 jolts of 3.5 magnitude or greater.

The highest sea wave caused by the 1964 earthquake occurred when an undersea slide near Shoup Glacier in Port Valdez triggered a wave that toppled trees 100 feet above tidewater and deposited silt and sand 220 feet above salt water.

Economy

Few states in the union have experienced the boom–and–bust cycles that have characterized Alaska's resource-rich economy. Driven by the oil, timber, mining, fishing and tourism industries, Alaska's economy expands when it is able to export its goods and services abroad or to the Lower 48. The peaks and troughs in Alaska's economy are seasonal and often dependent upon events outside the state's borders.

The oil and gas industry is by far the major player in the Alaskan economy. In terms of revenue to the state, no industry is as important to Alaska's economy as oil. About $2 billion a year, or 85 percent of every state dollar, is generated by taxes and royalties on North Slope crude oil. When oil prices are high, so are state revenues. For every one dollar per barrel increase in the price of oil, the state collects $150 million from royalty and severance taxes. Nearly 85 percent of the state budget is paid for by oil revenues and more than 20 percent of all jobs in the state are directly dependent on state government spending. The Alaska economy suffered a major blow with the drop in oil prices in 1986; few industries were spared during the recession. The recovery that began in 1989 was spurred on in part by higher oil prices. The Exxon Valdez oil spill cleanup effort added about $2 billion to the state's economy over 18 months. The fortunes of Alaska's oil industry, and therefore many sectors of the economy, are dependent on world oil prices.

In 1991, Alaska's economy posted a moderate 2.1 percent employment growth rate. This performance is weaker compared to the exceptional growth experienced in 1989 and 1990. Overall, Alaska's economy slowed down in 1991; however, the high growth rate of the previous two years was not expected to be sustained. According to the May 1992 issue of *Alaska Economic Trends*, continued expansion of tourist-related transportation, tourist-related trade and services, bottomfish industries, and retail trade project a positive outlook for at least 1992 and 1993.

Several factors contributed to Alaska's slowing economy in 1991— declining oil prices, troubles in the timber industry and little growth in the trade and services sector. State economists foresee a pattern of slow, but continued, growth in 1992. However, the state's economic outlook is based on the price of North Slope crude. If the price of oil drops below the projected $15–$17 per barrel, employment growth is likely to drop.

Mining and construction experienced no significant growth in employment in 1991. Nine out of ten wage and salary jobs in Alaska's mining industry are oil and gas related, so the outlook for mining is tied directly to the fortunes of the oil industry. Oil prices fell to $15 per barrel at the end of 1991. Entering 1992, the mood in the industry was somewhat troubled. Overall, the oil and gas industry is expected to experience employment decline during 1992–93 with Arco Alaska and BP Exploration's cost-cutting programs and consolidation efforts. But there are some important projects in the works: new well development in Cook Inlet; oil production on line at Point McIntyre; and construction of a facility designed to increase oil production, which will be completed in 1993.

In the fishing industry, recent booms in the shellfish and bottomfish harvests have also boosted employment in seafood processing to levels not seen since the king crab boom of the early 1980s. The commercial fishing industry in Alaska has been growing since the 1970s and is today a $1.2 billion industry. The bottomfish harvest in particular has experienced tremendous growth—700 percent in the last 10 years.

On the downside, the timber industry posted losses during 1991 as three sawmills—in Seward, Haines and Klawock—in Alaska were closed, and world markets for timber waned, a trend unlikely to change until 1993.

The transportation, communications and utilities sector became one of the fastest growing industries in 1991. Though several international air carriers stopped serving Anchorage, air cargo carriers such as Federal Express helped boost the industry, as well as MarkAir's expanded service into Seattle and Southeast Alaska.

Tourism in Alaska has experienced a steady annual growth of about 4 percent per year, attracting over a half million visitors last year. Steady growth is expected to continue. The industry is Alaska's second largest primary employer, directly employing 19,000 people and affecting 38,000 jobs indirectly. The Division of Tourism spent more than $11 million to market

Alaska's natural beauty and visitor potential. Most tourist dollars are spent between June 1 and August 31. But the state Division of Tourism is enticing more winter visitors these days. In fact, 4,000 Japanese tourists visited Alaska in the winter of 1990 to view the northern lights, compared to 1,000 Japanese in 1989. During the past three years, the number of tourists visiting Fairbanks for a northern lights vacation has increased more than 300 percent.

Outlook for the 1992 tourist season is optimistic; some segments of the industry predict about 30,000 more visitors, primarily due to the 50th anniversary of the Alaska Highway. However, low airfares to Europe are attracting some potential visitors from Alaska destinations. Lower gas prices will also aid the industry.

The outlook for most of Alaska's industries in 1992 and 1993 is for continued modest growth, though Alaska's economic fortune depends on the price and flow of oil through the pipeline.

Education

(*See also* School Districts *and* Universities and Colleges)

According to the 1991-92 *Alaska Education Directory*, Alaska has 472 public schools and approximately 80 private and denominational schools. The Bureau of Indian Affairs operated schools in Alaska until 1985.

The state Board of Education has seven members appointed by the governor. (In addition, two nonvoting members are appointed by the board to represent the military and public school students.) The board is responsible for setting policy for education in Alaska schools and appoints a commissioner of education to carry out its decisions. The 472 public schools are controlled by 54 school districts and each school district elects its own school board. There are 21 Regional Education Attendance Areas that oversee education in rural areas outside the 33 city and borough school districts.

Any student in grades kindergarten through 12 (K–12) may choose to study at home through the unique state-operated Centralized Correspondence School, which also serves traveling students, GED students, migrant students and students living in remote areas. Summer school classes are also available through correspondence; each year, up to 3,000 students are enrolled in this program. Home study has been an option for Alaskan students since 1939.

The state Department of Education also operates the Alaska Vocational Technical Center at Seward and a number of other education programs ranging from adult basic education to literacy skills.

Alaskans 7 through 16 years old are required to attend school. According to state regulations, a student must earn a minimum of 21 high school credits to receive a high school diploma. The state Board of Education has stipulated that four credits must be earned in language arts; three in social studies; two each in math and science; and one in physical education. Local school boards set the remainder of the required credits.

Since 1976, the state has provided secondary school programs to any community in which an elementary school is operated and one or more children of high school age wish to attend high school. This mandate was the result of a suit initiated on behalf of Molly Hootch, a high-school-age student from Emmonak. Prior to the so-called Molly Hootch Decree, high school-age students in villages without a secondary school attended high school outside their village. Of the 127 villages originally eligible for high school programs under the Molly Hootch Decree, only a few remain without one.

There were approximately 8,122 teachers and administrators in the public schools and approximately 110,000 students enrolled in K–12 in public schools in 1990–91. The size of schools in Alaska varies greatly, from a 1,973-student high school in Anchorage to one- or two-teacher, one-room schools in remote rural areas.

Of the school district's operating fund, 67 percent is provided by the state, 25 percent by local governments and 8 percent by the federal government. Alaska's average salary for teachers is among the highest in the nation.

51

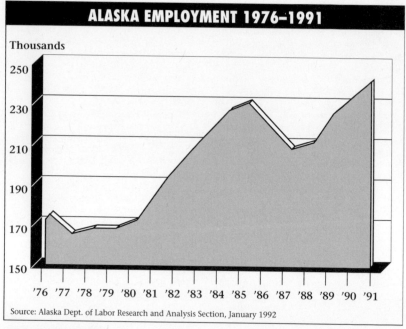

ALASKA EMPLOYMENT 1976–1991

Thousands

Source: Alaska Dept. of Labor Research and Analysis Section, January 1992

Employment

(*See also* Economy)

Alaska's economy showed a moderate increase in employment growth in 1991 of 2.1 percent. This slower growth followed two consecutive years of strong employment growth in 1989 and 1990.

In January 1992, the unemployment rate stood at 11.6 percent, the highest January rate reported since 1987. Factors that contributed to this rate hike were the seasonal layoffs in construction and retail trade industries.

The number of wage and salary jobs in Alaska in 1991 was about 243,000.

ALASKA EMPLOYMENT BY INDUSTRY 1991

Trade 19%

Transportation/Communications/Utilities 9%

Manufacturing 7%

Construction 4%

Mining (includes oil & gas) 5%

Finance/Insurance/Real Estate 4%

Government 29%

Services & Misc. 21%

Other 2%

Source: Alaska Dept. of Labor Research and Analysis Section, January 1992

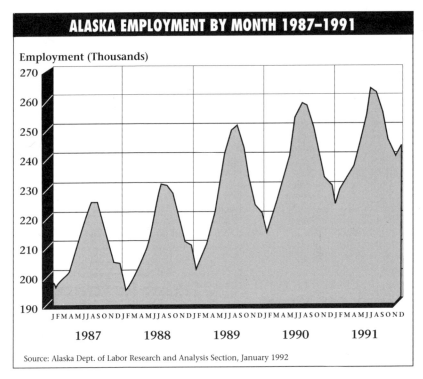

ALASKA EMPLOYMENT BY MONTH 1987–1991

Employment (Thousands)

JFMAMJJASOND JFMAMJJASOND JFMAMJJASOND JFMAMJJASOND JFMAMJJASOND

1987   1988   1989   1990   1991

Source: Alaska Dept. of Labor Research and Analysis Section, January 1992

The seafood-processing industry and transportation were the leaders in the employment field, adding 4,900 new jobs. Employment in seafood processing grew by almost 15 percent because of the related boom in shellfish and fish harvesting in southwestern Alaska.

Transportation employment grew 5.8 percent in 1991. Decreases in international air traffic were offset by increases in domestic air carrier expansion and freight traffic. Staff expansion at Alyeska Pipeline Service also helped boost the growth in the transportation sector.

Alaska's real estate market showed renewed activity after a several-year recession. As a result, employment at banks and lending institutions increased slightly as well.

Construction and mining remained about the same for 1991 as in 1990. There was also little or no growth in the oil and gas industries, with oil companies such as Arco Alaska and BP Exploration consolidating interests and laying off workers in the oil field. Layoffs in

the oil industry won't be completely reflected in the employment figures until sometime in 1992. Oil prices dropped to $15 per barrel by the end of 1991.

However, the most significant employment losses in 1991 were posted in the wood products industry, as sawmills were closed in Seward, Haines and Klawock. Southeast Alaska's logging industry also reported losses, mirroring the dwindling world markets for timber.

Alaska's unemployment rate is best characterized by a very seasonal labor market. Increased activity of all types in the summer makes unemployment fairly low, while a lack of activity in the winter months pushes up the unemployment rate. In addition, unemployment figures vary dramatically from one region to another. High unemployment rates in Alaska's rural areas are common. In interior Alaska, for example, the unemployment rate approaches 20 percent in the winter months. On the other hand, bustling seaports such as Kodiak experience unemployment rates below 3 percent during the summer.

Unemployment figures for December 1991 were 10.1 percent statewide; 7.3 percent for Anchorage; 11.3 percent for Fairbanks; 7.5 percent for Juneau; 13.7 percent for Kodiak; 12.6 percent for Nome; 13 percent for Ketchikan; 14.7 percent for Yukon–Koyukuk.

If you're seriously considering a move to Alaska to seek a job, first make a visit and explore the possibilities yourself. Jobs are scarce in Alaska and housing is expensive—there are now, and will be in the foreseeable future, plenty of Alaska residents out of work and anxious to find jobs. For additional information, write: Alaska Department of Labor, Alaska State Employment Service, P.O. Box 3-7000, Juneau 99802. Employment offices are located in most major communities.

Energy and Power

For the purposes of classifying power usage, the state of Alaska can be divided into three major regions, each having similar energy patterns, problems and resources: the Extended Railbelt region; the Southeast region; and the bush region. The Extended Railbelt region consists of major urban areas linked by the Alaska Railroad (Seward, Anchorage and Fairbanks). The southcentral area of this region uses relatively inexpensive natural gas in Cook Inlet and hydroelectrical power plants for electrical production and heating. The Fairbanks–Tanana Valley area uses primarily coal, and also oil, to meet its electrical needs. Future electrical demand for the Railbelt region will be met by a combination of hydropower and coal- and gas-fired generators. The Southeast region relies on hydro-

power for a large portion of its electrical generation. (Most of the existing hydroelectric power projects in Alaska are located in the Southeast region and more are planned.) In the smaller communities, diesel generators are used.

The bush region includes all communities that are remote from the major urban areas of the Extended Railbelt and Southeast regions. Electricity in bush communities is typically provided by small diesel generators. Where wind projects are feasible, such as at Lolo Bay and Unalakleet, wind power can be a viable, fuel-saving alternative to diesel-powered generators. Thermal needs in the bush are currently being met almost entirely by heating oil. Wood and kerosene heaters are used to a limited extent. Natural gas is available in Barrow.

Eskimo Ice Cream

Also called *akutak* (Yup'ik Eskimo word for Eskimo ice cream), this classic Native delicacy, popular throughout Alaska, is traditionally made of whipped berries, seal oil and snow. Sometimes shortening, raisins and sugar are added. In different regions, variations are found. One uses the soopalallie berry, *Shepherdia canadensis* (also called soapberry), a bitter species that forms a frothy mass like soapsuds when beaten.

Ferries

(*See also* Boating *and* Cruises)

The state Department of Transportation and Public Facilities, Marine Highway System, provides year-round scheduled ferry service for passengers and vehicles to communities in southeastern and southwestern Alaska. The Southeast and Southwest Alaska ferry systems do not connect with each other.

A fleet of six ferries on the southeastern system connects Bellingham, Washington, and Prince Rupert, British Columbia, with the southeastern Alaska ports of Hyder/Stewart, Ketchikan, Metlakatla, Hollis, Petersburg, Wrangell, Kake, Sitka, Angoon,

Pelican, Hoonah, Tenakee Springs, Juneau, Haines and Skagway. These southeastern communities—with the exception of Hyder, Haines and Skagway—are accessible only by boat, ferry or airplane. The six vessels of the southeastern system are the *Aurora, Columbia, LeConte, Malaspina, Matanuska* and *Taku.*

Southwestern Alaska is served by two ferries. The *Tustumena* serves Seward, Port Lions, Kodiak, Homer, Seldovia, Cordova and Valdez, with limited summer service to Chignik, Sand Point, King Cove, Cold Bay and Dutch Harbor. In summer, the *Bartlett* provides service between Valdez, Cordova and Whittier.

Scheduled state ferry service to southeastern Alaska began in 1963; ferry service to Kodiak Island began in 1964. The first three ferries of the Alaska ferry fleet were the *Malaspina, Matanuska* and *Taku.*

Reservations should be made for all sailings. Senior Citizen and Handicapped rates are available. The address of the main office of the Alaska Marine Highway System is P.O. Box 25535, Juneau 99802-5535; phone (907) 465-3941; or toll free, 1-800-642-0066.

Alaska State Ferry Data

Aurora: (235 feet, 14 knots), 250 passengers, 34 vehicles, no cabins. Began service in 1977.

Bartlett: (193 feet, 14 knots), 190 passengers, 30 vehicles, no cabins. Began service in 1969.

Columbia: (418 feet, 19 knots), 675 passengers, 140 vehicles, 91 cabins. Began service in 1974.

LeConte: (235 feet, 14 knots), 250 passengers, 34 vehicles, no cabins. Began service in 1974.

Malaspina: (408 feet, 16.5 knots), 500 passengers, 91 vehicles, 84 cabins. Began service in 1963 and was lengthened and renovated in 1972.

Matanuska: (408 feet, 16.5 knots), 500 passengers, 91 vehicles, 108 cabins. Began service in 1963.

Taku: (352 feet, 16 knots), 500 passengers, 73 vehicles, 44 cabins. Began service in 1963.

Tustumena: (296 feet, 14 knots), 220 passengers, 41 vehicles, 26 cabins. Began service in 1964.

Embarking Passenger and Vehicle Totals (in thousands) on Alaska Mainline Ferries*

Southeastern System

	Passengers	Vehicles
1965	123.7	25.8
1970	137.2	28.5
1972	162.7	39.4
1973	162.7	38.4
1974	174.7	41.4
1975	184.5	45.9
1976	181.7	46.3
1977	148.5	40.0
1978	222.1	53.7
1979	244.7	58.2
1980	275.8	63.2
1981	281.6**	65.6**
1982	299.5	73.2
1983	307.8	75.4
1984	311.5	80.0
1985	313.1	79.8
1986	296.1	76.0
1987	326.6	83.5
1988	344.2	90.7
1989	344.4	89.8
1990	363.1	94.7
1991	368.8	95.2

Southwestern System

	Passengers	Vehicles
1970	6.9	3.2
1971	25.8	7.7
1972	35.9	9.9
1973	40.7	11.3
1974	44.6	12.4
1975	45.0	12.8
1976	44.4	11.7
1977	38.8	12.5
1978	46.6	13.2
1979	49.4	13.9
1980	49.5	14.0
1981	55.8	15.1
1982	54.5	15.6
1983	55.5	15.9
1984	55.8	15.5
1985	56.3	16.5
1986	51.8	16.0

Southwestern System *(continued)*

	Passengers	Vehicles
1987	52.0	16.5
1988	50.3	16.6
1989	44.2	15.7
1990	50.5	16.5
1991	36.2	12.8

*Mainline ports for Southeast are: Seattle (until 1989), Bellingham (since 1989), Vancouver (1970 to 1973 only), Prince Rupert, Ketchikan, Wrangell, Petersburg, Sitka, Juneau, Haines and Skagway. Mainline ports for southwestern Alaska are: Anchorage (1970 to 1973 only), Cordova, Valdez, Whittier, Homer, Seldovia, Kodiak, Seward and Port Lions.
**Does not include totals of passengers (9.5) and vehicles (2.9) on the MV *Aurora*.

NAUTICAL MILES BETWEEN PORTS
Southeastern System
Bellingham–Ketchikan, 600
Prince Rupert–Ketchikan, 91
Ketchikan–Metlakatla, 16
Ketchikan–Hollis, 40
Hollis–Petersburg, 122
Hollis–Wrangell, 95
Ketchikan–Wrangell, 89
Wrangell–Petersburg, 41
Petersburg–Juneau, 108
Petersburg–Kake, 59
Kake–Sitka, 110
Sitka–Angoon, 66
Angoon–Tenakee, 33
Tenakee–Hoonah, 47
Angoon–Hoonah, 60
Hoonah–Juneau (Auke Bay), 45
Sitka–Hoonah, 115
Hoonah–Pelican via South Pass, 58
Hoonah–Juneau, 68
Juneau–Haines, 91
Haines–Skagway, 13
Juneau (Auke Bay)–Haines, 68
Petersburg–Juneau (Auke Bay), 120
Petersburg–Sitka, 156
Juneau (Auke Bay)–Sitka, 136

Southwestern System
Seward–Cordova, 146
Seward–Valdez, 143
Cordova–Valdez, 73
Valdez–Whittier, 84
Seward–Kodiak, 175
Kodiak–Port Lions, 27
Kodiak–Homer, 126
Homer–Seldovia, 16
Kodiak–Sand Point via Sitkinak
Strait, 353

Fires on Wild Land

The 1992 fire season marked 53 years of fire fighting in Alaska. In 1939, fire guards covered only 4 percent of the area needing protection. Today, no area goes unprotected. Village crews make up the backbone of Alaska's fire-fighting operations.

Fire season starts in April or May, when winter's dead vegetation is vulnerable to any spark. Lightning is the leading cause of wild land fires in Alaska. In June, thunderstorms bring as many as 3,000 lightning strikes a day to the Alaska Interior. By mid-July in a normal year, rainfall in interior Alaska increases.

When wildfires threaten inhabited areas, the Bureau of Land Management's (BLM) Alaska Fire Service (in the northern half of the state) and the State of Alaska Division of Forestry (in the southern half of the state) provide fire protection to lands managed by the BLM, National Park Service, U.S. Fish and Wildlife Service, Native corporations and the state.

All land management agencies in Alaska have placed their lands in one

of four protection categories—critical, full, modified and limited. These protection levels set priorities for fire fighting.

With its 586,000 square miles of land, Alaska is more than twice the size of Texas. Most of this vast area has no roads, and transportation for fire fighters is usually by airplane. Fire camps are remote. Mosquito repellent is a necessity, but headlamps are not required since the midnight sun shines all night. Aircraft bring in all supplies, even drinking water. Radios are the only means of communication with headquarters.

Black spruce is a fire-dependent species and burns very quickly. Fire fighters use chain saws to cut the trees and pulaskis to cut through the underlying vegetation. It is nearly impossible to transport heavy equipment to fires in remote areas. Bulldozers are not used because they damage the delicate permafrost layer, leading to dramatic erosion.

Fire fighters no longer depend on lookout towers in the wilderness to spot wildfires. Today, computers detect the ionization from a lightning strike anywhere in the state, determine the latitude and longitude of the strike and display it on a computer screen. Detection specialists then fly to the areas of greatest risk.

When a fire is reported, computers tell the dispatcher which agency manages the land and whether the fire should be aggressively attacked.

Remote automatic weather stations report weather conditions all over Alaska, enabling weather forecasters to predict thunderstorms in any part of the state. Smokejumpers and retardant airplanes are pre-positioned close to the predicted thunderstorm activity.

The largest single fire ever reported in Alaska burned 1,161,200 acres 74 miles northwest of Galena in 1957. In 1977, the Bear Creek fire was the largest in the United States that year, consuming 361,000 acres near the Farewell airstrip. Unusually dry weather in 1990 made it the most severe fire season on record in Alaska. Lightning was the primary cause of fires with an average of 2,000 strikes a day occurring between June 26 and July 5.

Calendar Year	No. of Fires	Acres Burned
1956	226	476,593
1957	391	5,049,661
1958	278	317,215
1959	320	596,574
1960	238	87,18057
1961	117	5,100
1962	102	38,975
1963	194	16,290
1964	164	3,430
1965	148	7,093
1966	256	672,765
1967	207	109,005
1968	442	1,013,301
1969	511	4,231,820
1970	487	113,486
1971	472	1,069,108
1972	641	963,686
1973	336	59,816
1974	869	662,960
1975	344	127,845
1976	622	69,119
1977	681	2,209,408
1978	356	7,757
1979	620	432,425
1980	417	188,778
1981	556	758,335
1982	283	70,798
1983	800	109,187*
1984	845	122,901*
1985	261	372,230
1986	396	395,169
1987	706	158,851*
1988	639	2,167,795*
1989	485	68,893*
1990	932	3,189,427*
1991	760	1,667,965*

*Combined AFS (federal) and state coverage.

Fish Wheel

The fish wheel is a machine fastened to a river shore and propelled by current, which scoops up fish heading upstream to spawn. Widely used for subsistence salmon fishing, the fish wheel provides an easy and inexpensive way of catching salmon without injuring them. Contrary to popular belief, Alaska Natives did not invent the fish wheel. Non-natives apparently first introduced the fish wheel on the Tanana River in 1904. Soon after, it appeared on the Yukon River, where it was used by both settlers and Natives. It first appeared on the Kuskokwim in

1914, when prospectors introduced it for catching salmon near Georgetown.

Today, subsistence fishing with the use of a fish wheel is allowed on the Copper River, as well as the Yukon River and its tributaries. Currently, there are 166 limited-entry permits for the use of fish wheels by commercial salmon fishermen on the Yukon River system—the only district where commercial and subsistence fishermen use the same gear. Fishing times with the wheels are regulated.

Prior to its appearance in Alaska, the fish wheel was used on the East Coast, on the Sacramento River in California and on the Columbia River in Washington and Oregon.

Fishing

COMMERCIAL

Alaska's commercial fish production is greater in value than that of any other state in the country and first in volume, according to the state Department of Fish & Game.

Value and Volume of Alaska Fish and Shellfish Landings*

Year	Value	Volume (in lbs.)
1976	$219,071,000	600,203,000
1977	333,844,000	658,754,000
1978	482,207,000	767,167,000
1979	622,284,000	854,247,000
1980	561,751,000	983,664,000
1981	639,797,000	975,245,000
1982	575,569,000	878,935,000
1983	543,941,000	963,765,000
1984	509,300,000	1,002,909,000
1985	590,751,000	1,184,807,000
1986	752,417,000	1,236,062,000
1987	941,690,000	1,697,547,000
1988	1,339,394,000	2,639,250,000
1989	1,332,000,000	5,213,100,000
1990	1,500,000,000	5,920,000,000
1991	1,216,482,000	5,144,800,000

*Source: National Marine Fisheries Service, U.S. Department of Commerce

Commercial fisheries in Alaska during 1991 harvested approximately 5.14 billion pounds of seafood, conservatively worth about $1.2 billion. The breakdown on the various commercial fisheries is as follows:

The 1991 commercial salmon harvest, at more than 189 million salmon (more than 729 million pounds), is the largest on record, surpassing the previous record of 155 million fish established in 1990. While the catch was up 12 percent over 1990, the total poundage increased by only about 5 percent, which can be attributed to a greater proportion of pink salmon in the current harvest. Salmon harvests have exceeded the 100 million fish mark since 1980, except for the 1987 harvest of 96.5 million fish.

The record harvest glutted the market, which depressed prices and sparked fishermen's boycotts statewide. Fishermen dumped 2.7 million pink salmon into Prince William Sound when no markets could be found for the fish. More than 1.5 million pink salmon from Prince William Sound were given to the people of the Soviet Union and to Alaska food banks.

Preliminary ex-vessel value estimates indicate that the 1991 salmon season was worth about $312 million, or about 40 percent less that that earned in 1990.

The 1991 record harvest was fueled by the catch of more than 129 million pink salmon, the largest ever recorded. This exceeds the previous record of 96.8 million pink salmon established in 1989, which is the parent year for this returning brood. Chinook catches statewide decreased from 1990. Chum salmon catches were mixed, with very poor landings in Prince William Sound, average to below anticipated landings in various Arctic–Yukon–Kuskokwim fisheries, and above-average landings in the Southeast and Westward regions. Coho salmon harvests were at the most recent 5-year average statewide level.

Herring fisheries in 1991 harvested about 106 million pounds, worth about $28 million. That's up a bit from 1990. The harvest includes sac roe, spawn-on-kelp, and food and bait catches.

Halibut fishermen landed more than 46 million pounds, worth about $91 million. Though halibut landings have been declining in recent years in Alaska, this season's catch reflects a 7 percent increase from 1990.

Shellfish fisheries resulted in the 1991 harvest of more than 400 million

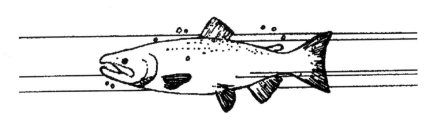

pounds—easily establishing a new record—of crab, shrimp and miscellaneous shellfish species, valued at $307 million. This surpasses the 1990 harvest by more than 52 percent, chiefly due to the record harvest of the *C. opilio* tanner crab at more than 325 million pounds. That was followed by the *C. bairdi* tanner crabs at more than 40 million pounds, followed by the king crab fisheries with landings of approximately 28 million pounds. The total value of all shellfish was about $308 million, a decrease from 1990 because of lower crab prices.

Groundfish fisheries in Alaska harvested about 3.8 billion pounds, worth $483 million. Bering Sea pollock accounted for 74 percent of the volume and half the value of the groundfish fisheries. Pacific cod made up 14 percent of the volume and 25 percent of the value.

In 1990, two Alaska ports, Dutch Harbor/Unalaska and Kodiak, were rated in the top 10 for the nation for quantity of seafood landed. Five Alaskan ports—Dutch Harbor/Unalaska, Kodiak, Naknek-South Naknek, Egegik and Kenai—were rated in the top 10 for value of product landed.

In 1991, several Alaskan ports received landing of more than 50 million pounds each: five individual ports of Dutch Harbor/Unalaska, Kodiak, Petersburg, Ketchikan and Dillingham; two combined ports on the Alaska Peninsula of Chignik, King Cove and Sand Point; and the combined southeastern ports of Gustavus, Hoonah, Kake, Metlakatla, Pelican, Tenakee Springs, Excursion Inlet and Yakutat.

Alaska's $1.2 billion fishing industry faces some hard choices in the future. Too many boats are chasing too few fish, according to some experts. Highly efficient trawlers with huge capacities have emphasized speed and volume fishing, increasing pressure for more and more fish to be harvested. In 1970, for example, halibut in the Gulf of Alaska were caught during a three-month fishing season by just 211 boats. In 1991, more than 2,500 boats compete for the halibut harvest, compressing the season to just two days.

Nowhere in the industry has the race for fish been as frenzied as for Alaska's groundfish, for which the number of harvesting permits has grown 700 percent in the last 10 years. Not so long ago, groundfish such as pollock and cod were considered low-value species. Groundfish today is a $500 million piece of the fisheries pie.

There is growing concern that over-exploitation of Alaska's fisheries could result in biological devastation of some species—a problem that New England fisheries now face. In the quest for quick, high-yield catches, accidental by-catch waste such as halibut, salmon and crab have been of growing concern. An estimated 3 percent of the halibut taken from the North Pacific in 1989 was the result of waste. In addition to by-catch waste and overfishing, illegal fishing, questions about the effects of concentrated harvesting during spawning season, and habitat pollution add to the potential biological difficulties that the Alaska fishing industry could face. The prospect is serious enough that regulators are considering an end to open access fishing by imposing a moratorium on the granting of new commercial permits and instituting a system of individual quotas. Individual fishermen would be allowed a set amount of fish to harvest each year.

Following on page 60 are Alaska Department of Fish & Game ex-vessel value figures:

Value of Alaska's Commercial Fisheries to Fishermen (in millions of dollars)

Species	1984	1985	1986	1987	1988	1989	1990	1991
Salmon	335.0	389.0	414.0	457.9	744.9	505.0	546.8	312.3
Shellfish	102.1	106.3	186.4	213.5	235.6	274.0	352.0	301.4
Halibut	24.9	40.3	63.2	60.9	66.1	76.1	85.0	91.6
Herring	19.8	38.0	38.5	41.8	56.0	20.3	27.0	28.6
Groundfish	108.8**	137.5**	197.9**	324.3	441.1	456.6	482.8	482.6

*Preliminary estimates.
**Includes international, joint-venture landings not previously shown in table.

1991 Preliminary Commercial Salmon Harvest (in thousands of fish)

Region	King	Red	Silver	Pink	Chum	Total
Southeast	327	2,058	2,347	61,515	2,949	69,196
Central (Prince William Sound, Cook Inlet, Kodiak,Chignik and Bristol Bay)	102	45,242	1,557	52,203	3,181	102,285
Arctic–Yukon–Kuskokwim	180	204	456	16	992	1,848
Western (Alaska Peninsula and Aleutian Islands)	30	4,811	499	3,662	1,349	10,351
Total	639	52,315	4,859	117,396	8,471	183,680

Note: Preliminary statistics are from ADF&G, 1992.

SPORT

There are 12 sportfishing management areas in Alaska, with varying bag and possession limits and possible special provisions. Current copies of *Alaska Sport Fishing Regulations Summary* are available from the Department of Fish and Game, Box 3-2000, Juneau 99802, or any sport fish office in the state.

Regulations

A sportfishing license is required for residents and nonresidents 16 years of age or older. (Alaskan residents 60 years of age or more who have been residents one year or more do not need a sportfishing license as long as they remain residents; a special identification card is issued for this exemption.)

Resident sportfishing licenses cost $10, valid for the calendar year issued (nonresident, $50; 1-day nonresident, $10; 3-day nonresident, $15; 14-day nonresident, $30). A resident is a person who has maintained a permanent place of abode within the state for 12 consecutive months and has continuously maintained a voting residence in the state. Military personnel on active duty permanently stationed in the state and their dependents can purchase a nonresident military sportfishing license ($10).

Nearly all sporting goods stores in Alaska sell fishing licenses. They are also available by mail from the Alaska Department of Revenue, Fish and Game License Section, 1111 W. Eighth St., Room 108, Juneau 99801.

The following sport fish species information includes the best bait or lure and the state record fish weight in pounds and ounces:

Arctic char: spoons, eggs, 17 lbs. 8 oz.

Arctic grayling: small spinners, flies, 4 lbs. 13 oz.

Burbot: bait, 24 lbs. 12 oz.

Chum salmon: spoons, 32 lbs.

Cutthroat trout: eggs, spinners, flies, 8 lbs. 6 oz.

Dolly Varden: eggs, spinners, flies, 17 lbs. 8 oz.

Halibut: octopus, herring, 450 lbs.

King salmon: eggs, herring, 97 lbs. 4 oz.

Kokanee: spinners, eggs, 2 lbs.

Lake trout: spoons, plugs, 47 lbs.

Northern pike: eggs, spoons, spinners, 38 lbs.

Pink salmon: small spoons, 12 lbs. 9 oz.

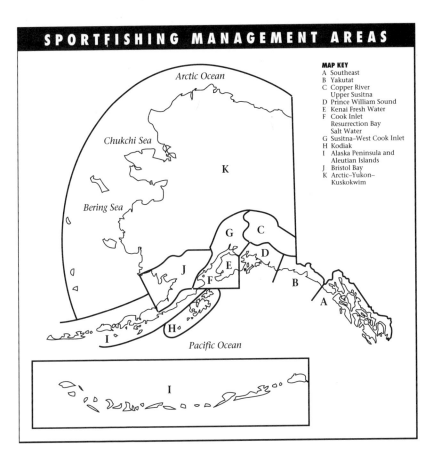

MAP KEY
A Southeast
B Yakutat
C Copper River
   Upper Susitna
D Prince William Sound
E Kenai Fresh Water
F Cook Inlet
   Resurrection Bay
   Salt Water
G Susitna–West Cook Inlet
H Kodiak
I Alaska Peninsula and
   Aleutian Islands
J Bristol Bay
K Arctic–Yukon–
   Kuskokwim

Arctic Ocean

Chukchi Sea

Bering Sea

Pacific Ocean

Rainbow/Steelhead trout: flies, lures, eggs, 42 lbs. 3 oz.

Red salmon: flies, 16 lbs.

Sheefish: spoons, 53 lbs.

Silver salmon: herring, spoons, 26 lbs.

Whitefish: flies, eggs, 9 lbs.

Furs and Trapping

According to the state furbearer biologist, the major sources of harvested Alaska furs are the Yukon and Kuskokwim valleys. The Arctic provides limited numbers of arctic fox, wolverine and wolf, but the gulf coast areas and Southeast Alaska are more productive. Southeast Alaska is a good source of mink and otter.

Trapping is seasonal work, and most trappers work summers at fishing or other employment. (Licenses are required for trapping. *See* Hunting section for cost of licenses.)

State regulated furbearers are beaver, coyote, red fox (includes cross, black or silver color phases), arctic fox (includes white or blue), lynx, marmot, marten, mink, muskrat, raccoon, river (land) otter, squirrel (parka or ground, flying and red), weasel, wolf and wolverine. Very little harvest or use is made of parka squirrels and marmots.

Flying squirrels are not caught deliberately, and raccoons, introduced in a couple of coastal locations years ago, appear to have been exterminated.

Prices for raw skins are widely variable and depend on the buyer, quality, condition and size of the fur. Pelts accepted for purchase are beaver,

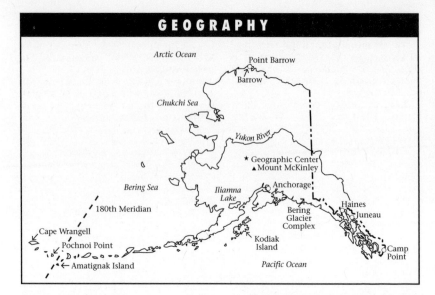

Arctic Ocean
Point Barrow
Barrow
Chukchi Sea
Yukon River
★ Geographic Center
▲ Mount McKinley
Bering Sea
Iliamna Lake
Anchorage
180th Meridian
Bering Glacier Complex
Haines
Juneau
Cape Wrangell
Pochnoi Point
Kodiak Island
Camp Point
← Amatignak Island
Pacific Ocean

coyote, lynx, marten, mink, muskrat, otter, red and white fox, red squirrel, weasel (ermine), wolf and wolverine. Check with a buyer for current market prices.

Related reading: *Trapline Twins,* by Julie and Miki Collins. Identical-twin sisters trap, canoe, dogsled and live off the land. *See* ALASKA NORTHWEST LIBRARY in the back of the book.

Geography

State capital: Juneau.
State population: 570,000
Land area: 586,412 square miles, or about 365,000,000 acres—largest state in the union; one-fifth the size of the Lower 48. Alaska is larger than the three next largest states in the United States combined.
Area per person: There are approximately 1.02 square miles per person.
Diameter: East to west, 2,400 miles; north to south, 1,420 miles.
Coastline: 6,640 miles, point to point; as measured on the most detailed maps available, including islands, Alaska has 33,904 miles of shoreline. Estimated tidal shoreline, including islands, inlets and shoreline to head of tidewater, is 47,300 miles.

Adjacent salt water: North Pacific Ocean, Bering Sea, Chukchi Sea, Arctic Ocean.
Alaska–Canada border: 1,538 miles long; length of boundary between the Arctic Ocean and Mount St. Elias, 647 miles; Southeast border with British Columbia and Yukon Territory, 710 miles; water boundary, 181 miles.
Geographic center: 63°50' north, 152° west, about 60 miles northwest of Mount McKinley.
Northernmost point: Point Barrow, 71°23' north.
Southernmost point: Tip of Amatignak Island, Aleutian Chain, 51°13'05" north.
Easternmost and westernmost point: It all depends on how you look at it. The 180th meridian—halfway around the world from the prime meridian at Greenwich, England, and the dividing line between east and west longitudes—passes through Alaska. According to one view, Alaska has both the easternmost and westernmost spots in the country! The westernmost is Amatignak Island, 179°10' west; and the easternmost, Pochnoi Point, 179°46' east. On the other hand, if you are facing north, east is to your right and west to your left. Therefore, the westernmost point is Cape Wrangell, Attu Island, 172°27' east; and the

easternmost is near Camp Point, in southeastern Alaska, 129°59' east.

Tallest mountain: Mount McKinley, 20,320 feet, and the tallest mountain in North America. Alaska has 39 mountain ranges, containing 17 of the 20 highest peaks in the U.S.

Largest natural freshwater lake: Iliamna, 1,150 square miles. Alaska has more than three million lakes more than 20 acres in size.

Longest river: Yukon, 1,400 miles in Alaska; 1,875 total. There are more than 3,000 rivers in the state. The Yukon River ranks third in length of U.S. rivers, behind the Mississippi and Missouri rivers.

Largest island: Kodiak, in the Gulf of Alaska, 3,588 square miles. There are 1,800 named islands in the state, 1,000 of which are located in Southeast Alaska.

Largest glacier: Bering Glacier complex, 2,250 square miles, which includes the Bagley Icefield. Ice fields cover about 5 percent of the state, or 29,000 square miles.

Largest city in population: Anchorage, population 226,338 (1990 census).

Largest city in area: Juneau, with 3,108 square miles (the largest city in square miles in North America).

Glaciers and Ice Fields

The greatest concentrations of glaciers are in the Alaska Range, Wrangell Mountains, and the coastal ranges of the Chugach, Coast, Kenai and St. Elias mountains, where annual precipitation is high. All of Alaska's well-known glaciers fall within these areas. (See map on page 64.)

Glaciers cover approximately 29,000 square miles—or 5 percent—of Alaska, which is 128 times more area covered by glaciers than in the rest of the United States. There are an estimated 100,000 glaciers in Alaska, ranging from tiny cirque glaciers to huge valley glaciers.

Glaciers are formed where, over a number of years, more snow falls than melts. Alaska's glaciers fall roughly into five general categories: alpine, valley, piedmont, ice fields and ice caps. Alpine (mountain and cirque) glaciers head high on the slopes of mountains and plateaus. Valley glaciers are an overflowing accumulation of ice from mountain or plateau basins. Piedmont glaciers result when one or more glaciers join to form a fan-shaped ice mass at the foot of a mountain range. Ice fields develop when large valley glaciers interconnect, leaving only the highest peaks and ridges to rise above the ice surface. Ice caps are smaller glaciers perched on plateaus.

Alaska's better-known glaciers accessible by road are: Worthington (Richardson Highway); Matanuska (Glenn Highway); Portage (Seward Highway) and Mendenhall (Glacier Highway). In addition, Childs and Sheridan glaciers may be reached by car from Cordova, and Valdez Glacier, also accessible by car, is only a few miles from the town of Valdez. The sediment-covered terminus of Muldrow Glacier in Denali National Park and Preserve is visible at a distance along several miles of the park road.

Many spectacular glaciers in Glacier Bay National Park and Preserve and in Prince William Sound are accessible by tour boat.

Glacier ice often appears blue because its great thickness absorbs all the colors of the spectrum except blue, which is reflected back.

Other facts about glaciers:

• About three-fourths of all the fresh water in Alaska is stored as glacial ice. This is many times greater than the volume of water stored in all the state's lakes, ponds, rivers and reservoirs.

• Longest tidewater glacier in North America is Hubbard, 76 miles in length (heads in Canada). In 1986, Hubbard rapidly advanced and blocked Russell Fiord near Yakutat. Later in the year, the ice dam gave way.

• Longest glacier is Bering (including Bagley Icefield), more than 100 miles in length.

• Southernmost active tidewater glacier in North America is LeConte.

• Greatest concentration of tidewater-calving glaciers is in Prince William Sound, with 20 active tidewater glaciers.

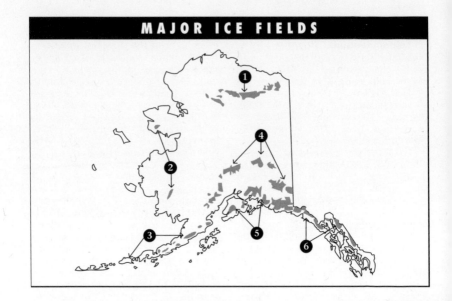

• Largest piedmont lobe glacier is Malaspina, 850 square miles; the Malaspina Glacier complex (including tributary glaciers) is approximately 2,000 square miles in area. The largest glacier is the Bering Glacier complex, about 2,250 square miles in size, which includes Bagley Icefield.

• La Perouse Glacier in Glacier Bay National Park is the only calving glacier in North America that discharges icebergs directly into the open Pacific Ocean.

• Iceberg production in Prince William Sound has increased fourfold recently, because Columbia Glacier is retreating.

• There are more than 750 glacier-dammed lakes in Alaska; the largest at the present time is 28-square-mile Chakachamna Lake west of Anchorage.

According to the U.S. Geological Survey, distribution of glacier ice is as follows (*see* map above):

Region	Sq. Miles (approx.)
1 **North:** Brooks Range	279
2 **West:** Seward Peninsula	2
Kilbuk Mountains	89
3 **Southwest:** Aleutian Islands	371
Alaska Peninsula	483
4 **Interior:** Alaska Range	5,367
Talkeetna Mountains	309
Wrangell Mountains	3,205
5 **Southcentral:** Kenai Mtns	1,776
Chugach Mountains	8,340
6 **Southeast:** St. Elias Mtns	4,556
Coast Mountains	4,055
Total	28,832

Gold

(*See also* Minerals and Mining)

The largest gold nugget ever found in Alaska was discovered near Nome. The nugget, weighing 155 troy ounces, was found Sept. 29, 1903, on Discovery Claim on Anvil Creek, Nome District. The nugget was 7 inches long, 4 inches wide and 2 inches thick.

Four other large nuggets have been found in Alaska, one of which also came from the Discovery Claim on Anvil Creek in 1899. It was the largest Alaska nugget found up to that time, weighing 82.2 troy ounces, and was 6 1/4 inches long, 3 1/4 inches wide, 1 3/8 inches thick at one end and 1/2 inch thick at the other.

In 1914, the second-largest nugget mined, weighing 138.8 troy ounces, was found near Discovery Claim on Hammond River, Wiseman District. Two of the top five nuggets have been discovered this decade, with one coming from Lower Glacier Creek, Kantishna District, in 1984, weighing 91.8 troy ounces, and the other from Ganes Creek, Innoko District, in 1986, weighing 122 troy ounces.

According to *Alaska's Mineral Industry 1991*, a publication of the Alaska Division of Geological and Geophysical Surveys, major operators produced 243,830 troy ounces of gold in 1991.

Following are volumes (in troy ounces) and value figures for recent years of Alaska gold production:

Gold Production in Alaska, 1980–91

Year	Vol. (in troy oz.)	Value
1980	75,000	$32,000,000
1981	134,000	55,200,000
1982	174,900	69,960,000
1983	169,000	67,600,000
1984	175,000	63,000,000
1985	190,000	61,175,000
1986	160,000	60,800,000
1987	229,700	104,500,000
1988	265,500	112,837,000
1989	297,900	113,796,000
1990	231,700	89,204,000
1991	243,900	88,291,000

The chart following shows the fluctuation in the price of gold after the gold standard was lifted in 1967. Note that these are average annual prices and do not reflect the highest or lowest prices during the year.

Average Annual Price of Gold, per Troy Ounce

Prior to 1934—$20.67	1979—$307.50
1934 to 1967— 35.00	1980— 569.73
1968— 39.26	1981— 548.90
1969— 41.51	1982— 461.00
1970— 36.41	1983— 400.00
1971— 41.25	1984— 360.00
1972— 58.60	1985— 325.00
1973— 97.81	1986— 380.00
1974—159.74	1989— 381.98
1975—161.49	1987— 447.00
1976—125.32	1990— 385.00
1977—148.31	1988— 425.00
1978—193.55	1991— 362.03

If you are interested in gold panning, sluicing or suction dredging in Alaska—for fun or profit—you'll have to know whose land you are on and familiarize yourself with current regulations.

Panning, sluicing and suction dredging on private property, established mining claims and Native lands is considered trespassing unless you have the consent of the owner. On state and federal lands, contact the agency for the area you are interested in for current restrictions on mining.

You can pan for gold for a small fee by visiting one of the commercial gold panning resorts in Alaska. These resorts rent gold pans and let you try your luck on gold-bearing creeks and streams on their property.

If you want to stake a permanent claim, the state Department of Natural Resources has a free booklet, *Regulations and Statutes Pertaining to Mining Rights of Alaska Lands,* which can be obtained by contacting the department office in Juneau, (907) 465-2400; Fairbanks, (907) 451-2790; and Anchorage, (907) 762-2518.

Gold Strikes and Rushes

1848—First Alaska gold discovery (Russian River on Kenai Peninsula)

1861—Stikine River near Telegraph Creek, British Columbia

1872—Cassiar district in Canada (Stikine headwaters country)

1872—Near Sitka

1874—Windham Bay near Juneau
1880—Gold Creek at Juneau
1886—Fortymile discovery
1887—Yakutat beach areas and Lituya Bay
1893—Mastodon Creek, starting Circle City
1895—Sunrise district on the Kenai Peninsula
1896—Klondike strike, Bonanza Creek, Yukon, Canada
1898—Anvil Creek near Nome; Atlin district
1898—British Columbia
1900—Porcupine rush out of Haines
1902—Fairbanks (Felix Pedro, Upper Goldstream Valley)
1906—Innoko
1907—Ruby
1908—Iditarod
1913—Marshall
1913—Chisana
1914—Livengood

Related reading: *Chilkoot Pass: The Most Famous Trail in the North,* revised and expanded edition, by Archie Satterfield. *See* ALASKA NORTHWEST LIBRARY in the back of the book.

Government

(*See also* Courts *and* Officials)

Alaska is represented in the U.S.Congress by two senators and one representative. The capital of Alaska is Juneau.

A governor and lieutenant governor are elected by popular vote for four-year terms on the same ticket. The governor is given extensive powers under the constitution. He administers 15 major departments: Administration, Commerce and Economic Development, Community and Regional Affairs, Corrections, Education, Environmental Conservation, Fish and Game, Health and Social Services, Labor, Law, Military and Veterans Affairs, Natural Resources, Public Safety, Revenue, and Transportation and Public Facilities.

The legislature is bicameral, with 20 senators elected from 14 senate districts for four-year terms, and 40 representatives from 27 election districts for two-year terms. Under the state constitution, redistricting is accomplished every 10 years, after the reporting of the decennial federal census. The latest redistricting occurred in 1981 and was carried out by the governor's office with assistance of an advisory apportionment board. The judiciary consists of a state supreme court, court of appeals, superior court, district courts and magistrates.

Alaska is unique among the 50 states in that most of its land mass has not been organized into political subdivisions equivalent to the county form of government. Local government is by a system of organized boroughs, much like counties in other states. Several areas of the state are not included in any borough because of sparse population. Boroughs generally provide a more limited number of services than cities. There are three classes. First- and second-class boroughs have three mandatory powers: education, land use planning, and tax assessment and collection. The major difference between the two classes is in how they may acquire other powers. Both classes have separately elected borough assemblies and school boards. A third-class borough has two mandatory powers: operation of public schools and taxation. All boroughs may assess, levy and collect real and personal property taxes. They may also levy sales taxes.

Incorporated cities are small units of local government, serving one community. There are two classes. First-class cities, generally urban areas, have six-member councils and a separately elected mayor. Taxing authority is somewhat broader than for second-class cities and responsibilities are broader. A first-class city that has adopted a home rule charter is called a home rule city; adoption allows the city to revise its ordinances, to the extent that the powers it assumes are those not prohibited by law or charter. Second-class cities, generally places with fewer than 400 people, are governed by a seven-member council, one of whom serves as mayor. Taxing authority is limited. A borough and all cities located within it may unite in a single unit of government called a unified municipality.

There are 246 federally recognized tribal governments in Alaska and one community organized under federal law. Originally an Indian reservation, Metlakatla was organized so municipal services could effectively be provided to its residents.

In 1991, there were 15 organized boroughs and unified home rule municipalities: three unified home rule municipalities, four home rule boroughs, seven second-class boroughs and one third-class borough.

Alaska's 150 incorporated cities include: 12 home rule cities, 22 first-class cities and 116 second-class cities. One city, Metlakatla, is organized under federal law.

BOROUGH ADDRESSES AND CONTACTS

Aleutians East Borough
P.O. Box 349, Sand Point 99661; phone (907) 383-5334

Municipality of Anchorage
Contact: Mayor's Office or Manager's Office, P.O. Box 196650, Anchorage 99519; phone (907) 343-4431

Bristol Bay Borough
Contact: Borough Clerk, P.O. Box 189, Naknek 99633; phone (907) 246-4224

Denali Borough
Contact: Mayor, P.O. Box 480, Anderson 99744; phone (907) 683-1330.

Fairbanks North Star Borough
Contact: Clerk, P.O. Box 71267, Fairbanks 99707; phone (907) 459-1000

Haines Borough
Contact: Borough Secretary, P.O. Box 1209, Haines 99827; phone (907) 766-2611

City and Borough of Juneau
Contact: City-Borough Manager, 155 S. Seward St., Juneau 99801; phone (907) 586-5240

Kenai Peninsula Borough
Contact: Borough Clerk, 144 N. Binkley St., Soldotna 99669; phone (907) 262-4441

Ketchikan Gateway Borough
Contact: Borough Manager, 344 Front St., Ketchikan 99901; phone (907) 225-6625

Kodiak Island Borough
Contact: Borough Mayor or Borough Clerk, 710 Mill Bay Road, Kodiak 99615; phone (907) 486-5736

Lake and Peninsula Borough
P.O. Box 495, King Salmon 99613; phone (907) 276-3421

Matanuska-Susitna Borough
Contact: Borough Manager, 350 E. Dahlia Ave., Palmer 99645-6488; phone (907) 745-4801

North Slope Borough
Contact: Borough Mayor, P.O. Box 69, Barrow 99723; phone (907) 852-2611

Northwest Arctic Borough
P.O. Box 1110, Kotzebue 99752; phone (907) 442-2500

City and Borough of Sitka
Contact: Administrator, 304 Lake St., Room 104, Sitka 99835; phone (907) 747-3294

Highways

(*See also* Alaska Highway *and* Dalton Highway)

As of Dec. 31, 1991, the state Department of Transportation and Public Facilities estimated total public road mileage in Alaska at 13,485 miles, including those in national parks and forests (1,950). The state also operates 2,229 miles of ferry routes. Highways in Alaska range from four-lane paved freeways to one-lane dirt and gravel roads. Approximately 47 percent of the roads in the Alaska Highway system are paved, with the exception of the following major highways that are gravel: Steese (Alaska Route 6), Taylor (Alaska Route 5), Elliott (Alaska Route 2), Dalton (Alaska Route 12) and Denali (Alaska Route 8). In addition, there were 2,200 miles of local city streets, 2,037 miles of borough roads and 541 miles listed as "other." Alaska's relative sparseness of roadway is accentuated by a comparison to Austria, a country only one-eighteenth the size of Alaska but with nearly twice as many public roads.

The chart on page 68 lists each major highway in Alaska, its route number, the year the highway opened to vehicle traffic and its total length within Alaska (most of the Alaska Highway, Haines Highway and Klondike Highway 2 lie within Canada). Also indicated is whether the highway is open all year or closed in winter:

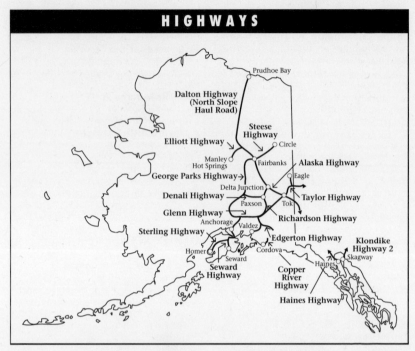

	Alaska Route	Year Opened	Total Length (miles)		Open
			Paved	Gravel	
Alaska	2	1942	298.2*		All year
Copper River	10 **		12.4	35.7	Apr.–Oct.
Dalton	12	1974		414	All year
Denali	8	1957	21	115	Apr.–Oct.
Edgerton	10	1923	35		All year
Elliott	2	1959	28	124	All year
George Parks	3	1971	322.7		All year
Glenn	1	1942	328*		All year
Haines	7	1947	40.5		All year
Klondike	2	1978	14.9		All year
Richardson	4	1923	368*		All year
Seward	1&9	1951	127		All year
Steese	6	1928	43.8	118.2	All year
Sterling	1	1950	135.8		All year
Taylor	5	1953		161	Apr.–Oct.

*The Richardson shares a common alignment with the Alaska Highway (for 98 miles) and with the Glenn (for 14 miles).

**Construction on the Copper River Highway—which was to link up with Chitina on the Edgerton—was halted by the 1964 Good Friday earthquake, which damaged the Million Dollar Bridge, and local Cordova citizens who desired semi-isolation.

Hiking

A variety of hiking trails for all levels of ability may be found in the state. The experienced hiker with proper topographic maps will find some of the best Alaska hiking is cross-country above tree line. Using both maps and tide tables, it is also feasible to hike along ocean shorelines at low tide.

Hikers in Alaska must plan for rapidly changing, inclement weather.

Take rain gear. If staying overnight in the back country, it's wise to carry a tent if a cabin is unavailable. Above tree line, snow can be encountered at any time of year.

Sporting goods stores in Alaska feature an excellent selection of hiking equipment. In addition, back country guides often furnish equipment on escorted expeditions.

Information on hiking in Alaska's national parks and monuments is available from the Alaska Public Lands Information Centers: 605 W. Fourth Ave., Suite 105, Anchorage 99501; 250 Cushman St., Suite 1A, Fairbanks 99701; and P.O. Box 359, Tok 99780; or from park headquarters for the area you're interested in. (*See* National Parks, Preserves and Monuments)

The Alaska Division of Parks (*see* State Park System) has information on hiking on the lands managed by that agency.

History

(*See also* Russian Alaska)

6,000–11,000 years ago—Human culture in southeastern, Aleutians, Interior and northwestern Arctic Alaska.

6,000 years ago—Most recent migration from Siberia across the land bridge. Earliest migration believed to have taken place up to 20,000 years ago.

3,000–5,000 years ago—Human culture present on the Bering Sea coast.

1725—Vitus Bering sent by Peter the Great to explore the North Pacific.

1741—On a later expedition, Bering in one ship and Alexei Chirikof in another ship, discover Alaska. Chirikof, probably sees land on July 15, a day ahead of his leader, who was perhaps 300 miles or more to the north. Georg Steller goes ashore on Kayak Island, becoming the first white man known to have set foot on Alaska soil.

1743—Russians begin concentrated hunting of sea otter, continuing until the species is almost decimated; fur seal hunting begins later.

1774–94—Explorations of Alaska waters by Juan Perez, James Cook and George Vancouver.

1784—First Russian settlement in

Alaska established at Three Saints Bay, Kodiak Island.

1794—Vancouver sights Mount McKinley.

1799—Alexander Baranof establishes the Russian post known today as Old Sitka. A trade charter is granted to the Russian–American Company.

1821—Russians prohibit trading in Alaska waters by other nations, making the Russian-American Company the sole trading firm.

1824–42—Russian exploration of the mainland leads to the discovery of the Kuskokwim, Nushagak, Yukon and Koyukuk rivers.

1847—Fort Yukon is established by Hudson's Bay Company.

1848—First mining begins in Alaska, on the Kenai Peninsula.

1853—Russian explorers-trappers find the first oil seeps in Cook Inlet.

1857—Coal mining begins at Coal Harbor, Kenai Peninsula, to supply steamers.

1859—Baron Edoard de Stoecki, minister and chargé d'affaires of the Russian delegation to the United States, is given authority to negotiate the sale of Alaska.

1867—United States under President Andrew Johnson buys Alaska from Russia for $7.2 million; the treaty is signed March 30 and formal transfer takes place on October 18 at Sitka. Fur seal population begins to stabilize. U.S. Army is given jurisdiction over the Department of Alaska the following year.

1869–70—The *Sitka Times*, first newspaper in Alaska, published.

1872—Gold is discovered near Sitka. Later discoveries include Windham, 1874; Juneau, 1880; Fortymile, 1886;

Circle City, 1893; Sunrise District (Kenai Peninsula), 1895; Nome, 1898; Fairbanks, 1902; Innoko, 1906; Ruby, 1907; Iditarod, 1908; Marshall, 1913; Chisana, 1913; and Livengood, 1914.

1878—First salmon canneries established at Klawock and Old Sitka.

1882—First commercial herring fishing begins; U.S. Navy destroys the Tlingit village of Angoon.

1887—Tsimshians, under Father William Duncan, arrive at Metlakatla from British Columbia.

1891—First oil claims staked in Cook Inlet area.

1897–1900—Klondike gold rush in Yukon Territory; heavy traffic through Alaska on the way to the gold fields.

1902—First oil production, at Katalla. Telegraph from Eagle to Valdez is completed.

1906—Peak gold production year. Alaska is granted a nonvoting delegate to Congress.

1911—Copper production begins at Kennicott.

1912—Territorial status for Alaska; first territorial legislature is convened the following year.

1913—First airplane flight in Alaska, at Fairbanks; first auto trip from Fairbanks to Valdez.

1914—President Wilson authorizes construction of the Alaska Railroad.

1916—First bill proposing Alaska statehood is introduced in Congress; peak copper production year.

1922—First pulp mill starts production at Speel River, near Juneau.

1923—President Warren Harding drives spike completing the Alaska Railroad.

1930—The first "talkie" motion picture is shown in Fairbanks, featuring the Marx Brothers in *The Cocoanuts.*

1935—Matanuska Valley Project, which establishes farming families in Alaska, begins. First Juneau to Fairbanks flight.

1936—All-time record salmon catch in Alaska—126.4 million fish.

1940—Military build-up in Alaska; Fort Richardson, Elmendorf Air Force Base are established. At this point there are only about 40,000 non-Native Alaskans and 32,458 Natives. Pan American Airways inaugurates twice-weekly service between Seattle,

Ketchikan and Juneau, using Sikorsky flying boats.

1942—Dutch Harbor is bombed and Attu and Kiska islands are occupied by Japanese forces. Alaska Highway is built—first overland connection to Lower 48.

1943—Japanese forces are driven from Alaska.

1944—Alaska–Juneau Mine shuts down.

1953—Oil well is drilled near Eureka, on the Glenn Highway, marking the start of modern oil history; first plywood mill at Juneau; first big pulp mill at Ketchikan.

1957—Kenai oil strike.

1958—Statehood measure is passed by Congress; statehood is proclaimed officially on Jan. 3, 1959. Sitka pulp mill opens.

1964—Good Friday earthquake, March 27, causes heavy damage throughout the gulf coast region; 131 people lose their lives.

1967—Alaska Centennial celebration; Fairbanks flood.

1968—Oil and gas discoveries at Prudhoe Bay on the North Slope; $900 million North Slope oil lease sale the following year; pipeline proposal follows.

1971—Congress approves Alaska Native Claims Settlement Act, granting title to 40 million acres of land and providing more than $900 million in payment to Alaska Natives.

1974—Trans-Alaska pipeline receives final approval; construction build-up begins.

1975—Population and labor force soar with construction of pipeline; Alaska Gross Products hits $5.8 billion—double the 1973 figure.

1976—Voters select Willow area for new capital site.

1977—Completion of the trans-Alaska pipeline from Prudhoe Bay to Valdez; shipment of first oil by tanker from Valdez to Puget Sound.

1978—A 200-mile off-shore fishing limit goes into effect. President Jimmy Carter withdraws 56 million acres to create 17 new national monuments as of Dec. 1, 1978.

1979—State of Alaska files suit to halt the withdrawal of 56 million acres of Alaska land by President Carter under the Antiquities Act.

1980—Special session of the Alaska Legislature votes to repeal the state income tax and provides for refunds of 1979 taxes. Legislature establishes a Permanent Fund as a repository for one-fourth of all royalty oil revenues for future generations. Census figures show Alaska's population grew by 32.4 percent during the 1970s. The Alaska Lands Act of 1980 puts 53.7 million Alaska acres into the national wildlife refuge system, parts of 25 rivers into the national wild and scenic rivers system, 3.3 million acres into national forest lands and 43.6 million acres into national park land.

1981—Legislature puts on the ballot a constitutional amendment proposal to limit state spending. Secretary of the Interior James Watt initiates plans to sell oil and gas leases on 130 million acres of Alaska's nonrestricted federal land and announces a tentative schedule to open 16 offshore areas of Alaska as part of an intense national search for oil and gas on the outer continental shelf.

1982—Oil revenues for state decrease. Vote for funds to move state capital from Juneau to Willow is defeated. First permanent fund dividend checks of $1,000 each are mailed to every six-month resident of Alaska.

1983—Time zone shift. All Alaska, except westernmost Aleutian Islands, moves to Alaska Standard Time, one hour west of Pacific Standard Time. Record-breaking salmon harvest in Bristol Bay. Building permits set a record at just under $1 billion.

1984—State of Alaska celebrates its 25th birthday.

1985—Anchorage receives the U.S. bid for the 1994 Olympics. Iditarod Sled Dog Race is won by Libby Riddles, the first woman to win in the history of the race.

1986—Mount Augustine in lower Cook Inlet erupts. World Championship Sled Dog Race held during Fur Rendezvous is canceled for the first time due to lack of snow. Iditarod Sled Dog Race is again won by a woman, Susan Butcher of Manley.

1987—Alaska is retained as America's choice for the 1994 Olympics. Iditarod Sled Dog Race is won by Susan

Mount Augustine

Butcher for the second straight year.

1988—The first successful solo winter ascent of Mount McKinley by Vern Tejas of Anchorage. The Iditarod Sled Dog Race is won by Susan Butcher for the third year in a row. Anchorage loses its bid to Norway for the 1994 Olympics.

1989—Worst oil spill in U.S. history occurs in Prince William Sound. Record-breaking cold hits entire state lasting for weeks. Soviets visit Alaska, and the Bering Bridge Expedition crosses the Bering Strait by dogsled and skis. Mount Redoubt begins erupting in December.

1990—Valdez sets a new record for snowfall. Susan Butcher wins her fourth Iditarod Sled Dog Race. Election upset as Walter J. Hickel becomes governor.

1991—Fairbanks sets a new record for snowfall. Rick Swenson claims fifth Iditarod win; Alaskan David Douthit killed in Gulf War.

1992—Alaska celebrates 50th anniversary of the Alaska Highway; Alaska's oldest newspaper, the *Anchorage Times*, shuts down; Mount Spurr erupts. (*See also* Yearly Highlights)

Holidays 1993

New Year's Day	January 1
Martin Luther King Day	January 18
Lincoln's Birthday	February 12
Washington's Birthday	
—holiday	February 15
—traditional	February 22
Seward's Day*	March 29

Memorial Day
—holiday ....May 31
—traditional ....May 30
Independence Day ....July 4
Labor Day ....September 6
Alaska Day* ....October 18
Veterans Day ....November 11
Thanksgiving Day............November 25
Christmas Day ....December 25

*Seward's Day commemorates the signing of the treaty by which the United States bought Alaska from Russia, signed on March 30, 1867. Alaska Day is the anniversary of the formal transfer of the territory and the raising of the U.S. flag at Sitka on Oct. 18, 1867.

Hooligan

Smelt, also known as eulachon or candlefish (because these oily little fish can be burned like candles), are known as "ooligan" in southeastern Alaska. Hooligan are caught by dip-netting as they travel upriver to spawn.

Hospitals and Health Facilities

(*See also* Pioneers' Homes)
Alaska has numerous hospitals, nursing homes and other health facilities. The only hospital in the state currently offering specialized care units is Providence Hospital in Anchorage, with its thermal unit (burn and frostbite), cancer treatment center and neonatal intensive care nursery.

A list of emergency medical services on Alaska's highways and marine highways is provided in a brochure available from the Office of Emergency Medical Services, Division of Public Health, Dept. of Health and Social Services, P.O. Box H, Juneau 99811.

MUNICIPAL, PRIVATE AND STATE HOSPITALS
Anchorage
Alaska Psychiatric Institute (176 beds), 2900 Providence Drive, 99508

Humana Hospital (238 beds), 2801 DeBarr Road, P.O. Box 143889, 99514

Providence Hospital (303 beds), 3200 Providence Drive, P.O. Box 196604, 99519

Cordova
Cordova Community Hospital (23 beds), Box 160, 99574

Fairbanks
Fairbanks Memorial Hospital (177 beds), 1650 Cowles St., 99701

Glennallen
Cross Road Medical Center (6 beds), Box 5, 99588

Homer
South Peninsula Hospital (38 beds), 4300 Bartlett St., 99603

Juneau
Bartlett Memorial Hospital (51 beds), 3260 Hospital Drive, 99801

Juneau Recovery Unit (15 alcoholism treatment beds), 3250 Hospital Drive, 99801

Ketchikan
Ketchikan General Hospital (92 beds), 3100 Tongass Ave., 99901

Kodiak
Kodiak Island Hospital (44 beds), 1915 E. Rezanof Drive, 99615

Palmer
Valley Hospital (36 beds), P.O. Box 1687, 99645

Petersburg
Petersburg General Hospital (25 beds), Box 589, 99833

Seward
Seward General Hospital (32 beds), Box 365, 99664

Sitka
Sitka Community Hospital (24 beds), 209 Moller Drive, 99835

Soldotna
Central Peninsula General Hospital (62 beds), 250 Hospital Place, 99669

Valdez
Harborview Developmental Center (state-operated residential center for the mentally handicapped; 80 beds), Box 487, 99686

Valdez Community Hospital (15 beds), Box 550, 99686

Wrangell
Wrangell General Hospital (14 beds), Box 1081, 99929

U.S. PUBLIC HEALTH SERVICE PHYSICIANS
Anchorage
Alaska Native Medical Center (170 beds), Box 107741, 99510

Barrow
PHS Alaska Native Hospital (14 beds), 99723

Bethel
Yukon–Kuskokwim Delta Service Unit (51 beds), 99559

Dillingham
Bristol Bay Area Kanakanak Hospital (15 beds), P.O. Box 130, 99576

Fairbanks
Chief Andrew Issac Health Center, 1638 Cowles, 99701

Juneau
SEARHC Medical Clinic, 3258 Hospital Drive, 99801

Ketchikan
PHS Alaska Native Health Center, 3289 Tongass Ave., 99901

Kodiak
Kodiak Area Native Association, 402 Center St., 99619

Kotzebue
Maniilaq Medical Center (31 beds), P.O. Box 256, 99752

Metlakatla
Annette Island Service Unit, P.O. Box 428, 99926

Nome
Norton Sound Regional Hospital (22 beds), P.O. Box 966, 99762

Sitka
SEARHC Regional Health Hospital (78 beds), 222 Tongass Drive, 99835

MILITARY PHYSICIANS
Adak
Branch Hospital, NAVSTA Adak, FPO Seattle, WA 98791

Eielson Air Force Base
Eielson Air Force Base Clinic, 99702

Elmendorf AFB
Elmendorf Air Force Base Hospital, 99506

Fort Greely
Fort Greely Dispensary, Box 488, APO Seattle, WA 98733

Fort Richardson
U.S. Army Health Clinic, 99505

Fort Wainwright
Bassett Army Hospital, 99703

Ketchikan
Coast Guard Dispensary, 99901

Kodiak
Coast Guard Dispensary, Box 2, 99619

Mount Edgecumbe
Sitka Coast Guard Air Station, Box 6-5000, 99835

NURSING HOMES AND HEALTH CARE FACILITIES
Anchorage
Alaska Surgery Center, 4001 Laurel St., 99508
Charter North Hospital (80 beds), 2530 DeBarr Road, 99514
Hope Cottage Inter. Care Facility (40 beds), 2805 Bering St., 99503
Mary Conrad Center (60 beds), 9100 Centennial Drive, 99504
North Star Hospital (34 beds), 1650 S. Bragaw, 99508
Our Lady of Compassion (224 beds), 4900 Eagle, 99503

Cordova
Cordova Community Hospital Nursing Home (10 beds), P.O. Box 160, 99574

Fairbanks
Denali Center (101 beds), 1949 Gillam Way, 99701

Glennallen

Cross Road Medical Center, P.O. Box 5, 99588

Homer

South Peninsula Hospital (38 beds), 4300 Bartlett St., 99603

Juneau

Saint Ann's Nursing Home (45 beds), 415 Sixth St., 99801

Ketchikan

Island View Manor (44 beds), 3100 Tongass Ave., 99901

Petersburg

Petersburg General Hospital (25 beds), P.O. Box 589, 99833

Seward

Wesleyan Nursing Home (66 beds), Box 430, 99664

Soldotna

Heritage Place (45 beds), 232 Rockwell Ave., 99669

Valdez

Harborview Development Center (80 beds), P.O. Box 487, 99686

Wrangell

Wrangell General Hospital (14 beds), P.O. Box 1081, 99929

Hostels

Alaska has 12 youth hostels, located as follows:

Alyeska International Home Hostel, P.O. Box 10-4099, Anchorage 99510; phone (907) 783-2099. Located 40 miles south of Anchorage on Alpina in Girdwood.

Anchorage International Hostel, 700 H St., Anchorage 99501; phone (907) 276-3635. Located on the corner of Seventh and H streets.

Bear Creek Camp and Hostel, P.O. Box 334, Haines 99827; phone (907) 766-2259. Located Mile 2 Small Tract Road.

Delta Youth Hostel, P.O. Box 971, Delta Junction 99737; phone (907) 895-5074. Located three miles from Milepost 272 on Richardson Highway.

Fairbanks Youth Hostel, P.O. Box 2196, 1641 Willow St., Fairbanks 99707; phone (907) 456-4159. Located near Tanana Valley Fairgrounds.

Juneau International Hostel, 614 Harris St., Juneau 99801; phone (907) 586-9559. Located four blocks northeast of the capitol building.

Ketchikan Youth Hostel, P.O. Box 8515, Ketchikan 99901; phone (907) 225-3319. Located in United Methodist Church, Grant and Main streets.

Sheep Mountain Lodge, SRC Box 8490, Palmer 99645; phone (907) 745-5121. Located at Mile 113.5 of the Glenn Highway.

Sitka Youth Hostel, P.O. Box 2645, Sitka 99835; phone (907) 747-8356. Located in United Methodist Church, Edgecumbe and Kimsham streets.

Skagway Home Hostel, Box 231, Skagway 99840; phone (907) 983-2131. Located on Third Avenue near Main Street.

Snow River International Hostel, HRC 64, Box 425, Seward 99664. Located at Mile 16 of the Seward Highway.

Tok International Youth Hostel, P.O. Box 532, Tok 99780. Located one mile south of Mile 1322.5 of the Alaska Highway on Pringle Drive.

The hostels in Alyeska, Anchorage, Haines, Juneau, Skagway and Seward are open year-round. All others are open only in the summer, and all of the hostels accept reservations by mail. Opening and closing dates, maximum length of stay and hours vary.

Hostels are available to anyone with a valid membership card issued by one of the associations affiliated with the International Youth Hostel Federation. Membership is open to all ages. By international agreement, each youth hostel member joins the association of his own country. A valid membership card, which ranges from $10 to $200 (life), entitles a member to use hostels.

Hostel memberships and a guide to American Youth Hostels can be purchased from the state office (Alaska Council, AYH, Box 240347, Anchorage 99524; phone (907) 562-7772), national office (American Youth Hostels, 1332 I St. N.W., Suite 800, Washington, D.C. 20005) or from most local hostels. For more information regarding Alaska

International Hostels, write the Alaska Council at the address listed above.

Hot Springs

The U.S. Geological Survey identifies 79 thermal springs in Alaska. Almost half of these hot springs occur along the volcanic Alaska Peninsula and Aleutian Chain. The second greatest regional concentration of such springs is in southeastern Alaska. Hot springs are scattered throughout the Interior and western Alaska, as far north as the Brooks Range and as far west as the Seward Peninsula.

Early miners and trappers were quick to use the naturally occurring warm waters for baths. Today approximately 25 percent of the recorded thermal springs are used for bathing, irrigation or domestic use. However, only a handful can be considered developed resorts.

Resorts (with swimming pools, changing rooms and lodging) are found at Chena Hot Springs, a 62-mile drive east from Fairbanks; and Circle Hot Springs, 136 miles northeast by road from Fairbanks. The less-developed Manley Hot Springs, in the small community of the same name at the end of the Elliott Highway, is privately owned, and the primitive bathhouse is used mainly by local residents. Developed, but not easily accessible, are the hot springs at Melozi Hot Springs Lodge, some 200 miles northwest of Fairbanks by air. The community of Tenakee Springs on Chichagof Island in southeastern Alaska maintains an old bathhouse near the waterfront. The state Marine Highway System provides ferry service to Tenakee Springs. Goddard Hot Springs near Sitka on Baranof Island was at one time owned by the Territory and operated as a Pioneers' Home for Alaska women. The temperature of the hot springs at Goddard Hot Springs is about 106°F/41°C. Also on Baranof Island is Baranof Hot Springs on the east shore of the island. Both Goddard and Baranof hot springs are accessible by private boat or by air; both have bathhouses.

Hunting

There are 26 game management units in Alaska with a wide variety of seasons and bag limits. Current copies of the *Alaska Game Regulations* with maps delineating game unit boundaries are available from the Alaska Department of Fish and Game (P.O. Box 3-2000, Juneau 99802) or from Fish and Game offices and sporting goods stores throughout the state.

Regulations

A hunting or trapping license is required for all residents and nonresidents with the exception of Alaska residents under 16 years or older than 60 years of age. A special identification card is issued for the senior citizen exemption.

A resident hunting license (valid for

the calendar year) costs $12; trapping license (valid until September 30 of the year following the year of issue), $10; hunting and trapping license, $22; hunting and sportfishing license, $22; hunting, trapping and sportfishing license, $32.

A nonresident (U.S. citizen) and alien hunting license (valid for calendar year) costs $85; hunting and sportfishing license, $135; hunting and trapping license, $250.

Military personnel stationed in Alaska may purchase a small game hunting license for $12, and a small game hunting and sportfishing license for $22. Military personnel must purchase a nonresident hunting license at full cost ($85) and pay nonresident military fees for big game tags (one-half the nonresident rate), unless they are hunting big game on military property.

Licenses may be obtained from any designated issuing agent or by mail from the Alaska Department of Fish and Game, Licensing Section, P.O. Box 3-2000, Juneau 99802. Licenses are also available at Fish and Game regional offices in Anchorage, Fairbanks, Juneau and Kodiak.

Big game tags and fees are required for residents hunting musk-oxen and brown/grizzly bear and for nonresidents and aliens hunting any big game animal. These nonrefundable, non-transferable, metal locking tags (valid for calendar year) must be purchased prior to the taking of the animal. A tag may, however, be used for any species for which the tag fee is of equal or less value. Fees quoted below are for *each* animal.

All residents (regardless of age), nonresidents and aliens intending to hunt brown/grizzly bear must purchase tags (resident, $25; nonresident, $500; alien, $650). Residents, nonresidents and aliens are also required to purchase musk-oxen tags (resident, $500 each bull taken on Nunivak Island, $25 each bull from Nelson Island or in Arctic National Wildlife Refuge, $25 cow; nonresident, $1,100; alien, $1,500).

Nonresident tag fees for other big game animals are as follows: deer, $150; wolf or wolverine, $175; black bear, $225; elk or goat, $300; caribou, $325; moose, $400; bison, $450; sheep, $425.

Nonresident alien tag fees for other big game animals are as follows: deer, $200; wolf or wolverine, $250; black bear, $300; elk or goat, $400; caribou, $425; moose, $500; bison, $650; and sheep, $550.

Nonresidents hunting brown/grizzly bear, Dall sheep or mountain goat are required to have a guide or be accompanied by an Alaska resident relative over 19 years of age within the second degree of kinship (includes parents, children, sisters or brothers). Nonresident aliens hunting big game must have a guide. A current list of registered Alaska guides is available for $5 from the Department of Commerce, Guide Licensing and Control Board, P.O. Box D-LIC, Juneau 99811.

Residents and nonresidents 16 years of age or older hunting waterfowl must have a signed federal migratory bird hunting stamp (duck stamp) and a state waterfowl conservation stamp. The Alaska duck stamp is available from agents who sell hunting licenses or by mail from the Alaska Department of Fish and Game, Licensing Section.

Trophy Game

Record big game in Alaska as recorded by the Boone and Crockett Club in the latest (1988) edition of *Records of North American Big Game* are as follows:

Black bear: Skull 13 $7/16$ inches long, 8 $6/16$ inches wide (1966).

Brown bear (coastal region): Skull 17 $15/16$ inches long, 12 $13/16$ inches wide (1952).

Grizzly bear (inland): Skull 16 $4/16$ inches long, 10 $5/16$ inches wide (1983).

Polar bear: Skull 18 $1/2$ inches long, 11 $7/16$ inches wide (1963). It is currently illegal for anyone but an Alaskan Eskimo, Aleut or Indian to hunt polar bear in Alaska.

Bison: Right horn 18 $1/8$ inches long, base circumference 15 inches; left horn 21 inches long, base circumference 15 $1/4$ inches; greatest spread 31 $7/8$ inches (1977).

Barren Ground caribou: Right beam 51 $1/4$ inches, 22 points; left beam 51 $5/8$ inches, 23 points (1967).

Moose: Right palm length 49 $5/8$ inches, width 20 $3/4$ inches; left palm length 49 $6/8$ inches, width 15 $5/8$ inches;

right antler 18 points, left 16 points; greatest spread 77 inches (1978).

Mountain goat: Right horn $11^5/8$ inches long, base circumference $5^3/4$ inches; left horn $11^5/8$ inches long, base circumference $5^5/8$ inches (1933).

Musk-oxen: Right horn $26^3/4$ inches; left horn $26^1/2$ inches; tip-to-tip spread 27 inches (1985).

Dall sheep: Right horn $48^5/8$ inches long, base circumference $14^5/8$ inches; left horn $47^7/8$ inches long, base circumference $14^3/4$ inches (1961).

Related reading: *Northwest Sportsman Almanac.* Writer-editor Terry Sheely has assembled the best works of writers and photographers in an informative guide to outdoor recreation. *See* ALASKA NORTHWEST LIBRARY in the back of the book.

Hypothermia

(*See also* Chill Factor)

Hypothermia develops when the body is exposed to cold and cannot maintain normal temperatures. In an automatic survival reaction, blood flow to the extremities is shut down in favor of preserving warmth in the vital organs. As internal temperature drops, judgment and coordination become impaired. Allowed to continue, hypothermia leads to stupor, collapse and death. Immersion hypothermia occurs in cold water.

Ice

(*See* Glaciers and Ice Fields *and* Icebergs)

Icebergs

Icebergs are formed in Alaska wherever glaciers reach salt water or a freshwater lake. Some accessible places to view icebergs include Glacier Bay, Icy Bay, Yakutat Bay, Taku Inlet, Endicott Arm, portions of northern Prince William Sound (College Fiord, Barry Arm, Columbia Bay), Mendenhall Lake and Portage Lake.

If icebergs contain little or no sediment, approximately 75 percent to 80 percent of their bulk may be underwater. The more sediment an iceberg contains, the greater its density, and an iceberg containing large amounts of sediment will float slightly beneath the surface. Glaciologists of the U.S. Geological Survey believe that some of these "black icebergs" may actually sink to the bottom of a body of water. Since salt water near the faces of glaciers may be liquid to temperatures as low as 28°F, and icebergs melt at 32°F, some of these underwater icebergs may remain unmelted indefinitely.

Alaska's icebergs are comparatively small compared to the icebergs found near Antarctica and Greenland. One of the largest icebergs ever recorded in Alaska was formed in May 1977, in Icy Bay. Glaciologists measured it at 346 feet long, 297 feet wide and 99 feet above the surface of the water.

Sea Ice

Sea water typically freezes at –1.8°C or 28.8°F. The first indication that sea water is freezing is the appearance of frazil—tiny needlelike crystals of pure ice—in shallow coastal areas of low current or areas of low salinity, such as near the mouths of rivers. Continued freezing turns the frazil into a soupy mass called grease ice and eventually into an ice crust approximately four inches thick. More freezing, wind and wave action thicken the ice and break it into ice floes ranging from a few feet to several miles across. In the Arctic Ocean, ice floes can be 10 feet thick. Most are crisscrossed with 6- to 8-foot-high walls of ice caused by the force of winds.

Sea salt that is trapped in the ice during freezing is leached out over time, making the oldest ice the least saline. Meltwater forming in ponds on multi-year-old ice during summer months is a freshwater source for native marine life.

Refreezing of meltwater ponds and the formation of new ice in the permanent ice pack (generally north of 72° north latitude) begins in mid-September. While the ice pack expands southward, new ice freezes to the coast (shorefast ice) and spreads seaward. Where the drifting ice pack grinds against the relatively stable shorefast ice, tremendous walls or ridges of ice are formed, some observed to be 100 feet thick and grounded in 60 feet of water. They are impenetrable by all but the most powerful icebreakers. By late March the ice cover has reached its maximum extent, approximately from Port Heiden on the Alaska Peninsula in the south to the northern Pribilof Islands and northwestward to Siberia. In Cook Inlet, sea ice, usually no more than two feet thick, can extend as far south as Anchor Point and Kamishak Bay on the east and west sides of the inlet, respectively. The ice season usually lasts from mid-November to mid-March.

The Navy began observing and forecasting sea ice conditions in 1954 in support of the construction of defense sites along the Arctic coast. In 1969, the National Weather Service began a low-profile sea ice reconnaissance program, which expanded greatly during the summer of 1975, when during a year of severe ice, millions of dollars of materials had to be shipped to Prudhoe Bay. Expanded commercial fisheries in the Bering Sea also heightened the problem of sea ice for crabbing and bottom fish trawling operations. In 1976, headquarters for a seven-day-a-week ice watch was established at Fairbanks; it was moved to Anchorage in 1981.

The National Weather Service operates a radio facsimile broadcast service that makes current ice analysis charts, special oceanographic charts and standard weather charts available to the public via standard radios equipped with "black box" receivers. Commercial fishing operators, particularly in the Bering Sea, use the radio-transmitted charts to steer clear of problem weather and troublesome ice formations. More information is available from the National Weather Service in Kodiak or Anchorage.

Ice Fog

Ice fog develops when air just above the ground becomes so cold, it can no longer retain water vapor and tiny, spherical ice crystals are formed. Ice fog is most common in Arctic and subarctic regions in winter when clear skies create an air inversion, trapping cold air at low elevations. It is most noticeable when man-made pollutants are also contained by the air inversion.

Iceworm

Although often regarded as a hoax, iceworms actually exist. These small, thin, segmented black worms, usually less than one inch long, thrive in temperatures just above freezing. Observers as far back as the 1880s reported that at dawn, dusk or on overcast days, the tiny worms, all belonging to the genus *Mesenchytraeus,* may literally carpet the surface of glaciers. When sunlight strikes them, they burrow back down into the ice.

The town of Cordova commemorates its own version of the iceworm each February in the Iceworm Festival, when a 150-foot-long, multilegged "iceworm" marches in a parade down Main Street.

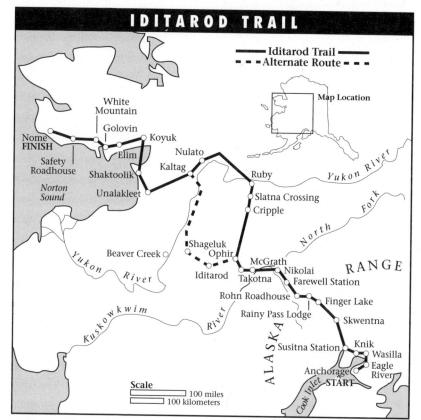

IDITAROD TRAIL

Iditarod Trail ━━━
■ ■ ■ Alternate Route ■ ■ ■

Map Location

White Mountain
Golovin
Nome FINISH
Koyuk
Safety Roadhouse
Elim
Nulato
Shaktoolik
Kaltag
Norton Sound
Unalakleet
Ruby
Yukon River
Slatna Crossing
Cripple
Shageluk
Beaver Creek
Ophir
Iditarod
McGrath
Takotna
Nikolai
Farewell Station
Rohn Roadhouse
Finger Lake
Rainy Pass Lodge
Skwentna
Susitna Station
Knik
Wasilla
Eagle River
Anchorage
START
North Fork
RANGE
Yukon River
Kuskokwim River
A L A S K A
Cook Inlet

Scale
100 miles
100 kilometers

Iditarod Trail Sled Dog Race

(*See also* Dog Mushing *and* Yukon Quest International Sled Dog Race)

Two of the longest sled dog races in the world take place in Alaska: the Yukon Quest and the Iditarod. The first Iditarod Trail Sled Dog Race, conceived and organized by Joe Redington, Sr., of Knik, and historian Dorothy Page, of Wasilla, was run in 1967 and covered only 56 miles. The race was lengthened in 1973, and the first ever 1,100-mile sled dog race began in Anchorage on March 3, 1973, and ended April 3 in Nome. Of the 34 who started the race, 22 finished. The Iditarod has been run every year since its inception. In 1976, Congress designated the Iditarod as a National Historic Trail.

Following the old dog team mail route blazed in 1910 from Knik to Nome, the trail crosses two mountain ranges, follows the Yukon River for about 150 miles, runs through several bush villages and crosses the pack ice of Norton Sound.

Strictly a winter trail because the ground is mostly spongy muskeg swamps, the route attracted national attention in 1925 when sled dog mushers, including the famous Leonhard Seppala, relayed 300,000 units of life-saving diphtheria serum to epidemic-threatened Nome. However, as the airplane and snowmobile replaced the sled dog team, the trail fell into disuse. Thanks to Redington and Page, the trail has been assured a place in Alaska history.

Each year the Iditarod takes a slightly different course, following an alternate southern route in odd years (*see* map). While the route is traditionally described as 1,049 miles long (a figure that was selected because Alaska is the 49th state), the actual distance run each year is close to 1,100 miles. Part of it is run on frozen river ice. The official length of the Iditarod National Historic Trail System, including northern and southern routes, is 2,350 miles.

The majority of the Iditarod purse is divided among the first 20 finishers. In 1992, Doug Swingley and Joe Runyan split $3,000 in silver ingots for simultaneously crossing the halfway checkpoint at Cripple ahead of all other racers. Rick Swenson won the Seppala Humanitarian Award. Other awards went to: Doug Swingley for Rookie of the Year; and Mike Williams, a Bethel-area Native who ran his race for Native sobriety, won the Most Inspirational Musher Award. Joe Runyan and Doug Swingley split the celebration dinner at

1992 Results

Place Musher	Days	Hrs.	Min.	Sec.	Prize
1. Martin Buser, Big Lake	10	19	17	15	$50,000
2. Susan Butcher, Eureka	11	05	36	03	40,000
3. Tim Osmar, Kasilof	11	05	49	39	35,000
4. Rick Swenson, Two Rivers	11	07	51	49	30,000
5. DeeDee Jonrowe, Willow	11	09	05	00	25,000
6. Jeff King, Denali Park	11	10	40	35	20,000
7. Vern Halter, Trapper Creek	11	13	08	40	18,000
8. Rick Mackey, Nenana	11	13	20	23	17,000
9. Doug Swingley, Simms, MT	11	13	47	00	16,000
10. Ketil Reitan, Kaktovik	11	14	38	00	15,000
11. Matt Desalernos, Nome	11	15	11	12	14,000
12. Bruce Lee, Denali Park	11	15	38	40	13,000
13. Claire Philip, By Thomery, France	11	15	43	20	12,000
14. Ed Iten, Ambler	11	16	01	43	11,500
15. Bill Cotter, Nenana	11	17	00	00	11,000
16. Kate Persons, Sikusuilaq Hatchery	11	20	14	42	10,500
17. Lavon Barve, Wasilla	11	21	38	03	10,000
18. John Barron, Sheep Creek	11	23	53	21	9,500
19. Dan MacEachen, Nenana	12	04	05	53	9,000
20. Joe Garnie, Willow	12	05	46	50	8,500

Winners and Times

Year Musher	Days	Hrs.	Min.	Sec.	Prize
1973 Dick Willmarth, Red Devil	20	00	49	41	$12,000
1974 Carl Huntington, Galena	20	15	02	07	12,000
1975 Emmitt Peters, Ruby	14	14	43	45	15,000
1976 Jerry Rilen, Nenana	18	22	58	17	7,000
1977 Rick Swenson, Eureka	16	16	27	13	9,600
1978 Dick Mackey, Wasilla	14	18	52	24	12,000
1979 Rick Swenson, Eureka	15	10	37	47	12,000
1980 Joe May, Trapper Creek	14	07	11	51	12,000
1981 Rick Swenson, Eureka	12	08	45	02	24,000
1982 Rick Swenson, Eureka	16	04	40	10	24,000
1983 Dick Mackey, Wasilla	12	14	10	44	24,000
1984 Dean Osmar, Clam Gulch	12	15	07	33	24,000*
1985 Libby Riddles, Teller	18	00	20	17	50,000
1986 Susan Butcher, Manley	11	15	06	00	50,000
1987 Susan Butcher, Manley	11	02	05	13	50,000
1988 Susan Butcher, Manley	11	11	41	40	30,000
1989 Joe Runyan, Nenana	11	05	24	34	50,000
1990 Susan Butcher, Manley	11	01	53	23	50,000
1991 Rick Swenson, Two Rivers	12	16	34	39	50,000
1992 Martin Buser, Big Lake	10	19	17	15	50,000

*Does not include $2,000 in silver ingots for reaching the halfway checkpoint first.

Ruby and the $3,500 cash prize for being the first mushers to the Yukon. Raymie Redington won a 1992 Dodge truck for being the first musher to reach Skwentna. Bob Hickel won the Eukanuba Sportsmanship Award for saving the life of his friend and fellow-musher Bob Ernisse, who was suffering from life-threatening frostbite about 30 miles from Nome.

In 1992, a record 76 mushers started the world's longest and richest sled dog race. Of those, a record 63 finished the Anchorage to Nome ordeal. Martin Buser of Big Lake won the Iditarod race, shaving off more than six hours from the previous record winning time. Joe Garnie was awarded the Golden Harness Award for the outstanding performance of his lead dog. Buser received the first-place check of $50,000 from a $387,000 purse. The 1992 race had the largest purse in the race's history and in dog mushing. There were no $1,000 checks issued to finishers beyond position 20.

Related reading: *Iditarod: The Great Race to Nome*. Photographs by Jeff Schultz, text by Bill Sherwonit. *Travelers of the Cold: Sled Dogs of the Far North*, by Dominique Cellura. A fascinating history of man and dog thriving in harsh climates. *See* ALASKA NORTHWEST LIBRARY at the back of the book.

Igloo

Also known as snowhouses, these snow block structures provided temporary shelter for Arctic Alaska Eskimos. Igloos are built in a spiral with each tier leaning inward at a greater angle. The entrance is a tunnel with a cold trap in front of the sleeping platform. A vent at the top allows for ventilation, and an ice window lets in light.

Imports and Exports

Alaska's most important trading region is Asia, to which it sent 91 percent of its exports in 1991. Other significant regions were Europe (5 percent) and Americas (2.7 percent). Alaska imports for 1991 were valued at $860 million. The largest importer to the state was Japan at $252 million, followed by Singapore ($151 million) and Canada ($107 million).

Exports for 1991 were valued at $4.42 billion by the Alaska Center for International Business. Of this total, state's most valuable exports were fish (35.6 percent), petroleum products (13.8 percent) and timber (12.2 percent).

Income

(*See also* Cost of Living)

On a per capita income basis, Alaska was ranked sixth in the nation at $21,932 per person in 1990, a slight gain from $21,656 per capita income in 1989. More than 70 percent of Alaska's personal income comes from earnings, which represents a larger portion than the rest of the nation. One reason could be that a larger percentage of Alaska's working age population is in the labor force and earning income from employment.

The average monthly wage reached $2,471 in 1990, the highest it has ever been in nominal terms. Mining still reflects the highest average monthly wage at $5,438, according to a 1990 report from the Alaska Department of Labor, Research and Analysis Section. Roughly 89 percent of these mining jobs are supplied through the oil and gas industry. Construction followed at $3,671 per month. The lowest average monthly wage remains in the retail trade at $1,394.

Median household income in Alaska in 1989 (latest available statistics) was $41,408, which ranks Alaska second in the nation. In terms of the number of Alaskans who live in poverty, the U.S. Census reported 11.4 percent of Alaska's population below the poverty level in 1990, which ranked Alaska 21st out of the 50 states in the percent of residents living in poverty. The figure nationwide was 13.5 percent. If Alaska's higher cost of living was taken into account in these statistics, it is likely that the state's rating would drop even more. A more comprehensive report from the Census Bureau on the poverty level is expected to be released sometime in 1992.

Though Alaska's per capita income

increased in 1990, the increase in cost of living was greater. But on a positive note, Alaskans still hold on to more of their income after taxes than residents in most other states.

Information Sources

Agriculture: State Division of Agriculture, P.O. Box 949, Palmer 99645; Cooperative Extension Service, University of Alaska, Fairbanks 99701.

Alaska Natives: Alaska Federation of Natives, 411 W. Fourth Ave., Anchorage 99501.

Boating, Canoeing and Kayaking: Alaska Dept. of Transportation and Public Facilities, P.O. Box Z, Juneau 99811; State of Alaska, Division of Parks and Outdoor Recreation, 3601 C St., Suite 1200, Anchorage 99503.

Business: Alaska Department of Commerce and Economic Development, P.O. Box D, Juneau 99811; State Chamber of Commerce, 217 Second St., Suite 201, Juneau 99801.

Camping and Hiking: U.S. Forest Service, P.O. Box 21628, Juneau 99802; Bureau of Land Management, 222 W. Seventh Ave., #13, Anchorage 99513; Supervisor, Chugach National Forest, 201 E. Ninth Ave., Suite 206, Anchorage 99501; National Park Service, 2525 Gambell St., Anchorage 99503; Supervisor, Tongass National Forest, P.O. Box 21628, Juneau 99802; U.S. Fish and Wildlife Service, 1011 E. Tudor Road, Anchorage 99503.

Census Data: Alaska Department of Labor, Research and Analysis, P.O. Box 107018, Anchorage 99510.

Climate: State Climatologist, University of Alaska, Arctic Environmental and Data Center, 707 A St., Anchorage 99501.

Education: Alaska Department of Education, P.O. Box F, Juneau 99811.

Gold Panning: State Division of Geological and Geophysical Surveys, Mines Information Office, 3601 C St., Anchorage 99503; Alaska Miners Association, 501 W. Northern Lights Blvd., Suite 203, Anchorage 99503.

Health: State Department of Health and Social Services, Division of Public Health, P.O. Box H, Juneau 99811.

Housing: State Housing Authority, P.O. Box 10080, Anchorage 99510.

Hunting and Fishing Regulations: State Department of Fish and Game, P.O. Box 3-2000, Juneau 99802.

Job Opportunities: State Employment Service, P.O. Box 3-7000, Juneau 99802.

Labor: State Department of Labor, P.O. Box 25501-5501, Juneau 99802.

Land: State Division of Lands, P.O. Box 107005, Anchorage 99510; Bureau of Land Management, 222 W. Seventh Ave., #13, Anchorage 99513; Alaska Public Lands Information Centers, 605 W. Fourth Ave., Suite 105, Anchorage 99501; 250 Cushman St., Suite 1A, Fairbanks 99701; P.O. Box 359, Tok 99780.

Legislature: Legislative Information Office, 3111 C St., Anchorage 99503.

Made in Alaska Products: Alaska Association of Manufacturers, P.O. Box 142831, Anchorage 99514.

Maps (topographic): U.S. Geological Survey, 4230 University Drive, Room 101, Anchorage 99508; 101 12th Ave., Room 126, Fairbanks 99701.

Military: Department of the Air Force, Headquarters, Alaskan Air Command, Elmendorf Air Force Base 99506; Department of the Army, Headquarters, 6th Infantry Brigade (Alaska), Fort Richardson 99505; State Department of Military Affairs, Office of the Adjutant General, 3601 C St., Anchorage 99503; Department of Transportation, U.S. Coast Guard, 17th Coast Guard District, P.O. Box 3-5000, Juneau 99802.

Mines and Petroleum: State Division of Geological and Geophysical Surveys, 3601 C St., Anchorage 99503; Petroleum Information Corp., P.O. Box 102278, Anchorage 99510; Alaska Miners Association, 501 W. Northern Lights Blvd., Suite 203, Anchorage 99503.

River Running: National Park Service, 2525 Gambell St., Anchorage 99503; U.S. Dept. of the Interior, Fish and Wildlife Service, 1011 E. Tudor Road, Anchorage 99503; Bureau of Land Management, 222 W. Seventh Ave., #13, Anchorage 99513.

Travel and Visitor Information: State Division of Tourism, P.O. Box E, Juneau 99811; Alaska Visitors Association, 501 W. Northern Lights Blvd., Anchorage 99503.

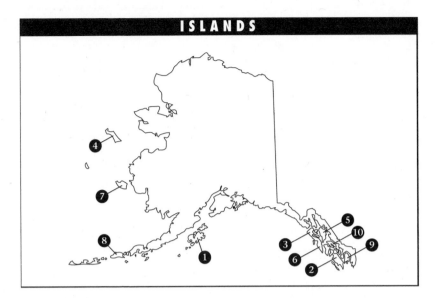

Islands

Southeastern Alaska contains about 1,000 of the state's 1,800 named islands, rocks and reefs; several thousand remain unnamed. The Aleutian Island chain, stretching southwest from the mainland, contains more than 200 islands.

Of the state's 10 largest islands, 6 are in southeastern Alaska. Of the remainder, Unimak is in the Aleutians, Nunivak and Saint Lawrence are in the Bering Sea off the west coast of Alaska, and Kodiak is in the Gulf of Alaska (*see* map above). The state's 10 largest islands, according to U.S. Geological Survey figures, are:

1. Kodiak, 3,588 sq. mi.
2. Prince of Wales, 2,731 sq. mi.
3. Chichagof, 2,062 sq. mi.
4. Saint Lawrence, 1,780 sq. mi.
5. Admiralty, 1,709 sq. mi.
6. Baranof, 1,636 sq. mi.
7. Nunivak, 1,600 sq. mi.*
8. Unimak, 1,600 sq. mi.
9. Revillagigedo, 1,134 sq. mi.
10. Kupreanof, 1,084 sq. mi.

*Estimate

Ivory

Eskimos traditionally carved ivory to make such implements as harpoon heads, dolls and ulu (fan-shaped knife) handles. For the past 80 years, however, most carvings have been made to be sold. Etching on ivory originally was done with hand tools and the scratches were filled in with soot. Today power tools supplement the hand tools and carvers may color the etching with India ink, graphite, hematite or commercial coloring.

The large islands of the Bering Sea—Saint Lawrence, Little Diomede and Nunivak—are home to the majority of Alaska's ivory carvers. Eskimos from King Island, renowned for their carving skill, now live in Nome along with talented artists from many other villages.

The bulk of the ivory used today comes from walrus tusks and teeth, seasoned for a few months. Old walrus ivory, often mistakenly called fossil ivory, is also used. This ivory has been buried in the ground or has been on beaches for years, and contact with various minerals has changed it from white to tan or any of a multitude of colors. Some highly prized old ivory exhibits rays of deep blue or areas of brown and gold that shine. Most old ivory comes from ancient sites or

beaches on Saint Lawrence Island and is sold by the pound to non-Native buyers, generally for use in some kind of artwork.

Mastodon tusks are often unearthed in the summer by miners or found eroding on river cutbanks where they have been buried for thousands of years. Although these tusks are enormous and their colorations often beautiful, the material cannot be used efficiently because it dries and then separates into narrow ridges.

Various federal prohibitions govern the collection of old walrus, mammoth and mastodon ivory. Such materials may be gathered from private or reservation lands, but may not be traded or sold if found on public lands. The taking of fresh walrus ivory is prohibited to non-Natives in accordance with the Marine Mammal Protection Act of 1972.

In the 19th century, Native artists who came in contact with whalers etched realistic scenes on sperm whale teeth. Today, with the ban on the taking of sperm whales, this type of ivory is not available to Native scrimshanders.

Walrus may be taken only by Alaska Natives (Aleuts, Eskimos and Indians) who dwell on the coast of the North Pacific Ocean or the Arctic Ocean, for subsistence purposes or for the creation and sale of authentic Native articles of handicrafts or clothing.

Raw walrus ivory and other parts can be sold only by an Alaska Native to an Alaska Native within Alaska, or to a registered agent for resale or transfer to an Alaska Native within the state. Only authentic Native-processed ivory articles of handicrafts or clothing may be sold or transferred to a non-Native, or sold in interstate commerce.

Beach ivory, which is found on the beach within one-fourth mile of the ocean, may, however, be kept by anyone. This ivory must be registered by all non-Natives with the U.S. Fish and Wildlife Service (USFWS) or the National Marine Fisheries Service within 30 days of discovery. Beach-found ivory must remain in the possession of the finder even if carved or scrimshawed.

Carved or scrimshawed walrus ivory (authentic Native handicraft) or other marine mammal parts made into clothing or other authentic Native handicrafts may be exported from the United States to a foreign country, but the exporter must first obtain an export permit from the USFWS. Even visitors from the Lower 48 simply traveling through, or stopping in Canada on their way home, are required to have a USFWS export and/or transit permit. Cost is $25. Mailing the carved ivory home will avoid the need for an export/transit permit. Importation of walrus or other marine mammal parts is illegal, except for scientific research purposes or for public display once a permit is granted.

For further information contact: Special Agent-in-Charge, U.S. Fish and Wildlife Service, 1011 E. Tudor Road, Anchorage 99503; phone (907) 786-3311; or Senior Resident, U.S. Fish and Wildlife Service, 1412 Airport Way, Fairbanks 99701; phone (907) 456-0239.

Jade

Most Alaskan jade is found near the Dall, Shungnak and Kobuk rivers, and Jade Mountain, all north of the Arctic Circle. The stones occur in various shades of green, brown, black, yellow, white and even red. The most valuable are those that are marbled black, white and green. Gem-quality jade, about one-fourth of the total mined, is used in jewelry making. Fractured jade is used for clock faces, table tops, book ends and other items. Jade is the Alaska state gem.

Kuspuk

A *kuspuk* is an Eskimo woman's parka, often made with a loosely cut

back so that an infant may be carried piggyback-style. Parkas are made from rabbit or fox skins; traditionally, the fur lining faces inward. The ruffs are generally made of wolverine or wolf fur. An outer shell, called a *qaspeg*, is worn over a fur parka to keep it clean and to prevent wear. This outer shell is usually made of brightly colored corduroy, cotton print or velveteenlike material, and may be trimmed with rickrack.

Labor and Employer Organizations

The Alaska State AFL–CIO *Alaska Labor Union Directory* lists the following organizations:

Anchorage

Alaska Federation of Teachers Local 8050

Alaska Metal Trades Council

Alaska Public Employees Association

Alaska State AFL-CIO

Alaska State District Council of Laborers

Alaska State Employees Association, AFSCME Local 52

American Federation of Government Employees, Anchorage Council, Local 121

Anchorage Central Labor Council

Anchorage Joint Crafts Council

Anchorage Municipal Employees Association

Anchorage Musicians Association Local 650

Anchorage Typographical Union Local 823

Asbestos Workers Local 97

Associated General Contractors of America

Boilermakers Local 502

Bricklayers and Allied Craftsmen Local 1

Brotherhood of Railroad Carmen of U.S.A. and Canada

Central and Southeastern Alaska District Council of Carpenters

Graphic Communications International Union Local 327

Hotel Employees, Restaurant Employees Union Local 878

International Alliance of Theatrical Stage Employees Local 918

International Association of Bridge, Structural and Ornamental Workers Local 751

International Association of Firefighters Local 1264

International Association of Machinists and Aerospace Workers Local 601

International Brotherhood of Electrical Workers Local 1547

International Brotherhood of Painters and Allied Trades Local 1140

International Brotherhood of Teamsters, Chauffeurs, Warehousemen and Helpers Local 959

International Union of Operating Engineers Local 302

Laborers International Union of North America Local 341

Laundry and Dry Cleaning Union Local 333

National Electrical Contractors Association

Operative Plasterers and Cement Masons Local 867

Piledrivers, Bridge, Dock Builders and Drivers Local 2520

Public Employees Local 71

Roofers and Waterproofers Local 190

Sheetmetal Workers International Association Local 23

United Association of Plumbers and Steamfitters Local 367

United Brotherhood of Carpenters and Joiners Local 1281

United Food and Commercial Workers Union Local 1496

United Transportation Union Local 1626

Western Alaska Building and Construction Trades Council

Cordova
Cordova District Fishermen United
International Longshoremen's and Warehousemen's Union Local 200

Craig
International Longshoremen's and Warehousemen's Union Local 200

Dillingham
Western Alaska Cooperative Marketing Association

Fairbanks
Alaska Public Employees Association
Fairbanks Building and Construction Trades
Fairbanks Central Labor Council
Fairbanks Firefighters Association Local 1324
Fairbanks Joint Crafts Council
Hotel Employees, Restaurant Employees Union Local 879
International Association of Bridge, Structural and Ornamental Workers Local 751
International Brotherhood of Electrical Workers Local 1547
International Brotherhood of Painters and Allied Trades Local 1555
International Brotherhood of Teamsters, Chauffeurs, Warehousemen and Helpers Local 959
International Printing and Graphic Communications Union Local 704
International Union of Operating Engineers Local 302
Laborers International Union of North America Local 942
Operative Plasterers and Cement Masons Local 867
Public Employees Local 71
Sheetmetal Union Local 72
United Association of Journeymen and Apprentices of the Plumbing and Pipefitting Industry Local 375
United Brotherhood of Carpenters and Joiners Local 1243
United Food and Commercial Workers Union Local 1496

Haines
International Longshoremen's and Warehousemen's Union Local 200

Juneau
Alaska Public Employees Association
Alaska State District Council of Laborers
Hotel Employees, Restaurant Employees Union Local 878
Inland Boatmen's Union of the Pacific, Alaska Region
International Association of Machinists and Aerospace Workers Local 2263
International Brotherhood of Electrical Workers Local 1547
International Brotherhood of Teamsters, Chauffeurs, Warehousemen and Helpers Local 959
International *Longshoremen's* and Warehousemen's Union Local 200
International Longshoremen's and *Warehousemen's* Union Local 200
International Union of Operating Engineers Local 302
Juneau Building and Construction Trades Council
Juneau Central Labor Council
Laborers International Union of North America Local 942
National Education Association
National Federation of Federal Employees Local 251
Operative Plasterers and Cement Masons Local 867
Public Employees Local 71
United Association of Journeymen and Apprentices of the Plumbing and Pipefitting Industry Local 262
United Brotherhood of Carpenters and Joiners Local 2247
United Fishermen of Alaska

Kenai
Hotel Employees, Restaurant Employees Union Local 878
International Brotherhood of Electrical Workers Local 1547
International Brotherhood of Teamsters, Chauffeurs, Warehousemen and Helpers Local 959
Kenai Peninsula Central Labor Council
Laborers International Union of North America Local 341

Ketchikan
Alaska Loggers Association
Associated Western Pulp and Paper Workers Local 783
Hotel Employees, Restaurant Employees Union Local 878

Inland Boatmen's Union of the Pacific, Alaska Region

International Brotherhood of Electrical Workers Local 1547

International *Longshoremen's* and Warehousemen's Union Local 200

International Longshoremen's and *Warehousemen's* Union Local 200

International Woodworkers of America Local 3-193

Ketchikan Building and Construction Trades Council

Ketchikan Central Labor Council

Laborers International Union of North America Local 942

United Brotherhood of Carpenters and Joiners Local 1501

Kodiak

Firefighters Local 3054

Hotel Employees, Restaurant Employees Union Local 878

Inland Boatmen's Union of the Pacific, Alaska Region

International Longshoremen's and Warehousemen's Union Local 200

Kodiak Labor Council

Laborers International Union of North America Local 341

Palmer

Laborers International Union of North America Local 341

Pelican

International Longshoremen's and Warehousemen's Union Local 200

Seward

International Longshoremen's and Warehousemen's Union Local 200

Sitka

Hotel Employees, Restaurant Employees Union Local 873

International Longshoremen's and Warehousemen's Union Local 200

United Brotherhood of Carpenters and Joiners Local 466

Unalaska

International Longshoremen's and Warehousemen's Union Local 200

Valdez

Hotel Employees, Restaurant Employees Union Local 878

Laborers International Union of North America Local 341

Ward Cove

Associated Western Pulp and Paper Workers Local 783

Wrangell

International Longshoremen's and Warehousemen's Union Local 200

United Paperworkers Local 1341

Lakes

There are 94 lakes with surface areas of more than 10 square miles among Alaska's more than 3 million lakes. According to the U.S. Geological Survey, the 10 largest (larger than 20 acres) natural freshwater lakes in square miles are: Iliamna, 1,000; Becharof, 458; Teshekpuk, 315; Naknek, 242; Tustumena, 117; Clark, 110; Dall, 100; Upper Ugashik, 75; Lower Ugashik, 72; and Kukaklek, 72.

Land Use

At first glance it seems odd that such a huge area as Alaska has not been more heavily settled. Thousands of acres of forest and tundra, miles and miles of rivers and streams, hidden valleys, bays, coves and mountains, are spread across an area so vast that it staggers the imagination. Yet, more than two-thirds of the population of Alaska remains clustered around two major centers of commerce and survival. Compared to the settlement of the western Lower 48, Alaska is not settled at all.

Visitors flying over the state are impressed by immense areas showing no sign of humanity. Current assessments indicate that approximately 160,000 acres of Alaska have been cleared, built on or otherwise directly altered by man, either by settlement or resource development, including mining, pipeline construction and agriculture. In comparison to the 365 million acres of land that make up the total of the state, the settled or altered area currently amounts to less than one-twentieth of 1 percent.

There are significant reasons for this lack of development in Alaska. Frozen for long periods in the dark of the Arctic, much of the land cannot support quantities of people or industry. Where the winters are "warm," the mountains, glaciers, rivers and oceans prevent easy access for commerce and trade.

The status of land is constantly changing, especially in Alaska. In most places, the free market affects patterns of land ownership, but in Alaska, all land ownership patterns until recently were the result of a century-long process of a single landowner, the United States government.

The Statehood Act signaled the beginning of a dramatic shift in land ownership patterns. It authorized the state to select a total of 104 million of the 365 million acres of land and inland waters in Alaska. (Under the Submerged Lands Act, the state has title to submerged lands under navigable inland waters.) In passing the Statehood Act, Congress cited economic independence and the need to open Alaska to economic development as the primary purposes for large Alaska land grants.

Alaska Native Claims Settlement Act

The issue of the Native claims in Alaska was cleared up with the passage of the Alaska Native Claims Settlement Act (ANCSA) on Dec. 18, 1971. This act of Congress provided for the creation of Alaska Native village and regional corporations, and gave the Alaska Eskimos, Aleuts and Indians nearly $1 billion and the right to select 44 million acres from a land "pool" of some 115 million acres.

Immediately after the settlement act passed, and before Native lands and National Interest Lands were selected, the state filed to select an additional 77 million acres of land. In September 1972, the litigation initiated by the state was resolved by a settlement affirming state selection of an additional 41 million acres.

Section 17 of the settlement act, in addition to establishing a Joint Federal–State Land Use Planning Commission, directed the secretary of the interior to withdraw from public use up to 80 million acres of land in Alaska for study as possible national parks, wildlife refuges, forests, and wild and scenic rivers. These were the National Interest Lands Congress was to decide upon, as set forth in Section 17(d)(2) of the settlement act, by Dec. 18, 1978. The U.S. House of Representatives passed a bill (HR39) that would have designated 124 million acres of national parks, forests and wildlife refuges, and designated millions of acres of these and existing parks, forests and refuges as wilderness. Although a bill was reported out of committee, it failed to pass the Senate before Congress adjourned.

In November 1978, the secretary of the interior published a draft environmental impact supplement, which listed the actions that the executive branch of the federal government could take to protect federal lands in Alaska until the 96th Congress could consider the creation of new parks, wildlife refuges, wild and scenic rivers and forests. In keeping with this objective, the secretary of the interior, under provisions of the 1976 Federal Land Policy and Management Act, withdrew about 114 million acres of land in Alaska from most public uses. On Dec. 1, 1978, the president, under the authority of the 1906 Antiquities Act, designated 56 million acres of these lands as national monuments.

In February 1980, the House of, Representatives passed a modified HR39. In August 1980, the Senate passed a compromise version of the Alaska lands bill that created 106 million acres of new conservation units and affected a total of 131 million acres of land in Alaska. In November 1980, the House accepted the Senate version of the Alaska National Interest Lands Conservation Act (ANILCA), which President Jimmy Carter signed into law on Dec. 2, 1980. This is also known as the d-2 lands bill or the compromise HR39. (See also National Parks, Preserves and Monuments; National Wilderness Areas; National Wildlife Refuges; National Forests; and National Wild and Scenic Rivers.)

Alaska's land ownership was complicated even further in 1982, when advocates for mental health programs in Alaska filed suit against the state of Alaska. Prior to statehood, Alaska was granted title to 1 million acres of fed-

eral land, with the provision that some revenues from the mental health trust were to be used to fund mental health programs for Alaskans.

In 1978, the legislature waived the trust status of mental health lands. In return, the mental health trust was to receive 1.5 percent of all income from state lands. However, this funding was not appropriated, and mental health advocates sued the state.

As of April 1992, a settlement of the lawsuit was pending before the court, and the state legislature was considering additional legislation. The proposed settlement has greatly curtailed the sale or exchange of state land for the forseeable future.

Land use in Alaska will continue to be a controversial and complex subject for some time. Implementation of the d-2 bill, and distribution of land to the Native village and regional corporations, the state of Alaska and private citizens in the state will require time. Much of this work is being done by the Bureau of Land Management, which also surveys federal land before a patent is issued. The passage of ANILCA 12 years ago set the stage for long-term management of resources, and the BLM is now moving forward to establish fish, wildlife and recreation resources as critical and necessary ingredients in a multiple-use mix. Balancing the needs of people, wildlife and the land itself will continue to challenge land use and management policies in the coming years.

Acquiring Land for Private Use

The easiest and fastest way to acquire land for private use is by purchase from the private sector, through real estate agencies or directly from individuals. Because of speculation, land claim conflicts and delays involving Native, state and federal groups, however, private land is considered by many people to be in short supply and often is very expensive.

Private land in Alaska, excluding land held by Native corporations, is estimated to be more than 1 million acres, but less than 1 percent of the state. Much of this land passed into private hands through the federal Homestead Acts and other public land laws, as well as land disposal programs of the state, boroughs or communities. Most private land is located along Alaska's small road network. Compared to other categories of land, it is highly accessible and constitutes some of the prime settlement land.

All laws related to homesteading on federal land (as opposed to state land) in Alaska were repealed as of 1986. Federal land is not available for homesteading or trade and manufacturing sites.

Following are programs that are in effect for the sale of state land. A one-year residency (except for the auction program) and an age of at least 18 is required for all programs.

Auction: The state has been selling land by public auction since statehood. The state may sell full surface rights, lease of surface or subsurface rights, or restricted title at an auction. There is a minimum bid of fair market value and the high bidder is the purchaser. Participants must be 18.

Homesite: The homesite program was passed in 1977 by the state legislature. Under its provisions, each Alaskan household is eligible for up to five acres. A person who has a homesite

entry permit, purchase contract or patent may not apply for another homesite, and neither can any member of that person's household. The land is free, but the individual must pay the cost of the application filing fee ($10), survey and platting, and appraisal, if purchasing. Persons enrolled in this program must live on the homesite for 35 months within seven years of entry and construct a permanent, single-family dwelling on the site within five years (this is called "proving up" on the land). After the dwelling is completed and approved by the division, the permit holder may purchase the land at fair market value at the date of purchase. The occupancy requirement is then waived.

Remote Parcels: This remote parcel program replaced the old open-to-entry program. It permitted entry upon designated areas to stake a parcel of up to 5, 20 or 40 acres, depending on the area, and to lease the area for five years with an option for a five-year renewal.

Remote parcels ended July 1, 1984, when the program was replaced by the 1983 homesteading bill. Alaskans leasing remote parcels, but who have not yet purchased them, may continue under the remote parcel lease agreement program to obtain patent.

Lottery: One year of residency is required to participate in the lottery program. Successful applicants are determined by a drawing and pay the appraised fair market value of the land. They repay the state over a period of up to 20 years, with interest set at the current federal land loan bank rate. Lotteries require a 5 percent down payment.

The state offered 100,000 acres of land to private ownership in each fiscal year from July 1, 1979, to July 1, 1982. Disposal levels from that time forward have been based on an annual assessment of the demand for state land. There are no land sales scheduled for 1992.

On April 1, 1983, the Department of Natural Resources discontinued a program that provided Alaska residents who were registered voters a 5-percent-per-year-of-residency discount (up to $25,000) on the sale of land purchased from the state. Recent legislation has changed U.S. military veteran benefits. A 90-day service now qualifies the veteran. It used to be that 15-year veteran residents had been eligible for up to $37,500 on this one-time program.

Homestead: Under state law, any resident of at least one year, who is 18 years or older and a U.S. citizen, has a chance to receive up to 40 acres of nonagricultural land or up to 160 acres of agricultural land without paying for the acreage itself. To receive title, however, the homesteader must pay a $10 application fee and either survey or reimburse the state for survey costs; brush and stake the parcel boundary, build a dwelling, occupy and improve the land in certain ways within specific time frames. This is called "proving up" on the homestead.

The state homestead act also allows homesteaders to purchase parcels at fair market value without occupying or improving the land. This option requires only that nonagricultural land be staked, brushed and surveyed, and that parcels designated for agricultural use also meet clearing requirements. There is a two-year purchase option available on the homesteads, or a five-year purchase option, which also requires a habitable dwelling to be built by the third year of the permit. Currently, there are no homesteads available.

Whether the homesteader chooses to prove up or purchase, all applicable requirements such as brushing, survey and agricultural clearing must be met. After homesteading areas have been designated, homesteaders must stake the corners and flag the boundaries of the land, pay a fee of $5 per acre and personally file a description of the land with the state. In order to acquire title to the land, homesteaders must brush the boundaries within 90 days after issuance of the entry permit, complete an approved survey of the land within two or five years (depending on purchase option), erect a habitable permanent dwelling on the homestead within three years, live on the parcel for 25 months within five years and, if the land is classified for agricultural use, clear and either put into production or prepare for cultivation 25 percent of the land within five years.

Up-to-date information and applications for state programs are available from the Department of Natural Resources Public Information Office:

Northern Region, 3700 Airport Way, Fairbanks 99709
Southcentral Region, 3601 C St., Suite 200, Anchorage 99503
Southeastern Region, 400 Willoughby Ave., Suite 400, Juneau 99801

Following is the amount of Alaska land owned by various entities as of April 1991:

Owner	Acreage (millions of acres)
U.S. Bureau of Land Management	92.4
State	84.7
U.S. Fish and Wildlife	75.4
National Park Service	50.6
Native	35.1
Forest Service	23.2
Military and other Federal	2.6
Private	1.0

(Source: U.S. Bureau of Land Management)

Languages

Besides English, Alaska's languages include 20 Native languages. Sixteen of these Native languages are at risk of extinction: Han, Haida, Eyak, Tanana, Tlingit, Dena'ina, Ahtna, Tanaina, Ingalik, Holikachuk, Tsimshian, Koyukon, Upper Kuskokwim, Upper Tanana, Kutchin and Aleut. The Eskimo language group—Yup'ik, Central Yup'ik, Siberian Yup'ik and Inupiaq—are widely spoken by many Natives in western and northern Alaska.

Mammals

Large Land Mammals

Black bear—Highest densities are found in Southeast, Prince William Sound, and southcentral coastal mountains and lowlands. Black bears also occur in interior and western Alaska, but are absent from Southeast islands north of Frederick Sound (primarily Admiralty, Baranof and Chichagof) and Kodiak archipelago. They are not commonly found west of about Naknek Lake on the Alaska Peninsula, in the Aleutian Islands or on the open tundra sloping into the Bering Sea and Arctic Ocean. (*See also* Bears)

Brown/grizzly bear—These large carnivores are found in most of Alaska. The grizzly is not found in the Southeast islands south of Frederick Sound and in the Aleutians (except for Unimak Island). (*See also* Bears)

Polar bear—There are two groups in Alaska's Arctic rim: an eastern group found largely in the Beaufort Sea and a western group found in the Chukchi Sea between Alaska and Siberia. The latter group are the largest polar bears in the world. Old males can exceed 1,500 pounds. (*See also* Bears)

American bison—In 1928, 23 bison were transplanted from Montana to Delta Junction to restore Alaska's bison population, which had died out some 500 years before. Today, several hundred bison graze near Delta Junction; other herds range at Farewell, Chitina and along the lower Copper River.

Barren Ground caribou—There are at least 13 distinct caribou herds, with some overlapping of ranges: Adak,

Alaska Peninsula, Arctic, Beaver, Chisana, Delta, Kenai, McKinley, Mentasta, Mulchatna, Nelchina, Porcupine and Fortymile. Porcupine and Fortymile herds range into Canada.

Sitka black-tailed deer—Sitka black-tailed deer range the coastal rain forests of southeastern Alaska. They have been successfully transplanted to the Yakutat area, Prince William Sound, and to Kodiak and Afognak islands.

Roosevelt elk—Alaska's only elk occur on Raspberry and Afognak islands and result from a 1928 transplant of Roosevelt elk from the Olympic Peninsula in Washington state. Other transplant attempts have failed.

Moose—Moose occur from the Unuk River in Southeast to the Arctic Slope, but are most abundant in second-growth birch forests, on timberline plateaus and along major rivers of Southcentral and Interior. They are not found on islands in Prince William Sound or Bering Sea, on most major islands in Southeast or on Kodiak or Aleutians groups.

Mountain goat—These white-coated animals are found in mountains throughout Southeast, and north and west along coastal mountains to Cook Inlet and Kenai Peninsula. They have been successfully transplanted to Kodiak and Baranof islands.

Musk-oxen—These shaggy, long-haired mammals were eliminated from Alaska by hunters by 1865. The species was reintroduced and first transplanted to Nunivak Island, and from there to the Arctic Slope around Kavik, Seward Peninsula, Cape Thompson and Nelson Island. (*See also* Musk-Oxen)

Reindeer—Introduced from Siberia just before the 20th century, reindeer roamed much of the Bering Sea Coast

region but are now confined to the Seward Peninsula and Nunivak Island.

Dall sheep—The only white, wild sheep in the world, Dall sheep are found in all major mountain ranges in Alaska except the Aleutian Range south of Iliamna Lake.

Wolf—Wolves are protected and managed as big game and valuable furbearers. Wolves are found throughout Alaska except Bering Sea islands, some Southeast and Prince William Sound islands, and the Aleutian Islands. The wolf succeeds in a variety of climates and terrains.

Wolverine—Shy, solitary creatures, wolverines are found throughout Alaska and on some Southeast islands; abundant in the Interior and on the Alaska Peninsula. They are not abundant in comparison with other furbearers.

Furbearers

Beaver—These large vegetarian rodents are found in most of mainland Alaska from Brooks Range to middle of Alaska Peninsula. Abundant in some major mainland river drainages in the Southeast and on Yakutat forelands, they have also been successfully transplanted to Kodiak area. Beaver dams are sometimes destroyed to allow salmon upstream; however, the beavers can rebuild their dams quickly and usually do so on the same site.

Coyote—The coyote is a relative newcomer to Alaska, showing up shortly after the turn of the century, according to old-timers and records. They are not abundant on a statewide basis, but are common in Tanana, Copper, Matanuska and Susitna river drainages and on Kenai Peninsula. The coyote is found as far west as Alaska Peninsula and the north side of Bristol Bay.

Fox—*Arctic* (white and blue phases): Arctic foxes are found almost entirely along the Arctic coast as far south as the northwestern shore of Bristol Bay. They have been introduced to Pribilof and Aleutian islands, where the blue color phase, most popular with fox farmers, predominates. The white color phase occurs naturally on Saint Lawrence and Nunivak islands. *Red:* Their golden fur coveted by trappers, the red fox is found throughout Alaska except for

most areas of Southeast and around Prince William Sound.

Lynx—These shy night-prowlers' main food source is the snowshoe hare. The lynx is found throughout Alaska, except on Yukon–Kuskokwim Delta, southern Alaska Peninsula and along coastal tidelands. It is relatively scarce along northern gulf coast and in southeastern Alaska.

Hoary marmot—Present throughout most of the mountain regions of Alaska and along the Endicott Mountains east into Canada, the hoary marmot lives in the high country, especially the warm slopes near and above timberline.

Marten—The marten must have climax spruce forest to survive, and its habitat ranges throughout timbered Alaska, except north of the Brooks Range, on treeless sections of the Alaska Peninsula, and on the Yukon–Kuskokwim Delta. It has been successfully introduced to Prince of Wales, Baranof, Chichagof and Afognak islands in this century.

Muskrat—Muskrats are found in greatest numbers around lakes, ponds, rivers and marshes throughout all of mainland Alaska south of the Brooks Range except for the Alaska Peninsula west of the Ugashik lakes. They were introduced to Kodiak Island, Afognak and Raspberry islands.

River otter—A member of the weasel family, the river otter occurs throughout the state except on Aleutian Islands, Bering Sea islands and on the Arctic coastal plain east of Point Lay. They are most abundant in southeastern Alaska, Prince William Sound coastal areas and on the Yukon–Kuskokwim Delta.

Raccoon—The raccoon is not native to Alaska and is considered an undesirable addition because of impact on native furbearers. It is found on the west coast of Kodiak Island, on Japonski and Baranof islands, and on other islands off Prince of Wales Island in Southeast.

Squirrel—*Northern Flying:* These small nocturnal squirrels are found in interior, southcentral and southeastern Alaska where coniferous forests are sufficiently dense to provide suitable habitat. *Red:* These tree squirrels inhabit spruce forests, especially along rivers, from Southeast north to the Brooks Range. They are not found on the Seward Peninsula, Yukon–Kuskokwim Delta and Alaska Peninsula south of Naknek River.

Weasel—Least weasels and short-tailed weasels are found throughout Alaska, except for Bering Sea and Aleutian islands. Short-tailed weasels are brown with white underparts in summer, becoming snow-white in winter (designated ermine).

Other Small Mammals

Bat—There are five common bat species in Alaska.

Northern hare (arctic hare or tundra hare)—This large hare inhabits western and northern coastal Alaska, weighs 12 pounds or more and measures 2$^{1}/_{2}$ feet long.

Snowshoe hare (or varying hare)—In winter, these animals become pure white; in summer, their coats are grayish to brown. The snowshoe hare occurs throughout Alaska except for lower portion of Alaska Peninsula, Arctic coast and most islands; it is scarce in southeastern Alaska. Cyclic population highs and lows of hares occur roughly every 10 years. Their big hind feet, covered

with coarse hair in winter, make for easy travel over snow.

Brown lemming—Lemmings are found throughout northern Alaska and the Alaska Peninsula; they are not present in Southeast, Southcentral or Kodiak archipelago.

Collared lemming—Resembling large meadow voles, collared lemmings are found from the Brooks Range north and from the lower Kuskokwim River drainage north.

Northern bog lemming (sometimes called lemming mice)—These tiny mammals, rarely observed, occur in meadows and bogs across most of Alaska.

Deer mouse—Inhabit timber and brush in southeastern Alaska.

House mouse—Extremely adaptive, familiar house mice are found in Alaska seaports and large communities in southcentral Alaska.

Meadow jumping mouse—These mice can jump six feet and are in the southern third of Alaska from Alaska Range to Gulf of Alaska.

Collared pika—Members of the rabbit family, pikas are found in central and southern Alaska; most common in Alaska Range.

Porcupine—These rodents are slow-moving animals that prefer forests and are found in most wooded regions of mainland Alaska.

Norway rat—The Norway rat came to Alaska on whaling ships to Pribilof Islands in mid-1800s; especially thriving in the Aleutians (the Rat Islands group is named for the Norway rats).

They are now found in virtually all Alaska seaports, and in Anchorage and Fairbanks and other population centers with open garbage dumps.

Shrew—Seven species of shrew range in Alaska.

Meadow vole (or meadow mouse)—Extremely adaptive, there are seven species of meadow vole attributed to Alaska that range throughout the state.

Red-backed vole—The red-backed vole prefers cool, damp forests and is found throughout Alaska from Southeast to Norton Sound.

Woodchuck—These large, burrowing squirrels, also called groundhogs, are found in the eastern Interior between Yukon and Tanana rivers, from east of Fairbanks to Alaska-Canada border.

Bushy-tailed woodrat—Commonly called pack rats because they tend to carry off objects to their nests, woodrats are found along mainland coast of southeastern Alaska.

Marine Mammals

Marine mammals found in Alaska waters are: **dolphin** (Grampus, Pacific white-sided and Risso's); **Pacific walrus**; **porpoise** (Dall and harbor); **sea otter**; **seal** (harbor, larga, northern elephant, northern fur, Pacific bearded or *oogruk*, ribbon, ringed and spotted); **Steller sea lion**; and **whale** (Baird's beaked or giant bottlenose, beluga, blue, narwhal, bowhead, Cuvier's beaked or goosebeaked, fin or finback, gray, humpback, killer, minke or little piked, northern right, pilot, sei, sperm and Stejneger's beaked or Bering Sea beaked).

The Marine Mammal Protection Act, passed by Congress on Dec. 21, 1972, provided for a complete moratorium on the taking and importation of all marine mammals. The purpose of the act was to give protection to population stocks of marine mammals that "are, or may be, in danger of extinction or depletion as a result of man's activities." Congress further found that marine mammals have "proven themselves to be resources of great international significance, aesthetic and recreational as well as economic, and it is the sense of the Congress that they should be protected and encouraged to develop to the greatest extent feasible commensurate with sound policies of resource management and that the primary objective of their management should be to maintain the health and stability of the marine ecosystem. Whenever consistent with this primary objective, it should be the goal to obtain an optimum sustainable population keeping in mind the carrying capacity of the habitat."

At the present time, the U.S. Fish and Wildlife Service (Department of the Interior) is responsible for the management of polar bears, sea otters and walrus in Alaska. The National Marine Fisheries Service (Department of Commerce) is responsible for the management of all other marine mammals. The state of Alaska assumed management of walrus in April 1976, and relinquished it back to the USFWS in July 1979. However, an amendment to the Marine Mammal Protection Act in 1981 makes it easier for states to assume management of marine mammals, and Alaska is currently going through the necessary steps to assume management of its marine mammals.

Masks

(*See also* Native Arts and Crafts)

Masks are integral to the cultures of the Eskimos, coastal Indians and Aleuts of Alaska.

Eskimo

Eskimo masks rank among the finest tribal art in the world. Ceremonialism and the mask-making that accompanied it were highly developed and practiced widely by the time the first Russians established trading posts in southeast Alaska in the early 1800s. By the early part of the 20th century, masks were made much less frequently and were rarely made for ceremonial use.

The shaman used masks during certain ceremonies, sometimes in conjunction with wooden puppets, in ways that frightened and entertained participants. Dancers wore religious masks in festivals that honored the spirits of animals and birds to be hunted or that needed to be appeased. Each spirit was interpreted visually in a different mask and each mask was thought to have a spirit, or *inua*, of its own. This *inua* tied the mask to the stream of spiritual beliefs present in Eskimo religion. Not all masks were benign; some were surrealistic pieces that represented angry or dangerous spirits.

The skill of ceremonial mask-making has remained popular in some regions, notably among King Islanders, on Nunivak Island and in other areas of southwest Alaska.

Indian

Several types of masks existed among the coastal Indians of Alaska, including simple single-face masks, occasionally having an elaborately carved totemic border; a variation of the face mask with the addition of moving parts; and transformation masks, which have several faces hidden behind the first.

Masked dancers were accompanied by a chorus of tribal singers who sang songs associated with the masks and reflecting the wealth of the host. Masks were the critical element in portraying the relationship of the tribe with spirits and projecting their power to spellbind their audiences.

Masks were always created to be worn, but not all members of the tribe held sufficient status or power to wear them. Ceremonial use of masks generally took place in the fall or winter, when the spirits of the other world were said to be nearby.

Crudely carved masks created for

fun were occasionally made among the Kwakiutl.

Northwest Coast Indian mask-makers primarily used alder, though red and yellow cedar were used at times.

Aleut

Examples of masks used on various islands of the Aleutian Chain for shamanistic and ceremonial purposes are reported as early as the mid-18th century. Some of these early masks were described as bizarre representations of various animals, but many were apparently destroyed after use and none survive today. Aleut legends maintain that some masks were associated with ancient inhabitants of the region, a people apparently considered unrelated.

On the Shumagin Islands, a group of cavelike chambers yielded important examples of Aleut masks late in the 19th century. A number of well-preserved masks, apparently associated with the burials of Aleut whalers, were found. All of them had once been painted. Some of them had attached ears and pegs where tooth grips for wearing the masks would have been placed. Other pegs and holes were used for inserting feathers or carved wooden appendages similar to those of Eskimo masks of southern Alaska today. Fragments of composite masks, those decorated with feathers, appendages or movable parts, have been found on Kagamil Island with earlier remains.

Early accounts of masked Aleut dances say each dance was accompanied by special songs. Most masks were apparently hidden in caves or secret places when the ceremony ended, possibly for good luck. Bone masks worn by members of burial parties in some regions were broken and discarded at the gravesite when funeral rites were completed.

Today, no Aleut mask-makers in the old tradition survive, so further explanation of the use and significance of masks already collected depends on future archaeological investigation.

Medal of Heroism

By a law established in 1965, the Alaska governor is authorized to award, in recognition of valorous and heroic deeds, a state medal of heroism to persons who have saved a life or, at risk to their lives, have served the state or community on behalf of the health, welfare or safety of other persons. The heroism medal may be awarded posthumously. Following are recipients of the Alaska Medal of Heroism:

Albert Rothfuss (1965), Ketchikan. Rescued a child from drowning in Ketchikan Creek.

Randy Blake Prinzing (1968), Soldotna. Saved two lives at Scout Lake.

Nancy Davis (1971), Seattle. A flight attendant who convinced an alleged hijacker to surrender to authorities.

Jeffrey Stone (1972), Fairbanks.

Saved the lives of two youths from a burning apartment.

Gilbert Pelowook (1975), Savoonga. An Alaska state trooper who aided plane crash victims on Saint Lawrence Island.

Residents of Gambell (1975). Provided aid and care for plane crash victims on Saint Lawrence Island.

George Jackinsky (1978), Kasilof. Rescued two persons from a burning aircraft.

Mike Hancock (1980), Lima, Ohio. In 1977, rescued a victim of a plane crash that brought down high-voltage lines.

John Stimson (1983), Cordova. A first sergeant in the Division of Fish and Wildlife Protection who died in a helicopter accident during an attempt to rescue others.

Robert Larson (1983), Anchorage. A Department of Public Safety employee who flew through hazardous conditions to rescue survivors of the crash that took John Stimson's life.

David Graham (1983), Kenai. Rescued a person from a burning car.

Darren Olanna (1984), Nome. Died while attempting to rescue a person from a burning house.

Esther Farquhar (1984), Sitka. Tried to save other members of her family from a fire in their home; lost her life in the attempt.

Billy Westlock (1986), Emmonak. Rescued a youngster from the Emmonak River.

Lt. Comm. Whiddon, Lt. Breithaupt, ASM2 Tunks, AD1 Saylor, AT3 Milne (1987), Sitka. Rescued a man and his son from their sinking boat during high seas.

Army and Air National Guard (1988), Gambell, Savoonga, Nome and Shishmaref. Searched for seven missing walrus hunters.

Evans Geary, Johnny Sheldon, Jason Rutman, Jessee Ahkpuk Jr. and Carl Hadley (1989), Buckland. These youth rescued two friends who, while ice skating on a frozen pond, had fallen through the ice.

Robert Cusack (1991), Lake Iliamna. Rescued a woman and a child who were trapped inside a floatplane that crashed and sank in Lake Iliamna.

Metric Conversions

As in the rest of the United States, metrics are slow in coming to Alaska. The conversion formulas on page 98 will help you to prepare for the metric system and to understand measurements in neighboring Yukon Territory.

Mileage Chart

See chart on page 99.

Military

(*See also* National Guard)

Until the rapid escalation of war in Europe in 1940–41, Congress saw little need for a strong military presence in Alaska. Spurred by World War II and a growing realization that Alaska could shorten the route to Asia for friend and foe, the government built and still maintains units of the Air Force, Army, Navy and Coast Guard at dozens of installations across the state and on floating units in Alaskan waters. At the state level are Air National Guard and Army National Guard units.

(Continued on page 99)

Approximate conversions from customary to metric and vice versa:

	When you know:	You can find:	If you multiply by:
Length	inches	millimeters	25.4
	feet	centimeters	30.5
	yards	meters	0.9
	miles	kilometers	1.6
	millimeters	inches	0.04
	centimeters	inches	0.4
	meters	yards	1.1
	kilometers	miles	0.6
Area	square inches	square centimeters	6.5
	square feet	square meters	0.09
	square yards	square meters	0.8
	square miles	square kilometers	2.6
	acres	square hectometers (hectares)	0.4
	square centimeters	square inches	0.16
	square meters	square yards	1.2
	square kilometers	square miles	0.4
	square hectometers (hectares)	acres	2.5
Weight	ounces	grams	28.4
	pounds	kilograms	0.45
	short tons	megagrams (metric tons)	0.9
	grams	ounces	0.04
	kilograms	pounds	2.2
	megagrams (metric tons)	short tons	1.1
Liquid Volume	ounces	milliliters	29.6
	pints	liters	0.47
	quarts	liters	0.95
	gallons	liters	3.8
	milliliters	ounces	0.03
	liters	pints	2.1
	liters	quarts	1.06
	liters	gallons	0.26
Temperature	degrees Fahrenheit	degrees Celsius	5/9 (after subtracting 32)
	degrees Celsius	degrees Fahrenheit	9/5 (then add 32)

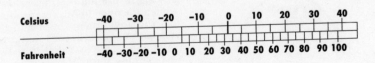

DRIVING MILEAGES BETWEEN PRINCIPAL POINTS	Anchorage, AK	Dawson City, YT	Dawson Creek, BC	Fairbanks, AK	Haines, AK	Homer, AK	Prince Rupert, BC	Seattle, WA	Skagway, AK	Valdez, AK	Whitehorse, YT
Anchorage, AK		515	1608	358	775	226	1605	2435	832	304	724
Dawson City, YT	515		1195	393	578	741	1192	2022	435	441	327
Dawson Creek, BC	1608	1195		1486	1135	1834	706	827	992	1534	884
Fairbanks, AK	358	393	1486		653	584	1483	2313	710	284	602
Haines, AK	775	578	1135	653		1001	1132	1962	359	701	251
Homer, AK	226	741	1834	584	1001		1831	2661	1058	530	950
Prince Rupert, BC	1605	1192	706	1483	1132	1831		1033	989	1531	881
Seattle, WA	2435	2022	827	2313	1962	2661	1033		1819	2361	1711
Skagway, AK	832	435	992	710	359	1058	989	1819		758	108
Valdez, AK	304	441	1534	284	701	530	1531	2361	758		650
Whitehorse, YT	724	327	884	602	251	950	881	1711	108	650	

(Continued from page 97)

U.S. ARMY

The Alaska District Corps of Engineers (COE) has three offices in Alaska: the Alaska District Office at Elmendorf Air Force Base, the Denali Area Office at Fort Richardson and the Fairbanks Resident Office at Fort Wainwright. There are also several offices across the state at Corps construction sites.

The Alaska District COE plans and designs military structures, runways and roads, utilities and other facilities for the Army, the 11th Air Force and the Alaska National Guard (Army and Air Force). Clear, Alaska, is the site of one of three Ballistic Missile Early Warning System (BMEWS) stations, which has been in operation since 1961. The two other BMEWS are in Greenland and England. The BMEWS station has three 400-foot-wide, 165-foot-high radar screens that scan the skies from the North Pole to China. The BMEWS supplies assistance to the Distant Early Warning (DEW) Line, which was originally designed to detect bombers crossing into North American air space. The Alaska sector of the DEW Line System is still in full operation.

The 6th Infantry Division (Light) is the primary Army unit in Alaska. The headquarters at Fort Richardson was moved to Fort Wainwright in 1990. Besides combat and combat support forces at those two posts, the division has research facilities and training grounds at Fort Greely. The division, supervised by a two-star general, must be prepared to move quickly to support other troops as needed. In late 1990 and early 1991, more than 200 Alaska-based soldiers were deployed to the Persian Gulf.

The primary units within the division include the 1st and 2nd Infantry Brigades in Alaska, and the 205th Infantry Brigade, which is a U.S. Army Reserve unit at Fort Snelling in St. Paul, Minnesota. In the event of a national emergency, the 205th will deploy to Alaska to "round out" the division. Other major units include the Aviation Brigade, Division Support Command, 6th Signal Battalion, the 6th Engineer Battalion and the 106th Military Intelligence Battalion.

In addition, 1117th Signal Battalion oversees all Army communications in the state; the Northern Warfare Training Center at Fort Greely trains soldiers, guardsmen and representatives from other services in arctic combat and survival; and the Cold Regions Test Center, also at Fort Greely, tests equipment for cold weather use.

The 6th Infantry Division (Light) conducts major midwinter exercises every other year. Other training includes unit-level exercises in Alaska, training at the Joint Readiness Training Center at Fort Chaffee, Arkansas, and at the National Training Center at Fort Irwin, California. The division also participates in exercises in Thailand and Japan.

Army helicopters in the state play an important role in search and rescue, as well as providing medical help to military and civilians. For example, the pilots of an Army OH-58 Scout helicopter from Fort Wainwright found an Italian hiker lost for four days near Fairbanks in August 1991. The M.A.S.T. (Military Assistance to Safety and Traffic) helicopters based at Forts Wainwright and Greely performed 47 missions, assisting 56 patients in fiscal year 1991 (October 1990 through September 1991). The Army's High Altitude Rescue Team (HART), flying specially equipped Chinook (CH-47) helicopters, went on three missions in the spring of 1990, rescuing nine people from Mount McKinley and other mountains within Denali National Park.

U.S. AIR FORCE

The 11th Air Force in Alaska was activated in 1990–91 during the same time the Alaskan Air Command was deactivated. The Commander, 11th Air Force, is also the Commander of the Alaskan Air Command, a subordinate unified command of the U.S. Pacific Command. Alaskan Air Command is responsible for the unified defense of Alaska's land and territorial waters, including the Aleutian Islands.

Alaskan Air Command's Air Force component belongs to the 11th Air Force at Elmendorf Air Force Base. It is the largest component in Alaska and provides support to all other Air Force units in the state. The 11th Air Force's largest subordinate units include the 21st Tactical Fighter Wing at Elmendorf Air Force Base and the 343rd Tactical Fighter Wing at Eielson Air Force Base. Other units are the 5073rd Air Base Group at Shemya Air Force Base, the 5072nd Combat Support Squadron at Galena Airport, the 5071st Combat Support Squadron at King Salmon Airport and the 17 long-range radar stations located throughout the state. The 11th Air Force provides combat-ready air forces to preserve the sovereignty of the United States' lands, waters and air space.

Other major Air Force components in Alaska include the Strategic Air Command with its KC-135 tanker fleet and other activities; Military Airlift Command with its fleet of C-130 "Hercules" cargo aircraft and Air Weather Service; Tactical Air Command with its E-3 Airborne Warning and Control System (AWACS) aircraft at Elmendorf Air Force Base; Air Force Space Command performing missile warning and space surveillance; the Air Force Communications Command providing major communications networks throughout the state; and Electronic Security Command.

U.S. COAST GUARD

The U.S. Coast Guard has been a part of Alaska since the mid-1800s, when it patrolled its extensive and unforgiving coastline with the wooden sailing and steam ships of its predecessor, the Revenue Cutter Service.

Since those early days, the service has changed names and those wooden ships have been replaced by today's modern fleet of ships, boats and aircraft, operated and maintained by Alaska's Coast Guard men and women.

The 17th Coast Guard District encompasses the entire state of Alaska, or 33,904 miles of coastline—more than all other states combined. As the nation's smallest military service, the U.S. Coast Guard performs its many missions in Alaska with 2,020 military and civilian employees at 40 units. District headquarters are located in Juneau, and the largest Coast Guard base and air station in the country is in Kodiak.

Major responsibilities in Alaska include enforcing the 200-mile fisheries conservation zone where the majority of the fish caught are sold to foreign countries. Search and rescue in Alaska is another task performed by Coast Guard units. The service maintains aids to navigation, including Long-Range Aids to Navigation (LORAN) lighthouses and buoys. Marine environmental pollution is also a major responsibility. The Coast Guard served as the Federal On-Scene Coordinator for the cleanup of the *Exxon Valdez* oil spill that occurred in Prince William Sound in 1989.

The Coast Guard also has an active role in the defense of Alaska. The

(Continued on page 102)

MILITARY INSTALLATIONS

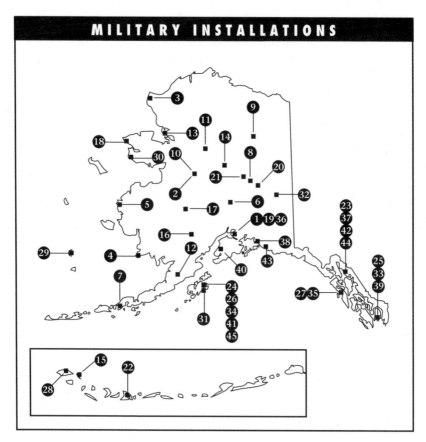

Map Key/Installation/Personnel

Air Force
1 Elmendorf AFB, 6,751
2 Campion AFS*
3 Cape Lisburne AFS*
4 Cape Newenham AFS*
5 Cape Romanzof AFS*
6 Clear AFS, 122
7 Cold Bay AFS*
8 Eielson AFB, 3,282
9 Fort Yukon AFS*
10 Galena Airport, 309
11 Indian Mountain AFS*
12 King Salmon, 275
13 Kotzebue AFS*
14 Murphy Dome AFS*
15 Shemya AFB, 598
16 Sparrevohn AFS*
17 Tatalina AFS*
18 Tin City AFS*

Army
19 Fort Richardson, 4,400

20 Fort Greely, 450
21 Fort Wainwright, 4,900

Navy
22 Adak, 1,677

Coast Guard
23 17th District Office Juneau, 170
24 Kodiak Support Center, 287
25 Base/Group Ketchikan, 101
26 Air Station Kodiak, 352
27 Air Station Sitka, 124
28 LORAN Station Attu, 24
29 LORAN Station Saint Paul, 21
30 LORAN Station Port Clarence, 27
31 LORAN Station Kodiak, 14
32 LORAN Station Tok, 7
33 LORAN Station Shoal Cove, 15
34 Communication Station Kodiak, 94
35 Marine Safety Detachment Sitka, 2
36 Marine Safety Office Anchorage, 25
37 Marine Safety Office Juneau, 12
38 Marine Safety Office Valdez, 40

Map Key/Installation/Personnel
(continued)
39 Marine Safety Detachment
   Ketchikan, 2
40 Marine Safety Detachment Kenai, 4
41 Marine Safety Detachment Kodiak,2
42 Station Juneau, 14
43 Seasonal Air Facility Cordova*, 4
44 Civil Engineering Unit Juneau, 26

45 Electronics Support Unit Kodiak, 20
*Now operated by civilian personnel

U.S. Coast Guard Cutters/Personnel
Anacapa, 16; *Elderberry,* 6; *Firebush,* 55;
Ironwood, 55; *Liberty,* 16; *Mustang,* 16;
Naushon, 16; *Planetree,* 55; *Sedge,*
Roanoke Island, 55; *Storis,* 75; *Sweetbrier,*
56; *Woodrush,* 55; *Yocona,* 82

Total Military Expenditures in Alaska by Agency for Fiscal Year 1990 (in millions of dollars)

Service	Pay	Construction	Operations & Maintenance	Other Procurement	Total
Air Force	$363.9	$ 36.6	$270.8	$97.3	$768.6
Army	315.3	66.3	132.3	27.9	541.8
Coast Guard	60.5	7.5	44.9	0.0	112.9
Corps of Engineers	22.7	0.0	7.7	23.9	54.3
National Guard	71.3	10.0	25.8	0.0	107.1
Navy*	67.7	39.8	32.7	0.1	140.3
Total	$903.6	$160.2	$514.4	$149.2	$1,727.4

*Includes Marines

Military Expenditures in Alaska for Fiscal Years 1985–1990 (in millions of dollars)

	1985	1986	1987	1988	1989	1990
Military Payroll	$ 503.1	$ 516.0	$ 567.5	$ 595.5	$605.3	$649.8
Civilian Payroll	189.7	181.5	212.4	204.9	204.0	214.8
Operations & Maintenance	389.1	493.3	645.3	485.1	527.1	514.4
Construction	204.0	180.3	204.9	167.6	227.0	160.2
Subtotal Appropriated Funds	$1,285.9	$1,371.1	$1,630.1	$1,453.1	$1,563.4	$1,539.2
Exchange & Nonappropriated Payrolls	32.8	35.7	32.5	29.5	30.7	39.0
Other Procurement.	136.9	149.5	105.4	194.5	176.7	149.2
Subtotal Other	$169.7	$185.2	$137.9	$224.0	$207.4	$188.2
DOD Retirement	113.1	122.3	130.4	139.5	146.4	175.9
Total	$1,568.7	$1,678.6	$1,898.4	$1,816.6	$1,917.2	$1,903.3

(Continued from page 100)
District Commander has recently been designated the Naval Component Commander for the Alaskan Command in addition to his responsibility as Commander, Maritime Defense Zone Sector Alaska.

MILITARY POPULATION

The total population of the uniformed services in Alaska on Sept. 30, 1990, was approximately 74,100. Population figures include active duty personnel, Department of Defense Civil Service employees, Nonappropriated Fund and Exchange personnel, and dependents. Of the total, 23,976 were active duty uniformed personnel and 4,695 were Civil Service employees of the Department of Defense.

The military services' work force consists of approximately 31,600 people, or roughly 12 percent of the state's estimated work force of 269,000 people. Military services stood as the third largest industry in the state in 1990. Total expenditures on behalf of the military services in Alaska had an estimated $2.7 billion impact on the Alaskan economy.

On a per capita basis, Alaska's veterans population of over 71,000 is the largest of any state. The Division of Veterans Affairs was established in 1984, as the state's official veterans advocate and coordinator of veterans issues and programs. It is also the liaison with federal and state agencies, veterans organizations, other states' veterans affairs organizations and the state's administration. The division ensures that Alaska's veterans and their dependents are aware of every state and federal benefit available to them and assists them in taking advantage of those benefits.

Minerals and Mining

(*See also* Coal; Gold; Oil and Gas; *and* Rocks and Gems)

In 1991, there were an estimated 3,638 people employed in mineral-related mining sectors in Alaska, according to the state Division of Geological and Geophysical Surveys. The early years of the 1970s were relatively quiet in the industry, with exploration primarily limited to geological reconnaissance. Late in 1974, restrictions on gold in the United States were lifted and the price of gold soared, spurring a revival of gold mining in the state.

By 1981, several large deposits containing minerals such as copper, chromite, molybdenum, nickel and uranium were the subject of serious exploration. Estimated exploration costs were in excess of $100 million for 1981, and more than 3,000 people were employed in the industry.

In 1991, the total value of Alaska's mineral industry, as measured by the sum of exploration and development expenditures and mineral production, amounted to $617 million. The industry experienced positive growth during 1991, especially in the hard-rock mining and development sectors, but suffered declines in mineral-exploration expenditures.

Zinc was the most valuable mineral commodity in 1991, accounting for 50 percent of Alaska's total mineral production revenues. Overall, metallic mineral production accounted for 80 percent of total mineral values, versus nonmetallic materials such as coal, sand and gravel, stone, peat and jade, which account for the remaining 20 percent of the values.

Usibelli Coal Mines near Healy continue as the state's only commercial coal mine. Production of coal in 1991 was estimated at 1.52 million tons, nearly unchanged from 1990. Of that total, about one-half was burned in interior Alaska power plants and the other half was shipped to Korea. During 1992, Usibelli will complete its 50th year of operation and will ship its 10 millionth ton of coal through the Port of Seward.

During 1989, the Greens Creek Mine on Admiralty Island began production and now employs 310 people. This is a modern, state of the art, underground mine producing silver along with some lead, zinc and gold. In 1990, Greens Creek produced 7.6 million ounces of silver, 37,000 ounces of gold, and was the largest silver producer in the U.S. Also in 1989, the Red Dog Mine began operation. In 1991, it continued as the largest zinc producer in the western world with production of 252,346 tons of zinc concentrates. The mine is a joint venture between Cominco Alaska and NANA Native Corporation and employs 340 people.

Until recently, Alaska was the only state to produce platinum, the fabled metal whose rarity exceeds that of gold. As of 1988, more than half a million ounces of platinum had been extracted by placer operations near the village of Goodnews Bay in southwestern Alaska.

Miss Alaska

The legislature has declared that the

young woman selected as Miss Alaska of the Miss America pageant each year will be the state's official hostess. Holders of the title are selected in Anchorage each spring in a competition sponsored by the nonprofit Miss Alaska Scholarship Pageant organization.

1959—Alansa Rounds Carr, Ketchikan
1960—June Bowdish, Anchorage
1961—Jean Ann Holm, Fairbanks
1962—Mary Dee Fox, Anchorage
1963—Colleen Sharon Kendall, Matanuska Valley
1964—Karol Rae Hommon, Anchorage
1965—Mary Ruth Nidiffer, Alaska Methodist University
1966—Nancy Lorell Wellman, Fairbanks
1967—Penny Ann Thomasson, Anchorage
1968—Jane Haycraft, Fairbanks
1969—Gwen Gregg, Elmendorf Air Force Base
1970—Virginia Walker, Kotzebue
1971—Linda Joy Smith, Elmendorf Air Force Base
1972—Deborah Wood, Elmendorf Air Force Base
1973—Virginia Adams, Anchorage
1974—Darby Moore, Kenai
1975—Cindy Suryan, Kodiak
1976—Kathy Tebow, Anchorage
1977—Lisa Granath, Kenai
1978—Patty-Jo Gentry, Fairbanks
1979—Lila Oberg, Matanuska Valley
1980—Sandra Lashbrook, Chugiak–Eagle River
1981—Laura Trollan, Juneau
1982—Kristan Sapp, Wasilla
1983—Jennifer Smith, Soldotna
1984—Marilin Blackburn, Anchorage
1985—Kristina Christopher Taylor, Palmer
1986—Jerri Morrison, Anchorage
1987—Teresa Murton, Anchorage
1988—Launa Middaugh, Anchorage
1989—Christine Rae McCubbins, Kenai
1990—Holly Ann Salo, Kenai
1991—Beth Gustafson, Anchorage
1992—Keri Baumgardner, Chugiak

Mosquitoes

At least 25 species of mosquito are found in Alaska (the number may be as high as 40), the females of all species feeding on people, other mammals or birds. Males and females eat plant sugar, but only the females suck blood, which they use for egg production. The itch that follows the bite comes from an anticoagulant injected by the mosquito. No Alaska mosquitoes carry diseases. The insects are present from April through September in many areas of the state. Out in the bush they are often at their worst in June, tapering off in July. The mosquito plague usually passes by late August and September. From Cook Inlet south, they concentrate on coastal flats and forested valleys. In the Aleutian Islands, mosquitoes are absent or present only in small numbers. The most serious mosquito infestations occur in moist areas of slow-moving or standing water, of the type found in the fields, bogs and forests of interior Alaska, from Bristol Bay eastward.

Mosquitoes are most active at dusk and dawn; low temperatures and high winds decrease their activity. Mosquitoes can be controlled by draining their breeding areas or spraying with approved insecticides. When traveling in areas of heavy mosquito infestations, it is wise to wear protective clothing, carefully screen living and camping areas and use a good insect repellent.

Mountains

Of the 20 highest mountains in the United States, 17 are in Alaska, which has 19 peaks over 14,000 feet. The U.S. Geological Survey lists them as follows:

Map Key/Elevation
1 McKinley, South Peak, 20,320 feet*
1 McKinley, North Peak, 19,470 feet*
2 Saint Elias, 18,008 feet**
3 Foraker, 17,400 feet
4 Bona, 16,500 feet
5 Blackburn, 16,390 feet
6 Sanford, 16,237 feet
1 South Buttress, 15,885 feet
7 Vancouver, 15,700 feet**
8 Churchill, 15,638 feet

9 Fairweather, 15,300 feet**
10 Hubbard, 15,015 feet**
11 Bear, 14,831 feet
1 East Buttress, 14,730 feet
12 Hunter, 14,573 feet
13 Alverstone, 14,565 feet**
1 Browne Tower, 14,530 feet
14 Wrangell, 14,163 feet
15 Augusta, 14,070 feet**

*Note: The two peaks of Mount McKinley are known collectively as the Churchill Peaks.
**On Alaska–Canada border.

Other Well-Known Alaska Mountains/Elevation

Augustine Volcano, 4,025 feet
Deborah, 12,339 feet
Devils Paw, 8,584 feet
Devils Thumb, 9,077 feet
Doonerak, 7,610 feet
Drum, 12,010 feet
Edgecumbe, 3,201 feet
Hayes, 13,832 feet
Kates Needle, 10,002 feet
Marcus Baker, 13,176 feet
Shishaldin, 9,372 feet

Mountain Ranges/Elevation

Ahklun Mountains, 1,000–3,000 feet

Mountain Ranges/Elevation

Alaska Range to 20,320 feet
Aleutian Range to 7,585 feet
Askinuk Mountains to 2,342 feet
Baird Mountains to 4,300 feet
Bendeleben Mountains to 3,730 feet
Brabazon Range to 5,515 feet
Brooks Range, 4,000–9,000 feet
Chigmit Mountains to 5,000 feet
Chugach Mountains to 13,176 feet
Coast Mountains to 18,000 feet
Darby Mountains to 3,083 feet
Davidson Mountains to 5,540 feet
De Long Mountains to 4,886 feet
Endicott Mountains to 7,000 feet
Fairweather Range to 15,300 feet
Igichuk Hills to 2,000 feet
Kaiyuh Mountains, 1,000–2,844 feet
Kenai Mountains to 6,000 feet
Kiglapak Mountains to 1,070 feet
Kigluaik Mountains to 4,714 feet
Kuskokwim Mountains to 3,973 feet
Lookout Range to 2,400 feet
Mentasta Mountains, 4,000–7,000 feet
Moore Mountains to 3,000 feet
Nutzotin Mountains, 5,000–8,000 feet
Ray Mountains, 2,500–5,500 feet
Romanzof Mountains to 8,700 feet
St. Elias Mountains to 18,000 feet

Mount McKinley

Mount McKinley in the Alaska Range is the highest mountain on the North American continent. The South Peak is 20,320 feet high; the North Peak has an elevation of 19,470 feet. The mountain was named in 1896 for William McKinley of Ohio, who at the time was the Republican candidate for president. An earlier name had been Denali, an Athabascan word meaning "the high one." The state of Alaska officially renamed the mountain Denali in 1975 and the state Geographic Names Board claims the proper name for the mountain is Denali. However, the federal Board of Geographic Names has not taken any action and congressional legislation has been introduced to retain the name McKinley in perpetuity.

Mount McKinley is within Denali National Park and Preserve (formerly Mount McKinley National Park). The park entrance is about 237 miles north of Anchorage and 121 miles south of Fairbanks via the George Parks Highway. (A 90-mile gravel road runs west from the highway through the park; vehicle traffic on the park road is restricted.) The park is also accessible via the Alaska Railroad and by aircraft.

The mountain and its park are one of the top tourist attractions in Alaska. The finest times to see McKinley up close are on summer mornings. August is best, according to statistics based on 13 summers of observation by park ranger Rick McIntyre. The mountain is rarely visible the entire day. The best view is from Eielson Visitor Center, located about 66 miles from the park entrance and 33 miles northeast of the summit. The center, open from early June through the second week in September, is accessible via free shuttle bus provided by the park.

Eleven climbers perished on Mount McKinley in May 1992, making it the deadliest climbing season in the mountain's history. The 11 climbers, including one American mountaineering guide, died in five separate incidents on the mountain. Since 1932 when the National Park Service began keeping records of climbers attempting to reach the summit of Mount McKinley, 75 climbers have been killed on the mountain. The five deadliest years on the mountain were 1981 and 1989, when six mountaineers were killed; 1967 and 1980, when eight mountaineers were killed, in addition to 1992, when 11 died.

The peak year for climbing the mountain was 1989, when 1,009 mountaineers scaled its heights. In 1991, 935 persons attempted to climb Mount McKinley, a drop of 6 percent from the year before. Of those 935 climbers, 557 or 59 percent were successful in reaching the summit. Foreign climbers numbered 531 (57 percent), with 28 countries represented. The largest number of foreign mountaineers came from Germany, with 51 climbers. The 1991 mountaineering season on Denali began with a rumble as a major earthquake hit the range on April 30. The earthquake measured 6.1 on the Richter scale, and its epicenter was just south of Mount Foraker. Huge avalanches were observed throughout the range, as well as several reports of close calls among climbers. There were no injuries reported, however.

In 1992, the National Park Service contracted an Areospatiale Lama helicopter to be stationed in Talkeetna for the mountaineering season. The Lama was successfully used on five major rescue missions. Its worthiness was proven after it was used for two successful rescues above 18,000 feet.

Related reading: *To the Top of Denali*, by Bill Sherwonit. A collection of Mount McKinley climbing stories. *See* ALASKA NORTHWEST LIBRARY in the back of the book.

Mukluks

Mukluks are lightweight boots designed to provide warmth in extreme cold. Eskimo mukluks are traditionally made with *oogruk* (bearded seal) skin bottoms and caribou tops and trimmed with fur. (Mukluk is also another name for *oogruk*.) Athabascan mukluks are traditionally made of moose hide and trimmed with fur and beadwork.

Muktuk

This Eskimo delicacy consists of the outer skin layers of whales. The two species of whale most often used for muktuk are the bowhead whale and the beluga, or white whale. The outer skin layers consist of a corky protective layer, the true skin and the blubber. In the case of beluga muktuk, the outer layer is white, the next layer is black and the blubber is pink. It may be eaten fresh, frozen, cooked or pickled.

Museums, Cultural Centers and Repositories

Visiting any of the following museums, historic sites, or other repositories offers a look into the rich diversity of Alaskan culture and history. For information about hours of operation and features of the collections, write to the addresses given or check with the Alaska State Division of Tourism, P.O. Box E, Juneau 99811; or Museums Alaska, Inc., 3779 Bartlett St., Homer 99603.

Adak Community Museum, P.O. Box 5244, NAV/STA, FPO Seattle, WA 98791

Alaska Indian Arts, Inc., P.O. Box 271, Haines 99827 (historic site)

Alaska Resources Library, 222 W. Seventh Ave., Anchorage 99513

Alaska State Museum, 395 Whittier St., Juneau 99801

Alaskaland Air Museum, P.O. Box 437, Fairbanks 99707

Alutiiq Cultural Center, 402 Center St., Kodiak 99615

Anchorage Museum of History & Art, 121 W. Seventh Ave., Anchorage 99501

Assumption of the Virgin Mary Church, Kenai 99611 (historic site)

Baranof Museum/Erskine House, 101 Marine Way, Kodiak 99615

Bristol Bay Historical Museum, P.O. Box 43, Naknek 99633

Carrie M. McLain Memorial Museum, P.O. Box 53, Nome 99762

Charlie Hubbard Museum, P.O. Box 552, Cooper Landing 99572

Circle District Historical Society, P.O. Box 1893, Central 99730

Clausen Memorial Museum, P.O. Box 708, Petersburg 99833

Cordova Museum, P.O. Box 391, Cordova 99574

Corrington Museum, P.O. Box 382, Skagway 99840

Damon Memorial Museum, P.O. Box 66, Soldotna 99669

Dorothy G. Page Museum, P.O. Box 870874, Wasilla 99687

Duncan Memorial Museum, P.O. Box 282, Metlakatla 99926

Eagle Historic Society, P.O. Box 23, Eagle 99738

Fort Kenay Museum, P.O. Box 580, Kenai 99611

Fort Richardson Fish and Wildlife Center, Building 600, Fort Richardson 99505

George I. Ashby Memorial Museum, P.O. Box 84, Copper Center 99573

Hoonah Cultural Center, P.O. Box 144, Hoonah 99829

House of Wickersham, Juneau. For information, write Alaska Division of Parks, P.O. Box M, Juneau 99811

Iditarod Museum, P.O. Box 870800, Wasilla 99687

The Imaginarium, 725 W. Fifth Ave., Anchorage 99501

Institute of Alaska Native Arts (IANA), P.O. Box 80583, Fairbanks 99708

Interior and Arctic Alaska Aeronautical Museum, P.O. Box 70437, Fairbanks 99707

Inupiat History, Language and Cultural Center, P.O. Box 69, Barrow 99723

Isabel Miller Museum, 330 Harbor Drive, Sitka 99835

Jessie Wakefield Memorial Library, P.O. Box 263, Port Lions 99550

Juneau Douglas City Museum, 155 S. Seward St., Juneau 99801

Juneau Mining Museum, 490 S. Franklin St., Juneau 99801

Klawock Totem Park, P.O. Box 113, Klawock 99925 (historic site)

Matanuska Valley Museum, Greater Palmer Chamber of Commerce, Palmer 99645

Museum of Alaska Transportation and Industry, P.O. Box 909, Palmer 99645

NANA Museum of the Arctic, P.O. Box 46, Kotzebue 99752

National Bank of Alaska Heritage Library Museum, P.O. Box 100600, Anchorage 99510

National Park Service, 2525 Gambell St., Anchorage 99503

Oscar Anderson House, 420 M St., Anchorage 99501

Pioneer Memorial Park, P.O. Box 70176, Fairbanks 99707

Pratt Museum, 3779 Bartlett St., Homer 99603

Rasmuson Library, University of Alaska, Fairbanks 99701

Resurrection Bay Historical Society Museum, P.O. Box 55, Seward 99664

Russian Bishop's House, P.O. Box 944, Sitka 99835

Saint Herman's Theological Seminary, P.O. Box 726, Kodiak 99615 (historic site)

Samuel K. Fox Museum, P.O. Box 3202, Dillingham 99576

Saxman Totem Park and Tribal House, P.O. Box 8558, Ketchikan 99901 (historic site)

Sheldon Jackson Museum, 104 College Drive, Sitka 99835

Sheldon Museum and Cultural Center, P.O. Box 239, Haines 99827

Simon Paneak Memorial Museum, P.O. Box 21085, Anaktuvuk Pass 99721

Southeast Alaska Indian Cultural Center, P.O. Box 944, Sitka 99835

Talkeetna Historical Society Museum, P.O. Box 76, Talkeetna 99676

Tanana Valley Agricultural Museum, P.O. Box 188, Fairbanks 99707

Tok Visitor Center, P.O. Box 335, Tok 99780

Tongass Historical Museum, 629 Dock St., Ketchikan 99901

Totem Bight, Ketchikan. For information, write Alaska Division of Parks, P.O. Box M, Juneau 99811 (historic site)

Totem Heritage Center, 629 Dock St., Ketchikan 99901 (historic site)

Trail of '98 Museum, P.O. Box 415, Skagway 99840

Tribal House of the Bear, P.O. Box 868, Wrangell 99929 (historic site)

University of Alaska Museum, 907 Yukon Drive, Fairbanks 99775

U.S. Historical Aircraft Preservation Museum, P.O. Box 6813, Anchorage 99502

Valdez Museum, P.O. Box 8, Valdez 99686

Visual Arts Center, 713 W. Fifth Ave., Anchorage 99501

Wales Museum, Wales 99783

Wasilla Historical Society, 323 Main St., Wasilla 99654

Whittier Historical Museum, P.O. Box 728, Whittier 99502

Wickersham House, P.O. Box 1794, Fairbanks 99707

Wildlife Museum, Elmendorf Air Force Base, Anchorage 99506

Wrangell Museum, P.O. Box 1050, Wrangell 99929

Yugtarvik Regional Museum, P.O. Box 388, Bethel 99559

Mushrooms

More than 500 species of mushroom grow in Alaska, and, while most are not common enough to be seen and collected readily by the amateur mycophile (mushroom hunter), many edible and choice species shoot up in any available patch of earth. Alaska's "giant arc of mushrooms" extends from Southeast's panhandle through Southcentral, the Alaska Peninsula and the Aleutian Chain and is prime mushroom habitat. Interior, western and northern Alaska also support mushrooms in abundance.

Mushroom seasons vary considerably according to temperature, humid-

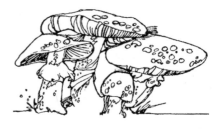

ity and available nutrients, but most occur from June through September. In a particularly cold or dry season, the crop will be scant.

There are relatively few poisonous mushrooms in relation to the number of species that occur throughout Alaska. Most toxic species are not fatal to healthy adults, but may produce severe symptoms such as heart palpitations, nausea, or may act as a laxative. Even edible mushrooms may disagree with one's digestion; the only test for an inedible or poisonous mushroom is positive identification. *If you can't identify it, don't eat it.*

Musk-Oxen

Musk-oxen are stocky, shaggy, long-haired mammals of the extreme northern latitudes. They remain in the open through Alaska's long winters. Their name is misleading, for they do not give musk and are more closely related to sheep and goats than to cattle. Adult males may weigh 500 to 900 pounds; females between 250 and 500 pounds. Both sexes have horns that droop down from their forehead and curve back up at the tips.

When threatened by wolves or other predators, musk-oxen form circles or lines with their young in the middle. These defensive measures did not protect them from man and his gun.

Musk-oxen were eliminated from Alaska in about 1865, when hunters shot and killed the last herd of 13. The species was reintroduced to the territory in the 1930s when 34 musk-oxen were purchased from Greenland and brought to the University of Alaska at Fairbanks. In 1935–36, the 31 remaining musk-oxen at the university were shipped to Nunivak Island in the Bering Sea, where the herd eventually thrived. Animals from the Nunivak herd have been transplanted to areas along Alaska's western and northern coasts; at least five herds—approximately 1,200 musk-oxen—now exist in the state.

Recent indications are that musk-oxen from Nelson Island are spreading to the mainland and that individuals from the eastern arctic herd have wandered west into adjacent Canada.

The soft underhair of musk-oxen is called qiviut and grows next to the skin, protected by long guard hairs. It is shed naturally every spring. Oomingmak Musk Ox Producers' Cooperative maintains a musk-oxen farm at Talkeetna, where workers gather the qiviut for cottage industry use. The hair is spun into yarn in Rhode Island and sent back to Alaska, where the cooperative arranges for knitters in villages in western Alaska, where jobs are scarce, to knit the yarn into clothing at their own pace.

Each village keeps its own distinct signature pattern for scarves knitted from qiviut. Villagers also produce stoles, tunics, hats and smoke rings, which are circular scarves that fit a person's head like a hood.

A domestic musk-oxen farm is located just outside Palmer. Guided tours operate daily from May to September and bring visitors face to face with these unique arctic animals. For more information, write: Musk–Ox Farm, P.O. Box 587, Palmer 99645.

Muskeg

Muskegs are deep bogs where little vegetation can grow except for sphagnum moss, black spruce, dwarf birch and a few other shrubby plants. Such swampy areas cover much of Alaska.

National Forests

Alaska has two national forests, the Tongass and the Chugach. The Tongass occupies the panhandle or southeast portion of the state. The Chugach extends south and east of Anchorage along the southcentral Alaskan coast, encompassing most of the Prince William Sound area.

These two national forests are managed by the U.S. Forest Service for a variety of uses. They provide forest products for national and international markets; minerals; recreational opportunities; wilderness experiences; and superb scenery and views for Alaska residents and visitors.

Nearly 200 public recreation cabins are maintained in the Tongass and Chugach national forests. They accommodate visitors from all over the world and are a vacation bargain at $20 per night, including firewood and on freshwater lakes, a boat. (*See also* Cabins)

Wildlife and fisheries are important Forest Service programs in the national forests of Alaska. The Tongass and Chugach national forests are also home to some of Alaska's most magnificent wildlife. It is here that the United States' national bird, the bald eagle, and large brown (grizzly) bears may be encountered in large numbers. All five species of Pacific salmon spawn in the rivers and streams of the forests, and smaller mammals and waterfowl abound. The Forest Service is charged with the management of this rich habitat; the Alaska Department of Fish and Game manages the wildlife species that this habitat supports.

There are many recreational opportunities in the national forests of Alaska, including backpacking, fishing, hunting, photography, boating, nature study and camping, to list just a few. For further information concerning recreational opportunities, contact the

U.S. Forest Service office nearest the area you are visiting.

The Alaska National Interest Lands Conservation Act of 1980—also referred to as ANILCA—and the Tongass Timber Reform Act (TTRA) of 1990 changed the status of certain lands in Alaska's national forests. (*See also* Land Use; National Parks, Preserves and Monuments; *and* National Wilderness Areas)

ANILCA created approximately 5.5 million acres of wilderness (consisting of 14 units) within the 17-million-acre Tongass National Forest. It also added three new areas to the forest: the Juneau Icefield, Kates Needle and parts of the Barbazon Range, totaling more than 1 million acres. The Tongass Timber Reform Act (TTRA) of 1990 amended ANILCA and designated five additional wilderness areas and an addition to the existing Kootznoowoo Wilderness.

The lands bill also provided extensive additions to the Chugach National Forest. These additions, totaling about 2 million acres, include the Nellie Juan area east of Seward, College Fiord extension, Copper/Rude rivers addition and a small extension at Controller Bay southeast of Cordova.

The Tongass Timber Reform Act of 1990 designated five more wilderness areas and expanded the existing Kootznoowoo Wilderness.

The following charts show the effect of the Alaska lands act on the Tongass and Chugach national forests:

Wilderness Units in Tongass National Forest (including acres)

Wilderness Areas Established Dec. 2, 1980 by ANILCA
  Kootznoowoo Wilderness (Admiralty Island National Monument)*, 955,921*
  Coronation Island Wilderness, 19,232
  Endicott River Wilderness, 98,729
  Maurelle Islands Wilderness, 4,937
  Misty Fiords National Monument**, 2,142,243
  Petersburg Creek–Duncan Salt Chuck Wilderness, 46,777
  Russel Fiord Wilderness, 348,701
  South Baranof Wilderness, 319,568
  South Prince of Wales Wilderness, 90,996
  Stikine–LeConte Wilderness, 448,926
  Tebenkof Bay Wilderness, 66,839
  Tracy Arm–Fords Terror Wilderness, 653,179
  Warren Island Wilderness, 11,181
  West Chichagof–Yakobi Wilderness, 264,747
Wilderness Areas Established Nov. 28, 1990 by TTRA
  Chuck River Wilderness, 74,298
  Karta Wilderness, 39,889
  Kuiu Wilderness, 60,581
  Pleasant–Lemusurier–Inian Islands Wilderness, 23,096
  South Etolin Wilderness, 83,371
Total Acreage, 5,753,211

*Kootznoowoo Wilderness includes 18,486 acres (including 24 acres of non-National Forest land) in the Young Lake Addition established by TTRA.
**Designated monuments under ANILCA; first areas so designated in the National Forest system. These wildernesses include only the public lands above mean high tide.

	Tongass	Chugach
Total Acreage Before ANILCA	15,555,388	4,392,646
Total Acreage After ANILCA	16,954,713	5,940,040*
Wilderness Acreage Created	5,453,366	none created
Wilderness Study	none created	2,019,999 acres
Wild and Scenic River Study	Situk River**	none created

*This lands act provides for additional transfers of national forest land to Native corporations, the state and the Fish and Wildlife Service of an estimated 296,000 acres on Afognak Island, and an estimated 242,000 acres to the Chugach Native Corporation.
**The lands act provides for a maximum of 640 acres on each side of the river, for each mile of river length.

National Guard

(*See also* Military)

The Department of Military Affairs administers the Alaska Army National Guard and the Air National Guard. The guard is charged with performing military reconnaissance, surveillance and patrol operations in Alaska; providing special assistance to civil authorities during natural disasters or civil disturbances; and augmenting regular Army and Air Force in times of national emergency. About 1,265 full-time employees work for the National Guard.

The Alaska Air National Guard has a headquarters unit located in Anchorage, a composite group made up of a tactical airlift squadron, an air refueling squadron and several support squadrons and flights. There are units based at Kulis Air National Guard Base on the west side of Anchorage International Airport, at Eielson Air Force Base in Fairbanks, and in Kotzebue, Bethel and Juneau.

Authorized staffing is 4,565 military personnel; about 35 percent are full-time technicians. When mobilized, the Air National Guard becomes an integral part of Alaska Command's Air Force component, and the Army National Guard becomes a part of Alaska Command's Army component.

The major unit of the Alaska Army National Guard, with a muster of 2,300, is the 207th Infantry Group, consisting of five Scout Battalions and detachments in almost 100 communities across the state. In addition, it has an airborne element, an air traffic control detachment and an aviation detachment. The Scout Battalions are authorized on Twin Otter aircraft and two helicopters in their aviation sections. In all, the Alaska Army National Guard operates 48 aircraft.

The scout teams are a unique element in the Alaska Army National Guard, performing a full-time active mission of intelligence gathering. Many scouts are subsistence hunters and whalers who constantly comb the coastal zones, offshore waters and inland areas. Reports of Soviet naval and air activities are common since Alaska and the USSR are separated by less than 50 miles across the Bering Strait.

The Alaska Division of Emergency Services administers statewide disaster preparedness and response programs. The division is the primary contact for obtaining emergency assistance from state, federal, military and independent services. Its personnel also provide guidance and financial assistance to state and local agencies to help them prepare for and recover from disasters. The agency responds to threats or occurrences of disasters, and directs disaster response in unincorporated areas where local government does not have the resources to respond adequately.

National Historic Places

(*See also* Archaeology)

A "place" on the National Register of Historic Places is a district, site, building, structure or object significant to the state for its history, architecture, archaeology or culture. The national register also includes National Historic Landmarks. NHLs are properties given special status by the secretary of the interior for the significance to the nation, as well as to the state. The register is an official list of properties recognized by the federal government as worthy of preservation. Listing on the register begins with owner's consent and entails a nomination process with reviews by the State Historic Preservation officer, the Alaska Historic Sites Advisory Committee and the keeper of the National Register. Limitations are *not* placed on a listed property: The federal government does not attach restrictive covenants to the property or seek to acquire it.

Listing on the register means that a property is accorded national recognition for its significance in American history or prehistory. Additional benefits include tax credits on income-producing properties and automatic qualification for federal matching funds for preservation, maintenance and restoration work when such funds are available. Listed properties are also guaranteed a full review process for potential adverse effects by federally funded, licensed or otherwise assisted projects. Such a review usually takes place while the project is in the planning stage: Alternatives are sought to avoid, if at all possible, damaging or destroying the particular property in question.

Southcentral

A.E.C. Cottage No. 23, Anchorage
Alaska Central Railroad Tunnel #1, Seward
Alaska Nellie's Homestead, Lawing vicinity
Alex (Mike) Cabin, Eklutna
American Cemetery, Kodiak
Anchorage City Hall, Anchorage
Anderson (Oscar) House, Anchorage
Ascension of Our Lord Chapel, Karluk
Bailey Colony Farm, Palmer
Ballaine House, Seward
Beluga Point Archaeological Site, North Shore, Turnagain Arm
Bering Expedition Landing Site NHL, Kayak Island
Berry House, Palmer
Brown & Hawkins Store, Seward
Campus Center Site, Palmer
Cape St. Elias Lighthouse, Kayak Island
Chilkat Oil Company Refinery Site, Katalla
Chisana Historic District, Chisana
Chitina Tin Shop, Chitina
Chugachik Island Archaeological Site, Kachemak Bay
Coal Village Site, Kachemak Bay
Cooper Landing Historic District, Cooper Landing
Cooper Landing Post Office, Cooper Landing
Copper River and Northwestern Railway, Chitina vicinity
Cordova Post Office and Courthouse, Cordova
Crow Creek Mine, Girdwood
Cunningham-Hall PT-6 NC692W (aircraft), Palmer
Dakah De'nin's Village Site, Chitina
David (Leopold) House, Anchorage
Diversion Tunnel, Lowell Creek, Seward
Eklutna Power Plant, Eklutna
Federal Building–U.S. Courthouse (Old), Anchorage
Fourth Avenue Theatre, Anchorage

Gakona Roadhouse, Gakona
Government Cable Office, Seward
Herried House, Palmer
Hirshey Mine, Hope vicinity
Holm (Victor) Cabin, Cohoe
Holy Assumption Russian Orthodox Church NHL, Kenai
Holy Resurrection Church, Kodiak
Holy Transfiguration of Our Lord Chapel, Ninilchik
Hope Historic District, Hope vicinity
Hyland Hotel, Palmer
Independence Mine Historic District, Hatcher Pass
Indian Valley Mine, Girdwood vicinity
KENI Radio Building, Anchorage
Kennecott Mines NHL, McCarthy vicinity
Kimball's Store, Anchorage
Knik Site, Knik vicinity
KOD-171 Archaeological Site, Kodiak
KOD-207 Archaeological Site, Kodiak
KOD-233 Archaeological Site, Kodiak
Kodiak Naval Operating Base (Fort Abercrombie and Fort Greely) NHL, Kodiak Island
Lauritsen Cabin, Seward Highway
Matanuska Colony Community Center, Palmer
McCarthy General Store, McCarthy
McCarthy Power Plant, McCarthy
Middle Bay Brick Kiln, Kodiak
Moose River Site, Naptowne, Kenai area
Nabesna Gold Mine, Nabesna area
Nativity of Holy Theotokos Church, Afognak Island
Nativity of Our Lord Chapel, Ouzinkie
Old St. Nicholas Russian Orthodox Church, Eklutna
Palmer Depot, Palmer
Palugvik Archaeological District, Hawkins Island
Patten Colony Farm, Palmer
Pioneer School House, Anchorage
Potter Section House, Anchorage
Protection of the Theotokos Chapel, Akhiok
Puhl House, Palmer
Rebarcheck (Raymond) Colony Farm, Palmer area
Reception Building, Cordova
Red Dragon Historic District, Cordova
Russian–American Company Magazin (Erskine House) NHL, Kodiak

St. Michael the Archangel Church, Cordova

St. Nicholas Chapel, Seldovia

St. Peter's Episcopal Church, Seward

Sts. Sergius and Herman of Valaam Chapel, Ouzinkie

Sts. Sergius and Herman of Valaam Church, English Bay

Selenie Lagoon Archaeological Site, Port Graham vicinity

Seward Depot, Seward

Sourdough Lodge NHL, Gulkana area

Susitna River Bridge, Alaska Railroad, Talkeetna vicinity

Swetman House, Seward

Tangle Lakes Archaeological District, Paxson vicinity

Teeland's Store, Wasilla

Three Saints Bay Site NHL, Kodiak Island

United Protestant Church, Palmer

Van Gilder Hotel, Seward

Wasilla Community Hall, Wasilla

Wasilla Depot, Wasilla

Wasilla Elementary School, Wasilla

Wendler Building, Anchorage

Yukon Island, Main Site NHL, Yukon Island

Southeast

Alaska Native Brotherhood Hall NHL, Sitka

Alaska Steam Laundry, Juneau

Alaska Totems, Ketchikan

Alaskan Hotel, Juneau

American Flag Raising Site NHL, Sitka

Bergmann Hotel, Juneau

Building No. 29 NHL, Sitka

Burkhart–Dibrell House, Ketchikan

Cable House and Station, Sitka

Cape Spencer Lighthouse, Cape Spencer

Chief Shakes House, Wrangell

Chilkoot Trail and Dyea NHL, Skagway

Davis (J.M.) House, Juneau

Duncan (Father William) Cottage, Metlakatla

Eldred Rock Lighthouse, Lynn Canal

Emmons House, Sitka

Etolin Canoe, Etolin Island

First Lutheran Church, Ketchikan

Fort Durham NHL, Taku Harbor, Juneau vicinity

Fort William H. Seward NHL, Haines

Frances House, Juneau

Fries Miners Cabins, Juneau

Gilmore Building, Ketchikan

Government Indian School, Haines

Governor's Mansion, Juneau

Holy Trinity Church, Juneau

Ketchikan Ranger House, Ketchikan

Klondike Gold Rush National Historic Park, Skagway area

Mayflower School, Douglas

Mills (May) House, Sitka

Mills (W.P.) House, Sitka

New Russia Archaeological Site NHL, Yakutat

Old Sitka NHL, Sitka

Pleasant Camp, Haines Highway

Porcupine Historic District, Skagway vicinity

Russian Bishop's House NHL, Sitka

St. John the Baptist Church, Angoon

St. Michael the Archangel Cathedral NHL, Sitka

St. Nicholas Church (Russian Orthodox), Juneau

St. Peter's Church, Sitka

St. Philip's Episcopal Church, Wrangell

Saxman Totem Park, Ketchikan

See House, Sitka

Sheldon Jackson Museum, Sitka

Sitka National Historical Park, Sitka

Sitka Naval Operating Base NHL, Sitka

Sitka Pioneers' Home, Sitka

Skagway and White Pass Historic District NHL, Skagway vicinity

Sons of Norway Hall, Petersburg

Totem Bight, Ketchikan

Twin Glacier Camp, Juneau

U.S. Army Corps of Engineers, Storehouse #3, Portland Canal

U.S. Army Corps of Engineers, Storehouse #4, Hyder

Governor's Mansion, Juneau

U.S. Coast and Geodetic Survey House, Sitka
Valentine Building, Juneau
Walker-Broderick House, Ketchikan
Wickersham House, Juneau
Wrangell Public School, Wrangell
Ziegler House, Ketchikan

Western

Adak Army and Naval Operating Bases NHL, Adak
Anangula Site NHL, Aleutian Islands
Ananiuliak Island Archaeological District, Aleutian Islands
Anvil Creek Gold Discovery Site, Nome
Archaeological Site 49 Af 3, Katmai National Park and Preserve
Archaeological Site 49 MK 10, Katmai National Park and Preserve
Atka B-24 Liberator, Aleutian Islands
Attu Battlefield and U.S. Army and Navy Airfields NHL, Attu
Brooks River Archaeological District, Katmai National Park and Preserve
Cape Field at Fort Glenn NHL, Aleutian Islands
Cape Krusenstern Archaeological District NHL, Kotzebue vicinity
Cape Nome Mining District Discovery Sites NHL, Nome
Cape Nome Roadhouse, Nome vicinity
Carrighar (Sally) House, Nome
Chaluka Site NHL, Umnak Island
Christ Church Mission, Anvik
Discovery Saloon, Nome
Dutch Harbor Operating Base and Fort Mears NHL, Aleutian Islands
Elevation of the Holy Cross Church, Naknek
Fairhaven Ditch, Imruk Lake
First Mission House, Bethel
Fort St. Michael Site, Unalakleet vicinity
Fure's Cabin, Katmai National Park and Preserve
Gambell Sites, Gambell
Holy Ascension Orthodox Church NHL, Unalaska
Holy Resurrection Church, Belkofski
Iyatayet Archaeological Site NHL, Norton Sound
Japanese Occupation Site, Kiska NHL, Aleutian Islands
Kaguyak Village Site, Katmai National Park and Preserve

Arctic Brotherhood Hall, Skagway Historic District

Kijik Historic District, Lake Clark National Park and Preserve
Kolmakov Redoubt Site, Kuskokwim River, Aniak vicinity
Kukak Village, Katmai National Park and Preserve
Norge Storage Site, Teller
Old Savonoski Site, Katmai National Park and Preserve
Onion Portage Archaeological District NHL, Noatak vicinity
Pilgrim 100B N709Y Aircraft, Dillingham
Pilgrim Hot Springs, Seward Peninsula
Port Moller Hot Springs Village Site, Alaska Peninsula
Presentation of Our Lord Chapel, Nikolai
Redoubt St. Michael Site, Unalakleet vicinity
St. George the Great Martyr Orthodox Church, St. George Island
St. Jacob's Church, Napaskiak
St. John the Baptist Chapel, Naknek
St. John the Theologian Church, Perryville
St. Nicholas Chapel, Ekuk
St. Nicholas Chapel, Igiugig
St. Nicholas Chapel, Nondalton
St. Nicholas Chapel, Pedro Bay
St. Nicholas Chapel, Sand Point
St. Nicholas Church, Kwethluk (ROC)
St. Nicholas Church, Nikolski
St. Nicholas Church, Pilot Point
St. Seraphim Chapel, Lower Kalskag
St. Sergius Chapel, Chuathbaluk

St. Michael the Archangel Cathedral NHL, Sitka

Sts. Constantine and Helen Chapel, Lime Village

Sts. Peter and Paul Russian Orthodox Church, St. Paul Island

Savonoski River District, Katmai National Park and Preserve

Seal Islands Historic District NHL, Pribilof Islands

Sir Alexander Nevsky Chapel, Akutan

Sitka Spruce Plantation NHL, Amaknak Island

Snow Creek Placer Claim No. 1, Nome vicinity

Solomon Roadhouse, Solomon

Takli Island Archaeological District, Katmai National Park and Preserve

TEMNAC P-38G Lightning Aircraft, Aleutian Islands

Transfiguration of Our Lord Chapel, Nushagak

Wales Archaeological District NHL, Wales vicinity

Interior

Biederman (Ed) Fish Camp, Eagle area

Big Delta State Historic District, Delta Junction

Campus Center Site, Fairbanks

Central Roadhouse, Central

Chatanika Gold Camp, Chatanika

Chena Pump House, Fairbanks

Chugwater Archaeological Site, Fairbanks

Clay Street Cemetery, Fairbanks

Creamer's Dairy, Fairbanks

Davis (Mary Lee) House, Fairbanks

Dry Creek Archaeological Site NHL, Healy vicinity

Eagle Historic District NHL, Eagle

Ester Camp Historic District, Fairbanks

Ewe Creek Ranger Cabin #8, Denali National Park

Fairview Inn, Talkeetna

Federal Building, U.S. Post Office, Courthouse (Old), Fairbanks

Goldstream Dredge #8, Mile 9, Old Steese Hwy.

Harding Railroad Car, Alaskaland, Fairbanks

Igloo Creek Cabin #25, Denali National Park

Immaculate Conception Church, Fairbanks

Joslin (Falcon) House, Fairbanks

The Kink, Fortymile River

Lacey Street Theatre, Fairbanks

Ladd Field NHL (Fort Wainwright), Fairbanks

Lower East Fork Ranger Cabin #9, Denali National Park

Lower Toklat River Ranger Cabin #18, Denali National Park

Lower Windy Creek Ranger Cabin #15, Denali National Park

Main School, Fairbanks

Masonic Temple, Fairbanks

McGregor (George) Cabin, Eagle vicinity

Mission Church, Arctic Village

Mission House (Old), Fort Yukon

Moose Creek Ranger Cabin #19, Denali National Park

Mount McKinley National Park Headquarters, Denali National Park

Nenana Depot, Nenana

Oddfellows Hall (First Avenue Bathhouse), Fairbanks

Rainey's Cabin, Fairbanks

Riley Creek Ranger Cabin #20, Denali National Park

Ruby Roadhouse, Ruby

Sanctuary River Cabin #31, Denali National Park

Slaven, (Frank), Roadhouse, Eagle vicinity

Steele Creek Roadhouse, Fortymile

Sternwheeler Nenana NHL, Fairbanks

Sullivan Roadhouse, Fort Greely

Sushana River Ranger Cabin #17, Denali National Park

Tanana Mission, Tanana

Taylor (James) Cabins, Eagle vicinity

Teklanika Archaeological District, Denali National Park and Preserve

Thomas (George C.) Memorial Library NHL, Fairbanks

Tolovana Roadhouse, Tanana vicinity

Toklat Ranger Station (Pearson Cabin) #4, Denali National Park

Upper East Fork Cabin #29, Denali National Park

Upper Savage River Cabin, Denali National Park

Upper Toklat River Ranger Cabin #24, Denali National Park

Upper Windy Creek Ranger Cabin #7, Denali National Park

Wickersham House, Fairbanks

Woodchopper Roadhouse, Eagle vicinity

Yukon River Lifeways District, Eagle vicinity

Far North

Aluakpak Site, Wainwright vicinity

Anaktuuk Site, Wainwright vicinity

Atanik District, Wainwright vicinity

Avalitkuk Site, Wainwright vicinity

Birnirk Site NHL, Barrow

Gallagher Flint Station Archaeological Site NHL, Sagwon

Ipiutak Archaeological District, Point Hope

Ipiutak Site NHL, Point Hope

Ivishaat Site, Wainwright vicinity

Kanitch, Wainwright vicinity

Leffingwell Camp NHL, Flaxman Island

Napanik Site, Wainwright vicinity

Negilik Site, Barrow

Point Barrow Refuge–Cape Smythe Whaling and Trading Station, Barrow vicinity

Utkeagvik Presbyterian Church Manse, Barrow

Uyagaagruk, Wainwright vicinity

Will Rogers–Wiley Post Site, Barrow vicinity

National Parks, Preserves and Monuments

The National Park Service administers approximately 54 million acres of land in Alaska, consisting of 15 units classified as national parks, national preserves and national monuments. The Alaska National Interest Lands Conservation Act of 1980—also referred to as ANILCA (*see* Land Use)—created 10 new National Park Service units in Alaska and changed the size and status of the three existing Park Service units: Mount McKinley National Park, now Denali National Park and Preserve; Glacier Bay National Monument, now a national park and preserve; and Katmai National Monument, now a national park and preserve. (*See* map, pages 118–19.)

In 1991, Alaska's national parks, preserves and monuments experienced a slight increase of visitors over the 1,200,000 numbers in 1989 and 1990. Kenai Fjords National Park showed the biggest gain in visitations in 1991, reaching 107,000 visitors, an increase of 62 percent from 1990. Denali is still the most popular destination, with Glacier Bay the second-most visited park. Visitors from cruise ships helped boost the number of visitors to the Sitka National Historical Park to a record 136,110. The

(Continued on page 120)

NATIONAL INTEREST LANDS

(Numbers refer to accompanying map)

NATIONAL WILDLIFE REFUGE SYSTEM
1 Alaska Maritime NWR*
    Chuckchi Sea Unit
    Bering Sea Unit
    Aleutian Island Unit
    Alaska Peninsula Unit
    Gulf of Alaska Unit
2 Alaska Peninsula
3 Arctic
4 Becharof
5 Innoko
6 Izembek
7 Kanuti
8 Kenai
9 Kodiak
10 Koyukuk
11 Nowitna
12 Selawik
13 Tetlin
14 Togiak
15 Yukon Delta
16 Yukon Flats

NATIONAL PARK SYSTEM
17 Aniakchak Natl. Monument and Preserve
18 Bering Land Bridge Nat'l. Preserve
19 Cape Krusenstern Nat'l. Monument
20 Denali Nat'l. Park and Preserve
21 Gates of the Arctic Nat'l. Park and Preserve
22 Glacier Bay Nat'l. Park and Preserve
23 Katmai Nat'l. Park and Preserve
24 Kenai Fjords Nat'l. Park
25 Kobuk Valley Nat'l. Park
26 Lake Clark Nat'l. Park and Preserve
27 Noatak Nat'l. Preserve
28 Wrangell-St. Elias Nat'l. Park and Preserve
29 Yukon-Charley Rivers Nat'l. Preserve
30 Klondike Gold Rush Nat'l. Historical Park
31 Sitka Nat'l. Historical Park

BUREAU OF LAND MANAGEMENT SYSTEM
32 Steese Nat'l. Conservation Areas
33 White Mountains Nat'l. Recreation Area

NATIONAL FOREST SYSTEM
34 Chugach Nat'l. Forest
35 Tongass Nat'l. Forest
36 Admiralty Island Nat'l. Monument**
37 Misty Fiords Nat'l. Monument**

NATIONAL WILD AND SCENIC RIVERS SYSTEM
There are 26 rivers designated wild and
scenic by the 1980 Alaska National
Interest Lands Conservation Act.

*The Alaska Maritime National Wildlife Refuge
consists of all the public lands in the coastal
waters and adjacent seas of Alaska including
islands, islets, rocks, reefs, capes and spires.
**Admiralty Island and Misty Fiords national
monuments are part of the Tongass National
Forest, which includes 12 other wilderness areas.

Chukchi Se

Bering

Aleutian Islands

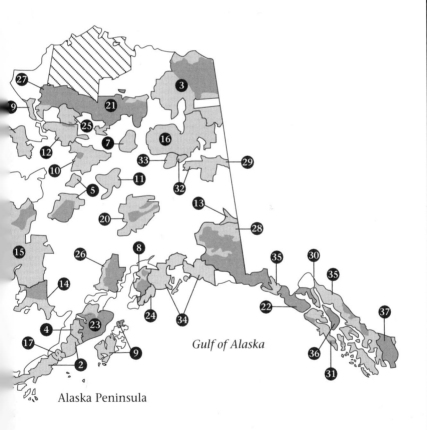

(Continued from page 117)

Klondike Gold Rush National Historical Park also marked a record year with 110,597 visitors. Visitations to the national parks in Alaska were expected to increase in 1992, with an estimated 30,000 additional travelers visiting the state for the celebrations commemorating the 50th anniversary of the Alaska Highway.

National parks are traditionally managed to preserve scenic, wildlife and recreational values; mining, cutting of house logs, hunting and other resource exploitation are carefully regulated within park monument and preserve boundaries, and motorized access is restricted to automobile traffic on authorized roads. However, regulations for National Park Service units in Alaska recognize that these units contain lands traditionally occupied and used by Alaska Natives and rural residents for subsistence activities. Therefore, management of *some* parks, preserves and monuments in Alaska provides for subsistence hunting, fishing and gathering activities, and the use of such motorized vehicles as snow machines, motorboats and airplanes where such activities are customary. National preserves do permit sport hunting.

Following is a list of National Park Service parks, preserves and monuments. (The U.S. Forest Service manages another two national monuments: Admiralty Island National Monument, 937,000 acres; and Misty Fiords National Monument, 2.1 million acres. Both are in Southeast and part of the National Wilderness Preservation System. *See also* National Wilderness Areas *and* National Wild and Scenic Rivers.)

Information on the parks, preserves and monuments is available at the Alaska Public Lands Information Centers: 605 W. Fourth Ave., Suite 105, Anchorage 99501; 250 Cushman St., Suite 1A, Fairbanks 99701; and P.O. Box 359, Tok 99780.

National Park Service Units are followed by address, acreage and major features or recreations:

Aniakchak National Monument and Preserve, Superintendent, Katmai National Park and Preserve, P.O. Box 7, King Salmon 99613 (603,000 acres). Aniakchak dry caldera.

Bering Land Bridge National Preserve, National Park Service, P.O. Box 220, Nome 99762 (2,785,000 acres). Lava fields, archaeological sites, migratory waterfowl.

Cape Krusenstern National Monument, National Park Service, P.O. Box 1029, Kotzebue 99752 (660,000 acres). Archaeological sites.

Denali National Park and Preserve, National Park Service, P.O. Box 9, Denali Park 99755 (6,028,000 acres). Mount McKinley, abundant wildlife.

Gates of the Arctic National Park and Preserve, National Park Service, P.O. Box 74680, Fairbanks 99707 (8,472,000 acres). Brooks Range, wild and scenic rivers, wildlife.

Glacier Bay National Park and Preserve, National Park Service, P.O. Box 140, Gustavus 99826 (3,283,000 acres). Glaciers, marine wildlife.

Katmai National Park and Preserve, National Park Service, P.O. Box 7, King Salmon 99613 (4,090,000 acres). Valley of Ten Thousand Smokes, brown bears.

Kenai Fjords National Park, National Park Service, P.O. Box 1727, Seward 99664 (580,000 acres). Fjords, Harding Icefield, Exit Glacier.

Klondike Gold Rush National Historical Park, National Park Service, P.O. Box 517, Skagway 99840 (2,721 acres). Chilkoot Trail.

Kobuk Valley National Park, National Park Service, P.O. Box 1029, Kotzebue 99752 (1,750,000 acres). Archaeological sites, Great Kobuk Sand Dunes, river rafting.

Lake Clark National Park and Preserve, National Park Service 4230 University Drive, Suite 311, Anchorage 99508 (4,044,000 acres). Backcountry recreation, fishing, scenery.

Noatak National Preserve, National Park Service, P.O. Box 1029, Kotzebue 99752 (6,574,000 acres). Abundant wildlife, river floating.

Sitka National Historical Park, National Park Service , P.O. Box 738, Sitka 99752 (106 acres). Russian Bishop's House, trails.

Wrangell–St. Elias National Park and Preserve, National Park Service, P.O. Box 29, Glennallen 99588 (13,188,000 acres). Rugged peaks, glaciers, expansive wilderness.

Yukon–Charley Rivers National Preserve, National Park Service, P.O. Box 164, Eagle 99738 (2,523,000 acres). Backcountry recreation, river floating.

National Petroleum Reserve

(*See also* Oil and Gas)

In 1923, President Warren G. Harding signed an executive order creating Naval Petroleum Reserve Number 4 (NPR-4), the last of four petroleum reserves to be placed under control of the U.S. Navy. The secretary of the Navy was charged to "explore, protect, conserve, develop, use, and operate the Naval Petroleum Reserves," including NPR-4, on Alaska's North Slope. (*See* map, pages 118–19.)

The U.S. Geological Survey (USGS) had begun surface exploration in the area in 1901; following creation of the 23-million-acre reserve, exploration programs were conducted by the Navy. From 1944 to 1953, extensive geological and geophysical surveys were conducted and 36 test wells were drilled. Nine oil and gas fields were discovered; the largest oil field, near Umiat, contains an estimated 70 million to 120 million barrels of recoverable oil. Active exploration was suspended in 1953.

In 1974, the Arab oil embargo, coupled with the knowledge of large petroleum reserves at nearby Prudhoe Bay, brought about renewed interest in NPR-4, and Congress directed the Navy to resume its exploration program.

In 1976, all lands within NPR-4 were redesignated the National Petroleum Reserve Alaska (NPR-A) and jurisdiction was transferred to the secretary of the interior. In 1980, Congress authorized the secretary of the interior to prescribe an expeditious program of competitive leasing of oil and gas tracts in the reserve, clearing the way for private development of the area's resources.

By mid-1983, three competitive bid lease sales, involving a total of 7.2 million acres of NPR-A, had been held. Dates of the sales and the number of acres involved were: January 1982, 1.5 million acres; May 1982, 3.5 million acres; and July 1983, 2.2 million acres. As oil prices have dropped, interest from the oil companies has lessened and leases have expired. As of mid-1989, there were 24 leases covering 558,950 acres.

The Interior Department, through USGS, continued exploration of NPR-A into the 1980s. Past naval explorations and those conducted by USGS resulted in the discovery of oil at Umiat and Cape Simpson, and several gas fields, including Walakpa, Gubic and Point Barrow. The North Slope Borough is developing the reserves in the Walakpa field to provide gas for heating and electrical generation for Barrow. The Borough plans to drill up to eight wells to produce the gas. Data gathered indicates NPR-A may contain recoverable reserves of 1.85 billion barrels of crude oil and 3.74 trillion cubic feet of natural gas.

National Wild and Scenic Rivers

(*See also* Rivers)

The Alaska National Interest Lands Conservation Act (ANILCA) of Dec. 2, 1980, gave wild and scenic river classification to 13 streams within the National Park System, six in the National Wildlife Refuge System and two in Bureau of Land Management Conservation and Recreation areas. (*See* map, pages 118–19.) An additional five rivers are located outside designated preservation units. Twelve more rivers were designated for further study and possible wild and scenic classification.

The criteria for wild and scenic river classification cover more than just float trip possibilities. Scenic features, wilderness characteristics and recreational opportunities that would be impaired by alteration, development or impoundment are also considered.

Rivers are classified into three categories under the Wild and Scenic Rivers Act. The wild classification is most restrictive of development or incompatible uses—it stresses the wilderness aspect of the rivers. The scenic classification permits some intrusions upon

the natural landscape, and recreational classification is the least restrictive category. A specified amount of land back from the river's banks is also put in protected status to ensure access, use and the preservation of aesthetic values for the public.

For those desiring to float these rivers, special consideration must be given to put-in and take-out points because most of the designated wild and scenic rivers are not accessible by road. This means that voyagers and their crafts have to be flown in and picked up by charter bush planes. Because Federal Aviation Administration regulations prohibit the lashing of canoes and kayaks to pontoons of floatplanes when carrying passengers, inflatable rafts and folding canvas or rubber kayaks are often more convenient and less expensive to transport.

Further information on rivers and river running can be obtained from the Alaska Public Lands Information Centers: 605 W. Fourth Ave., Suite 105, Anchorage 99501; 250 Cushman St., Suite 1A, Fairbanks 99701; and P.O. Box 359, Tok 99780; the U.S. Fish and Wildlife Service, 1011 E. Tudor Road, Anchorage 99503; and the Bureau of Land Management, 222 W. Seventh Ave., #13, Anchorage 99513. Information for rivers within park units or managed by the National Park Service is also available from the particular park headquarters. (*See also* National Parks, Preserves and Monuments)

Rivers Within National Park Areas

Alagnak—Katmai National Preserve

Alatna—Gates of the Arctic National Park

Aniakchak—Aniakchak National Monument; Aniakchak National Preserve

Charley—Yukon–Charley Rivers National Preserve

Chilikadrotna—Lake Clark National Park and Preserve

John—Gates of the Arctic National Park and Preserve

Kobuk—Gates of the Arctic National Park and Preserve

Mulchatna—Lake Clark National Park and Preserve

Noatak—Gates of the Arctic National Park and Noatak National Preserve

North Fork Koyukuk—Gates of the Arctic National Park and Preserve

Salmon—Kobuk Valley National Park

Tinayguk—Gates of the Arctic National Park and Preserve

Tlikakila—Lake Clark National Park

Rivers Within National Wildlife Refuges

Andreafsky—Yukon Delta National Wildlife Refuge

Ivishak—Arctic National Wildlife Refuge

Nowitna—Nowitna National Wildlife Refuge

Selawik—Selawik National Wildlife Refuge

Sheenjek—Arctic National Wildlife Refuge

Wind—Arctic National Wildlife Refuge

(General information on rivers not listed in refuge brochures may be obtained from respective refuge offices by addressing queries to refuge managers. Addresses for refuges are given in the brochures.)

Rivers Within Bureau of Land Management Units

Beaver Creek—The segment of the main stem from confluence of Bear and Champion creeks within White Mountains National Recreation Area to the Yukon Flats National Wildlife Refuge boundary.

Birch Creek—The segment of the main stem from the south side of Steese Highway downstream to the bridge at Milepost 147.

Rivers Outside of Designated Preservation Units

Alagnak—Those segments or portions of the main stem and Nonvianuk tributary lying outside and westward of Katmai National Park and Preserve.

Delta River—The segment from and including all of the Tangle Lakes to a point one-half mile north of Black Rapids.

Fortymile River—The main stem within the state of Alaska, plus tributaries.

Gulkana River—The main stem from the outlet of Paxson Lake to the confluence with Sourdough Creek; various segments of the west fork and middle fork.

Unalakleet River—Approximately 80 miles of the main stem.

Rivers Designated for Study for Inclusion in Wild and Scenic Rivers System

Colville River
Etivluk–Nigu Rivers
Kanektok River
Kisaralik River
Koyuk River
Melozitna River
Porcupine River
Sheenjek River (lower segment)
Situk River
Squirrel River
Utukok River
Yukon River (Rampart section)

National Wilderness Areas

Passage of the Alaska National Interest Lands Conservation Act (ANILCA) on Dec. 2, 1980, added millions of acres to the National Wilderness Preservation System. Administration of these wilderness areas is the responsibility of the agency under whose jurisdiction the land is situated. Agencies that administer wilderness areas in Alaska include the National Park Service, U.S. Fish and Wildlife Service and the U.S. Forest Service. Although the Bureau of Land Management has authority to manage wilderness in the public domain, no BLM wilderness areas exist in Alaska. (*See* map, pages 118–19.)

In addition, passage of the Tongass Timber Reform Act (TTRA) on Nov. 28, 1990, designated an additional 299,721 acres of the Tongass National Forest as wilderness.

Wilderness allocations to different agencies in Alaska are: U.S. Forest Service, approximately 5,753,211 acres; National Park Service, approximately 32,848,564 acres; and U.S. Fish and Wildlife Service, approximately 18,676,320 acres.

Wilderness, according to the federal Wilderness Act of 1964, is land sufficient in size to enable the operation of natural systems without undue influence from activities in surrounding areas and should be places in which people are visitors who do not remain. Alaska wilderness regulations follow the stipulations of the Wilderness Act as amended by the Alaska lands act. Specifically designed to allow for Alaska conditions, the rules are considerably more lenient about transportation access, human-made structures and use of mechanized vehicles. The primary objective of a wilderness area continues to be the maintenance of the wilderness character of the land.

In Alaska wilderness areas, the following uses and activities are permitted:

• Fishing, hunting and trapping will continue on lands within the national forests, national wildlife refuges and national park preserves. National park wilderness does not allow sport hunting, or sport or commercial trapping.

• Subsistence uses, including hunting, fishing, trapping, berry gathering and use of timber for cabins and firewood, may be allowed but are not permitted in all wilderness areas. Contact the particular land manager for the most up-to-date rules on subsistence activity.

• Public recreation or safety cabins in wilderness areas in national forests, national wildlife refuges and national park preserves will continue to be maintained and may be replaced. A limited number of new public cabins may be added if needed.

• Existing special use permits and leases on all national forest wilderness lands for cabins, homesites or similar structures may continue. Use of temporary campsites, shelters and other temporary facilities and equipment related to hunting and fishing on national forest lands will continue.

• Fish habitat enhancement programs, including construction of buildings, fish weirs, fishways, spawning channels and other accepted means of maintaining, enhancing, and rehabilitating fish stocks, will be allowed in national forest wilderness areas.

• Special use permits for guides and outfitters operating within wilderness areas in the national forests and national wildlife refuges will be allowed to continue.

• Private, state and Native lands surrounded by wilderness areas will be guaranteed access through the wilderness area.

• Use of fixed wing airplanes, motorboats, snow machines, and nonmotorized methods of surface transportation for *traditional* activities and for access to villages and homesites will be allowed to continue.

National Wildlife Refuges

There are approximately 77 million acres of National Wildlife Refuge lands in Alaska administered by the U.S. Fish and Wildlife Service. (National wildlife refuge acreage in Alaska increased nearly fourfold with the signing of the Alaska National Interest Lands Conservation Act, ANILCA, in December 1980.) Wildlife refuges are designed to protect the habitats of representative populations of birds, fish and mammals. The 16 refuges vary widely in size. (*See* map, pages 118–19.)

Among the public recreational uses permitted within national wildlife refuges are sightseeing, nature observation and photography, sport hunting and fishing (under state law), boating, camping, hiking and picnicking. Trapping can be carried out under applicable state and federal laws. Commercial fishing and related facilities (campsites, cabins, etc.) are authorized by special use permits.

Subsistence activities within national wildlife refuges are all protected under the lands bill. Use of snowmobiles, motorboats and other means of surface transportation traditionally relied upon by local rural residents for subsistence is generally permitted. Fixed-wing aircraft access to wildlife refuges is usually allowed, though certain areas within the Kenai National Wildlife Refuge have been closed to aircraft (a map is available from the refuge manager). A special use permit is required for all helicopter access.

National Wildlife Refuge administrative addresses are followed by acreage and major features:

Alaska Maritime National Wildlife Refuge, 2355 Kachemak Drive, Homer 99603 (3,548,956 acres). Seabirds, sea lions, sea otters, harbor seals.

Alaska Peninsula National Wildlife Refuge, P.O. Box 277, King Salmon 99613 (3,500,000 acres). Brown bears, caribou, moose, sea otters, bald eagles, peregrine falcons.

Arctic National Wildlife Refuge, 101 12th Ave., Box 20, Fairbanks 99701 (19,351,000 acres). Caribou, polar bears, grizzly bears, wolves, Dall sheep, peregrine falcons.

Becharof National Wildlife Refuge, P.O. Box 277, King Salmon 99613 (1,200,000 acres). Brown bears, bald eagles, caribou, moose, salmon.

Innoko National Wildlife Refuge, P.O. Box 69, McGrath 99627 (3,850,000 acres). Migratory birds, furbearers, moose.

Izembek National Wildlife Refuge, P.O. Box 127, Cold Bay 99571 (321,000 acres). Black brant, brown bears.

Kanuti National Wildlife Refuge, 101 12th Ave., Box 20, Fairbanks 99701 (1,430,000 acres). Migratory birds, furbearers, moose.

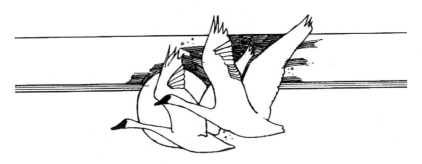

Kenai National Wildlife Refuge, Box 2139, Soldotna 99669 (1,970,000 acres). Moose, salmon, mountain goats, Dall sheep, bears.

Kodiak National Wildlife Refuge, 1390 Buskin River Road, Kodiak 99615 (1,865,000 acres). Brown bears, black-tailed deer, bald eagles, salmon.

Koyukuk National Wildlife Refuge, P.O. Box 287, Galena 99741 (3,550,000 acres). Wolves, caribou, bear, moose.

Nowitna National Wildlife Refuge, P.O. Box 287, Galena 99741 (1,560,000 acres). Migratory waterfowl, caribou, moose, bears, furbearers.

Selawik National Wildlife Refuge, P.O. Box 270, Kotzebue 99752 (2,150,000 acres). Migratory birds, caribou.

Tetlin National Wildlife Refuge, P.O. Box 779, Tok 99780 (700,000 acres). Migratory waterfowl, Dall sheep, moose.

Togiak National Wildlife Refuge, P.O. Box 270, Dillingham 99576 (4,105,000 acres). Nearly every major wildlife species of Alaska is represented.

Yukon Delta National Wildlife Refuge, P.O. Box 346, Bethel 99559 (19,624,458 acres). Migratory birds, musk-oxen are found on Nunivak Island.

Yukon Flats National Wildlife Refuge, 101 12th Ave., Box 14, Fairbanks 99701 (8,630,000 acres). Waterfowl.

Native Arts and Crafts

(*See also* Baleen; Baskets; Beadwork; Masks; Potlatch; Skin Sewing; *and* Totems)

The traditional arts and crafts of Alaska's Natives were produced for ceremonial and utilitarian reasons. This work was not thought of as art in the Western sense but as objects and designs to fulfill specific functions. Native art also reflected spiritual values and the physical environment each group inhabited. Alaska's Natives are known for their ingenious use and manipulation of natural materials to supply life's needs. Roots, bark, grasses, wood, fur, skins, feathers and the sea's resources are still used to produce containers, clothing, hunting implements, ceremonial regalia and many other items.

Today, most Native utilitarian objects are modern adaptations using plastic, metal and glass. But many traditional Native designs and materials are still used to create ceremonial objects, and Alaska Native arts and crafts are widely sought by collectors, museums and tourists. This new market for their work has proven beneficial to Native artists and therefore to Native culture as a whole, which is experiencing the transition from a subsistence lifestyle to a contemporary Western economy.

The Inupiat and Yup'ik Eskimo people, like all of the Alaska Native groups, are divided geographically and linguistically. Because their coastal environment offers few forest resources, the Eskimo people have learned to rely on the tundra and the sea for cultural materials. The Inupiat of northern Alaska are known for making objects out of sea mammal parts—especially ivory, baleen and whale bone. Their ivory carving and scrimshaw work is world renowned, and more contemporary work in which stiff baleen is coiled into elegant baskets is also gaining recognition.

The Yup'ik of western Alaska also utilize sea mammal materials in their art. In addition, they rely heavily on the coastal rye grass for their intricate coiled baskets and mat work. Yup'ik ceremonial masks, which are carved primarily of wood, assembled and painted, are distinctive in the global tribal mask-making tradition. Both the Inupiat and Yup'ik groups produce warm, beautiful clothing using the furs and skins of indigenous land and sea mammals.

The Aleut people of the Aleutian Islands also make beautiful baskets from rye grass, but they use a twining technique. The Aleut are known for their traditional capes made of sea mammal gut and their bentwood hats and visors.

The Athabascan Indians of Alaska's Interior live in a region abundant with forest and river resources. They make decorative beaded clothing and other items, often on tanned, smoked moose-hide, and they form the bark of the birch tree into a variety of containers. They are also known for their skill sewing skins into clothing.

The Tlingit, Haida and Tsimshian people of southeastern Alaska are part of the Pacific Northwest Coast Indian culture, which extends down the coast of British Columbia and into Washington state. Each person in this culture is given at birth his or her own totemic crest—an animal form representing the family clan. These crests are reproduced in many art forms, such as elaborate ceremonial regalia; carvings in wood, metal or stone; paintings or prints; and jewelry. The carvers of the Northwest Coast, best known for boldly carved monumental totem poles, record legendary happenings and honor important people or events. Their artwork, which adheres to a complex, formal design system, is highly stylized and dramatic. Fine Northwest Coast pieces such as carved and painted wood masks and bentwood boxes are sought worldwide by collectors and museums.

Native People

Alaska's 85,698 Native people make up about 15.6 percent of the state's total population. Of those, the majority are Eskimo, Indian and Aleut. Although many live in widely scattered villages along the coastline and great rivers of Alaska, 14,569 Native persons lived in Anchorage in 1990, and Fairbanks had a Native population of nearly 5,330 that year.

At the time Europeans came in contact with the Natives of Alaska in 1741, the Indian, Eskimo and Aleut people lived within well-defined regions, with little mixing of ethnic groups. All were hunting and gathering people who did not practice agriculture.

In southeastern Alaska, the salmon, deer and other plentiful foods permitted the Tsimshian, Haida and Tlingit Indians to settle in permanent villages and develop a culture rich in art. The Athabascan Indians migrated from one village site to another to take advantage of seasonal abundance of fish, waterfowl and other game. The Aleut and coastal Eskimo subsisted primarily on the rich resources of the rivers and the sea.

The Tsimshians moved in 1887 from their former home in British Columbia

Eskimo

Athabascan

Eskimo

Tlingit

Aleut

Haida →

Tsimshian

to Annette Island in Southeast Alaska, under Anglican minister Father William Duncan. About 1,200 now live in Metlakatla. They are primarily fishermen, as are most southeastern people.

Approximately 1,000 Haida live in Alaska, about 300 of whom live in Hydaburg on the south end of Prince of Wales Island. They migrated to the coast from Canada in the 1700s. The Haida excell in the art of totem carving and are noted for precise and delicate working of wood, bone, shell, stone and silver.

Today, about 10,000 Tlingit live throughout southeastern Alaska; approximately another 1,000 live in other parts of the state, primarily in the Anchorage area. The Tlingit, who migrated west from what is now Canada before the first European contact, commercially dominated the interior Canadian Indians, trading eulachon oil, copper pieces and Chilkat blankets for various furs. Like the Haida, they are part of the totem culture; totems provide a historic record of major events in the life of a family or clan.

Athabascan Indians, who occupied the vast area of interior Alaska, were nomadic people whose principal source of food was land animals. Hard times and famines were frequent for all Athabascans, except the Tanaina and Ahtna groups who lived along the Gulf of Alaska and could rely on salmon as their basic food.

The Eskimo have traditionally lived in villages along the harsh Bering Sea and Arctic Ocean coastlines, and along a thin strip of the Gulf of Alaska coast, including Kodiak Island. They took salmon, waterfowl, berries, ptarmigan and a few caribou, but it was the sea and its whales, walruses and seals that provided the foundation for their existence. Houses were igloos—dwellings built partially underground and covered with sod. They did not live in snow igloos.

The Aleut have traditionally lived on the Alaska Peninsula and along the Aleutian Chain. When the Russians reached the Aleutians in the 1740s, practically every island was inhabited. Decimated by contact with the white man, there are only a few Aleut settlements, including two on the Pribilof Islands, where Natives work handling seal herds for the government.

The Aleut lived in permanent villages, taking advantage of sea life and land mammals for food. Their original dwellings were large, communal structures, housing as many as 40 families. After Russian occupation they lived in much smaller houses, called barabaras. Today many Aleuts are commercial fishermen.

Rapid advances in communications, transportation and other services to remote villages have altered Native life in Alaska. Economic changes, from a subsistence to a cash economy, culminated in the passage of the Alaska Native Claims Settlement Act. It gave Alaska Natives $962.5 million and 44 million acres of land as compensation for the loss of lands historically occupied by their people.

NATIVE REGIONAL CORPORATIONS

Twelve regional business corporations were formed under the 1971 Alaska Native Claims Settlement Act to manage money and land received from the government. (*See* map on page 118–19.) A 13th corporation was organized for those Natives residing outside Alaska. Following is a list of corporations and the area or region each administers:

Ahtna Incorporated (Copper River Basin), Drawer G, Copper Center 99573 or 2701 Fairbanks St., Anchorage 99503

Aleut Corporation (Aleutian Islands), 1 Aleut Plaza, 4000 Old Seward Highway, Suite 300, Anchorage 99503

Arctic Slope Regional Corporation (Arctic Alaska), P.O. Box 129, Barrow 99723, or 313 E St., Suite 5, Anchorage 99501

Bering Straits Native Corporation (Seward Peninsula), P.O. Box 1008, Nome 99762

Bristol Bay Native Corporation (Bristol Bay area), P.O. Box 198, Dillingham 99576 or P.O. Box 100220, Anchorage 99510

Calista Corporation (Yukon-Kuskokwim Delta), P.O. Box 408, Bethel 99559 or 516 Denali St., Anchorage 99501

Chugach Alaska Corporation (Prince William Sound), 3000 A St.,

Suite 400, Anchorage 99503

Cook Inlet Region, Incorporated (Cook Inlet region), 2525 C St., Anchorage 99503

Doyon, Limited (interior Alaska), 201 First Ave., Suite 200, Fairbanks 99701

Koniag, Incorporated (Kodiak area), 4300 B St., Anchorage 99503

NANA Regional Corporation (Kobuk region), P.O. Box 49, Kotzebue 99752 or 4706 Harding Drive, Anchorage 99503

Sealaska Corporation (southeastern Alaska), One Sealaska Plaza, Juneau 99801

Thirteenth Regional Corporation (outside Alaska), 13256 Northup Way, Suite 12, Bellevue, WA 98005

Regional Nonprofit Corporations

Aleutian–Pribilof Islands Association, Incorporated (Aleut Corporation), 1689 C St., Anchorage 99501

Association of Village Council Presidents (Calista Corporation), P.O. Box 219, Bethel 99559

Bristol Bay Native Association (Bristol Bay Native Corporation), P.O. Box 237, Dillingham 99756

Central Council of Tlingit-Haida Indian Tribes (Sealaska Corporation), One Sealaska Plaza, Suite 200, Juneau 99801

Cook Inlet Native Association (Cook Inlet Region, Incorporated), 670 W. Fireweed Lane, Anchorage 99503

Copper River Native Association (Ahtna Incorporated), Drawer H, Copper Center 99573

Inupiat Community of the Arctic Slope (Arctic Slope Regional Corporation), P.O. Box 437, Barrow 99723

Kawerak, Incorporated (Bering Straits Native Corporation), P.O. Box 948, Nome 99762

Kodiak Area Native Association (Koniag, Incorporated), P.O. Box 172, Kodiak 99615

Maniilaq (formerly Mauneluk) Association (NANA Regional Corporation), P.O. Box 256, Kotzebue 99752

North Pacific Rim Native Association (Chugach Alaska Corporation), 3000 A St., Suite 400, Anchorage 99503

Tanana Chiefs Conference (Doyon, Limited), 201 First Ave., Fairbanks 99701

NATIVE REGIONAL CORPORATIONS

Arctic Slope Regional Corp.

NANA Regional Corp.

Bering Straits Native Corp.

Doyon Limited

Cook Inlet Region Inc.

Calista Corp.

Ahtna Inc.

Bristol Bay Native Corp.

Chugach Natives Inc.

Sealaska Corp.

The Aleut Corp.

Koniag Inc.

Other Native Organizations

Alaska Eskimo Whaling Commission, P.O. Box 570, Barrow 99723

Alaska Federation of Natives, 411 W. Fourth Ave., Suite 1-A, Anchorage 99501

Alaska Native Brotherhood, P.O. Box 112, Juneau 99801

Alaska Native Commission on Alcoholism and Drug Abuse, P.O. Box 4-2463, Anchorage 99509

Alaska Native Foundation, 411 W. Fourth Ave., Suite 314, Anchorage 99501

Alaska Native Health Board, 1135 W. Eighth, Suite 2, Anchorage 99501

Central Council of Tlingit and Haida Indian Tribes of Alaska, One Sealaska Plaza, Suite 200, Juneau 99801

Fairbanks Native Association, Incorporated, 310 First Ave., Fairbanks 99701

Interior Village Association, 127-1/2 Minnie St., Fairbanks 99701

Inuit Circumpolar Conference, Barrow 99723

Norton Sound Health Corporation,

P.O. Box 966, Nome 99762

Southeast Alaska Regional Health Corporation, P.O. Box 2800, Juneau 99803

Yukon-Kuskokwim Health Corporation, P.O. Box 528, Bethel 99559

Yupiktat Bista (a branch of the Association of Village Council Presidents), Bethel 99559

Native Village Corporations

In addition to the 12 regional corporations managing money and land received as part of the Alaska Native Claims Settlement Act, eligible Native villages were required to form corporations and to choose lands made available by the settlement act by December 1974. The 203 Native villages that formed village corporations eligible for land and money benefits are listed under their regional corporation.

Ahtna Incorporated: Cantwell, Chistochina, Chitina, Copper Center, Gakona, Gulkana, Mentasta Lake, Tazlina.

Aleut Corporation: Akutan, Atka, Belkofski, False Pass, King Cove, Nelson

Lagoon, Nikolski, Saint George, Saint Paul, Sand Point, Unalaska, Unga.

Arctic Slope Regional Corporation: Anaktuvuk Pass, Atkasook, Barrow, Kaktovik, Nuiqsut, Point Hope, Point Lay, Wainwright.

Bering Straits Native Corporation: Brevig Mission, Council, Golovin, Inalik/Diomede, King Island, Koyuk, Marys Igloo, Nome, Saint Michael, Shaktoolik, Shishmaref, Stebbins, Teller, Unalakleet, Wales, White Mountain.

Bristol Bay Native Corporation: Aleknagik, Chignik, Chignik Lagoon, Chignik Lake, Clarks Point, Dillingham, Egegik, Ekuk, Ekwok, Igiugig, Iliamna, Ivanof Bay, Kokhanok, Koliganek, Levelock, Manokotak, Naknek, Newhalen, New Stuyahok, Nondalton, Pedro Bay, Perryville, Pilot Point, Portage Creek, Port Heiden, South Naknek, Togiak, Twin Hills, Ugashik.

Calista Corporation: Akiachak, Akiak, Alakanuk, Andreafsky, Aniak, Atmautluak, Bethel, Bill Moores, Chefornak, Chevak, Chuathbaluk, Chuloonwick, Crooked Creek, Eek, Emmonak, Georgetown, Goodnews Bay, Hamilton, Hooper Bay, Kasigluk, Kipnuk, Kongiganak, Kotlik, Kwethluk, Kwigillingok, Lime Village, Lower Kalskag, Marshall, Mekoryuk, Mountain Village, Napaimiute, Napakiak, Napaskiak, Newtok, Nightmute, Nunapitchuk, Ohogamiut, Oscarville, Paimiut, Pilot Station, Pitkas Point, Platinum, Quinhagak, Red Devil, Russian Mission, Saint Marys, Scammon Bay, Sheldons Point, Sleetmute, Stony River, Toksook Bay, Tuluksak, Tuntutuliak, Tununak, Umkumiut, Upper Kalskag.

Chugach Natives, Incorporated: Chenaga, English Bay, Eyak, Port Graham, Tatitlek.

Cook Inlet Region, Incorporated: Chickaloon, Knik, Eklutna, Ninilchik, Seldovia, Tyonek.

Doyon, Limited: Alatna, Allakaket, Anvik, Beaver, Bettles Field, Birch Creek, Chalkyitsik, Circle, Dot Lake, Eagle, Fort Yukon, Galena, Grayling, Healy Lake, Holy Cross, Hughes, Huslia, Kaltag, Koyukuk, Manley Hot Springs, McGrath, Minto, Nenana, Nikolai, Northway, Nulato, Rampart, Ruby, Shageluk, Stevens Village, Takotna, Tanacross, Tanana, Telida.

Koniag, Incorporated: Afognak, Akhiok, Kaguyak, Karluk, Larsen Bay, Old Harbor, Ouzinkie, Port Lions, Woody Island.

NANA Regional Corporation, Incorporated: Ambler, Buckland, Deering, Kiana, Kivalina, Kobuk, Kotzebue, Noatak, Noorvik, Selawik, Shungnak.

Sealaska Corporation: Angoon, Craig, Hoonah, Hydaburg, Kake, Kasaan, Klawock, Saxman, Yakutat.

Related reading: *Shamans and Kushtakas*, by Mary Giraudo Beck, illustrations by Martin Oliver. Tales in Tlingit and Haida mythology provide a powerful mix of history, legend and adventure. *See* ALASKA NORTHWEST LIBRARY in the back of the book.

Nenana Ice Classic

(*See also* Breakup)

The Ice Classic is a gigantic betting pool offering $165,000 in 1992 in cash prizes to the lucky winner who guessed the time, to the nearest minute, of the ice breakup on the Tanana River at the town of Nenana. Official breakup time each spring is established when the surging ice dislodges a tripod and breaks an attached line, which stops a clock set to Yukon standard time. The Nenana Ice Classic was 76 years old in 1992.

Tickets for the classic are sold for $2 each, entitling the holder to one guess. Ice Classic officials estimate over $7 million has been paid to lucky guessers through the years.

The primary intention of the Ice Classic was never as a fund-raiser for the town, but as a statewide lottery, which was officially sanctioned by the first state legislature in one of its first actions back in 1959. But over the years the contest has benefited the town. Fifty percent of the gross proceeds goes to the winners. Nenana residents are paid salaries for ticket counting and compilation, and about 15 percent is earmarked for upkeep of the Nenana Civic Center and as donations to local groups such as the Dog Mushers, to the Visitors Center and to other activities or organizations.

The U.S. Internal Revenue Service

also gets a large chunk of withholding taxes on the $140,000 payroll and a huge bite of each winner's share. In 1991, the money was split between two winners. In 1992, there was only one winner of the $165,000 prize.

Another pool, the Kuskokwim Ice Classic, has been a tradition in Bethel since 1924. Initially, it was said that the winner was paid 20 fish or 20 furs, but stakes are considerably higher now, with the winner receiving 40 percent of the total ticket sales.

Breakup times for the Nenana Ice Classic from 1918 through 1992, arranged in order of day and time of breakup, are:

April 20, 1940— 3:27 p.m.
24, 1990— 5:19 p.m.
26, 1926— 4:03 p.m.
28, 1969—12:28 p.m.
28, 1943— 7:22 p.m.
29, 1939— 1:26 p.m.
29, 1958— 2:56 p.m.
29, 1953— 3:54 p.m.
29, 1983— 6:37 p.m.
30, 1936—12:58 p.m.
30, 1980— 1:16 p.m.
30, 1942— 1:28 p.m.
30, 1934— 2:07 p.m.
30, 1978— 3:18 p.m.
30, 1951— 5:54 p.m.
30, 1979— 6:16 p.m.
30, 1981— 6:44 p.m.
May 1, 1991—12:04 a.m.
1, 1932—10:15 a.m.
1, 1956—11:24 a.m.
1, 1989— 8:14 p.m.
2, 1976—10:51 a.m.
2, 1960— 7:12 p.m.
3, 1941— 1:50 a.m.
3, 1919— 2:33 p.m.
3, 1947— 5:53 p.m.
4, 1967—11:55 a.m.
4, 1973—11:59 a.m.
4, 1944— 2:08 p.m.
4, 1970—10:37 p.m.
5, 1957— 9:30 a.m.
5, 1961—11:31 a.m.
5, 1987— 3:11 p.m.
5, 1929— 3:41 p.m.
5, 1946— 4:40 p.m.
5, 1963— 6:25 p.m.
6, 1977—12:46 p.m.
6, 1974— 3:44 p.m.
6, 1950— 4:14 p.m.
6, 1928— 4:25 p.m.
6, 1954— 6:01 p.m.

May 6, 1938— 8:14 p.m.
7, 1925— 6:32 p.m.
7, 1965— 7:01 p.m.
8, 1959—11:26 a.m.
8, 1966—12:11 p.m.
8, 1930— 7:03 p.m.
8, 1933— 7:30 p.m.
8, 1968— 9:26 p.m.
8, 1986— 9:31 p.m.
8, 1971—10:50 p.m.
9, 1923— 2:00 p.m.
9, 1955— 2:31 p.m.
9, 1984— 3:33 p.m.
10, 1931— 9:23 a.m.
10, 1972—11:56 a.m.
10, 1975— 1:49 p.m.
10, 1982— 5:36 p.m.
11, 1921— 6:42 a.m.
11, 1918— 9:33 a.m.
11, 1920—10:45 a.m.
11, 1985— 2:36 p.m.
11, 1924— 3:10 p.m.
12, 1927— 5:42 a.m.
12, 1922— 1:20 p.m.
12, 1952— 5:04 p.m.
12, 1937— 8:04 p.m.
12, 1962—11:23 p.m.
13, 1948—11:13 a.m.
14, 1992— 6:26 a.m.
14, 1949—12:39 p.m.
15, 1935— 1:32 p.m.
16, 1945— 9:41 a.m.
20, 1964—11:41 a.m.

Newspapers and Periodicals

(*Rates are subject to change*)
Advocate, 3933 Geneva Place, Anchorage 99503. Biweekly. Annual rates: $30.

Air Guardian, 600 Air Guard Road, Anchorage 99502. Monthly. Annual rates: free.

Alaska Bar Rag, 310 K St., #602, Anchorage 99501. Bimonthly. Annual rates: $25.

Alaska Business Monthly, P.O. Box 241288, Anchorage 99524. Monthly. Annual rates: $21.95.

Alaska Commercial Fisherman, 3709 Spenard Road, #200, Anchorage 99503. Biweekly. Annual rates: $30.

Alaska Designs, P.O. Box 103115, Anchorage 99510. Monthly. Annual rates: free to members.

Alaska Directory of Attorneys, 203 W. 15th Ave., Suite 102, Anchorage 99501. Semiannually. Annual rates: $25 per issue.

Alaska Economic Report, 3037 S. Circle, Anchorage 99507. Biweekly. Annual rates: $225.

Alaska Fisherman's Journal, 1115 NW 46th St., Seattle, WA 98107. Monthly. Annual rates: $18.

The Alaska Geographic Society, P.O. Box 93370, Anchorage 99509. Quarterly. Annual rates: $39; outside the U.S., $44.

Alaska Journal of Commerce, P.O. Box 91419, Anchorage 99509. Weekly. Annual rates: $49.

Alaska Land & Home, 801 Barnette St., Fairbanks 99701. Bimonthly. Annual rates: $18.

Alaska Legislative Digest, 3037 S. Circle, Anchorage 99507. Weekly during session. Annual rates: $225.

ALASKA magazine, 808 E St., Suite 200, Anchorage 99501. Monthly. Annual rates: $26; outside the U.S., $31.

Alaska Media Directory, 6200 Bubbling Brook, Anchorage 99516. Annually. Annual rates: $68.

Alaska Outdoors, P.O. Box 190324, Anchorage 99519. Monthly. Annual rates: $23.95.

Alaska Public Affairs Journal, P.O. Box 92560, Anchorage 99509. Quarterly. Annual rates: $24.

Alaska Travel News, P.O. Box 202622, Anchorage 99520. May through August. Annual rates: free.

Alaska Wilderness Milepost, P.O. Box 3007, Bothell, WA 98041-3007. Annually. Annual rates: $14.95.

AlaskaMen, 201 Danner St., Suite 100, Anchorage 99518. Bimonthly. Annual rates: $24.95.

Alaskan, 134th Public Affairs Team, 3601 C St., Suite 620, Anchorage 99503. Bimonthly. Annual rates: free.

Alaskan Southeaster, P.O. Box 240557, Douglas 99824. Monthly. Annual rates: $28.

Alaskan Viewpoint, HCR 64, Box 453, Seward 99664. Quarterly. Annual rates: $10.

Aleutian Eagle, 3933 Geneva Place, Anchorage 99503. Weekly. Annual rates: $45.

The All-Alaska Weekly, P.O. Box 70970, Fairbanks 99707. Weekly. Annual rates: $24.

Anchorage Daily News, P.O. Box 149001, Anchorage 99514. Daily. Annual rates: Anchorage home delivery, $102; second-class mail, $300.

Anchorage Visitors Guide, 1600 A St., Suite 200, Anchorage 99501. Annually. Annual rates: free.

Aniak Paper, P.O. Box 116, Aniak 99577. Bimonthly. Annual rates: $15.

Arctic Soldier Magazine, Public Affairs Office, HQ, 6th Infantry Division (Light), Fort Richardson 99505. Quarterly. Annual rates: free.

Arctic Sounder, P.O. Box 290, Kotzebue 99752. Biweekly. Annual rates: $30.

Arctic Star, Public Affairs Office, HQ, 6th Infantry Division (Light), Fort Wainwright 99703. Weekly. Annual rates: free.

Barrow Sun, 3933 Geneva Place, Anchorage 99503. Weekly. Annual rates: $45.

Boat Broker, P.O. Box 22163, Juneau 99802. Monthly. Annual rates: free.

Borough Post, 3709 Spenard Road, Anchorage 99503. Weekly. Annual rates: $45.

Bristol Bay News, 3933 Geneva Place, Anchorage 99503. Weekly. Annual rates: $45.

Bristol BayTimes, P.O. Box 1129, Dillingham 99576. Weekly. Annual rates: $40.

Bush Buyers Guide, 3709 Spenard Road, Anchorage 99503. Monthly. Annual rates: free.

Capitol City Weekly, 8365 Old Dairy Road, Juneau 99801. Weekly. Annual rates: home delivery, free; mail delivery, $52/year.

Chilkat Valley News, P.O. Box 630, Haines 99827. Weekly. Annual rates: $32.

Chugiak-Eagle River Star, 16941 North Eagle River Loop, Eagle River 99577. Weekly. Annual rates: $16.

Commercial Buyers Guide, P.O. Box 112955, Anchorage 99511. Annually. Annual rates: $20.

Commercial Fisherman's Guide, P.O. Box 119, Port Ludlow, WA 98365. Annually. Annual rates: $12.95.

Copper River Country Journal, P.O. Box 336, Glennallen 99588. Bimonthly. Annual rates: $25.

Cordova Times, P.O. Box 200, Cordova 99574. Weekly. Annual rates: $50.

Daily Sitka Sentinel, P.O. Box 799, Sitka 99835. Monday through Friday. Annual rates: $60.

The Delta Paper, P.O. Box 988, Delta Junction 99737. Weekly. Annual rates: $45.

Eagles Call, Box 2 NAS Adak, FPO Seattle 98791. Weekly. Annual rates: free.

Fairbanks Daily News–Miner, P.O. Box 70710, Fairbanks 99707. Daily, except Saturday. Annual rates: $252.

Fairbanks Magazine, 921 Woodway, Fairbanks 99709. June-October. Annual rates: $2.25.

Fairbanks Tribune, 455 3rd Ave., Box 202, Fairbanks 99701. Weekly. Annual rates: $30.

The Frontiersman, 1261 Seward Meridian, Wasilla 99687. Semiweekly. Annual rates: $26.

Great Lander Bush Mailer, 3110 Spenard Road, Anchorage 99503. Monthly. Annual rates: free.

Greater Anchorage Tomorrow, 437 E St., Suite 300, Anchorage 99501. Monthly. Annual rates: $12.

Haines Sentinel, P.O. Box 630, Haines 99827. Annually. Annual rates: free.

Homer News, 3482 Landings St., Homer 99603. Weekly. Annual rates: Kenai Peninsula Borough, $24.

Island News, P.O. Box 19430, Thorne Bay 99919. Weekly. Annual rates: $55.

Joint Venture News, 3581 Kachemak Circle, Anchorage 99515. Monthly. Annual rates: $49.

Juneau Empire, 3100 Channel Drive, Juneau 99801. Monday through Friday. Annual rates: $76.

Ketchikan Daily News, P.O. Box 7900, Ketchikan 99901. Monday through Saturday. Annual rates: $84.

Kodiak Daily Mirror, 1895 Mission, Kodiak 99615. Monday through Friday. Annual rates: $85.

The MILEPOST®, P.O. Box 3007, Bothell, WA 98041. Annual edition, available in March. $16.95 plus $2.50 for fourth-class postage; $4.50 for first-class mail.

Mukluk News, P.O. Box 90, Tok 99780. Bimonthly. Annual rates: $20.

Mushing, P.O. Box 149, Ester 99725. Bimonthly. Annual rates: $21.

The New Alaska Outdoors Magazine, 400 D St., Suite 200, Anchorage 99501. Monthly. Annual rates: $23.95.

New Alaskan, 8339 Snug Harbor Lane NTG, Ketchikan 99901. Quarterly. Annual rates: $7 outside of Ketchikan.

Nome Nugget, P.O. Box 610, Nome 99762. Weekly. Annual rates: $50.

North Pole Independent, P.O. Box 55757, Fairbanks 99705. Weekly. Annual rates: $25.

Northern Adventures Magazine, 400 Denali, Wasilla 99687. Biannually. Annual rates: Write for information.

Northland News, P.O. Box 70710, Fairbanks 99707. Monthly. Annual rates: free.

Peninsula Clarion, P.O. Box 3009, Kenai 99611. Monday through Friday. Annual rates: $64.

Petersburg Pilot,P.O. Box 930, Petersburg 99833. Weekly. Annual rates: $28.

Ptarmigan Ptimes, Box 5545, NAS Adak, AK, FPO Seattle 98791. Biweekly. Annual rates: free.

Senior Voice, 325 E. Third Ave., Anchorage 99501. Monthly. Annual rates: $15 seniors; $20 under 55.

Seward Phoenix Log, P.O. Box 89, Seward 99664. Weekly. Annual rates: $30.

The Skagway News, P.O. Box 1898, Skagway 99840. Biweekly. Annual rates: $30.

Sourdough Sentinel, 21st TFW, Public Affairs, Elmendorf Air Force Base 99506. Weekly. Annual rates: free.

Tundra Drums, P.O. Box 868, Bethel 99559. Weekly. Annual rates: $20.

Tundra Times, P.O. Box 104480, Anchorage 99510. Weekly. Annual rates: $20.

Valdez Pioneer, P.O. Box 367, Valdez 99686. Weekly. Annual rates: $45.

Valdez Vanguard, P.O. Box 98, Valdez 99686. Weekly. Annual rates: $90.

Valley Courier, P.O. Box 28, Healy 99743. Monthly. Annual rates: $15.

Valley Sun, 1261 Seward Meridian, Wasilla 99687. Weekly. Annual rates: free to Matanuska-Susitna Borough box holders.

Village Voice, P.O. Box 1615, Bethel 99559. Weekly. Annual rates: $45.

Who's Who In Alaskan Arts & Crafts, HCR 64, Box 453, Seward 99664. Annually. Annual rates: Write for information.

Wrangell Sentinel, P.O. Box 798, Wrangell 99929. Weekly. Annual rates: $27.50.

Your Personal Guide to Anchorage, P.O. Box 1581, Anchorage 99510. Monthly. Annual rates: free.

Your Personal Guide to Fairbanks, P.O. Box 1581, Anchorage 99510. Monthly. Annual rates: free.

No-see-ums

In its usual swarms this tiny, gray-black, silver-winged gnat is a most persistent pest and annoys all creatures. But, when alone, each insect is difficult to see. While no-see-ums don't transmit disease, their bites are irritating. Protective clothing, netting and a good repellent are recommended while in the bushes or near still-water ponds. Tents and recreational vehicles should be well screened.

Nuchalawoya

Nuchalawoya means "where the great waters meet"; it was originally a meeting of Athabascan chiefs held near the time of the summer solstice. Nuchalawoya today is a festival held in June at Tanana, a town located at the confluence of the Tanana and Yukon rivers. The festival is open to the public.

Obituaries

See page 207 for listings.

Officials

UNDER RUSSIA
Emperor Paul of Russia grants the Russian–American Company an exclusive trade charter in Alaska.
Chief Managers,
Russian–American Company
Alexander Andrevich Baranof, 1799–1818

Leontil Andreanovich Hagemeiste, January–October 1818
Semen Ivanovich Yanovski, 1818–1820
Matxei I. Muravief, 1820–1825
Peter Egorovich Chistiakov, 1825–1830
Baron Ferdinand P. von Wrangell, 1830–1835
Ivan Antonovich Kupreanof, 1835–1840
Adolph Karlovich Etolin, 1840–1845
Michael D. Tebenkof, 1845–1850
Nikolai Y. Rosenberg, 1850–1853
Alexander Ilich Rudakof, 1853–1854
Stephen Vasili Voevodski, 1854–1859
Ivan V. Furuhelm, 1859–1863
Prince Dmitri Maksoutoff, 1863–1867

UNDER UNITED STATES
U.S. purchases Alaska from Russia in 1867; U.S. Army given jurisdiction over Department of Alaska.
Army Commanding Officers
Bvt. Maj. Gen. Jefferson C. Davis, Oct. 18, 1867–Aug. 31, 1870
Bvt. Lt. Col. George K. Brady, Sept. 1, 1870–Sept. 22, 1870
Maj. John C. Tidball, Sept. 23, 1870–Sept. 19, 1871
Maj. Harvey A. Allen, Sept. 20, 1871–Jan. 3, 1873
Maj. Joseph Stewart, Jan. 4, 1873–April 20, 1874
Capt. George R. Rodney, April 21, 1874–August 16, 1874
Capt. Joseph B. Campbell, Aug. 17, 1874–June 14, 1876
Capt. John Mendenhall, June 15, 1876–March 4, 1877
Capt. Arthur Morris, March 5, 1877–June 14, 1877

U.S. Army troops leave Alaska; the highest ranking federal official left in Alaska is the U.S. collector of customs. Department of Alaska is put under control of the U.S. Treasury Department.
U.S. Collectors of Customs
Montgomery P. Berry, June 14, 1877–Aug. 13, 1877
H.C. DeAhna, Aug. 14, 1877–March 26, 1878
Mottrom D. Ball, March 27, 1877–June 13, 1879

U.S. Navy is given jurisdiction over the Department of Alaska.

Navy Commanding Officers

Captain L.A. Beardslee, June 14, 1879–Sept. 12, 1880

Comdr. Henry Glass, Sept. 13, 1880–Aug. 9, 1881

Comdr. Edward Lull, Aug. 10, 1881–Oct. 18, 1881

Comdr. Henry Glass, Oct. 19, 1881–March 12, 1882

Comdr. Frederick Pearson, March 13, 1882–Oct. 3, 1882

Comdr. Edgar C. Merriman, Oct. 4, 1882–Sept. 13, 1883

Comdr. Joseph B. Coghlan, Sept. 15, 1883–Sept. 13, 1884

Lt. Comdr. Henry E. Nichols, Sept. 14, 1884–Sept. 15, 1884

Congress provides civil government for the new District of Alaska in 1884; on Aug. 24, 1912, territorial status is given to Alaska.

Presidential Appointments

John H. Kinkead (President Arthur), July 4, 1884–May 7, 1885. (He did not reach Sitka until Sept. 15, 1884.)

Alfred P. Swineford (President Cleveland), May 7, 1885–April 20, 1889

Lyman E. Knapp (President Harrison), April 20, 1889–June 18, 1893

James Sheakley (President Cleveland), June 18, 1893–June 23, 1897

John G. Brady (President McKinley), June 23, 1897–March 2, 1906

Wilford B. Hoggatt (President Roosevelt), March 2, 1906–May 20, 1909

Walter E. Clark (President Taft), May 20, 1909–April 18, 1913

John F.A. Strong (President Wilson), April 18, 1913–April 12, 1918

Thomas Riggs Jr. (President Wilson), April 12, 1918–June 16, 1921

Scott C. Bone (President Harding), June 16, 1921–Aug. 16, 1925

George A. Parks (President Coolidge), June 16, 1925–April 19, 1933

John W. Troy (President Roosevelt), April 19, 1933–Dec. 6, 1939

Ernest Gruening (President Roosevelt), Dec. 6, 1939–April 10, 1953

B. Frank Heintzleman (President Eisenhower), April 10, 1953–Jan. 3, 1957

Mike Stepovich (President Eisenhower), April 8, 1957–Aug. 9, 1958

Alaska becomes a state Jan. 3, 1959.

Elected Governors

William A. Egan, Jan. 3, 1959–Dec. 5, 1966

Walter J. Hickel,* Dec. 5, 1966–Jan. 29, 1969

Keith H. Miller,* Jan. 29, 1969–Dec. 7, 1970

William A. Egan, Dec. 7, 1970–Dec. 2, 1974

Jay S. Hammond, Dec. 2, 1974–Dec. 6, 1982

Bill Sheffield, Dec. 6, 1982–Dec. 1, 1986

Steve Cowper, Dec. 1, 1986–Dec. 3, 1990

Walter J. Hickel, Dec. 3, 1990–

*Hickel resigned before completing his first full term as governor in order to accept the position of secretary of the interior. He was succeeded by Miller.

In 1906, Congress authorized Alaska to send a voteless delegate to the House of Representatives.

Delegates to Congress

Frank H. Waskey, 1906–1907

Thomas Cale, 1907–1909

James Wickersham, 1909–1917

Charles A. Sulzer, 1917–contested election

James Wickersham, 1918, seated as delegate

Charles A. Sulzer, 1919, elected; died before taking office

George Grigsby, 1919, elected in a special election

James Wickersham, 1921, seated as delegate, having contested election of Grigsby

Dan A. Sutherland, 1921–1930

James Wickersham, 1931–1933

Anthony J. Dimond, 1933–1944

E.L. Bartlett, 1944–1958

Unofficial delegates to Congress to promote statehood, elected under a plan first devised by Tennessee. The Tennessee Plan delegates were not seated by Congress but did serve as lobbyists.

Senators:

Ernest Gruening, 1956–1958

William Egan, 1956–1958

Representative:

Ralph Rivers, 1956–1958

Alaska becomes 49th state in 1959 and sends two senators and one representative to U.S. Congress.

Senators:

E.L. Bartlett, 1958–1968

Ernest Gruening, 1958–1968

Mike Gravel, 1968–1980
Ted Stevens, 1968–
Frank H. Murkowski, 1980–

Representatives:
Ralph Rivers, 1958–1966
Howard Pollock, 1966–1970
Nicholas Begich, 1970–1972
Donald E. Young, 1972–

Correspondence Addresses
The Honorable Walter J. Hickel, Office of the Governor, P.O. Box A, Juneau 99811
The Honorable John B. "Jack" Coghill, Office of the Lieutenant Governor, P.O. Box AA, Juneau 99811

Alaska's Delegation in U.S. Congress:
The Honorable Ted Stevens, United States Senate, 522 Hart Bldg., Washington, D.C. 20510
The Honorable Frank H. Murkowski, United States Senate, 709 Hart Bldg., Washington, D.C. 20510
The Honorable Donald E. Young, House of Representatives, 2331 Rayburn House Office Bldg., Washington, D.C. 20515

Alaska State Legislature
Members of the Alaska Legislature as of the end of the 1991 session are listed below. During sessions, members of the legislature receive mail at P.O. Box V, Juneau 99811.

House of Representatives
District 1: Robin L. Taylor (Seat A, Republican); Cheri Davis (Seat B, Republican)
District 2: Jerry Mackie (Democrat)
District 3: Ben F. Grussendorf (Democrat)
District 4: Bill Hudson (Seat A, Republican); Fran Ulmer (Seat B, Democrat)
District 5: Mike Navarre (Seat A, Democrat); Gail Phillips (Seat B, Republican)
District 6: Gene Kubina (Democrat)
District 7: Jim Zawacki (Republican)
District 8: Betty Bruckman (Seat A, Democrat); Dave Choquette (Seat B, Republican)
District 9: Loren Leman (Seat A, Republican); Mark S. Hanley (Seat B, Republican)
District 10: Larry Baker (Seat A, Republican); Pat Parnell (Seat B, Democrat)
District 11: Dave Donley (Seat A, Democrat); Max F. Gruenberg Jr. (Seat B, Democrat)
District 12: Kay Brown (Seat A, Democrat); Johnny Ellis (Seat B, Democrat)
District 13: David Finkelstein (Seat A, Democrat); Terry Martin (Seat B, Republican)
District 14: Ramona Barnes (Seat A, Republican); Bettye J. Davis (Seat B, Democrat)
District 15: Mary Miller (Seat A, Republican); Randy E. Phillips (Seat B, Republican)
District 16: Pat Carney (Seat A, Democrat); Ronald L. Larson (Seat B, Democrat)
District 17: John Gonzales (Republican)
District 18: Mike W. Miller (Republican)
District 19: Tom Moyer (Democrat)
District 20: Bert M. Sharp (Seat A, Republican); Mark Boyer (Seat B, Democrat)
District 21: Niilo Koponen (Democrat)
District 22: Eileen Panigeo MacLean (Democrat)
District 23: Richard Foster (Democrat)
District 24: Georgianna Lincoln (Republican)
District 25: Ivan (Martin) Ivan (Democrat)
District 26: George G. Jacko Jr. (Democrat)
District 27: Cliff Davidson (Democrat)

Senate
District A: Lloyd Jones (Republican)
District B: Richard I. Eliason (Republican)
District C: Jim Duncan (Democrat)
District D: Paul A. Fischer (Republican)
District E: Jalmar M. "Jay" Kerttula (Seat A, Democrat); Curt Menard (Seat B, Democrat)
District F: Arliss Sturgulewski (Seat A, Republican); Virginia Collins (Seat B, Republican)
District G: Drue Pearce (Seat A, Republican); Patrick M. Rodey (Seat B, Democrat)
District H: Pat Pourchot (Seat A, Democrat); Rick Uehling (Seat B, Republican)
District I: Rick Halford (Seat A, Republican); Sam Cotten (Seat B, Democrat)
District J: Dick Shultz (Republican)

District K: Steve Frank (Seat A, Republican); Bettye M. Fahrenkamp (Seat B, Democrat)
District L: Al Adams (Democrat)
District M: Lyman F. Hoffman (Democrat)
District N: Fred F. Zharoff (Democrat)

Oil and Gas

Alaska's first exploratory oil well was drilled in 1898 on the Iniskin Peninsula, Cook Inlet, by Alaska Petroleum Company. According to the Alaska Oil and Gas Association, oil was encountered in this first hole at about 700 feet, but a water zone beneath the oil strata cut off the oil flow. Total depth of the well was approximately 1,000 feet.

The first commercial oil discovery was made in 1902 near Katalla, near the mouth of the Bering River east of Cordova. This field produced until 1933.

As early as 1921, oil companies surveyed land north of the Brooks Range for possible drilling sites. In 1923, the federal government created Naval Petroleum Reserve Number 4 (now known as National Petroleum Reserve-Alaska, see National Petroleum Reserve), a 23-million-acre area of Alaska's North Slope. Wartime needs speeded up exploration. In 1944, the Navy began drilling operations on the petroleum reserve and continued until 1953, but made no significant oil discoveries. Since 1981, the U. S. Department of the Interior has leased out oil and gas tracts in the reserve.

Atlantic Richfield discovered oil in 1957 on the Kenai Peninsula, at a depth of approximately 2 miles, about 20 miles northeast of Kenai at what became known as the Swanson River Oilfield. Later, Union Oil Company found a large gas field at Kalifonsky Beach (the Kenai Gas Field) and Amoco found the first oil offshore at a location known as Middle Ground Shoals in Cook Inlet in 1962. Since 1957, the oil and gas industry has invested $45 billion in Alaska. The money has gone toward exploration and development of North Shore oil fields, and construction of the trans-Alaska pipeline.

Currently, there are 15 production platforms in Cook Inlet, one of which produces only gas. Built to contend with extreme tides, siltation and ice floes, the Cook Inlet platforms are in one of three successful areas of offshore oil production in the United States. Hundreds of miles of pipeline with diameters up to 20 inches link the offshore platforms with onshore facilities at Kenai and Drift River. The deepest producing oil well in the state is in the

OIL AND GAS FACTS

	Cook Inlet	North Slope
Producing Fields:		
Oil	6	5
Gas	11	0
Number of Active Wells:		
Oil	221	1,261
Gas	110	0
Injectors	72	458
Average Production Rates Per Well:		
Oil	182 barrels/D	1,532 barrels/D
Water	590 barrels/D	1,105 barrels/D
Gas (gas wells only)	5.7 million CF/D	—
Cumulative Production:		
Oil	1,129 million barrels	8,133 million barrels
Water	547 million barrels	1,785 million barrels
Gas (net)	3,763 billion CF	1,466 billion CF
Remaining Reserves:		
Oil	66 million barrels	7,555 million barrels
Gas	3,417 billion CF	27,822 billion CF

/D=per day
CF=cubic feet

Swanson River Oilfield on the Kenai Peninsula; total depth is 17,689 feet. By late 1990, Alaska had 1,512 producing wells, according to the Alaska Oil and Gas Conservation Commission.

A fertilizer plant, the largest of its kind on the West Coast, is located at Nikiski, near Kenai. It uses natural gas as a feed stock to manufacture ammonia and urea. One refinery is located at Kenai and two at North Pole near Fairbanks. Gasoline, diesel fuel, heavy fuel oil, propane, JP-4, Jet A and asphalt are produced for use within and outside of Alaska. Crude oil topping plants located at Prudhoe Bay; Kuparuk; and at pump stations 6, 8 and 10 provide diesel oil for oil field and pipeline use. Liquified natural gas is produced at a special Philips LNG plant and is the only LNG export facility in the U.S.

The Prudhoe Bay oil field, largest in North America, was discovered in 1968 by Atlantic Richfield Company and Exxon. Recoverable reserves are now estimated to be 12 billion barrels of oil and 26 trillion cubic feet of natural gas. Peak production of 1.5 million barrels per day has begun to decline and is transported from North Slope fields via the trans-Alaska pipeline from Prudhoe Bay to Valdez. (*See also* Pipeline.)

In spring of 1988, it was estimated that one-half of the Prudhoe Bay recoverable oil reserve had been pumped. A $2 billion waterflood project was installed to maximize oil recovery by forcing additional oil out of the reservoir rock and into producing wells. The Central Gas Facility, built at Prudhoe Bay, is currently capable of processing 5.4 billion cubic feet of natural gas and yielding more than 54,000 barrels of natural gas liquids daily. By 1994, the processing capacity will be up to 7.2 billion cubic feet daily. The facility is the largest gas plant in the world. Two new fields, Endicott and Lisburne, are in production, with Lisburne beginning production in 1986. Endicott began production in February 1986, and is owned by BP Exploration (56.7 percent), Exxon (21 percent), Amoco (10.5 percent) and Union (10.5 percent). The remaining 1.3 percent is owned by ARCO; Cook Inlet Region, Incorporated; Doyon, Limited; and NANA Regional Corporation, and is the first offshore commercial development in the United States portion of the Beaufort Sea. Endicott is estimated to have 350 million barrels of oil, and in early 1990 became the sixth largest field in the nation in terms of production. Milne Point, located 35 miles northwest of Prudhoe Bay, is a field operated by Conoco. Economically, this is a marginal field with estimated reserves of 100 million barrels. Conoco suspended drilling operations in February 1985, but resumed production in October 1990, at the rate of 20,000 barrels per day. In 1991, production also began from the shallow Schrader Bluff formation, which added 5,000 barrels per day.

The Kuparuk River Field, 40 miles west of Prudhoe Bay, is being developed by ARCO. The field went into production in mid-December 1981; approximately 303,740 barrels a day are being delivered to the trans-Alaska pipeline. Alaska's North Slope oil fields amount to 25 percent of U.S. oil production and about 12 percent of U.S. oil consumption. In February 1989, ARCO and

Exxon announced the discovery of a 300-million-barrel oil field at Point McIntyre, which is about two miles north of the Prudhoe Bay field. The reservoir for the field lies offshore beneath the Beaufort Sea, and if the estimates of the amount of recoverable reserves are correct, the field would be the largest domestic discovery since the discovery of the Endicott field in the late 1970s. Production start-up is scheduled for 1993.

In 1984, Shell Western discovered oil at Seal Island, 12 miles northwest of Prudhoe Bay. Northstar Island, five miles to the west, was the site of delineation drilling in 1985, and in the same region, Sandpiper Island reported another strike in 1985. Texaco hit a strike on the Colville River Delta about eight miles northwest of the Kuparuk River field. Exploration in Navarin Basin began when Amoco drilled five wells, Exxon drilled two wells and ARCO drilled one well. The average well took 60 days to drill and the average cost per well was $20 million to 30 million. Although none of the wells is considered commercially feasible, drilling was halted by legal action. In October 1985, the 9th Circuit Court of Appeals in San Francisco ruled that drilling must stop in Navarin Basin until a lawsuit filed by the villages of Gambell and Stebbins was fully heard. In a significant decision in early 1987, the Supreme Court overturned the 9th Circuit ruling and held that the aboriginal rights of Alaska Natives were extinguished by Section 4(b) of the Alaska Native Claims Settlement Act, and that Section 810(a) of the Alaska National Interest Lands Conservation Act (ANILCA), which provides protection for subsistence resources, did not extend to the outer continental shelf.

The Alaska Natural Gas Transportation System (proposed Alaska gas pipeline) was authorized by the federal government in 1977. Estimated cost was $10 billion with a completion date of 1983. A two-year delay in the northern part of the project was announced in May 1982 by Northwest Alaskan, the consortium building the project. Recent cost estimates for the gas pipeline have risen to more than $40 billion. A completion date is not set for the fore-seeable future, due to problems in financing the project. Now, most industry observers feel that the proposed trans-Alaska gas system is the most viable idea for transporting North Slope gas to Valdez for shipment to market.

Alaska Oil and Natural Gas Liquid Production (in millions of barrels)

Year	Oil*	Natural Gas**
1972	73.6	0.608
1973	73.1	0.812
1974	72.2	0.793
1975	72.0	0.765
1976	67.0	0.770
1977	171.3	0.863
1978	444.8	0.815
1979	511.3	0.635
1980	591.6	0.735
1981	587.3	0.988
1982	618.9	0.999
1983	625.6	0.692
1984	630.4	0.678
1985	666.2	0.986
1986	681.3	1.600
1987	716.0	16.500
1988	738.1	20.300
1989	684.0	18.045
1990	647.3	18.19
1991	656.3	23.88

*Oil production for the years 1902–71 totaled 396,537,603 barrels; for the years 1902–82, total production amounted to 3,682,769,004 barrels.
**Natural gas liquid production for the years 1902–71 totaled 1,312,113 barrels; for the years 1902–83, total production was 9,218,705 barrels.
Source: 1983 Statistical Report, Alaska Oil and Gas Conservation Commission, 3001 Porcupine Drive, Anchorage 99501.

Since 1987, Alaska and Texas have alternated as the number one state in oil production. The top five oil-producing states are: Alaska, Texas, Louisiana, California and Oklahoma. According to the State Division of Oil and Gas, Alaska currently provides about 25 percent of the nation's oil.

The state of Alaska receives approximately 85 percent of its general revenue from petroleum taxes and royalties, and since 1959, the state has collected more than $38 billion in oil and gas revenues. In early 1986, the price of oil dropped. Oil industry employment then declined rather than increased, and the state government was in a more tenuous fiscal situation. By early 1990, oil prices had improved, but Prudhoe Bay production had begun to decline.

While crude oil produced in the North Slope cannot be exported, there are no such restrictions on natural gas, but so far, no transportation system has been constructed for North Slope gas. In 1990, natural gas and products derived from it (ammonia and urea) made up about 12.5 percent of all Alaska exports. Most natural gas produced in Alaska is either locally consumed or reinjected back into oil wells.

Natural gas provides a relatively low-cost source of energy for certain Railbelt residents and businesses of Alaska. There are four refineries in Alaska, which satisfy 75 percent of gasoline, diesel and jet fuel consumption in the state.

Oil and gas leasing on state land in Alaska is managed by the Department of Natural Resources, Division of Oil and Gas. The secretary of the interior is responsible for establishing oil and gas leasing on federal lands in Alaska, including the outer continental shelf. In 1986, Chevron, in partnership with a Native corporation, completed its well at Kaktovik on the coastal plain of the Arctic National Wildlife Refuge. The land was obtained in a swap with the U.S. Department of the Interior, but Congress will have to approve any development within the boundaries of the refuge.

Oil Spill

Prince William Sound was the site of the largest oil spill in U.S. history, when the 987-foot *Exxon Valdez* oil tanker struck Bligh Reef on March 24, 1989. Before the tanker leak could be stopped, more than 40,000 barrels, or about 11 million gallons, of crude oil oozed into Prince William Sound. The oil, which poured out of the tanker at a rate of 20,000 barrels per hour, contaminated more than 1,200 miles of coastline in Prince William Sound, the Gulf of Alaska and lower Cook Inlet.

At the time the tanker hit the reef, the third mate was piloting the tanker. He apparently veered from the ship's normal route out of Valdez to avoid icebergs.

Within hours of the spill, skimmer ships began to vacuum oil off the water's surface; booms were set up strategically to prevent the oil spill from contaminating salmon fisheries. Other fishing vessels assisted in attempts to capture oiled and wounded wildlife, and transport those animals to rehabilitation centers.

Five days after the spill, the oil slick extended 45 miles, hitting islands, beaches and fish hatcheries throughout the sound, an area known for its rich commercial herring and salmon hatcheries. Oil from the tanker also was found later to have fouled beaches on the Alaska Peninsula, almost 600 miles from the spill's original site.

Cleanup efforts involved armies of cleaning crews, who used techniques ranging from washing the rocks by hand to washing the shore rocks with highly pressurized hot water. Bioremediation was another cleanup technique, which involved applying fertilizer to oiled shorelines to accelerate oil-metabolizing bacteria. Winter storms proved to assist the cleanup of many beaches throughout the oil spill area. Cleanup efforts were resumed in the spring of 1990.

Thousands of marine mammals, birds and other wildlife perished as a result of the oil spill. Carcasses of 1,011 sea otters were recovered from the sound in 1989, and estimates of the number of otters that died range from about 3,500 to 5,500. About 31,000 birds were reported to have been killed, caused by the spill.

But scientists believe these figures represent only a fraction of the total loss, since many birds were thought to have floated out to sea, sank, or simply have not been found. Preliminary figures fix the loss at between 350,000 and 390,000 birds, according to a report produced by the federal agencies, including the U.S. Department of Fish and Wildlife, in charge of damage assessment and restoration.

Exxon Corp. accepted full responsibility for the spill on March 25, 1989. More than 29,000 claims were filed for damages related to the oil spill. Many of the claims were from fishermen, canneries, Natives and business owners in the region whose livelihood was curtailed by the oil spill: in 1989, the red salmon season was canceled in Prince William Sound.

Litigation continues to this day as a result of the oil spill. The state of Alaska sued Exxon and Alyeska Pipeline Service Company in 1989; Exxon countersued, alleging that state officials hampered cleanup efforts. In October 1991, the state of Alaska and the federal government settled their suits with Exxon, splitting $1.025 billion. In addition, the state is scheduled to receive another $900 million from Exxon during the next 10 years.

It is estimated that the Exxon Valdez oil spill infused about $2 billion into the Alaska economy in 1989 and 1990, as well as adding about 2,500 jobs in the cleanup effort in 1989. But conclusive figures for the long-term damage to the environment, wildlife, fishing industry and tourism have not been calculated.

Parka

Pronounced PAR-kee, this over-the-head garment worn by Eskimos was made in several versions. The work

parka most often came from caribou fawn skin, while the fancy parka, reserved for special occasions, used the skin of the male ground squirrel (the male offering grayer fur than the female). The rain parka was made from *oogruk* (bearded seal) intestine. A person's wealth was judged by the quality of his/her best parka.

Related reading: *Secrets of Eskimo Skin Sewing,* by Edna Wilder. The complete book on the art of Eskimo skin sewing, with how-to-do-it instructions and things-to-make ideas. *See* ALASKA NORTHWEST LIBRARY in the back of the book.

Permafrost

Permafrost is defined as ground that remains frozen for two or more years. In its continuous form, permafrost underlies the entire Arctic region to depths of 2,000 feet. In broad terms, continuous permafrost occurs north of the Brooks Range and in the alpine

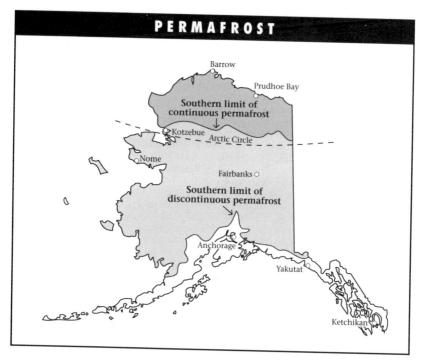

PERMAFROST

Barrow
Prudhoe Bay
Southern limit of continuous permafrost
Kotzebue
Arctic Circle
Nome
Fairbanks
Southern limit of discontinuous permafrost
Anchorage
Yakutat
Ketchikan

region of mountains (including those of the Lower 48).

Discontinuous permafrost occurs south of the Brooks Range and north of the Alaska Range. Much of the Interior and parts of southcentral Alaska are underlain by discontinuous permafrost.

Permafrost affects many man-made structures and natural bodies. It influences construction in the Arctic because building on it may cause the ground to thaw and if the ground is ice-rich, structures will sink. Arctic and subarctic rivers typically carry 55 percent to 65 percent of the precipitation that falls onto their watersheds, roughly 30 percent to 40 percent more than rivers of more temperate climates. Consequently, northern streams are prone to flooding and have high silt loads. Permafrost is responsible for the thousands of lakes dotting the arctic tundra because groundwater is held on the surface.

A tunnel excavated in permafrost near Fox, north of Fairbanks, during the early 1960s is maintained cooperatively by the University of Alaska Fairbanks, and the U.S. Army Cold Regions Research and Engineering Laboratory. It is one of the few such tunnels in the world; it offers unique research opportunities on a 40,000-year-old accumulation of sediments and ice.

The tunnel is open to the general public from June 1 through August 31 each year, by appointment only, through the CRREL office.

Permanent Fund

In 1976, state voters approved a constitutional amendment to establish the Alaska Permanent Fund. This provides that a percentage of all mineral lease rentals, royalties, royalty sales proceeds, federal mineral revenue sharing payments and bonuses shall be placed in a Permanent Fund. Essentially a trust fund for all Alaskans, money from the fund may be used in income-producing investments, but may not be used for state operating expenses (interest income from the Permanent Fund can go into the state's General Fund).

In 1980, the legislature established a Permanent Fund dividend payment program that provides for distribution of the fund's earnings (interest income and capital gains on any liquidation of assets) among the people of Alaska. Eligible residents were to receive a $50 dividend for each year of residency since 1959. The U.S. Supreme Court declared the 1980 program unconstitutional on the grounds that it discriminated against short-term residents, and in 1982, a new state program was signed into law. Under the plan, an initial $1,000 dividend was paid to applicants who had lived in the state for at least six months prior to applying. Dividends are distributed each year to every resident who applies and qualifies, and the amount is decided by adding together the Fund's net income for the last five years, multiplying that number by 21 percent, and dividing that number in half.

If Alaska's Permanent Fund were a Fortune 500 company, it would rank in the top 5 percent in terms of net income. It is the largest pool of money in the country, and the only fund that pays dividends to residents. By the year 2000, it is projected that the Permanent Fund will be producing more revenues for the state than Prudhoe Bay, and as of February 1991, the principal on the Fund was at $11.6 billion. The 1992 dividend payment to residents will be over $850.

Pioneers' Homes

"The state of Alaska recognizes the invaluable contributions of its older citizens and seeks to offer a place for them in which they can live in comfort and security, while remaining active members of the Alaska community. The companionship of other pioneer Alaskans whose earlier years have been spent in the exciting days of the territory is one of the advantages of living in the Pioneers' Homes." These words were taken from a state brochure describing Pioneers' Homes. The six state-supported homes offer a comfortable, secure residence for several hundred older Alaskans. The homes provide space for 294 ambulatory residents, 60 assisted-

Sitka Pioneers' Home

living residents and 273 nursing residents.

Applicants must be 65 years or older, have lived continuously in Alaska for 15 years immediately preceding application for admission and agree to pay the rent established by the Department of Administration. (Some exceptions are made for Alaskans who have lived in the state more than 30 years.) Race, sex, national origin and religion are not considered when determining eligibility. Some people are under the mistaken impression that to qualify for the Pioneers' Homes, one must be a member of the Pioneers of Alaska. This is not the case. Pioneers of Alaska is a private, fraternal organization and is not connected with the state-operated Pioneers' Homes.

The first Pioneers' Home was established in Sitka in 1913 for "indigent prospectors and others who have spent their years in Alaska." With the coming of statehood in 1959, the homes were officially opened to women and Alaska Natives.

For additional information about Pioneers' Homes, contact the Director of Pioneers' Benefits, P.O. Box CLMS0211, Juneau 99811; phone (907) 465-4400.

Following are the locations of the six homes:

Anchorage Pioneers' Home, 923 W. 11th Ave., Anchorage 99501; phone (907) 276-3414.

Fairbanks Pioneers' Home, 2221 Eagan Ave., Fairbanks 99701; phone (907) 456-4372.

Juneau Pioneers' Home, 4675 Glacier Highway, Juneau 99801; phone (907) 780-6422.

Ketchikan Pioneers' Home, 141 Bryant, Ketchikan 99901; phone (907) 225-4111.

Palmer Pioneers' Home, 250 E. Fireweed, Palmer 99645; phone (907) 745-4241.

Sitka Pioneers' Home, 120 Katlian St., Sitka 99835; phone (907) 747-3213.

Pipeline

The trans-Alaska pipeline designer, builder and operator is the Alyeska Pipeline Service Company, a consortium of the following seven oil companies:

BP Pipeline Company, 50.01%

ARCO Transportation Alaska, Inc., 21.35%

Exxon Pipeline Company, 20.34%

Mobil Alaska Pipeline Company, 4.08%

Unocal Pipeline Company, 1.36%

Phillips Alaska Pipeline Corporation, 1.36%

Amerada Hess Pipeline Corporation, 1.50%

Pipeline length: 800 miles, slightly less than half that length is buried, the remainder is on 78,000 above ground supports, located 60 feet apart, built in a flexible zigzag pattern. More than 800 river and stream crossings. Normal burial of pipe was used in stable soils and rock; above ground pipe—insulated and jacketed—was used in

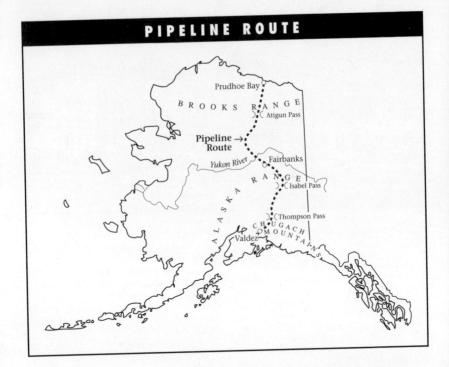

thaw unstable permafrost areas. Thermal devices prevent thawing around vertical supports. Has 151 stop flow valves.

Pipe: specially manufactured coated pipe with zinc anodes installed to prevent corrosion. Size is 48 inches in diameter, with thickness from 0.462 to 0.562 inch. Pipe sections before construction in lengths of 40 and 60 feet.

Cost: $8 billion, which includes terminal at Valdez, but does not include interest on money raised for construction.

Amount of oil pumped through pipeline: As of Dec. 28, 1990, 8 billion barrels of crude oil. In 1990, the 10,000th tanker sailed from the Marine Terminal at Valdez with a cargo of Alaska North Slope crude oil destined for U.S. markets.

Operations: Control center at Valdez terminal and 11 operating pump stations along line monitor and control pipeline.

Pipeline throughput: 1.8 million barrels a day, average.

Estimated crude oil reserves recoverable on the North Slope: approximately 8 billion barrels as of Jan. 1, 1991.

Terminal: 1,000-acre site at Port Valdez, northernmost ice-free harbor in the U.S., with 18 tanks providing storage capacity of 9,180,000 barrels of oil.

Valdez ship-loading capacity: 110,000 barrels per hour for each of three berths; 80,000 barrels per hour for one berth.

Length and cost of pipeline haul road built by Alyeska: 360 miles, from the Yukon River to Prudhoe Bay, $150 million.

Yukon River bridge: first bridge (2,290 feet long) spanning the Yukon in Alaska.

Important dates: July 1968, Prudhoe Bay oil field discovery confirmed; **1970**, suits filed to halt construction, Alyeska Pipeline Service Company formed; **Nov. 16, 1973**, presidential approval of pipeline legislation; **April 29, 1974**, construction begins on North Slope Haul Road (now the Dalton Highway) and is completed 154 days later; **March 27, 1975**, first pipe installed at Tonsina River; **June 20, 1977**, first oil leaves Prudhoe Bay, reaches Valdez terminal July 28; **Aug. 1, 1977**, first tanker load of oil shipped aboard the SS *ARCO Juneau*; **June 13, 1979**, tanker number 1,000 (SS *ARCO Heritage*) sails; **July 15, 1983**, 3 billionth barrel of oil leaves pump station; **Sept. 15, 1986**, 5 billionth barrel of oil leaves pump station; **April 19, 1987**, 7,000th tanker sails from Marine Terminal with Prudhoe Bay crude oil; **Feb. 16, 1988**, 6 billionth barrel arrives at the Marine Terminal; **May 2, 1988**, *Chevron Mississippi* is 8,000th tanker to load crude oil at Marine Terminal; **June 30, 1989**, 7 billionth barrel was loaded on the *Mobil Arctic*, and the 9,000th tanker sailed from the Marine Terminal at Valdez with a full load of crude oil; **Dec. 28, 1990**, 8 billionth barrel was pumped from the North Slope into the pipeline and arrived in Valdez on Jan. 1, 1991.

Place Names

Alaska has a rich international heritage of place names. Throughout the state, names of British (Barrow), Spanish (Valdez), Russian (Kotzebue), French (La Perouse), American (Fairbanks) and Native Alaskan (Sitka) origin dot the map. Some Alaska place names are quite common. There are about 70 streams called Bear Creek in Alaska (not to mention Bear Bay, Bear Bluff, Bear Canyon, Bear Cove and Bear Draw) and about 50 called Moose Creek. Many place names have an unusual history. In 1910, geologist Lawrence Martin named Sherman Glacier in the Chugach Mountains after Gen. William Tecumseh Sherman, with the explanation, "He [Sherman] said, 'War is hell'; so I put him on ice, near the Sheridan Glacier."

For a comprehensive listing, description and history of Alaska's usual and unusual place names, from Aaron Creek to Zwinge Valley, see Donald Orth's *Dictionary of Alaska Place Names*, U.S. Geological Survey Professional Paper 567.

Poisonous Plants

Alaska has few poisonous plants, considering the total number of plant species growing in the state. Nonetheless, some extremely poisonous plants are found in the state. Baneberry (*Actaea rubra*), water hemlock (*Cicuta douglasii* and *C. mackenzieana*), fly agaric mushroom (*Amanita muscaria*) monkshood (*Aconitum* species) and false hellebore (*Veratrum* species) are the most dangerous. Be sure you have properly identified plants before harvesting for food.

Alaska has no plants poisonous to the touch, such as poison ivy and poison oak, found in almost all other states.

Related reading: *Discovering Wild Plants, Alaska, Western Canada, the Northwest*, by Janice Schofield. More than 130 species are described, along with traditional Native American and European uses of wild plants; includes recipes, color photographs and illustrations. *See* ALASKA NORTHWEST LIBRARY at the back of the book.

Political Parties

There are four recognized political parties in Alaska. To become recognized in the state, a political party must be an organized group of voters that represents a particular political program and that nominated a candidate for governor who received at least 3 percent of the total votes cast at the preceding general election for governor.

Alaska's four political parties are:

Alaska Independence Party, Chairperson Joe Vogler, P.O. Box 40, Fairbanks 99707; phone (907) 479-2344.

Democratic Party of Alaska, Chairperson Rhonda Roberts, P.O. Box 104199, Anchorage 99510-4199; phone (907) 258-3050.

Green Party of Alaska, Chairperson Joni Whitmore, Decentralized Coordinating Office, 106 W. Bunnell Ave., Homer 99603; phone (907) 235-7601.

Republican Party of Alaska, Chairperson Connie Zawacki, P.O. Box 243732, Anchorage 99524-3732; phone (907) 276-4467.

Populations and Zip Codes

According to the U.S. Census Bureau, Alaska's population grew 3.7 percent from April 1990 to July 1991 to 570,000 people. This rate increase makes Alaska the second-fastest growing state after Nevada for this same period.

From 1980–89, Alaska's population increased 31.1 percent. According to the Alaska Department of Labor, this growth was the result, in part, of the economic boom of the early 1980s driven by increased state oil revenues and federal government expenditures. The boom fueled high immigration to the state from 1981 through 1983.

Natural increase also plays a role in Alaska's population growth. In 1987, the state's birth rate was 22.2 births per 1,000 population, ranking Alaska first, ahead of Utah at 21.0 births per 1,000 population. However, that trend may now be slowing. According to 1991 fig-ures, Alaska's population under the age of 5 is growing at a rate of only 1.3 percent, almost 50 percent lower than the national rate of 2.5 percent.

Between April 1990 and July 1991, the state's population aged 46 to 64 increased 7.1 percent, compared to the national rate of 1.2 percent. Likewise, Alaska's residents 65 and older increased 7.2 percent, compared to the national rate of 2.2 percent for the same period. Alaska's residents aged 25 to 44 grew 2.9 percent, compared to 1.9 percent for the nation between April 1990 and July 1991.

Increased growth rates of older residents are attributed to a number of factors, including the financial benefits of the state's longevity bonus, property tax rebates, Permanent Fund dividend, as well as Alaska's lack of a state income tax.

The populations for cities and communities in the following lists are taken from the Alaska Department of Labor 1990 census (NA=Not Available):

Community	Year Incorporated	Population	Zip
Akhiok (AH-key-ok)	1972	77	99615
Akiachak (ACK-ee-a-chuck)	1974	481	99551
Akiak (ACK-ee-ack)	1970	285	99552
Akutan (ACK-oo-tan)	1979	589	99553
Alakanuk (a-LACK-a-nuk)	1969	544	99554
Aleknagik (a-LECK-nuh-gik)	1973	185	99555
Allakaket (alla-KAK-it)	1975	170	99720
Ambler	1971	311	99786
Anaktuvuk Pass (an-ak-TU-vuk)	1957	259	99721
Anchor Point	—	866	99556
Anchorage (Municipality)	1920	226,338	99510
Eastchester Station	—	—	99501
Fort Richardson	—	—	99505
Elmendorf AFB	—	—	99506
Mountain View	—	—	99508
Spenard Station	—	—	99509
Downtown Station	—	—	99510
South Station	—	—	99511
Alyeska Pipeline Co	—	—	99512
Federal Building	—	—	99513
Anderson	1962	628	99744
Angoon	1963	638	99820
Aniak (AN-ee-ack)	1972	540	99557
Annette	—	43	99926
Anvik	1969	82	99558
Arctic Village	—	96	99722
Atka	—	73	99502
Atmautluak (at-MAUT-loo-ack)	1976	258	99559
Atqasuk	1983	216	99791

Community	Year Incorporated	Population	Zip
Auke Bay	—	NA	99821
Barrow	1959	3,469	99723
Beaver	—	103	99724
Bethel	1957	4,674	99559
Bettles Field	1985	36	99726
Big Delta	—	400	99737
Big Lake	—	1,417	99652
Birch Creek	—	42	99790
Border	—	NA	99780
Brevig Mission	1969	198	99785
Buckland	1966	318	99727
Butte	—	2,039	NA
Cantwell	—	147	99729
Cape Yakataga	—	NA	99574
Central	—	52	99730
Chalkyitsik (chawl-KIT-sik)	—	90	99788
Chase	—	38	NA
Chefornak (cha-FOR-nack)	1974	320	99561
Chenega	—	94	99574
Chevak	1967	598	99563
Chickaloon	—	145	99674
Chicken	—	NA	99732
Chignik	1983	188	99564
Chignik Lagoon	—	53	99565
Chignik Lake	—	133	99564
Chiniak	—	69	99615
Chistochina	—	60	NA
Chitina (CHIT-nah)	—	49	99566
Chuathbaluk (chew-ATH-ba-luck)	1975	97	99557
Chugiak (CHOO-gee-ack)	—	NA	99567
Circle	—	73	99733
Clam Gulch	—	79	99568
Clarks Point	1971	60	99569
Clear	—	NA	99704
Coffman Cove	—	186	99950
Cohoe	—	508	99669
Cold Bay	1982	148	99571
College	—	11,249	99709
Cooper Landing	—	243	99572
Copper Center	—	449	99573
Copperville	—	163	NA
Cordova	1909	2,110	99574
Covenant Life	—	47	NA
Craig	1922	1,260	99921
Crooked Creek	—	106	99575
Crown Point	—	62	NA
Cube Cove	—	156	NA
Deadhorse	—	26	NA
Deering	1970	157	99736
Delta Junction	1960	652	99737
Denali Park	—	NA	99755
Dillingham	1963	2,017	99576
Diomede (DY-o-mede)	1970	178	99762
Dora Bay	—	57	99950
Dot Lake	—	70	99737
Douglas	1902	NA	99824
Dry Creek	—	106	NA

147

Community	Year Incorporated	Population	Zip
Dutch Harbor	1942	NA	99692
Eagle	1901	168	99738
Eagle River	—	NA	99577
Eagle Village	—	35	NA
Edna Bay	—	86	99825
Eek	1970	254	99578
Egegik (EEG-gah-gik)	—	122	99579
Ekwok (ECK-wok)	1974	77	99580
Elfin Cove	—	57	99825
Elim (EE-lum)	1970	264	99739
Emmonak (ee-MON-nuk)	1964	642	99581
English Bay	—	158	99695
Ester	—	147	99725
Evansville	—	33	99726
Eyak	—	172	NA
Fairbanks	1903	30,843	9970–
Main Office	—	—	99701
Eielson AFB	—	5,251	99702
Fort Wainwright	—	—	99703
Main Office Boxes	—	—	99706
Downtown Station	—	—	99707
College Branch	—	—	99708
Salcha	—	—	99714
False Pass	—	68	99583
Ferry	—	56	NA
Flat	—	NA	99584
Fort Greely	—	1,147	99790
Fort Yukon	1959	580	99740
Fox	—	275	99712
Fox River	—	382	NA
Freshwater Bay	—	68	NA
Fritz Creek	—	1,426	99603
Gakona (ga-KOH-na)	—	25	99586
Galena (ga-LEE-na)	1971	833	99741
Gambell	1963	525	99742
Game Creek	—	61	NA
Girdwood	—	NA	99587
Glennallen	—	451	99588
Golovin (GAWL-uh-vin)	1971	127	99762
Goodnews Bay	1970	241	99589
Grayling	1969	208	99590
Gulkana	—	103	99586
Gustavus (ga-STAY-vus)	—	258	99826
Haines	1910	1,238	99827
Halibut Cove	—	78	99603
Happy Valley	—	309	NA
Harding Lake	—	27	99714
Healy	—	487	99743
Healy Lake	—	47	NA
Hobart Bay	—	187	99850
Hollis	—	111	99950
Holy Cross	1968	277	99602
Homer	1964	3,660	99603
Hoonah	1946	795	99829
Hooper Bay	1966	845	99604
Hope	—	161	99605
Houston	1966	697	99694

Community	Year Incorporated	Population	Zip
Hughes	1973	54	99745
Huslia (HOOS-lee-a)	1969	207	99746
Hydaburg	1927	384	99922
Hyder	—	99	99923
Iliamna (ill-ee-YAM-nuh)	—	94	99606
Iquigig	—	33	99613
Ivanof Bay	—	35	99502
Jakolof Bay	—	28	99603
Juneau	1900	26,751	9980–
Main Office	—	—	99801
Main Office Boxes	—	—	99802
Mendenhall Station	—	—	99803
State Government Offices	—	—	99811
Kachemak (CATCH-a-mack)	1961	365	99603
Kake	1952	700	99830
Kaktovik (kack-TOE-vik)	1971	224	99747
Kalifonsky	—	285	99669
Kalskag	1975	NA	99607
Kaltag	1969	240	99748
Karluk	—	71	99608
Kasaan (Ka-SAN)	1976	54	99924
Kasigluk (ka-SEEG-luk)	1982	425	99609
Kasilof (ka-SEE-loff)	—	383	99610
Kenai (KEEN-eye)	1960	6,327	99611
Kenny Lake	—	4,253	NA
Ketchikan	1900	8,263	99901
Kiana (Ky-AN-a)	1964	385	99749
King Cove City	1947	451	99612
King Salmon	—	696	99613
Kipnuk (KIP-nuck)	—	470	99614
Kivalina	1969	317	99750
Klawock (kla-WOCK)	1929	722	99925
Klukwan	—	129	99827
Knik	—	272	99687
Kobuk	1973	69	99751
Kodiak	1940	6,365	99615
U.S. Coast Guard Station	—	2,025	99619
Kokhanok (KO-ghan-ock)	—	152	99606
Koliganek (ko-LIG-a-neck)	—	181	99576
Kongiganak (kon-GIG-a-nuck)	—	294	99559
Kotlik	1970	461	99620
Kotzebue (KOT-sa-bue)	1958	2,751	99752
Koyuk	1970	231	99753
Koyukuk (KOY-yuh-kuck)	1973	126	99754
Kupreanof (ku-pree-AN-off)	1975	23	99833
Kwethluk (KWEETH-luck)	1975	558	99621
Kwigillingok (kwi-GILL-in-gock)	—	278	99622
Labouchere Bay	—	149	NA
Lake Minchumina (min-CHOO-min-a)	—	32	99757
Larsen Bay	1974	147	99624
Lazy Mountain	—	838	NA
Levelock (LEH-vuh-lock)	—	105	99625
Lignite	—	99	NA
Lime Village	—	42	99627
Long Island	—	198	NA
Lower Kalskag	1969	291	99626
Lutak	—	45	NA

Community	Year Incorporated	Population	Zip
Manley Hot Springs	—	96	99756
Manokotak (man-a-KO-tack)	1970	385	99628
Marshall	1970	273	99585
McCarthy	—	25	99588
McGrath	1975	528	99627
McKinley Park		171	99755
Meadow Lakes	—	2,374	NA
Mekoryuk (ma-KOR-ee-yuk)	1969	177	99630
Mendeltna	—	37	NA
Mentasta Lake	—	96	99780
Metlakatla	1944	1,407	99926
Meyers Chuck	—	37	99903
Minto	—	218	99758
Moose Creek	—	610	99705
Moose Pass	—	81	99631
Mosquito Lake	—	80	NA
Mountain Village	1967	674	99632
Naknek (NACK-neck)	1962	575	99633
Napakiak (NAP-uh-keey-ack)	1970	318	99634
Napaskiak (na-PASS-kee-ack)	1971	328	99559
Naukati Bay	—	93	NA
Nelson Lagoon	—	83	99571
Nenana (nee-NA-na)	1921	393	99760
New Stuyahok (STU-ya-hock)	1972	391	99636
Newhalen	1971	160	99606
Newtok	1976	207	99559
Nightmute	1974	153	99690
Nikiski	—	2,743	99635
Nikolaevsk	—	371	99556
Nikolai	1970	109	99691
Nikolski	—	35	99638
Ninilchik	—	456	99639
Noatak	—	333	99761
Nome	1901	3,500	99762
Nondalton	1971	178	99640
Noorvik	1964	531	99763
North Pole	1953	1,456	99705
Northway	—	123	99764
Northway Junction	—	88	NA
Northway Village	—	113	NA
Nuiqsut (noo-IK-sut)	1975	354	99789
Nulato	1963	359	99765
Nunapitchuk (NU-nuh-pit-CHUCK)	1983	378	99641
Nyac (NY-ack)	—	NA	99642
Old Harbor	1966	284	99643
Oscarville	—	57	99695
Ouzinkie (u-ZINK-ee)	1967	209	99644
Palmer	1951	2,866	99645
Paxson	—	30	99737
Pedro Bay	—	42	99647
Pelican	1943	222	99832
Pennock Island	—	108	99928
Perryville	—	108	99648
Petersburg	1910	3,207	99833
Pilot Point	1992	53	99649
Pilot Station	1969	463	99650
Pitkas Point	—	135	99658

Community	Year Incorporated	Population	Zip
Platinum	1975	64	99651
Pleasant Valley	—	401	NA
Point Baker	—	39	99927
Point Hope	1966	639	99766
Point Lay	—	139	99759
Polk Inlet	—	135	NA
Port Alexander	1974	119	99836
Port Alice	—	30	NA
Port Alsworth	—	55	99653
Port Clarence	—	26	99762
Port Graham	—	166	99603
Port Heiden	1972	119	99549
Port Lions	1966	222	99550
Port Protection	—	62	99950
Primrose	—	63	NA
Prudhoe Bay	—	47	99734
Quinhagak (QUIN-a-gak)	1975	501	99655
Rampart	—	68	99767
Red Devil	—	53	99656
Ridgeway	—	2,018	NA
Rowan Bay	—	133	99850
Ruby	1973	170	99768
Russian Mission	1970	246	99657
Saint George	1983	138	99591
Saint John Harbor	—	69	NA
Saint Marys	1967	441	99658
Saint Michael	1969	295	99659
Saint Paul	1971	763	99660
Salamatof	—	999	99611
Salcha	—	354	99714
Sand Point	1966	878	99661
Savoonga (suh-VOON-guh)	1969	519	99769
Saxman	1930	369	99901
Saxman East	—	490	99901
Scammon Bay	1967	343	99662
Selawik (SELL-a-wick)	1977	596	99770
Seldovia	1945	316	99663
Seward	1912	2,699	99664
Shageluk (SHAG-a-look)	1970	139	99665
Shaktoolik (shack-TOO-lick)	1969	178	99771
Sheldon Point	1974	109	99666
Shishmaref (SHISH-muh-reff)	1969	456	99772
Shungnak (SHOONG-nack)	1967	223	99773
Sitka (City and Borough)	—	8,588	99835
Skagway	1900	692	99840
Skwentna	—	85	99667
Slana	—	63	99586
Sleetmute	—	106	99668
Soldotna	1967	3,482	99669
South Naknek	—	136	99670
Stebbins	1969	400	99671
Sterling	—	3,802	99472
Stevens Village	—	102	99774
Stony River	—	51	99557
Sutton	—	308	99674
Takotna (Tah-KOAT-nuh)	—	38	99675
Talkeetna (Tal-KEET-na)	—	250	99676

Community	Year Incorporated	Population	Zip
Tanacross	—	106	99776
Tanana (TAN-a-nah)	1961	345	99777
Tatitlek	—	119	99677
Teller	1963	151	99778
Tenakee Springs	1971	94	99841
Tetlin	—	87	99779
Thorne Bay	1982	569	99919
Togiak (TOE-gee-yack)	1969	613	99678
Tok (TOKE)	—	935	99780
Toksook Bay	1972	420	99637
Tonsina	—	38	99573
Trapper Creek	—	296	99683
Tuluksak (tu-LOOK-sack)	1970	358	99679
Tuntutuliak (TUN-too-TOO-li-ack)	—	300	99680
Tununak	1975	316	99681
Twin Hills	—	66	99576
Two Rivers	—	453	99716
Tyonek (ty-O-neck)	—	154	99682
Unalakleet (YOU-na-la-kleet)	1974	714	99684
Unalaska (UN-a-LAS-ka)	1942	3,089	99685
Upper Kalskag	1975	172	99607
Valdez (val-DEEZ)	1901	4,068	99686
Venetie (VEEN-a-tie)	—	182	99781
Wainwright	1962	492	99782
Wales	1964	161	99783
Wasilla (wah-SIL-luh)	1974	4,028	99687
Whale Pass	—	75	99950
White Mountain	1969	107	99784
Whitestone Logging Camp	—	164	NA
Whittier	1969	243	99693
Willow	—	285	99688
Wrangell	1903	2,479	99929
Yakutat (YAK-a-tat)	1948	534	99689

Census Populations of Major Cities

City	1900	1920	1940	1950	1970	1980	1990
Anchorage	*	1,856	4,229	11,254	48,081	174,431	226,338
Barrow	*	*	*	*	2,104	2,207	3,469
Cordova	*	955	938	1,165	1,164	1,879	2,110
Fairbanks	*	1,155	3,455	5,771	14,771	22,645	30,843
Juneau	1,864	3,058	5,729	5,956	6,050	19,528	26,751
Kenai	290	332	303	321	3,533	4,324	6,327
Ketchikan	459	2,458	4,695	5,305	6,994	7,198	8,263
Kodiak	341	374	864	1,710	3,798	4,756	6,365
Nome	12,488	852	1,559	1,876	2,357	2,301	3,500
Petersburg	*	879	1,323	1,619	2,042	2,821	3,207
Seward	*	652	949	2,114	1,587	1,843	2,699
Sitka	1,396	1,175	1,987	1,985	3,370	7,803	8,588
Valdez	315	466	529	554	1,005	3,079	4,068
Wrangell	868	821	1,162	1,263	2,029	2,184	2,479

*Population figures unavailable. Source: Alaska Department of Labor

Population by Census Areas (*See* map on following page)

Map Key	Census Area	1990	1980	1970
	Alaska	550,043	401,851	302,583
1	North Slope Borough	5,979	4,199	NA

152

CENSUS AREAS

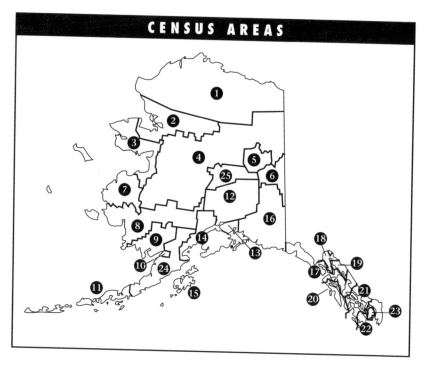

Map Key	Census Area	1990	1980	1970
2	Northwest Arctic Borough	6,113	4,831	4,434
3	Nome	8,288	6,537	5,749
4	Yukon-Koyukuk	8,478	7,873	NA
5	Fairbanks North Star Borough	77,720	53,983	45,864
6	Southeast Fairbanks	5,913	5,676	NA
7	Wade Hampton	5,791	4,665	3,917
8	Bethel	13,656	10,999	NA
9	Dillingham	4,012	4,616	NA
10	Bristol Bay Borough	1,410	1,094	1,147
11	Aleutian Islands	11,942	7,768	NA
12	Matanuska-Susitna Borough	39,683	17,816	6,509
13	Anchorage Borough	226,338	174,431	126,385
14	Kenai Peninsula Borough	40,802	25,282	NA
15	Kodiak Island Borough	13,309	9,939	NA
16	Valdez-Cordova	9,952	8,348	NA
17	Skagway-Yakutat-Angoon	4,385	3,478	NA
18	Haines Borough	2,117	1,680	NA
19	Juneau Borough	26,751	19,528	13,556
20	Sitka Borough	8,588	7,803	3,370
21	Wrangell-Petersburg	7,042	6,167	NA
22	Prince of Wales-Outer Ketchikan	6,278	3,822	NA
23	Ketchikan Gateway Borough	13,828	11,316	10,041
24	Lake and Peninsula Borough	1,668	—	—
25	Denali Borough	1,750	—	—

Source: March 15, 1991, estimates, Alaska Department of Labor

153

Potlatch

This Native gathering, primarily an Indian custom, is held to commemorate major life events. Traditional Native foods are served, songs and dances are performed and gifts are distributed to everyone who attends. A funeral potlatch might result in the giving away of the deceased's possessions to relatives or to persons who had done favors for the deceased during his or her lifetime.

Before the U.S. and Canadian governments outlawed the practice in the 1880s, potlatches were a focal point of Native society. The host family might give away all its possessions in an attempt to demonstrate its wealth to the guests. Each guest in turn would feel an obligation to hold an even bigger potlatch. The outlawing of potlatches resulted in the disintegration of all aspects of Native culture. Potlatch restrictions were repealed in 1951.

Radio Stations

Alaska's radio stations broadcast a wide variety of music, talk shows, religious and educational programs. Many radio stations in Alaska also broadcast personal messages, long a popular and necessary form of communication in Alaska—especially in the bush. It was in consideration of these messages—and the importance of radio stations in providing the sole source of vital weather information to fishermen and hunters—that the United States and Canada agreed to grant some Alaska radio stations international communication status. The "clear channel" status provides protection against interference from foreign broadcasters. Personal message broadcasts are heard on: KYAK's Bush Pipeline, **Anchorage**; KBRW's Tundra Drums, **Barrow**; KYUK's Tundra Drums, **Bethel**; KDLG's Bristol Bay Messenger, **Dillingham**; KIAK's Pipeline of the North, **Fairbanks**; KIYU's Yukon Wireless, **Galena**; KCAM's Caribou Clatter, **Glennallen**; KHNS's Listener Personals, **Haines**; KBBI's Bay Bush Lines, **Homer**; KRBD's Muskeg Messenger, **Ketchikan**; KTKN's Public Service Announcements,

Ketchikan; KVOK-KJJZ-FM's Highliner Crabbers, **Kodiak**; KOTZ's Messages, **Kotzebue**; KSKO's Messages, **McGrath**; KICY's Ptarmigan Telegraph, **Nome**; KNOM's Hot Lines, **Nome**; KJNP's Trapline Chatter, **North Pole**; KFSK's Muskeg Messages, **Petersburg**; KRSA's Channel Chatters, **Petersburg**; KCAW-FM's Muskeg Messages, **Sitka**; KSRM's Tundra Tom Tom, **Soldotna**; and KSTK-FM's Radiograms, **Wrangell**.

A complete listing of Alaska's radio stations follows:

Anchorage

KATB-FM 89.3 MHz; P.O. Box 210389, 99521

KBYR 700 kHz; KNIK-FM 105.3 MHz; P.O. Box 102200, 99510

KEAG-FM 97.3 MHz; 3700 Woodland Park Drive, Suite 300, 99517

KENI 550 kHz; KBFX-FM 100.5 MHz; 1777 Forest Park Drive, 99517

KFQD 750 kHz; KWHL-FM 106.5 MHz; 9200 Lake Otis Parkway, 99507

KHAR 590 kHz; KKLV-FM 104.1 MHz; P.O. Box 111566, 99511

KJAM-FM 94.5 MHz; 3605 Arctic Blvd., Suite 945, 99503

KKSD 1080 kHz; KASH-FM 107.5 MHz; 1300 E. 68th, Suite 208, 99518

KLEF-FM 98.1 MHz; 3601 C St., Suite 290, 99503

KPXR-FM 102.1 MHz; 3700 Woodland Drive, #300, 99517

KSKA-FM 91.1 MHz; 4101 University Drive, 99508

KYAK 650 kHz; KGOT-FM 101.3 MHz; 2800 E. Dowling Road, 99507

KYMG-FM 98.9 MHz; 500 L St., Suite 200, 99501

Barrow

KBRW 680 kHz; P.O. Box 109, 99723

Bethel

KYKD-FM 100.1 MHz; P.O. Box 905, 99559

KYUK 640 kHz; P.O. Box 468, 99559

Cordova

KCHU-FM 88.1 MHz; P.O. Box 467, Valdez 99686

KLAM 1450 kHz; P.O. Box 60, 99574

Dillingham

KDLG 670 kHz; P.O. Box 670, 99576

Eagle River

KCFA 1020 kHz; P.O. Box 773527, 99577

Fairbanks

KAYY-FM 101.1 MHz; 3504 Industrial Ave., 99701

KCBF 820 kHz; P.O. Box 950, 99707

KFAR 660 kHz; KWLF-FM 98.1 MHz; P.O. Box 70910, 99707

KIAK 970 kHz; KIAK-FM 1025 MHz; P.O. Box 73410, 99707

KSUA-FM 103.9 MHz; P.O. Box 83831, 99708

KUAC-FM 104.7 MHz; University of Alaska, 312 Tanana Dr., 99775

KUWL-FM 91.5 MHz; P.O. Box 70339, 99707

KXLR-FM 95.9 MHz; P.O. Box 950, 99707

Galena

KIYU 910 kHz; P.O. Box 165, 99741

Glennallen

KCAM 790 kHz; P.O. Box 249, 99588

Haines

KHNS-FM 102.3 MHz; P.O. Box 1109, 99827

Homer

KBBI 890 kHz; 3913 Kachemak Way, 99603

KGTL 620 kHz; KWVV-FM, 103.5 MHz; P.O. Box 103, 99603

Juneau

KINY 800 kHz; 1107 W. Eighth St., 99801

KJNO 630 kHz; 3161 Channel Drive, Suite 2, 99801

KSUP-FM 106.3 MHz; 1107 W. Eighth St., 99801

KTKU-FM 105.1 MHz; 3161 Channel Drive, Suite 2, 99801

KTOO-FM 104.3 MHz; 224 Fourth St., 99801

Kenai

KCZP-FM 91.9 MHz; P.O. Box 2111, 99611

KPEN-FM 101.7 MHz; P.O. Box 103, Homer 99603

KZXX 980 kHz; 6672 Kenai Spur Road, 99611

Ketchikan

KRBD-FM 105.9 MHz; 716 Totem Way, 99901

KTKN 930 kHz; KGTW-FM 106.7 MHz; 526 Stedman, 99901

Kodiak

KMXT-FM 100.1 MHz; 718 Mill Bay Road, 99615

KVOK 560 kHz; KJJZ-FM 101.1 MHz; P.O. Box 708, 99615

Kotzebue

KOTZ 720 kHz; P.O. Box 78, 99752

McGrath

KSKO 870 kHz; P.O. Box 70, 99627

Naknek

KAKN-FM 100.9 MHz; P.O. Box O, 99633

Nenana

KIAM 630 kHz; P.O. Box 474, 99760

Nome

KICY 850 kHz; KICY-FM 100.3 MHz; P.O. Box 820, 99762

KNOM 780 kHz; P.O. Box 988, 99762

North Pole

KJNP 1170 kHz; KJNP-FM 100.3 MHz; P.O. Box 0, 99705

Petersburg

KFSK-FM 100.9 MHz; P.O. Box 149, 99833

KRSA 580 kHz; P.O. Box 650, 99833

Saint Paul

KUHB-FM 91.9 MHz; Pouch 5, 99660

Sand Point

KSDP 840 kHz; P.O. Box 328, 99661

Seward

KSWD 950 kHz; P.O. Box 405, 99664

Sitka

KCAW-FM 104.7 MHz; 2-B Lincoln St., 99835

KIFW 1230 kHz; KSBZ-FM 103.1 MHz; P.O. Box 299, 99835

Soldotna

KCSY 1140 kHz; 374 Lovers Lane, 99669

KSRM 920 kHz; **KWHQ-FM** 100.1 MHz; R2, Box 852, 99669

Unalakleet

KNSA 930 kHz; P.O. Box 178, 99684

Unalaska

KIAL 1450 kHz; P.O. Box 181, 99685

Valdez

KCHU 770 kHz; P.O. Box 467, 99686

KVAK 1230 kHz; P.O. Box 367, 99686

Wasilla

KMBQ-FM 99.7 MHz; P.O. Box 871890, 99687

Whittier

KCHU-FM 88.3 MHz; P.O. Box 467, 99686

Wrangell

KSTK-FM 101.7 MHz; P.O. Box 1141, 99929

Yakutat

KJFP-FM 103.9 MHz; P.O. Box 388, 99689

In addition to the preceding commercial and public radio stations, the Detachment 8, Air Force Pacific Broadcasting Squadron at Elmendorf Air Force Base (Elmendorf AFB 99506) operates the Alaskan Forces Radio Network. AFRN is the oldest broadcast network in the U.S. military. It began in January 1942 on Kodiak Island, with a volunteer crew that pieced together a low-power station from second-hand parts, borrowed records and local talent. Eventually, the servicemen generated enough interest in Hollywood and Washington, D.C., to receive "official" status. Those early efforts resulted in the Armed Forces Radio and Television Service, a far-flung system of broadcast outlets serving U.S. forces around the world.

Nearly all the programming heard at AFRN locations in Alaska originates at Elmendorf AFB, although it is not broadcast in the Elmendorf vicinity. (In addition to network programming, Fort Greely originates about six hours of programming a day at their location.)

Following is a list of AFRN outlets:

Fort Greely, **AFRN-FM** 90.5 MHz, 93.5 MHz

Galena Airport, **AFRN-FM** 90.5 MHz, 101.1 MHz

King Salmon Airport, **AFRN-FM** 90.5 MHz, 101.7 MHz

Shemya Air Force Base, **AFRN-FM** 90.5 MHz, 101.1 MHz

Tok Coast Guard Station, **AFRN-FM** 90.5 MHz, 101.1 MHz

Railroads

The Alaska Railroad is the northernmost railroad in North America and was for many years the only one owned by the United States government. Ownership now belongs to the state of Alaska. The ARR rolls on 470 miles of mainline track from the ports of Seward and Whittier to Anchorage, Cook Inlet and Fairbanks in the Interior.

The Alaska Railroad began in 1912 when Congress appointed a commission to study transportation problems in Alaska. In March 1914, the president authorized railroad lines in the territory of Alaska to connect open harbors on the southern coast of Alaska with the Interior. The Alaska Engineering Commission surveyed possible railroad routes in 1914 and, in April 1915, President Woodrow Wilson announced the selection of a route from Seward north 412 miles to the Tanana River (where Nenana is now located), with branch lines to Matanuska coal fields. The main line was later extended to Fairbanks. Construction of the railroad began in 1915. On July 15, 1923, President Warren G. Harding drove the golden spike, signifying completion of the railroad, at Nenana.

The railroad offers year-round passenger, freight and vehicle service. The ARR features flag-stop service along the Anchorage-to-Fairbanks corridor, as well as summer express trains to Denali National Park and Preserve. Passenger service is daily between mid-May and early September, and in winter, weekly service is available between Anchorage and Fairbanks. A one-day excursion to Seward is provided daily, mid-May to

early September. Additionally, daily service to Whittier is offered from May through September and four days a week in winter. In 1991, 471,217 passengers rode the Alaska Railroad. For more information contact The Alaska Railroad, P.O. Box 107500, Anchorage 99510.

The privately owned White Pass and Yukon Route provided a narrow-gauge link between Skagway, Alaska, and Whitehorse, Yukon Territory. At the time it was built—1898 to 1900—it was the farthest north any railroad had operated in North America. The railway maintained one of the steepest railroad grades in North America, climbing to 2,885 feet at White Pass in only 20 miles of track. The White Pass and Yukon Route provided both passenger and freight service until 1982, when it suspended service. In May 1988, it began operating again as an excursion train only, going from Skagway to the summit of White Pass and eight miles beyond to Fraser, British Columbia. For more information contact the White Pass & Yukon Route, P.O. Box 435, Skagway 99840.

Regions of Alaska

Southeast

Southeast, Alaska's panhandle, stretches approximately 500 miles from Icy Bay, northwest of Yakutat, to Dixon

Entrance at the United States–Canada border beyond the southern tip of Prince of Wales Island. Massive ice fields, glacier-scoured peaks and steep valleys, more than a thousand named islands, and numerous unnamed islets and reefs characterize this vertical world where few flat expanses break the steepness. Spruce, hemlock and cedar, the basis for the region's timber industry, cover many of the mountainsides.

Average temperatures range from 50°F to 60°F in July and from 20°F to 40°F in January. Average annual precipitation varies from 80 to more than 200 inches. The area receives from 30 to 200 inches of snow in the lowlands and more than 400 inches in the high mountains.

The region's economy revolves around fishing and fish processing, timber and tourism. Mining is taking on increasing importance with development of a world-class molybdenum mine near Ketchikan and a base metals mine on Admiralty Island.

Airplanes and boats provide the principal means of transportation. Only three communities in Southeast are connected to the road system: Haines via the Haines Highway to the Alaska Highway at Haines Junction; Skagway, via Klondike Highway 2 to the Alaska Highway; and Hyder, to the continental road system via the Cassiar Highway in British Columbia. Juneau, on the Southeast mainland, is the state capital; Sitka,

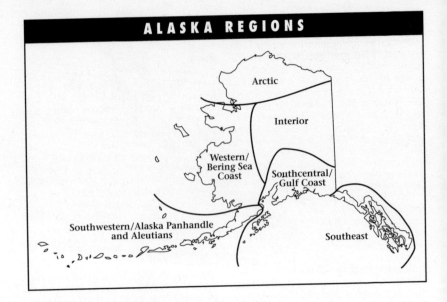

Arctic

Interior

Western/
Bering Sea
Coast

Southcentral/
Gulf Coast

Southwestern/Alaska Panhandle
and Aleutians

Southeast

on Baranof Island, was the capital of Russian America.

Southcentral/Gulf Coast

The Southcentral/Gulf Coast region curves 650 miles north and west of Southeast to Kodiak Island. About two-thirds of the state's residents live in the arc between the Gulf of Alaska on the south and the Alaska Range on the north, the region commonly called Southcentral. On the region's eastern boundary, only the Copper River valley breaches the mountainous barrier of the Chugach and St. Elias mountains. On the west rise lofty peaks of the Aleutian Range. Within this mountainous perimeter course the Susitna and Matanuska rivers.

The irregular plain of the Copper River lowland has a colder climate than the other major valley areas, with January temperatures hitting –16°F compared with average lows of 0°F in the Susitna Valley. July temperatures average 50°F to 60°F in the region.

Precipitation in the region ranges from a scant 17 inches annually in drier areas to more than 76 inches a year at Thompson Pass in the coastal mountains.

Vegetation varies from the spruce-hemlock forests of Prince William

Sound to mixed spruce and birch forests in the Susitna Valley to tundra in the highlands of the Copper River–Nelchina Basin.

Alaska agriculture historically has been most thoroughly developed in the Matanuska Valley. The state's dairy industry is centered there and at a new project at Point MacKenzie across Knik Arm from Anchorage. Vegetables thrive in the area and Matanuska Valley is well known for its giant cabbages.

Hub of the state's commerce, transportation and communications is Anchorage, on a narrow plain at the foot of the Chugach Mountains, and bounded by Knik Arm and Turnagain Arm, offshoots of Cook Inlet. The population of this, Alaska's largest, city is closely tied to shifts in the state's economy.

Alaska's major banks and oil companies have their headquarters in Anchorage, as does the Alaska Railroad. The city's port handles much of the shipping in and out of the state. Anchorage International Airport saw over 4.5 million passengers pass through in 1991. Valdez, to the east of Anchorage on Prince Willam Sound, is the southern terminal of the trans-Alaska pipeline, which brings oil from Prudhoe Bay on the North Slope.

Interior

Great rivers have forged a broad low-land, known as the Interior, in the central part of the state between the Alaska Range on the south and the Brooks Range on the north. The Yukon River carves a swath across the entire state. In the Interior, the Tanana, Porcupine, Koyukuk and several other rivers join with the Yukon to create summer and winter highways. South of the Yukon, the Kuskokwim River rises in the hills of the western Interior before beginning its meandering course across the Bering Sea coast region.

Winter temperatures in the Interior commonly drop to –50°F and –60°F. Ice fog sometimes hovers over Fairbanks and other low-lying communities when the temperature falls below zero. Controlled by the extremes of a continental climate, summers usually are warmer than in any other region; high temperatures are in the 80s and 90s. The climate is semi-arid, with about 12 inches of precipitation recorded annually.

Immense forests of birch and aspen bring vibrant green and gold to the Interior's landscape. Spruce cover many of the slopes and cottonwood thrive near river lowlands. But in northern and western reaches of the Interior, the North American taiga gives way to tundra. In highlands above tree line and in marshy lowlands, grasses and shrubs replace trees.

Gold lured the first large influx of non-Natives to Alaska's Interior. Fairbanks, largest community in the region, was once a booming gold-mining camp. Now the city on the banks of Chena Slough is a transportation and supply center for eastern and northern Alaska. The main campus of the University of Alaska overlooks the city.

About 100 miles east of Fairbanks, farmers at the Delta project hope to build a foundation for agriculture based on barley. With barley for feed, Alaska farmers look for development of a beef cattle industry. At Healy, southwest of Fairbanks, the state's only operating coal mine produces coal used to generate electricity for the Interior. The rest of the Interior relies primarily on a subsistence economy, sometimes combined with a cash economy where fishing or seasonal government jobs are available.

Arctic

Beyond the Brooks Range, more than 80,000 square miles of tundra interlaced with meandering rivers and countless ponds spread out along the North Slope. In far northwestern Alaska, the Arctic curves south to take in Kotzebue and other villages of the Kobuk and Noatak river drainages.

Short, cool summers with temperatures usually between 30°F and 40°F allow the permanently frozen soil to thaw only a few inches. Winter temperatures range well below zero, but the Arctic Ocean moderates temperatures in coastal areas. Severe winds sweep along the coast and through mountain passes. The combination of cold and wind often drops the chill-factor temperature far below the actual temperature. Most areas receive less than 10 inches of precipitation a year, but the terrain is wet in summer because of little evaporation and frozen ground.

Traditionally the home of Inupiat Eskimos, the Arctic was inhabited by few non-Natives until oil was discovered at Prudhoe Bay in the 1960s. Today the region's economy is focused on Prudhoe Bay and neighboring Kuparuk oil fields. Petroleum-related jobs support most of the region's residents either directly or indirectly. Subsistence hunting and fishing fill any economic holes left by the oil industry.

The largest Inupiat Eskimo community in the world, Barrow is the center of commerce and government activity for the region. Airplanes, the major means of transportation, fan out from there to the region's far-flung villages.

The 416-mile Dalton Highway, formerly the North Slope Haul Road, connects the Arctic with the Interior. The road is open to the public to Disaster Creek near Dietrich Camp, about 200 miles north from the junction with the Elliott Highway in the Interior. Only permit holders can travel the road north of Disaster Creek.

Western/Bering Sea Coast

Western Alaska extends along the Bering Sea coast from the Arctic Circle south to where the Alaska Panhandle

joins the mainland near Naknek on Bristol Bay. Home of Inupiat and Yup'ik Eskimos, the region centers around the immense Yukon-Kuskokwim river delta, the Seward Peninsula to the north and Bristol Bay to the south.

Summer temperatures range from the 30s to low 60s. Winter readings generally range from just above zero to the low 30s. Wind chill lowers temperatures considerably. Total annual precipitation is about 20 inches with northern regions drier than those to the south.

Much of the region is covered with tundra, although a band of forests covers the hills on the eastern end of the Seward Peninsula and Norton Sound. In the south near Bristol Bay, the tundra once again gives way to forests. In between, the marshy flatland of the great Yukon-Kuskokwim delta spreads out for more than 200 miles.

Gold first attracted non-Natives to the hills and creeks of the Seward Peninsula. To the south, only a few anthropologists and wildlife biologists entered the world of the Yup'ik Eskimos of the delta. At the extreme south, fish, including the world's largest sockeye salmon run, drew fishermen to the riches of Bristol Bay.

The villages of western Alaska are linked by air and water, dogsled and snow machine. Commerce on the delta radiates out from Bethel, largest community in western Alaska. To the north, Nome dominates commerce on the Seward Peninsula, while several fishing communities take their livelihood from the riches of Bristol Bay.

Southwestern/Alaska Peninsula and Aleutians

Southwestern Alaska includes the Alaska Peninsula and Aleutian Islands. From Naknek Lake, the peninsula curves southwest about 500 miles to the first of the Aleutian Islands; the Aleutians continue south and west more than 1,000 miles. Primarily a mountainous region with about 50 volcanic peaks, only on the Bering Sea side of the peninsula does the terrain flatten out.

More than 200 islands, roughly 5,500 square miles in area, form the narrow arc of the Aleutians, which separate the North Pacific from the Bering Sea. Nearly the entire chain is in the Alaska Maritime National Wildlife Refuge. Unimak Island, closest to the Alaska Peninsula mainland, is 1,000 miles from Attu, the most distant island. Five major island groups make up the Aleutians, all of which are treeless except for a few scattered stands that have been transplanted on the islands.

The Aleutian climate is cool, with summer temperatures up to the 50s and winter readings in the 20s and lower. Winds are almost constant and fog is common. Precipitation ranges from 21 to more than 80 inches annually. The peninsula's climate is somewhat warmer than the islands' in summer and cooler in winter.

Aleuts, original inhabitants of the chain, still live at Atka, Atka Island; Nikolski, Umnak Island; Unalaska, Unalaska Island; Akutan, Akutan Island; and False Pass, Unimak Island.

The quest for furs first drew Russians to the islands and peninsula in the 1700s. The traders conquered the Aleuts and forced them to hunt marine mammals. After the United States purchased Alaska, fur traders switched their efforts to fox farming. Many foxes were turned loose on the islands, where they flourished and destroyed native wildlife. With the collapse of the fur market in the 1920s and 1930s, the islands were left to themselves. This relative isolation was broken during World War II when Japanese military forces bombed Dutch Harbor and landed on Attu and Kiska islands. The United States military retook the islands, and after the war the government resettled Aleuts living in the western Aleutians to villages in the eastern Aleutians, closer to the mainland.

Today fishing provides the main economic base for the islands and the peninsula. Many Aleuts go to Bristol Bay to fish commercially in summer.

Religion

Nearly every religion practiced in American society is found in Alaska. Following is a list of addresses for some of the major ones:

Alaska Baptist Convention, 1750 O'Malley Road, Anchorage 99516

Alaska Moravian Church, Bethel 99559

Assemblies of God,1048 W. International Airport Road, Anchorage 99502

Baha'i Faith, 13501 Brayton Drive, Anchorage 99516

Christian Science Church, 1347 L St., Anchorage 99501

Church of God, 1348 Bennington Drive, Anchorage 99508

Church of Jesus Christ of Latter-day Saints, 13111 Brayton Drive, Anchorage 99516

Congregation Beth Sholom, 7525 E. Northern Lights Blvd., Anchorage 99504

Episcopal Diocese of Alaska, 1205 Denali Way, Fairbanks 99701

Presbyterian Churches, 616 W. 10th Ave., Anchorage 99501

Roman Catholic Archdiocese of Anchorage, 225 Cordova, Anchorage 99501

Russian Orthodox Diocese of Alaska, 414 Mission Road, Kodiak 99615

The Salvation Army, 726 E. Ninth Ave., Anchorage 99501

United Methodist Church, Alaska Missionary Conference, 3402 Wesleyan Drive, Anchorage 99508

Unity of Anchorage, 10821 Totem Road, Anchorage 99516

Reptiles

For all practical purposes, reptiles are not found in Alaska outside of captivity. The northern limits of North American reptilian species may be the latitude at which their embryos fail to develop during the summer. Three sightings of a species of garter snake, *Thamnophis sirtalis,* have been reported on the banks of the Taku River and Stikine River.

Rivers

(*See also* National Wild and Scenic Rivers)

There are more than 3,000 rivers in Alaska. The major navigable Alaska inland waterways are as follows:

Chilkat—Navigable by shallow-draft vessels to village of Klukwan, 25 miles above mouth.

Kobuk—Controlling channel depth is about 5 feet through Hotham Inlet, 3 feet to Ambler and 2 feet to Kobuk Village, about 210 river miles.

Koyukuk—Navigable to Allakaket by vessels drawing up to 3 feet during normally high river flow and to Bettles during occasional higher flows.

Kuskokwim—Navigable (June 1 to September 30) by 18-foot draft ocean-going vessels from mouth upriver 65 miles to Bethel. Shallow-draft (4-foot) vessels can ascend river to mile 465. McGrath is at Mile 400.

Kvichak—The river is navigable for vessels of 10-foot draft to Alaganak River, 22 miles above the mouth of

Kvichak River. Remainder of this river (28 miles) navigable by craft drawing 2 to 4 feet, depending on stage of river. Drains into Lake Iliamna, which is navigable an additional 70 miles.

Naknek—Navigable for vessels of 12-foot draft for 12 miles with adequate tide. Vessels with 3-foot draft can continue an additional 7.5 miles.

Noatak—Navigable (late May to mid-June) for shallow-draft barges to a point about 18 miles below Noatak village. Shallow-draft vessels can continue on to Noatak.

Nushagak—Navigable (June 1 to August 31) by small vessels of $2^{1}/_{2}$-foot draft to Nunachuak, about 100 miles above the mouth. Shallow-draft, ocean-going vessels can navigate to mouth of Wood River at mile 84.

Porcupine—Navigable to Old Crow, Yukon Territory, by vessels drawing 3 feet, during spring runoff and fall rain floods.

Stikine—Navigable (May 1 to October 15) from mouth 165 miles to Telegraph Creek, British Columbia, by shallow-draft, flat-bottom riverboats.

Susitna—Navigable by sternwheelers and shallow-draft, flat-bottom riverboats to confluence of Talkeetna River, 75 miles upstream, but boats cannot cross bars at mouth of river. Not navigable by ocean-going vessels.

Tanana—Navigable by shallow-draft (4-foot), flat-bottom vessels and barges from the mouth to Nenana and by smaller river craft to the Chena River 201 miles above the mouth. Craft of 4-foot draft can navigate to Chena River on high water to University Avenue Bridge in Fairbanks.

Yukon—Navigable (June 1 to September 30) by shallow-draft, flat-bottom riverboats from the mouth to near the head of Lake Bennett. It cannot be entered or navigated by ocean-going vessels. Controlling depths are 7 feet to Stevens Village and 3 to 5 feet from there to Fort Yukon.

Following are Alaska's 10 longest rivers (*see* map above):

Map Key

1 Yukon, 1,400 miles*
2 Porcupine, 555 miles**

   3 Koyukuk, 554 miles
   4 Kuskokwim, 540 miles
   5 Tanana, 531 miles
   6 Innoko, 463 miles
   7 Colville, 428 miles
   8 Noatak, 396 miles
   9 Kobuk, 347 miles
  10 Birch Creek, 314 miles

*The Yukon flows about 1,400 miles in Alaska; the remainder is in Canada. It ranks fourth in North America in length (1,875 miles total), fifth in drainage area (327,600 square miles).
**The Porcupine, a major tributary of the Yukon River, flows from Canada into Alaska.

Roadhouses

An important part of Alaska history, roadhouses were modest quarters that offered bed and board to travelers along early-day Alaska trails. The majority provided accommodations for sled dog teams, as most travel occurred in winter. By 1920, there were roadhouses along every major transportation route in Alaska. Most roadhouses have vanished, though a few of the historic roadhouses survive, including: Sourdough Roadhouse on the Richardson Highway; Gakona Lodge on the Glenn Highway; Paxson Lodge at the junction of the Richardson and Denali highways; and Talkeetna Roadhouse. Several roadhouses are included in the National Register of Historic Places. Some of these historic roadhouses are occupied by modern businesses.

Rocks and Gems

(*See also* Gold; Jade; *and* Minerals and Mining)

Gemstones are not easy to find in Alaska—you have to hunt for them and often walk quite a distance. The easiest ones to collect are float-rocks that were scattered millions of years ago by glaciers. These rocks are found on ocean beaches and railroad beds, and in creeks and rivers all over Alaska. In most rock-hunting areas, every instance of high water, wind, heavy rain and a melting patch of snow and ice uncovers a new layer, so you can hunt in the same area over and over and make new finds.

The easiest gemstones to search out are in the crypto-crystalline group of quartz minerals. These gems have crystals not visible to the naked eye. They are the jaspers, agates, cherts and flints.

Thunder eggs, geodes and agatized wood (all in the chalcedony classification) occur in Alaska. Thunder eggs have a jasper rind enclosing an agate core; harder-to-find geodes usually have an agate rind with a hollow core filled with crystals; agatized and petrified woods come in various colors and often show the plant's growth rings. Sometimes even the bark or limb structure is visible on agatized and petrified woods.

Crystalline varieties of quartz can also be found: amethyst (purple), citrine (yellow), rose quartz (pink), rock crystal (clear) and smoky quartz (brown).

Other gems to search for in Alaska are: onyx, feldspar, porphyry, jade, serpentine, soapstone, garnet, rhodonite, sapphire, marble, amethyst, staurolite, malachite and covelite (blue copper).

Russian Alaska

(*See also* History)

Russian presence in Alaska began with the 1741 voyages of Vitus Bering and Alexei Chirikof. Their exploration of the Aleutian Islands and the Alaska mainland spurred dozens of voyages by Russian fur hunters, or *promyshlenniki*. By the mid-1800s, Russians had explored most of the coast of southern and southwestern Alaska and some of the Interior. Their interest in Alaska lay primarily in exploiting the rich fur resources of the region, especially sea otters and fur seals. In 1799, the Russian post known today as Old Sitka was established. That same year, a trade charter was granted to the Russian-American Company, a monopoly authorized by the Czar in 1790 to control activities in Alaska.

During the entire Russian period, which lasted from 1741 to 1867, there were rarely more than about 500 Russians in Alaska at any one time. Nevertheless, the Aleut, Eskimo and Indians whom the Russians encountered felt the devastating effects of foreign contact. Native populations declined drastically from introduced diseases. The population of the Aleut people, the first to succumb to Russian occupation, was reduced to less than 20 percent of the precontact level through warfare, disease and starvation. The Tlingit, Haida and Chugach may have been reduced by 50 percent. The Russians also brought to the new land their customs, religion and language, which, through subjugation and the efforts of the missionaries, brought great changes in traditional technologies, social patterns and religious beliefs.

In 1867, facing increasing competition and frustrated in their efforts to expand its territory, the Russians sold Alaska to the United States for $7.2 million.

Today, one of the foremost legacies of the Russian period is the Russian Orthodox Church, still a vital aspect of Native culture in Southwest, Southcentral and Southeast Alaska. Visitors to Kodiak, Sitka and smaller Native communities can see the familiar onion-shaped domes of the Russian Orthodox churches.

Related reading: *Where the Sea Breaks Its Back,* by Corey Ford. This epic story tells the history of early naturalist Georg W. Steller and the Russian exploration of Alaska. *See* ALASKA NORTHWEST LIBRARY in the back of the book.

School Districts

(*See also* Education)

Alaska's 54 public school districts served approximately 110,366 pre-elementary through 12th grade students in the 1990-91 school year. There are two types of school districts: city and borough school districts and Regional Educational Attendance Areas (REAA). The 33 city and borough school districts are located in municipalities, each contributing funds for the operation of its local schools. The 21 REAAs are located in the unorganized boroughs and have no local government to contribute funds to their schools. The REAAs are almost solely dependent upon state funds for school support. City and borough school districts are supported by about 67 percent state, 25 percent local and 8 percent federal funding.

The Centralized Correspondence School (CCS), Alaska Department of Education, 3134 Channel Drive, #100, Juneau 99801-7897, provides courses by correspondence to students in grades K–12.

Following are the names and addresses of Alaska's 54 public school districts:

Adak Region Schools, PSC 486, Box 1234, FPO AP 96506-0005, Intra-Alaska Mail, Adak

Alaska Gateway Schools, Box 226, Tok 99780

Aleutian Region Schools, Pouch 790, Unalaska 99685

Aleutians East Borough Schools, P.O. Box 429, Sand Point 99661

Anchorage Schools, 4600 DeBarr Road, Box 196614, Anchorage 99519

Annette Island Schools, Box 7, Metlakatla 99926

Bering Strait Schools, Box 225, Unalakleet 99684

Bristol Bay Borough Schools, Box 169, Naknek 99633

Chatham Schools, Box 109, Angoon 99820

Chugach Schools, 165 E. 56th Ave., Suite D, Anchorage 99518

Copper River Schools, Box 108, Glennallen 99588

Cordova City Schools, Box 140, Cordova 99574

Craig City Schools, Box 800, Craig 99921

Delta/Greely Schools, Box 527, Delta Junction 99737

Dillingham City Schools, Box 170, Dillingham 99576

Fairbanks North Star Borough Schools, Box 71250, Fairbanks 99707

Galena City Schools, Box 299, Galena 99741

Haines Borough Schools, Box 1289, Haines 99827

Hoonah City Schools, Box 157, Hoonah 99829

Hydaburg City Schools, Box 109, Hydaburg 99922

Iditarod Area Schools, Box 90, McGrath 99627

Juneau City Schools, 10014 Crazy Horse Drive, Juneau 99801

Kake City Schools, Box 450, Kake 99830

Kashunamiut School District, 985 KSD Way, Chevak 99563

Kenai Peninsula Borough Schools, 148 N. Binkley St., Soldotna 99669

Ketchikan Gateway Borough Schools, Pouch Z, Ketchikan 99901

Klawock City Schools, Box 9, Klawock 99925

Kodiak Island Borough Schools, 722 Mill Bay Road, Kodiak 99615

Kuspuk Schools, Box 49, Aniak 99557

Lake and Peninsula Schools, Box 498, King Salmon 99613

Lower Kuskokwim Schools, Box 305, Bethel 99559

Lower Yukon Schools, Box 32089, Mountain Village 99632

Matanuska–Susitna Borough Schools, 125 W. Evergreen, Palmer 99645

Nenana City Schools, Box 10, Nenana 99760

Nome City Schools, Box 131, Nome 99762

North Slope Borough Schools, Box 169, Barrow 99723

Northwest Arctic Borough Schools, Box 51, Kotzebue 99752

Pelican City Schools, Box 90, Pelican 99832

Petersburg City Schools, Box 289, Petersburg 99833

Pribilof Schools, Pouch 5, Saint Paul Island 99660

Railbelt School District, Drawer 280, Healy 99743

Saint Marys School District, Box 171, Saint Marys 99658

Sitka Borough Schools, Box 179, Sitka 99835

Skagway City Schools, Box 497, Skagway 99840

Southeast Island Schools, Box 8340, Ketchikan 99901

Southwest Region Schools, Box 90, Dillingham 99576

Tanana Schools, Box 89, Tanana 99777

Unalaska City Schools, Pouch 260, Unalaska 99685

Valdez City Schools, Box 398, Valdez 99686

Wrangell City Schools, Box 2319, Wrangell 99929

Yakutat City Schools, Box 427, Yakutat 99689

Yukon Flats Schools, Box 359, Fort Yukon 99740

Yukon/Koyukuk Schools, Box 309, Nenana 99760

Yupiit Schools, Box 100, Akiachak 99551

Shipping

Vehicles

Persons shipping vehicles between Seattle and Anchorage are advised to shop around for the carrier that offers the services and rates most suited to the shipper's needs. Not all carriers offer year-round service and freight charges vary greatly depending upon the carrier, and the weight and height of the vehicle. Rates quoted here are only approximate. Sample fares per unit: northbound, Seattle to Anchorage, under 66 inches in height, $823; over 66 inches and under 87 inches, $1,070. Southbound, Anchorage to Seattle, any unit under 84 inches, $600. Fuel surcharges may be applied.

Not all carriers accept rented moving trucks and trailers, and a few of those that do accept them require authorization from the rental company to carry its equipment to Alaska. Check with the carrier and your rental company before booking service.

Make your reservation at least two weeks in advance, and prepare to have the vehicle at the carrier's loading facility two days prior to sailing. Carriers differ on what items they allow to travel inside the vehicle, from nothing at all to goods packaged and addressed separately. Coast Guard regulations forbid the transport of vehicles holding more than one-quarter tank of gas and none of the carriers listed allows owners to accompany their vehicles in transit. *Remember to have fresh antifreeze installed in your car or truck prior to sailing.*

At a lesser rate, you can ship your vehicle aboard a state ferry to southeastern ports. However, you must accompany your vehicle or arrange for someone to drive it on and off the ferry at departure and arrival ports.

Carriers that will ship cars, truck campers, house trailers and motor-homes from Anchorage to Seattle/Tacoma include:

The Alaska Railroad, P.O. Box

107500, Anchorage 99510; phone (907) 265-2490.

Sea-Land Freight Service, Inc., 1717 Tidewater Ave., Anchorage 99501; phone (907) 274-2671, or vehicle rates hotline (907) 263-5900.

Totem Ocean Trailer Express, 2511 Tidewater Ave., Anchorage 99501; phone (907) 276-5868.

In the Seattle/Tacoma area, contact:
A.A.D.A. Systems, P.O. Box 2323, Auburn, WA 98071; phone (206) 762-7840.

Alaska Railroad, 2203 Airport Way S., Suite 215, Seattle, WA 98134; phone (206) 624-4234.

Sea-Land Service, Inc., 3600 Port of Tacoma Road, Tacoma, WA 98424; phone (206) 922-3100, or 1-800-426-4512 (outside Washington).

Totem Ocean Trailer Express, P.O. Box 24908, Seattle, WA 98124; phone (206) 628-9280 or 1-800-426-0074 (outside Washington, Alaska and Hawaii).

Vehicle shipment between southeastern Alaska and Seattle is provided by:
Alaska Marine Lines, 5615 W. Marginal Way SW, Seattle, WA 98106; phone (206) 763-4244 or 1-800-443-4343 (serves Ketchikan, Wrangell, Petersburg, Sitka, Juneau, Haines, Skagway, Yakutat, Excursion Inlet and Hawk Inlet).

Boyer Alaska Barge Line, 7318 Fourth Ave. S., Seattle, WA 98108; phone (206) 763-8575 (serves Ketchikan and Wrangell).

Household Goods and Personal Effects
Many moving van lines have service to and from Alaska through their agency connections in most Alaska and Lower 48 cities. To initiate service, contact the van line agents nearest your starting point.

Northbound goods are shipped to Seattle and transferred through a port agent to a water-borne vessel for transportation to Alaska. Few shipments go over the road to Alaska. Southbound shipments are processed in a like manner through Alaska ports to Seattle, then on to the destination.

Haul-it-yourself companies provide service to Alaska for those who prefer to move their goods themselves. It is possible to ship a rented truck or trailer into southeastern Alaska aboard the carriers that accept privately owned vehicles (*see* Vehicles, *preceding*). A few of the carriers sailing between Seattle and Anchorage also carry rented equipment. However, shop around for this service, for it has not been common practice in the past—rates can be very high if the carrier does not yet have a specific tariff established for this type of shipment. *You will not be allowed to accompany the rented equipment.*

Sitka Slippers

Also known as Alaska tennis shoes, Wrangell sneakers or Petersburg sneakers, Sitka slippers are heavy-duty rubber boots worn by residents of rainy southeastern Alaska.

Skiing

Both cross-country and downhill skiing are popular forms of outdoor recreation in Alaska from November through May. There are developed ski facilities in several Alaska communities, backcountry powder skiing is available by charter helicopter or ski-equipped aircraft and cross-country skiing opportunities are virtually limitless throughout the state. It is also possible to ski during the summer months by chartering a plane to reach glacier skiing spots.

In the 1992 Winter Olympics, Hilary Lindh of Juneau turned all eyes to the state of Alaska when she won the silver medal for the downhill. This was the first individual merit Olympic medal that an Alaskan has ever won.

Anchorage

There are two major downhill ski areas in the Anchorage area: Alyeska Resort and Alpenglow at Arctic Valley. Alyeska Resort, 40 miles southeast of Anchorage, is the state's largest ski resort, offering five chair lifts with runs up to a mile long. Chair No. 3 is equipped for night skiing and a fifth chair lift is reserved for racer training. The resort also has two rope tows and cross-country skiing. Alyeska is open year-round, with skiing from November through April and sightseeing during the summer. Hours of operation depend on daylight, except for chair No. 3.

Alpenglow, a few miles from Anchorage, is owned and operated by the Anchorage Ski Club, a nonprofit corporation. Arctic Valley is open on winter weekends and holidays. Facilities include two double chair lifts, a T-bar/Poma lift combination and three rope tows on beginner slopes.

Several smaller alpine slopes maintained by the municipality of Anchorage include: Far North Bicentennial Park; Russian Jack Springs Park, with rope tows; and Hilltop, south of town, featuring the closest chair lift to the Anchorage area.

There are several popular cross-country ski trails in the Anchorage area in city parks that are maintained by the municipality. These include: Russian Jack Springs, with nearly 5 miles of trails, all lighted; Kincaid Park, site of the first World Cup and U.S. National races in Alaska and the U.S. in March 1983, with 24 miles of trails, 6 miles lighted, and a warm-up facility; Far North Bicentennial Park, with 3 miles of trails, about 2 miles lighted; Hillside Park, with 10.8 miles of trails, 1.5 miles lighted; Tony Knowles Coastal Trail, with 9 miles of trails, none lighted; and Chester Creek Greenbelt, with 10 kilometers of trails, none lighted. Cross-country skiers can find trails in Chugach State Park and in the Turnagain Pass area in Chugach National Forest, about 57 miles south of Anchorage.

Palmer

Hatcher Pass, site of the Independence Mine State Park, north of Palmer, is an excellent cross-country ski area with several maintained trails. The lodge has a coffee shop and warm-up area. The ski area is open from October through May.

Fairbanks

Fairbanks has a few downhill ski areas, but none as large as Alyeska resort. Cleary Summit and Skiland, about 20 miles from town on the Steese Highway, both privately owned and operated, have rope tows, with a chair lift at Cleary Summit; Ski Boot Hill at 4.2 mile on Farmer's Loop Road has a rope tow; Birch Hill, located on Fort Wainwright, is mainly for military use; the University of Alaska has a small slope and rope tow; and Chena Hot Springs Resort at mile 57 on the Chena Hot Springs Road has a small alpine ski area that uses a tractor to transport skiers to the top of the hill.

Popular cross-country ski trails in the Fairbanks area include: Birch Hill recreation area, about 3 miles north of town on the Steese Expressway to a well-marked turnoff, then 2 miles in; the University of Alaska, Fairbanks, with 26 miles of trails that lead out to Ester Dome; Creamers Field trail near downtown; Salcha cross-country ski area, about 40 miles south of town on the Richardson Highway, with a fairly large trail system also used for ski races;

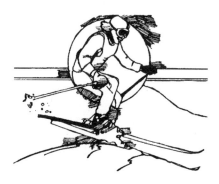

Two Rivers trail area, near the elementary school at mile 10 Chena Hot Springs Road; and Chena Hot Springs Resort, offering cross-country ski trails for both novice and more experienced skiers.

Juneau

Eaglecrest Ski Area on Douglas Island, 12 miles from Juneau, has a 4,800-foot-long chair lift, a Platter Pull lift, a 3,000-foot-long chair lift and a day lodge. Cross-country ski trails are also available. Eaglecrest is open from November to May. A few smaller alpine ski areas are located at Cordova, Valdez, Ketchikan and Homer. All have rope tows.

Several cross-country ski races are held each year. The largest, the Alaska Nordic Ski Cup Series, determines contestants for the Arctic Winter Games and Junior Olympic competitions. The series of five races is held in Anchorage, Homer, Salcha and Fairbanks. The World Masters Cross Country Ski Championships also were held in Anchorage in February 1992, and Valdez is now home to the World Extreme Ski Championships in April.

Skin Sewing

(See also Beadwork; Mukluks; and Parka)

The craft of sewing tanned hides and furs was a highly developed skill among Alaska's Natives. Although commercially made garments are now often worn by Eskimo villagers, women who are exceptional skin sewers still not only ensure the safety of family members who must face the harsh outdoors, but are regarded as a source of pride for the entire community.

Sewers place great importance on the use of specific materials, some of which are only available seasonally. For instance, winter-bleached sealskin can only be tanned during certain seasons. Blood, alder bark and red ochre

are traditionally used for coloring on garments and footgear. Most sewers prefer sinew as thread, although in some areas sinew cannot be obtained and waxed thread or dental floss is substituted. Skins commonly used for making parkas and mukluks include seal, reindeer, caribou and polar bear. Wolf and wolverine are prized for ruffs.

Parka styles, materials used and ornamentation (such as pieced calfskin or beadwork trim) vary from village to village, and between Yup'ik, Inupiat and Siberian Yup'ik sewers. The cut of parkas changes from north to south.

In most regions, mukluk styles and material vary with changes in season and weather conditions. The mukluks advertise the skill of their makers and the villages where they were made.

The manufacture of children's toys, primarily clothed dolls and intricately sewn balls, still reflects the traditional ingenuity of skin sewers.

Skookum

Skookum is a word meaning strong or serviceable. It originated with the Chehalis Indians of western Washington and was incorporated into the Chinook jargon, a trade language dating from the early 1800s. A skookum chuck is a narrow passage between a saltwater lagoon and the open sea. In many areas of Alaska, because of extreme tides, skookum chucks may resemble fast-flowing river rapids during changes of the tide.

Soapstone

This soft, easily worked stone is often carved into art objects by Alaskans. Most of the stone, however, is imported. Alaska soapstone is mined in the Matanuska Valley by blasting. This process creates in the stone a tendency to fracture when being worked; therefore, it is not as desirable as imported soapstone.

Sourdough

Carried by many early-day pioneers,

this versatile, yeasty mixture was used to make bread and hot cakes. Sourdough cookery remains popular in Alaska today. Because the sourdough supply is replenished after each use, it can remain active and fresh indefinitely. A popular claim of sourdough cooks is that their batches trace back to pioneers at the turn of the century. The name also came to be applied to any Alaska or Yukon old-timer.

Related reading: *Alaska Sourdough: The Real Stuff by a Real Alaskan,* by Ruth Allman. *Cooking Alaskan,* hundreds of time-tested recipes, including a section on sourdough. *See* ALASKA NORTHWEST LIBRARY at the back of the book.

Speed Limits

The basic speed law in Alaska states the speed limit is "no speed more than is prudent and reasonable."

The maximum speeds are 15 miles per hour in an alley, 20 miles per hour in a business district or school zone, 25 miles per hour in a residential area and 55 miles per hour on any other roadway.

Locally, municipalities and the state may, and often do, reduce or alter maximums as long as no maximum exceeds 55 miles per hour.

Squaw Candy

Squaw candy is salmon that has been dried or smoked for a long time until it's very chewy. It's a staple food in winter for rural Alaskans and their dogs.

State Forest

Created in 1983, the 1.81-million-acre Tanana Valley State Forest is located almost entirely within the Tanana River basin and includes 200 miles of the Tanana River. It extends from near the Canadian border approximately 265 miles west to Manley Hot Springs, encompasses areas as far south as Tok, and is interspersed with private and other state lands throughout the basin. The Bonanza Creek Experimental Forest near Nenana is located within the state forest.

Hardwood and hardwood-spruce trees dominate almost 90 percent of the forest, and 22 percent (392,000 acres) is suitable for harvest. There are 44 rivers, streams and lakes within the forest with significant fish, wildlife, recreation and water values. Nearly all of the land will remain open for mineral development.

Approximately 85 percent of the forest is located within 20 miles of a highway, making it one of the more accessible public lands in the Interior. Rivers and trails throughout the river basin provide additional access to areas in the forest. The Eagle Trail State Recreation Site is the only developed facility in the Tanana Valley State Forest and has 40 campsites. For more information, contact the Regional Forester, Northcentral District, 3726 Airport way, Fairbanks 99701.

State Park System

The Alaska state park system began in July 1959 with the transfer of federally managed campgrounds and recreation sites from the Bureau of Land Management to the new state of Alaska. These sites were managed by the state Division of Lands until 1970—under Forestry, Parks and Recreation until 1966; then under Parks and Recreation. The Division of Parks was created in October 1970.

The Alaska state park system consists of approximately 116 individual units divided into six park management districts. There are 48 recreation sites, 15 recreation areas, 6 historic parks, 3 historic sites, 2 state trails, 7 state parks (Chugach, Denali, Chilkat,

Kachemak Bay, Point Bridget, Shuyak Island and Wood-Tikchik) and the 49,000-acre Alaska Chilkat Bald Eagle Preserve. Wood-Tikchik State Park is Alaska's most remote state park and, with 1.5 million acres of wilderness, is the largest state park in the United States.

Campsites are available on a first-come, first-served basis for $6 or $8 per night, except Bird Creek and Eklutna ($10) and Eagle River ($12), all in Chugach State Park, and Chena River State Recreation Site in Fairbanks ($12). A yearly pass is also available for $75. In addition to camping and picnicking, many units offer hiking trails and boat launching ramps; most developed campgrounds have picnic tables and toilets. General information on the state park system is available from the Division of Parks, P.O. Box 107001, Anchorage 99510.

State park units are listed by park management districts on the following pages. Designations for units of the Alaska state park system are abbreviated as follows: SP–State Park, SHP–State Historical Park, SHS–State Historic Site, SRA–State Recreation Area, SRS–State Recreation Site, ST–State Trail, SMP–State Marine Park, P–Preserve, WP–Wilderness Park, PUF–Public Use Facility. Park units designated "undeveloped" may have camping, hiking trails and limited facilities. Parks that indicate no developed campsites or picnic sites may offer fishing or river access, hiking and other activities. (*See* map pages 172–73.)

Map Key	Acreage	Campsites	Picnic Sites	Nearest Town

Southeast District (400 Willoughby Bldg., Juneau 99801)

Map Key	Acreage	Campsites	Picnic Sites	Nearest Town
1 Totem Bight SHP	11	—	—	Ketchikan
2 Refuge Cove SRS	13	—	14	Ketchikan
3 Settlers Cove SRS	38	12	—	Ketchikan
4 Pioneer Park SRS	3	—	—	Sitka
5 Baranof Castle SHS	1	—	—	Sitka
6 Halibut Point SRS	22	—	9	Sitka
7 Old Sitka SHP	51	—	—	Sitka
8 Juneau Trail Sys. ST	15	—	—	Juneau
9 Johnson Crk SRS	65	—	—	Juneau
10 Wickersham SHS	0.5	—	—	Juneau
11 Point Bridget SP	2,800	—	—	Juneau
12 Chilkoot Lake SRS	80	32	—	Haines
13 Portage Cove SRS	7	9	3	Haines
14 Chilkat SP	6,045	15	—	Haines
15 Ak-Chilkat Bald Eagle P	49,320	—	—	Haines
16 Mosquito Lake SRS	5	10	—	Haines
17 Gruening SHP	12	—	—	Juneau
18 Dall Bay SMP	585	—	—	Ketchikan
19 Thom's Place SMP	1,198	—	—	Wrangell
20 Beecher Pass SMP	660	—	—	Wrangell
21 Joe Mace Island SMP	62	—	—	Wrangell
22 Security Bay SMP	500	—	—	Petersburg
23 Taku Harbor SMP	700	—	—	Juneau
24 Oliver Inlet SMP	560	—	—	Juneau
25 Funter Bay SMP	162	—	—	Juneau
26 Shelter Island SMP	3,560	—	6	Juneau
27 St. James Bay SMP	10,220	—	—	Juneau
28 Sullivan Island SMP	2,163	—	—	Juneau
29 Chilkat Islands SMP	6,560	—	—	Haines
30 Magoun Islands SMP	—	—	—	Sitka
31 Big Bear/Baby Bear SMP	—	—	—	Sitka

Northern District (3700 Airport Way, Fairbanks 99709)

Map Key	Acreage	Campsites	Picnic Sites	Nearest Town
32 Tok River SRS	38	50	—	Tok

Map Key	Acreage	Campsites	Picnic Sites	Nearest Town
33 Eagle Trail SRS	640	40	4	Tok
34 Moon Lake SRS	22	15	—	Tok
35 Fielding Lake SRS	300	7	—	Delta Junction
36 Donnelly Creek SRS	42	12	—	Delta Junction
37 Clearwater SRS	27	18	—	Delta Junction
38 Delta SRS	7	22	6	Delta Junction
39 Big Delta SHP	10	—	—	Delta Junction
40 Quartz Lake SRA	600	16	—	Delta Junction
41 Birch Lake SRS	191	10	—	Delta Junction
42 Harding Lake SRA	169	89	52	Delta Junction
43 Salcha River SRS	61	25	20	Delta Junction
44 Chena River SRS	27	59	30	Fairbanks
45 Chena River SRA	254,080	—	—	Fairbanks
46 Upper Chatanika Rvr SRS	73	25	—	Fairbanks
47 Lower Chatanika Rvr SRA	570	—	—	Fairbanks

Mat-Su/Copper Basin District (HC 32, Box 6706, Wasilla 99687)

Map Key	Acreage	Campsites	Picnic Sites	Nearest Town
48 Denali SP	324,240	—	—	Trapper Creek
49 Montana Creek SRS	82	89	28	Talkeetna
50 Willow Creek SRA	3,583	—	—	Willow
51 Nancy Lake SRA	22,685	—	—	Willow
52 Nancy Lake SRS	36	30	30	Willow
53 Rocky Lake SRS	48	10	—	Big Lake
54 Big Lake North SRS	19	60	24	Big Lake
55 Big Lake South SRS	16	20	10	Big Lake
56 Little Susitna River PUF	—	145	41	Wasilla
57 Kepler-Bradley Lakes SRA	344	—	—	Palmer
58 Finger Lake SRS	47	41	10	Palmer
59 Wolf Lake SRS	23	4	4	Palmer
60 Independence Mine SHP	761	—	—	Palmer
61 Summit Lake SRS	360	—	—	Palmer
62 Moose Creek SRS	40	12	4	Palmer
63 King Mountain SRS	20	22	2	Palmer
64 Bonnie Lake SRS	129	8	—	Palmer
65 Long Lake SRS	480	9	—	Palmer
66 Matanuska Glacier SRS	229	12	—	Palmer
67 Little Nelchina SRS	22	11	—	Glennallen
68 Lake Louise SRA	90	36	—	Glennallen
69 Tolsona Creek SRS	600	10	—	Glennallen
70 Dry Creek SRS	372	58	4	Glennallen
71 Porcupine Creek SRS	240	12	—	Tok
72 Liberty Falls SRS	10	8	—	Chitina
73 Squirrel Creek SRS	350	14	—	Copper Center
74 Little Tonsina SRS	103	8	—	Copper Center
75 Worthington Glacier SRS	113	—	—	Valdez
76 Blueberry Lake SRS	192	15	—	Valdez

Chugach/Southwest District (P.O. Box 107001, Anchorage 99510)

Map Key	Acreage	Campsites	Picnic Sites	Nearest Town
77 Chugach SP	495,204	—	—	Anchorage
78 Potter Section House SHS	0.5	—	—	Anchorage
79 Wood-Tikchik SP	1,555,200	3	—	Dillingham

Kenai Peninsula District (P.O. Box 1247, Soldotna 99669)

Map Key	Acreage	Campsites	Picnic Sites	Nearest Town
80 Bettles Bay SMP	680	—	—	Whittier
81 Zeigler Cove SMP	720	—	—	Whittier
82 Surprise Cove SMP	2,280	—	—	Whittier

(Continued on page 174)

STATE PARKS

(Numbers refer to accompanying list)

SP = State Park
SRS = State Recreation Site
SRA = State Recreation Area
SHP = State Historical Park
SHS = State Historic Site
ST = State Trail
WP = Wilderness Park
SMP = State Marine Park
P = Preserve
PUF = Public Use Facility

Circle

NORTHERN

Steese Highway

Elliott Highway

Fairbanks

Delta Junction

Alaska Highway

Tok Jun

Denali Highway

Paxson

Richardson Highway

Highway

COPI BASI

George Parks Highway

MAT-SU

SOUTHCENTRAL

Glennallen

Glenn

CHUGACH

Edgerton Highw

Palmer

Anchorage

Valdez

Richardson Highwa

Kenai

Soldotna

Seward

Sterling Highway

Seward Highway

Homer

KENAI PENINSULA

KODIAK

Kodiak

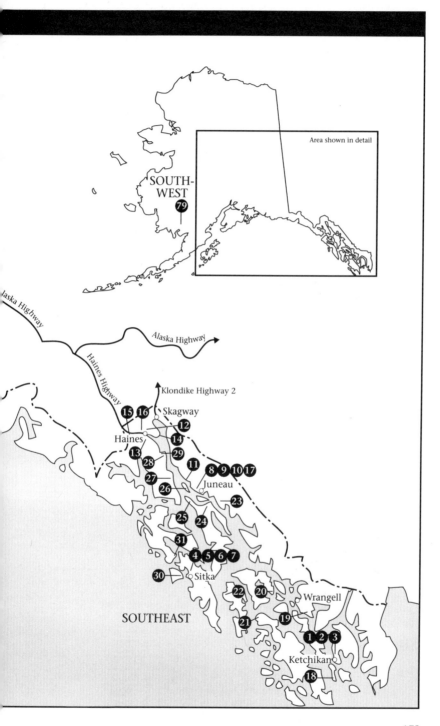

SOUTH-WEST
79

Area shown in detail

Alaska Highway

Alaska Highway

Haines Highway

Klondike Highway 2

15 16 Skagway

12

14

Haines

13

28

29

27

26

11

8 9 10 17

Juneau

23

25

24

31

4 5 6 7

30 Sitka

22 20

Wrangell

SOUTHEAST

21

19

1 2 3

Ketchikan

18

(Continued from page 171)

Map Key	Acreage	Campsites	Picnic Sites	Nearest Town
83 S. Esther Island SMP	3,360	—	—	Whittier
84 Horseshoe Bay SMP	970	—	—	Seward
85 Sawmill Bay SMP	2,320	—	—	Valdez
86 Shoup Bay SMP	4,560	—	—	Valdez
87 Jack Bay SMP	811	—	—	Valdez
88 Boswell Bay SMP	799	—	—	Cordova
89 Canoe Passage SMP	2,735	—	—	Cordova
90 Decision Point SMP	460	—	—	Whittier
91 Entry Cove SMP	370	—	—	Whittier
92 Granite Bay SMP	2,105	—	—	Whittier
93 Kayak Island SMP	1,437	—	—	Cordova
94 Driftwood Bay SMP	840	—	—	Seward
95 Safety Cove SMP	660	—	—	Seward
96 Sandspit Point SMP	600	—	—	Seward
97 Sunny Cove SMP	300	—	—	Seward
98 Thumb Cove SMP	300	—	—	Seward
99 Kenai River Special Management Area	2,770	—	—	Sterling
100 Caines Head SRA	5,961	4	4	Seward
101 Bernice Lake SRS	152	11	1	Kenai
102 Captain Cook SRA	3,466	—	—	Kenai
103 Crooked Creek SRS	49	75	30	Soldotna
104 Kasilof River SRS	50	16	—	Soldotna
105 Johnson Lake SRA	324	50	25	Soldotna
106 Clam Gulch SRA	129	116	—	Soldotna
107 Ninilchik SRA	97	165	—	Homer
108 Deep Creek SRA	155	300	—	Homer
109 Stariski SRS	30	13	—	Homer
110 Anchor River SRA	213	38	—	Homer
111 Anchor River SRS	53	9	—	Homer
112 Kachemak Bay SP&WP	368,290	8	1	Homer

Kodiak District (SR Box 3800, Kodiak 99615)

Map Key	Acreage	Campsites	Picnic Sites	Nearest Town
113 Fort Abercrombie SHP	183	14	—	Kodiak
114 Buskin River SRS	196	18	—	Kodiak
115 Pasagshak SRS	20	10	—	Kodiak
116 Shuyak Island SP	11,000	—	—	Kodiak

State Symbols

Flag

Alaska's state flag was designed in 1926 by Benny Benson, a seventh-grade student who entered his design in a territorial flag contest. The Alaska Legislature adopted his design as the official flag of the Territory of Alaska on May 2, 1927.

The flag consists of eight gold stars—the Big Dipper and the North Star—on a field of blue. In Benny Benson's words, "The blue field is for the Alaska sky and the forget-me-not, an Alaska flower. The North Star is for the future state of Alaska, the most northerly of the Union. The Great Bear—symbolizing strength."

Alaska was proclaimed the 49th state of the Union on Jan. 3, 1959. The drafters of the constitution for Alaska stipulated that the flag of the territory would be the official flag of the state of Alaska. When the flag was first flown over the capital city on July 4, 1959, Benny Benson proudly led the parade that preceded the ceremony, carrying the flag of eight stars on a field of blue, which he had designed 33 years before.

Seal

The first governor of Alaska designed a seal for the then–District of Alaska in

1884. In 1910, Gov. Walter E. Clark redesigned the original seal, which became a symbol for the new Territory of Alaska in 1912. The constitution of Alaska adopted the territorial seal as the Seal for the State of Alaska in 1959.

Represented in the state seal are icebergs, northern lights, mining, agriculture, fisheries, fur seal rookeries and a railroad. The seal is $2^1/8$ inches in diameter.

Song

Alaska's Flag

Eight stars of gold on a field of blue—
Alaska's flag.
May it mean to you the blue of the sea, the
evening sky,
The mountain lakes, and the flow'rs
nearby;
The gold of the early sourdough's dreams,
The precious gold of the hills and streams;
The brilliant stars in the northern sky,
The "Bear"—the "Dipper"—and, shining
high,
The great North Star with its steady light,
Over land and sea a beacon bright.
Alaska's flag—to Alaskans dear,
The simple flag of a last frontier.

The lyrics were written by Marie Drake as a poem that first appeared on the cover of the October 1935 *School*

Bulletin, a territorial Department of Education publication that she edited while assistant commissioner of education.

The music was written by Mrs. Elinor Dusenbury, whose husband, Col. Ralph Wayne Dusenbury, was commander of Chilkoot Barracks at Haines from 1933 to 1936. Mrs. Dusenbury wrote the music several years after leaving Alaska because, she was later quoted as saying, "I got so homesick for Alaska I couldn't stand it." She died Oct. 17, 1980, in Carlsbad, California.

The territorial legislature adopted *Alaska's Flag* as the official song in 1955.

Other Symbols

Bird: Willow ptarmigan, *Lagopus lagopus*, a small arctic grouse that lives among willows and on open tundra and 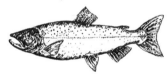 muskeg. Its plumage changes from brown in summer to white in winter; feathers cover the entire lower leg and foot. Common from southwestern Alaska into the Arctic. Adopted in 1955.

Fish: King salmon, *Oncorhynchus tshawytscha*, an important part of the Native subsistence fisheries and a significant species to the state's commercial salmon fishery. This anadromous fish

ranges from beyond the southern extremes of Alaska to as far north as Point Hope. Adopted in 1962.

Flower: Forget-Me-Not. Adopted in 1949.

Fossil: Woolly mammoth. Adopted in 1986.

Gem: Jade. (*See* Jade.) Adopted in 1968.

Marine Mammal: Bowhead whale. Adopted in 1983.

Mineral: Gold. (*See* Gold.) Adopted in 1968.

Motto: North to the Future, adopted in 1967.

Sport: Dog mushing. (*See* Dog Mushing.) Adopted in 1972.

Tree: Sitka spruce, *Picea sitchensis,* the largest and one of the most valuable trees in Alaska. Sitka spruce grows to 160 feet in height and 3 to 5 feet in diameter. Its long, dark-green needles surround twigs that bear cones. It is found throughout Southeast and the Kenai Peninsula, along the gulf coast, and along the west coast of Cook Inlet. Adopted in 1962.

Subsistence

Alaska is unique among states in that it has established the subsistence use of fish and game as the highest priority consumptive use of the resource. Alaska's legislature passed subsistence priority laws in 1978 and 1986. In addition, Congress passed a priority subsistence law in 1980 for federal lands in Alaska. Studies by the Alaska Department of Fish and Game have shown that many rural communities in Alaska depend upon subsistence hunting and fishing for a large portion of their diets.

Subsistence, a controversial issue and a difficult concept to define, is defined by federal law as "the customary and traditional uses by rural Alaska residents of wild, renewable resources for direct personal or family consumption as food, shelter, fuel, clothing, tools or transportation; for the making and selling of handicraft articles out of nonedible byproducts of fish and wildlife resources taken for personal or family consumption; and for the customary trade, barter or sharing for personal or family consumption."

According to Alaska State Subsistence Statutes passed in 1986, only rural residents can be considered subsistence users. In addition to the rural requirement, subsistence uses can be identified by a variety of other criteria, such as long-term traditional use, local area use and frequent sharing of harvests. Subsistence also depends upon the biological status of fish and game resources, and is not authorized if harvesting will damage the resources.

In December 1989, the Alaska Supreme Court ruled that the rural subsistence preference in the state law was unconstitutional. This placed the state out of compliance with requirements of the federal law. Consequently, the federal government took over management of subsistence on federal lands in Alaska on July 1, 1990, and began to develop its own set of subsistence regulations. Although the state desires to regain this management authority, no resolution to the issue was reached in 1991.

State subsistence fishing regulations are available as a separate pamphlet from the Alaska Department of Fish and Game, P.O. Box 3-2000, Juneau 99802. State subsistence hunting regulations are included with the annually published state hunting regulations, also available from the ADF&G.

Sundog

Sundogs are "mock suns" (parhelia) usually seen as bright spots on opposite sides of the winter sun. This optical phenomenon is created by the refraction of sunlight through tiny ice crystals suspended in the air. The ice crystals are commonly called "diamond dust."

Taiga

Taiga is a moist coniferous forest that begins where the tundra ends. Taken from a Russian word that means "land of little sticks," this name is applied to the spindly white spruce and black spruce forests found in much of southcentral and interior Alaska.

Telecommunications

History
Alaska's first telecommunications project, begun in the 1860s, was designed to serve New York, San Francisco and the capitals of Europe, not particularly the residents of Nome or Fairbanks. It was part of Western Union's ambitious plan to link California to Russian America (Alaska) with an intercontinental cable that would continue under the Bering Strait to Siberia and on to Europe. Men and material

were brought together on both sides of the Bering Sea, but with the first successful Atlantic cable crossing in 1867, the trans-Siberian intercontinental line was abandoned.

The first operational telegraph link in Alaska was laid in September 1900, when 25 miles of line were stretched from military headquarters in Nome to an outpost at Port Safety. It was one part of a $450,000 plan by the Army Signal Corps to connect scattered military posts in the territory with the United States. By the end of 1903, land lines linked western Alaska, Prince William Sound, the Interior and southeastern Alaska (where underwater cable was used).

Plagued by blocks of ice that repeatedly tore loose the underwater cables laid across Norton Sound, the military developed "wireless telegraphy" to span the icy water in 1903. It was the world's first application of radio-telegraph technology and marked the completion of a fragile network connecting all military stations in Alaska with the United States and each other. Sitka, Juneau, Haines and Valdez were connected by a line to Whitehorse, Yukon Territory. Nome, Fort Saint Michael, Fort Gibbon (Tanana) and Fort Egbert (Eagle) were linked with Dawson, Yukon Territory. A line from Dawson to Whitehorse continued on to Vancouver, British Columbia, and Seattle.

In 1905, the 1,500 miles of land lines, 2,000 miles of submarine cables and the 107-mile wireless link became the Washington-Alaska Military Cable and Telegraph System. This, in turn, became the Alaska Communications System in 1935, reflecting a shift to greater civilian use and a system relying more heavily on wireless stations than land lines. The Alaska Communications System operated under the Department of Defense until RCA Corporation, through its division RCA Alascom, took control in 1971.

Alascom

Alascom, Inc., is the original long lines carrier for the state and provides a full range of modern long-distance telecommunications services to all Alaska. When Alascom purchased Alaska Communications Systems, about 5 million calls were being handled each year. Today, with more than 200 satellite communication sites in operation, Alascom handles nearly 70 million toll calls each year. To complement its satellite communications, Alascom also maintains hundreds of miles of terrestrial microwave routes.

On Oct. 27, 1982, Alascom launched its own telecommunications satellite, *Aurora,* into orbit from Cape Canaveral, Florida. The launching marked several firsts for Alaska: It was the first telecommunications satellite dedicated to a single state; it was the first completely solid-state satellite to be placed in orbit; and it was the first satellite to be named by a youngster in a contest. Sponsored by Alascom and the Alaska Chamber of Commerce, the contest drew some 5,000 entries from schoolchildren across Alaska. The winner was 8-year-old Nick Francis of Eagle River, who chose "aurora" for the name "because it's our light in the sky to tell us we are special people."

On May 29, 1991, Alascom launched its second satellite, *Aurora II,* from Cape Canaveral. Designed to replace the original *Aurora,* which had reached the end of its lifespan, *Aurora II* uses a similar design updated with modern technology to increase its lifespan. Alascom also began offering service in 1991 on its new fiber optic telecommunications cable, which as part of its parent company's North Pacific fiber optic cable, links Alaska to the Lower 48 and Japan. The 17,000-circuit capacity cable can handle up to 85,000 simultaneous messages.

A typical long-distance telephone call between two points in rural Alaska may travel nearly 100,000 miles in what engineers call a "double hop," in which a signal travels from a village to the *Aurora II,* back to toll facilities in Fairbanks, Juneau or Anchorage, up again to *Aurora II* and down to a receiving antenna in another village. The signals are relayed at almost the speed of light.

Improvements over the past 10 years have made long-distance telephone service available to every community of 25 persons or more in Alaska. Live or same-day television is now available to 90 percent of the state's population. In addition to message toll service and television transmissions, Alascom also provides the following services to the residents of Alaska: discounted calling plans, computer data transmission and access, Wide Area Telecommunications Service (WATS), fax service, national and in-state 800 toll-free numbers, dedicated line service, marine radio, foreign exchange service, and transportable satellite earth stations. Alascom is one of the largest private employers in the state.

General Communication Inc.

General Communication Inc. (GCI) provides long-distance telephone service to national and international destinations. In May 1991, GCI began providing in-state long-distance service to Alaska customers.

GCI transmits calls via a communications satellite, tying in with the AT&T, MCI and US Sprint national phone networks.

Telephone Numbers in the Bush

Although most Alaskan bush communities now have full telephone service, a few villages still have only one telephone. For those villages, call the information number, 555-1212. The area code for all of Alaska is 907.

Television Stations

Television in Alaska's larger communities, such as Anchorage and Fairbanks, was available years before satellites were sent into orbit. The first satellite broadcast to the state was Neil Armstrong's moon walk in July 1969. Television reached the bush in the late 1970s with the construction of telephone earth stations that could receive television programming via satellite transmissions. The state funds Satellite Television Project (TVP), which supplies general programming to more than 250 rural communities. For more information about TVP, contact the Department of Administration, Information Services, 5900 E. Tudor Road, Anchorage 99507.

Tapes of programming from the LearnAlaska Instructional Television Network, which is no longer on the air, are available to teachers through the state library system.

Regular network programming (ABC, CBS, NBC and PBS) from the Lower 48 reaches Alaska on a time-delayed basis. Most of the stations listed here carry a mixture of network programming, with local broadcasters specifying programming. Some stations, such as KJNP, carry locally produced programming.

Cable television is available in many communities, with the cable companies offering dozens of channels. At least one cable system offers a complete satellite earth station and 24-hour programming. Local television viewing in Bethel, for example, includes Channel 4 (KYUK), which carries ITV programming such as PBS's "NOVA" series and "Sesame Street," and local news; cable Channel 8, which carries regular network programming; and a half-dozen other cable channels carrying specialized programming such as movies, sports and specials.

The following list shows the commercial and public television stations in Alaska:

Anchorage

KAKM Channel 7 (public television); 2677 Providence Drive, 99508

KIMO Channel 13; 2700 E. Tudor Road, 99507

KTBY Channel 4; 1840 S. Bragaw, Suite 101, 99508

KTUU Channel 2; P.O. Box 102880, 99510

KTVA Channel 11; P.O. Box 102200, 99510

KYES Channel 5; 3700 Woodland Drive, #600, 99517

Bethel

KYUK Channel 4 (public television); P.O. Box 468, 99559

Fairbanks

KATN Channel 2; 516 Second Ave., 99707

KTVF Channel 11; P.O. Box 950, 99707

KUAC Channel 9 (public television); University of Alaska, 99775

KO7UU Channel 7; 3650 Braddock St., 99707

Juneau

KJUD Channel 8; 1107 W. Eighth St., 99801

KTOO Channel 3 (public television); 224 Fourth St., 99801

Kenai

UHF Channel 17; P.O. Box 4665, 99611

North Pole

KJNP Channel 4; P.O. Box O, 99705

Sitka

KTNL Channel 13; 520 Lake St., 99835

Tides

(*See also* Bore Tide)

In southeastern Alaska, Prince William Sound, Cook Inlet and Bristol Bay, salt water undergoes extreme daily fluctuations, creating powerful tidal currents. Some bays may go totally dry at low tide. The second greatest tide range in North America occurs in upper Cook Inlet near Anchorage, where the maximum diurnal range during spring tides is 38.9 feet. (The greatest tide range in North America is Nova Scotia's Bay of Fundy, with spring tides to 43 feet.)

Here are diurnal ranges for some coastal communities: Bethel, 4 feet; Cold Bay, 7.1 feet; Cordova, 12.4 feet; Haines, 16.8 feet; Herschel Island, 0.7 feet; Ketchikan, 15.4 feet; Kodiak, 8.5 feet; Naknek River entrance, 22.6 feet; Nikiski, 20.7 feet; Nome, 1.6 feet; Nushagak, 19.6 feet; Point Barrow, 0.4 feet; Port Heiden, 12.3 feet; Port Moller, 10.8 feet; Sand Point, 7.3 feet; Sitka, 9.9 feet; Valdez, 12 feet; Whittier, 12.3 feet; Wrangell, 15.7 feet; Yakutat, 10.1 feet.

Timber

According to the U.S. Forest Service, Anchorage Forestry Sciences Lab, 129 million acres of Alaska's 365 million acres of land surface are forested, 21 million acres of which are classified as timberland. Timberland is defined as forest land capable of producing in excess of 20 cubic feet of industrial wood per acre per year in natural stands and not withdrawn from timber utilization.

Alaska has two distinct forest ecosystems: the interior forest and the coastal rain forest. The vast interior forest covers 115 million acres, extending from the south slope of the Brooks Range to the Kenai Peninsula, and from Canada to Norton Sound. More than 13 million acres of white spruce, paper birch, quaking aspen, black cottonwood and balsam poplar stands are considered timberland, comparing favorably in size and growth with the forests of the lake states of Minnesota, Wisconsin and Michigan. However, 3.4 million acres of this timberland are unavailable for harvest because they are in designated parks or wilderness.

The interior's land management policies and the region's remoteness from large markets have limited timber use to approximately 20 sawmills, a few of which have estimated capacities of 1 million to 5 million board feet per year, but most cutting less than 300,000 board feet per year. In 1991, a mill with an estimated capacity of 70 million board feet per year has been producing intermittently. There are some exports of sawlogs, cants and chips.

The coastal rain forests extend from Cook Inlet to the Alaska-Canada border south of Ketchikan, and they continue to provide the bulk of commercial timber volume in Alaska. Of the 13.6 million acres of forested land, 7.6 million acres support timberland. About 1.9 million acres of these commercial stands are in parks and wilderness and therefore are not available for harvest. Western hemlock and Sitka spruce provide most of the timber harvest for domestic and export lumber and pulp markets. Western red cedar and Alaska cedar make up most of the balance, along with mountain hemlock and some lodgepole pine and other species. Southeastern Alaska has two pulp mills, five major sawmills and about as many smaller mills, some operating intermittently.

Lands from which substantial volumes of timber are harvested are divided into two distinct categories:

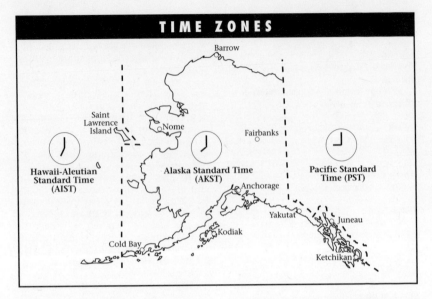

Saint
Lawrence
Island

Barrow

Nome

Fairbanks

Anchorage

Yakutat

Juneau

Kodiak

Ketchikan

Cold Bay

**Hawaii-Aleutian
Standard Time
(AIST)**

**Alaska Standard Time
(AKST)**

**Pacific Standard
Time (PST)**

privately owned by Native corporations and villages under the 1971 Native Claims Settlement Act; and publicly owned and managed federal, state and borough lands. Timber harvests from publicly owned lands are carried through short- and long-term sales offered by government agencies. Harvests on Native lands are scheduled for accelerated cutting through the early 1990s, tapering off to a lower sustained harvest in the following years.

The forest products of Alaska are also divided somewhat along the same lines as land ownership. By federal law, timber harvested from federal lands (more than 85 percent of all timber harvested on public lands) cannot be exported without processing. Consequently, while processors dependent on federal lands produce roughly sawn lumber, pulpwood and chips, the Native corporations primarily produce round logs, which find more buyers along the Pacific Rim, especially Japan. Given that the Alaska forest products industry is almost entirely dependent on the Japanese market, the processing requirement has had considerable effect on some sections of the forest industry, as it limits responsiveness to varying market conditions. Pulp mills provide a market for wood chips and for lower-quality timber from both public

and private lands. A market for this so-called utility wood is critical to all operators.

In 1990, more than 480 million board feet of timber were harvested from publicly owned or managed lands in Alaska (excluding Bureau of Land Management lands). Approximately 85 percent of the harvest was sawtimber. An estimated 547 million board feet of sawlogs, mostly for export, were harvested from private lands. In addition, there was a pulplog harvest from private lands of more than 67 million board feet. The total 1990 timber harvest exceeded 1.1 billion board feet. Alaska timber exports in 1990 were valued at more than $625 million, accounting for nearly 17 percent of the state's export revenue.

Time Zones

On Sept. 15, 1983, Transportation Secretary Elizabeth Dole signed a plan to reduce the number of time zones in Alaska from four to two. The plan, which became effective Oct. 30, 1983, when daylight saving time reverted to standard time, places 90 percent of Alaska residents on Alaska (same as Yukon) time, only one hour behind the West Coast. The far reaches of the Aleutian Islands and Saint Lawrence Island enter Hawaii–Aleutian time.

Before the change, Alaska's time zones were Pacific time (southeastern Alaska), Yukon time (Yakutat) and Alaska time (from just east of Cold Bay and west of Yakutat northward, including Nome). The shift was accomplished to facilitate doing business in Alaska, improve communications and unify residents. It had the support of the governor, the state legislature and the majority of Alaskans.

Totems

(*See also* Native Arts and Crafts *and* Potlatch)

In the early days of southeastern Alaska and the Pacific Northwest coast, the Native way of life was based on the rich natural resources of the land, on respect for all living things, and on a unique and complex social structure. The totemic art of the Indians reflects this rich culture.

Totem poles, carved from the huge cedar trees of the northern coast, are a traditional art form among the Natives of the Pacific Northwest and southeastern Alaska. Although the best-known type of totem pole is tall and freestanding, totemic art also is applied to houseposts, house frontal poles and mortuary poles. Totem poles are bold statements that make public records of the lives and history of the people who had them carved and represent pride in clans and ancestors.

Animals of the region are most often represented on the poles. Commonly depicted are eagles, ravens, frogs, bears, wolves, thunderbirds and whales. Also represented are figures from Native mythology: monsters with animal features, humanlike spirits and legendary ancestors. Occasionally included are objects, devices, masks and charms, and more rarely, art illustrating plants and sky phenomena.

The poles were traditionally painted with natural mineral and vegetable pigments. Salmon eggs were chewed with cedar bark to form the binder for the ground pigment. Traditional colors are black, white and red-brown; green, blue-green, blue and yellow are also used, depending on tribal convention. The range of colors broadened when modern paints became available. Totem art grew rapidly in the late 18th century, with the introduction of steel European tools acquired from explorers and through the fur trade. Large totem poles were a thriving cultural feature by the 1830s, having become a means by which the Natives displayed their social standing.

Totem pole carving almost died out between the 1880s and 1950s during the enforcement of a law forbidding the "potlatch," the core of Northwest Coast Indian culture. The potlatch is a ceremony in which major events are celebrated, such as marriages; guests are invited from near and far, dancing and feasting take place, property is given away and often poles are raised to commemorate the event. Since the anti-potlatching law was repealed in

1951, a revival of Native culture and the arts has taken place, and many tribes are actively carving and raising poles again.

Totem poles were left to stand as long as nature would permit, usually no more than 50 to 60 years. Once a pole became so rotten that it fell, it was left to decay naturally or used for firewood. Some totem poles still standing in parks today are 40 to 50 years old. Heavy precipitation and acid muskeg soils hasten decomposition, even though cedar is resistant to decay.

Collections of fine totem poles may be seen in several Alaska communities, either outdoors or in museums, including Ketchikan, Wrangell and Sitka. Carvers can be seen practicing their art at cultural centers in those towns as well as in Haines.

Tourism

Although Alaska has been attracting tourists for over 100 years, people are surprised that the visitor industry has quietly become the state's second largest primary employer. The visitor industry employs 19,000 Alaskans directly and affects 38,000 Alaskan jobs. Over 2,500 businesses in Alaska derive most of their income from visitor sales. Tourism is a renewable resource that brings dollars to all regions of Alaska. The visitor industry is expected to play a greater role in Alaska's future as the state's petroleum production decreases.

State government has long recognized the value of the visitor industry and supports this growing segment of the state's economy through the Division of Tourism.

For the fiscal year 1991–92, the Division of Tourism received $3.5 million and the Alaska Tourism Marketing Council received $7.5 million from the legislature to promote Alaska as a visitor destination.

While the oil spill in Prince William Sound threatened the 1989 tourism season, the negative image shown by the media was countered by a $4 million emergency marketing program developed by the Alaska Visitors Association. In 1992, tourism officials estimate that 30,000 more visitors would come to Alaska for celebrations surrounding the 50th anniversary of the Alaska Highway.

The continental United States provided 84.5 percent of Alaska's visitors in 1991, Canadian visitors formed 8.9 percent and 5.9 percent came from overseas. Of these travelers, 60 percent had independent itineraries while the remainder came on package tour programs. The most popular mode of entry for visitors was domestic air (53 percent), cruise ships (27 percent), personal vehicles (10 percent) and the ferry system (4 percent). The remainder arrived by international air (2.5 percent) and motor coach tours (1 percent). Total arrivals for summer 1991 were 651,700.

Alaska's scenic beauty, abundant wildlife and colorful history remain its biggest attractions. The adventure travel market is growing rapidly in Alaska, with an increasing number of visitors participating in river rafting, backcountry trekking and other wilderness experiences.

Trees and Shrubs

According to the U.S. Department of Agriculture, the number of native tree species in Alaska is less than in any

Nonresident Visitor Volume and Impact: Summer Seasons

Year	Visitor Volume	In-State Sales (in millions)*
1985	497,300	—
1986	552,900**	$285.0
1987	515,300	—
1988	536,300	—
1989	559,300	311.4
1990	629,700	—
1991	651,700	—

*Does not include travel to and from the state, expenditure studies done only in 1986 and 1989
**Affected by Expo '86 in Vancouver

other state. Species of trees and shrubs in Alaska fall under the following families: yew, pine, cypress, willow, bayberry, birch, mistletoe, gooseberry, rose, maple, elaeagnus, ginseng, dogwood, crowberry, pyrola, heath, dispensia, honeysuckle and composite.

Commercial timber species include white spruce, Sitka spruce, western hemlock, mountain hemlock, western red cedar, Alaska cedar, balsam poplar, black cottonwood, quaking aspen and paper birch.

Rare tree species include the Pacific yew, Pacific silver fir, subalpine fir, silver willow and Hooker willow.

Tundra

Characteristic of arctic and subarctic regions, tundra is a treeless plain that consists of moisture-retaining soils and permanently frozen subsoil. Tundra climates, with frequent winds and low temperatures, are harsh on plant species attempting to grow there. Soils freeze around root systems and winds wear away portions exposed above rocks and snow. Consequently, the three distinct types of Alaska tundra—wet, moist and alpine—support low-growing vegetation that includes a variety of delicate flowers, mosses and lichens.

According to a report in *Alaska Science Nuggets*, every acre of arctic tundra contains more than 2 tons of live fungi that survive by feeding on, thus decomposing, dead organic matter. Since the recession of North Slope ice age glaciers 12,000 years ago, a vegetative residue has accumulated a layer of peat 3- to 6-feet thick overlying the tundra.

Ulu

A traditional Eskimo woman's knife designed for scraping and chopping,

this fan-shaped tool was originally made of stone with a bone handle. Today, an ulu is often shaped from an old saw blade and a wood handle is attached.

Umiak

An umiak is a traditional Eskimo skin-covered boat, whose design has changed little over the centuries. Although the umiak is mostly powered by outboard motors today, paddles are still used when stalking game and when ice might damage the propeller. Because umiaks must often be pulled for long distances over the ice, the boats are designed to be lightweight and easily repairable. The frames are wood, often driftwood found on the beaches, and the covering can be sewn should it be punctured. The bottom is flat and the keel is bone, which prevents the skin from wearing out as it is pulled over the ice.

Female walrus skins are the preferred covering because they are the proper thickness when split (bull hides are too thick) and because it only takes two to cover a boat. However, sometimes female walrus skins are unavailable, so the Eskimos substitute skins of the bearded seal, or *oogruk*. But *oogruk* skins are smaller and it takes six or seven skins to cover an umiak.

Once the skins are stretched over the frame and lashed into place, the outside is painted with marine paint for waterproofing. Historically, the skin would have been anointed with seal oil or other fats, but the modern waterproofing is now universally accepted because it does not have to be renewed after each trip.

Umiak is the Inupiat word for skin boat and is commonly used by the coastal Eskimos throughout Alaska. The Saint Lawrence Islanders, however, speak the Yup'ik dialect and their word for skin boat is *angyaq*.

Universities and Colleges

Higher education in Alaska is provided by the University of Alaska system and private institutions. The university system includes three multicampus universities, one community college and a network of service for rural Alaska. University of Alaska institutions enroll more than 30,000 people each year.

The three regional institutions are the University of Alaska Anchorage, which includes Kenai Peninsula College, Kodiak College, Matanuska–Susitna College and Prince William Sound Community College; University of Alaska Fairbanks with campuses in Bethel, Dillingham, Kotzebue and Nome; and University of Alaska Southeast with campuses in Juneau, Ketchikan and Sitka. These schools offer developmental, certificate, associate, baccalaureate and graduate degree programs. Student housing is available in Anchorage, Bethel, Fairbanks and Juneau.

University of Alaska Fairbanks research facilities include the Agricultural and Forestry Experiment Station, Arctic Research Consortium of the United States (ARCUS), Center for Cross-Cultural Studies, Center for Global Change & Arctic System Research, Geophysical Institute, Juneau Center for Fisheries and Ocean Sciences, Mineral Industry Research and Petroleum Development laboratories, Office of Sponsored Programs, University of Alaska Museum, Institutes of Arctic Biology, Marine Science and Northern Engineering, Polar Ice Coring Office, and Water Research Center.

The University of Alaska Anchorage is the home of the Alaska Center for International Business, Arctic Environmental Information & Data Center, Institute for Circumpolar Health Studies, Institute for Social and Economic Research, Justice Center, and centers for Alcohol and Addiction Studies, High Latitude Health Research, Economic Education, and Information Technology.

Through the university's Cooperative Extension Service and Marine Advisory Program, research results are interpreted and transferred to people of the state.

For information on state colleges and universities, contact the following institutions:

University of Alaska Anchorage, 3211 Providence Drive, Anchorage 99508: **Kenai Peninsula College,** 34820 College Drive, Soldotna 99669; **Kodiak College,** 117 Benny Benson Drive, Kodiak 99615; **Matanuska–Susitna College,** P.O. Box 2889, Palmer 99645; **Prince William Sound Community College,** P.O. Box 97, Valdez 99686

University of Alaska Fairbanks, Fairbanks 99775: **Bristol Bay Campus,** P.O. Box 1070, Dillingham 99576; **Chukchi Campus,** P.O. Box 297, Kotzebue 99752; **Interior Campus,** 4280 Geist Road, Fairbanks 99775; **Kuskokwim Campus,** P.O. Box 368, Bethel 99559; **Northwest Campus,** Pouch 400, Nome 99762

University of Alaska Southeast, Juneau Campus, 11120 Glacier Highway, Juneau 99801: **Ketchikan Campus,** Seventh and Madison, Ketchikan 99901; **Sitka Campus,** 1332 Seward Ave., Sitka 99835

For information on private institutions of higher learning, contact the following:
Alaska Bible College, P.O. Box 289, Glennallen 99588
Alaska Pacific University, 4101 University Drive, Anchorage 99508
Sheldon Jackson College, 801 Lincoln St., Sitka 99835

Many additional schools and institutes in Alaska offer religious, vocational and technical study. For a complete listing of these and other schools, write for the *Directory of Postsecondary Educational Institutions in Alaska,* Alaska Commission on Postsecondary Education, P.O. Box FP, Juneau 99811.

Volcanoes

The state's 10 tallest volcanic peaks, nearly all of which are known to have erupted within the last 10,000 years (information from the Smithsonian Institution and the Alaska Volcano Observatory), are as follows:

Fairbanks ○

❶ Mount Wrangell

❷ Mount Spurr
❸ Redoubt Volcano
Anchorage
❹ Iliamna Volcano

❿ Mount Denison
❾ Mount Griggs

❻ Pavlof Volcano
❼ Mount Veniaminof
❺ Shishaldin
❽ Isanotski Peaks

Map Key

1 Mount Wrangell, 14,163 feet
2 Mount Spurr, 11,070 feet
3 Redoubt Volcano, 10,197 feet
4 Iliamna Volcano, 10,016 feet
5 Shishaldin Volcano, 9,372 feet
6 Pavlof Volcano, 8,261 feet
7 Mount Veniaminof, 8,225 feet
8 Isanotski Peaks, 8,025 feet
9 Mount Griggs, 7,600+ feet
10 Mount Denison, 7,500+ feet

Volcanoes on the Aleutian Islands, the Alaska Peninsula and in the Wrangell Mountains are part of the "Ring of Fire" that surrounds the Pacific Ocean basin. There are more than 80 potentially active volcanoes in Alaska, about half of which have had at least one eruption since 1760, the date of earliest recorded eruptions. Pavlof Volcano is one of the most active of Alaskan volcanoes, having had more than 41 reported eruptions since 1760. One recent spectacular eruption of Pavlof in April 1986 sent ash 10 miles high, causing black snow to fall on Cold Bay. The eruption of Augustine

Volcano (elev. 4,025 feet) in lower Cook Inlet on March 27, 1986, sent ash 8 miles high and disrupted air traffic in southcentral Alaska for several days. Most recently, Mount Redoubt erupted on Dec. 14, 1989, its first eruption since 1968. The biggest eruptions sent ash throughout most of southcentral Alaska and disrupted air traffic. Periodic eruptions occurred from December 1989 to April 1990. Mount Spurr erupted in June, August and September 1992. Anchorage received the brunt of the ash fallout from the August eruption, which halted air traffic out of the city for several day. It was briefly interrupted again with the September eruption.

The most violent Alaskan eruption recorded occurred over a 60-hour period in June 1912 from Novarupta Volcano. The eruption darkened the sky over much of the Northern Hemisphere for several days, deposited almost a foot of ash on Kodiak, 100 miles away, and filled the Valley of Ten Thousand Smokes (now contained within Katmai National Park) with more than 2.5 cubic miles of ash during its brief but extremely explosive duration.

Waves

(*See also* Earthquakes; Bore Tide; *and* Tides)

Alaska's seismic history is very short, yet extremely active. Alaska responds to movement in the Aleutian–Alaska megathrust zone, where the edge of the Pacific plate descends under the North American plate. These vertical movements of the earth's crust result in vertical motion of the sea floor, which can produce great tsunamis. In fact, these crustal movements in the Alaska Peninsula, Aleutians and Gulf of Alaska can produce Pacific-wide tsunamis.

In southeastern Alaska, the Fairweather Fault lies inland. Though this fault has not triggered tectonic tsunamis as in other Alaskan areas, it can trigger nearby underwater landslides, which can cause tsunamis, even without an earthquake.

According to the Alaska Tsunami Warning Center in Palmer, Alaska has had seven tsunamis that caused fatalities in recorded history. These were of local origin and occurred between 1788 and 1964. Tsunamis originating in Alaska Pacific waters have caused all of the fatalities reported on the West Coast and in Alaska, and most of those in Hawaii. The most recent tsunami was in 1964 following the March 27, Good Friday earthquake. That wave completely destroyed three Alaskan villages before reaching Washington, Oregon and California, and continued to cause damage as far away as Hawaii, Chile and Japan.

Tsunami is taken from the Japanese words "tsu" meaning harbor and "nami" meaning great wave. Although often called tidal waves, tsunamis are not caused by tides. Generated by earthquakes occurring on or below the sea floor, tsunamis can race across the Pacific Ocean at speeds up to 600 miles per hour. Tsunamis rarely cross the Atlantic. Traveling across the open ocean, the waves are only a few feet high and can be up to 100 miles from crest to crest. They cannot be seen from an airplane or felt in a ship at sea. Once they approach shore, however, shallower water causes the waves to grow taller by increasingly restricting their forward motion. Thus, a 2-foot wave traveling 500 miles per hour in deep water becomes a 100-foot killer at 30 miles per hour as it nears the shore. The wave action of a tsunami can repeat every 15 to 30 minutes and the danger for a given area is generally not considered over until the area has been free from damaging waves for two hours.

Providing information, and timely warnings, on tsunamigenic earthquakes (those quakes measuring above 7.0 on the Richter scale and lasting 30 seconds or longer) is the job of the Alaska Tsunami Warning Center (ATWC), located in Palmer. Established in 1967, the ATWC now makes loss of life unnecessary for Alaska, Canada and the West Coast of the United States, and ensures the avoidance of such a tragedy as the April 1, 1946, earthquake at Scotch Cap on Unimak Island, Alaska. Within minutes after the quake struck, waves measuring 100 feet high completely destroyed the lighthouse on the island, killing five people. In less than five hours, the first wave hit Hawaii, killing 159 people. More recently, in

March 1985, after an 8.1 quake in Chile, tsunami warnings alerted coastal Alaskans in plenty of time to take precautionary measures. Normally, tsunamis from remote Pacific sources will not be destructive in Alaska.

Another type of wave action that occurs in Alaska is a seiche. A seiche is a long, rhythmic wave in a closed or partially closed body of water. Caused by earthquakes, winds, tidal currents or atmospheric pressure, the motion of a seiche resembles the back and forth movement of a tipped bowl of water. The water moves only up and down, and can remain active from a few minutes to several hours. The highest recorded wave in Alaska, 1,740 feet, was the result of a seiche that took place in Lituya Bay on July 9, 1958. This unusually high wave was due to an earthquake-induced landslide that cleared trees from the opposite side of the bay.

Whales and Whaling

(*See also* Baleen)

Fifteen species of both toothed and baleen whales are found in Alaskan waters. Baleen refers to the hundreds of strips of flexible bonelike material that hangs from the gum of the upper jaw. The strips are fringed and act as strainers that capture krill, the tiny shrimplike organisms upon which the whales feed. Once the baleen fills with krill, whales force water back out through the sides of their mouth, swallowing the food left behind. Baleen whale cows are usually larger than bulls.

Baleen whales that inhabit Alaskan waters include blue, bowhead, northern right, fin or finback, humpback, sei, minke or little piked and gray. Toothed whales include sperm, beluga, killer, pilot, beaked (three species), dolphins (two species) and porpoises (two species). Another toothed whale, the narwhal, a full-time resident of the Arctic, is almost never seen in Alaskan waters. Saint Lawrence Islanders call narwhals *bousucktugutalik*, or "beluga with tusk," due to a tusk that grows from the left side of the upper jaw on bulls only. Spiraling in a left-hand direction, the tusk can reach lengths of 7 to 8 feet on an adult.

A few facts on three of the whales indigenous to Alaska, and the whales residents and tourists are most likely to see in Alaska's waters, are interesting to note. According to the Alaska Department of Fish and Game, gray whales have the distinction of being the most primitive of the living *mysticete* ("moustached") or baleen whales. They can regularly be observed in large numbers from Alaskan shores, and are found in the North Pacific Ocean and adjacent waters of the Arctic Ocean. There are two geographically isolated stocks: the Korean or western Pacific stock, and the California or eastern Pacific stock. The California stock migrates between Baja California and the Bering and Chukchi seas, a round-trip distance of 10,000 miles, and the longest migration of any marine mammal.

Grays are mottled gray in color and covered with scars, abrasions and clusters of parasitic barnacles that are most abundant on their heads and backs, the parts that are exposed to air when they breathe.

The estimated daily consumption of an adult gray whale is about 2,600 pounds. In the approximately five months spent in Alaskan waters, one whale eats about 396,000 pounds of food, primarily amphipod crustaceans. Gray whales feed on the bottom by sucking tube-dwelling amphipods out of the sandy sediment and leaving large oval feeding imprints behind. Scientists can study these imprints and gain knowledge about the feeding habits of these whales. Muddy feeding trails are often seen when gray whales surface after feeding dives. Gray whales were called "devil fish" by early whalers because they were so aggressive and protective of their young when hunted.

Adult grays are about 36 to 50 feet long and weigh from 16 to 45 tons, with females larger than males at any given age. They have been known to live up to 70 years, but the average lifespan is 40 to 50 years.

The beluga, or white whale, belongs to the *odontocetes* ("toothed") group, which includes sperm and killer whales, dolphins and porpoises. Its closest relative is the narwhal. Belugas range widely in arctic and subarctic waters,

and two populations occur in Alaska. The Cook Inlet population can be found in the inlet and in the Shelikof Straits region, although some belugas have been seen east to Yakutat Bay and west to Kodiak Island. Belugas of the Western Arctic population range throughout the Bering, Chukchi and Beaufort seas. These whales winter in the ice of the Bering Sea, moving in summer over 1,500 miles to concentrated areas along the coast from Bristol Bay to the Mackenzie River delta in northwestern Canada. In Alaska, major concentrations occur in the Bristol Bay area, Norton Sound, Kotzebue Sound and Kasegaluk Lagoon. In Bristol Bay, they sometimes swim more than 100 miles per day.

Belugas are very vocal animals, producing a variety of grunts, clicks, chirps and whistles, which are used for navigating, finding prey and communicating. Because of their talkative nature, they were called "sea canaries" by whalers. Belugas are also masters of echolocation, using their sophisticated sonar to detect fish and to navigate in shallow waters or among gill nets without getting stranded. In some areas, they may dive more than 1,000 feet to feed on the bottom. At birth, belugas are dark blue-gray in color, lightening to white by the age of five or six. Adult males are 11 to 16 feet long and weigh 1,000 to 2,000 pounds; adult females are smaller, reaching 12 feet in length. Belugas can live up to 40 years.

Killer whales, also known as orcas, or wolves of the sea, are carnivorous cetaceans. They range from the Beaufort Sea to Antarctica and are most abundant off the Aleutians. It is thought that killers migrate, riding cold currents south in the winter. The most unusual feature of the killer whale is the high dorsal fin on its back, which has no muscle, but may serve the whale as a keel would a boat. The fin on older males can grow to six feet in height.

Killers are thought to be very intelligent and to possess all mammalian senses except smell. To sleep, they take catnaps on the surface of the water, and they hunt in pods using complex, cooperative patterns in an attack. Prey includes sea lions, salmon, seals, porpoises, halibut, shark, squid, belugas and other whales. Male killer whales average 23 feet in length, with females being smaller. Average lifespan is 30 to 40 years.

Whaling

Bowhead whales have been protected from commercial whaling by the Convention for the Regulation of Whaling of 1931, the International Convention for the Regulation of Whaling of 1947, the Marine Mammal Protection Act of 1972, the Endangered Species Act of 1973, and the Convention of International Trade in Endangered Species of Wild Fauna and Flora.

Commercial whaling for gray whales has been banned by the International Convention for the Regulation of Whaling since 1947. These conventions and acts have, however, allowed for a subsistence harvest by Alaska Indians, Aleut and Eskimo.

Since 1978, the International Whaling Commission (IWC) has regulated the take of bowheads by establishing an annual catch limit for Alaska Eskimo. Also in 1978, the IWC reclassified the eastern stock of gray whales from a protected species to a sustained management stock with an annual catch limit of about 179 whales, based on the average known removals during the period 1968–77. The entire catch limit has been reserved for taking by Natives or by member governments on behalf of Natives.

Other species of large baleen whales, such as minke and fin whales, are occasionally taken by Alaska Eskimos for food. It is not necessary to report gray and minke harvests. The only toothed whale taken by Eskimo is the beluga and its harvest is monitored by the Alaska and Inuvialuit Beluga Whale Committee (AIBWC), which is currently developing a management plan.

According to the National Marine Mammal Laboratory and the Alaska Department of Fish and Game, harvest figures for beluga whales for the years 1979–1991 are as follows:

Year	Beluga
1980	233–245*
1981	179–231*
1982	307–354*
1983	226–236*
1984	186–211
1985	256–352
1986	174–191
1987	133–190*
1988	352–388*
1989	229–259*
1990	217–*
1991	50*

*Approximate figures

Wildflowers

Wildflowers in Alaska are seldom gaudy; they are usually rather small and delicate. More than 1,500 plant species occur in the state, including trees, shrubs, ferns, grasses and sedges, as well as flowering plants.

Alpine regions are particularly rich in flora and some of the alpine species are rare. Anywhere there is tundra there is apt to be a bountiful population of flowers. The Steese Highway (Eagle Summit), Richardson Highway (Thompson Pass), Denali Highway (MacLaren Summit), Denali National Park and Preserve (Polychrome Pass), Seward Highway (Turnagain Pass), Glenn Highway just north of Anchorage (Eklutna Flats) and a locale near Wasilla (Hatcher Pass) are wonderful wildflower-viewing spots. These are all readily accessible by car. Less easily accessible floral Edens are some of the Aleutian Islands, Point Hope, Anvil Mountain and the Nome-Teller Road (both near Nome), Pribilof Islands and other remote areas.

Alaska's official flower, the forget-me-not (*Myosotis alpestris*), is a delicate little beauty found throughout much of the state in alpine meadows and along streams. Growing to 18 inches tall, forget-me-nots are recognized by their bright blue petals surrounding a yellow "eye." A northern "cousin," the arctic forget-me-not (*Eritrichium aretioides*), grows in sandy soil on the tundra, or in the mountains, and reaches only 4 inches in height.

Related reading: *Discovering Wild Plants: Alaska, Western Canada, the Northwest,* by Janice Schofield. Descriptions, historical uses, harvest information and recipes of more than 130 plants. Full color photographs and drawings. *The Alaska–Yukon Wild Flowers Guide,* edited by Helen A. White. An invaluable information source on Alaska's wildflowers. *See* ALASKA NORTHWEST LIBRARY in the back of the book.

Winds

Some of Alaska's windiest weather has been recorded on the western islands of the Aleutian chain. Overall, the causes are the same as elsewhere, incorporating planet rotation and the tendency of the atmosphere to equalize the difference between high and low pressure fronts (*See also* Climate). A few winds occur often and significantly enough to be given names: chinook, taku and williwaws.

Chinook

Old-timers describe chinook winds as unseasonably warm winds that can cause thaw in the middle of winter. What they also cause are power outages and property damage, especially in the Anchorage bowl, where in recent years hundreds of homes have sprung up on the Chugach Mountain hillsides over which the chinook winds howl. One such wind occurred on April Fool's Day in 1980, causing $25 million in property damage and nominating the city as a disaster area. Parts of Anchorage were without power for 60 hours.

Until recently, it was not possible to predict the coming of a chinook wind. Today, however, Anchorage meteorologists can tell if the winds are gathering, when they will arrive and their relative strength. It was discerned that such a warm wind could only originate in Prince William Sound and that its speed had to be at least 55 miles per hour or faster just to cross the 3,500-foot Chugach Mountains. Other factors that need to be present are a storm near Bethel and relatively stable air over Anchorage. Meteorologists predict the coming of chinook winds 55 percent of the time.

Taku

Taku winds are the sudden, fierce gales that sweep down from the icecap behind Juneau and Douglas, and plague residents there. Takus are shivering cold winds capable of reaching 100 miles per hour. They have been known to send a 2-by-4 timber flying through the wall of a frame house.

Williwaws

Williwaws are sudden gusts of wind that can reach 113 miles per hour after the wind "builds up" on one side of a mountain and suddenly spills over into what may appear to be a relatively protected area. Williwaws are considered the bane of Alaska mariners. The term was originally applied to a strong wind in the Strait of Magellan.

World Eskimo–Indian Olympics

An audience of thousands watches the annual gathering of several hundred Native athletes from Alaska and the circumpolar nations competing in the World Eskimo–Indian Olympics (WEIO) in Fairbanks. Held over four days during the second-to-last weekend in July, the self-supporting games draw

participants from all of Alaska's Native populations (Eskimo, Aleut, Athabascan, Tlingit, Haida and Tsimshian). Canadian, Greenlandic and Soviet Eskimos are also invited to participate, as well as Natives from the contiguous 48 states.

Spectators thrill to the sight of such feats as the knuckle hop and the ear-weight competition. Other traditional Native sports and competitions include the greased pole walk, fish cutting, stick pull, Indian–Eskimo dancing, men's and women's blanket toss, and the spectacular two-foot and one-foot high kicks. Each year the judges choose a Native queen to reign over the four-day Olympics. She reigns through the year, making several appearances throughout the state, and represents the WEIO at the National Congress of American Indians. The judges also pick the most authentic Native costumes. Some of the more boisterous games include the lively white men/Native women tug of war and the muktuk-eating contest.

The games will be held on Wednesday, Thursday, Friday and Saturday evenings at the Big Dipper Recreation Arena in Fairbanks July 21–24, 1993. Advance tickets may be purchased from the World Eskimo–Indian Olympics Committee, P.O. Box 2433, Fairbanks 99707.

Yukon Quest International Sled Dog Race

(*See also* Dog Mushing *and* Iditarod Trail Sled Dog Race)

The Yukon Quest International Sled Dog Race was begun by Roger Williams and LeRoy Shank in November 1983, with the purpose of supporting a long-distance sled dog race of international character between Fairbanks, Alaska, and Whitehorse, Yukon Territory. The first race took place in February 1984, with 26 teams competing, and had a purse of $50,000.

Named for the old-time "Highway of the North," the Yukon River, the 1,000-mile trek takes between 11 and 14 days to complete, depending on the weather. During their journey between the two cities, the teams retrace the footsteps of Gold Rush trappers, miners, explorers and missionaries. They cross four major summits, over diverse and challenging terrain, travel 250 miles on the frozen Yukon River and cross the longest unguarded international border in the world.

The direction of the race alternates each year, and between the start and (Continued on page 193)

Winners and Times

Year	Musher	Days	Hrs.	Min.	Prize
1984	Sonny Lindner, Johnson River	12	00	05	$15,000
1985	Joe Runyan, Nenana	11	11	55	15,000
1986	Bruce Johnson	14	09	17	15,000
1987	Bill Cotter, Nenana	12	04	34	15,000
1988	David Monson	12	05	06	20,000
1989	Jeff King, Denali	11	20	51	20,000
1990	Vern Halter, Trapper Creek	11	17	09	20,000
1991	Charlie Boulding, Nenana	10	21	12	25,000
1992	John Schandelmeier, Paxson	11	21	40	29,837

1992 Results

Place	Musher	Days	Hrs.	Min.	Prize*
1	John Schandelmeier, Paxson	11	21	40	$29,837
2	Sonny Lindner, Fairbanks	11	23	10	20,270
3	Charlie Boulding, Nenana	12	01	38	15,202
4	Linda Forsberg, Denali Park	12	01	45	10,135
5	David Sawatzky, Healy	12	04	01	6,587
6	Frank Turner, Pelly Crossing, YT	12	07	06	4,054
7	Peter Butteri, Tok	12	14	42	3,040
8	John Peep, Fairbanks	13	08	30	2,280
9	John Gourley, Healy	13	10	40	2,128

1992 Results (continued)

Place	Musher	Days	Hrs.	Min.	Prize*
10	Tim Mowry, Fairbanks	13	10	59	1,925
11	Lucy Nordlum, Kotzebue	13	12	55	1,722
12	Jeffrey Mann, Fairbanks	13	18	35	1,520
13	Jack Berry, Anchor Point	14	05	40	1,317
14	Ned Cathers, Whitehorse, YT	14	07	40	1,114
15	Jennine Cathers, Whitehorse, YT	14	16	34	912
16	Jim Kublin, Marquette, MI	16	00	30	850
17	Jeff Bouton, Fairbanks	16	01	00	800
18	George Cook, Ashland, NH	16	03	19	750

*The top 20 finishers were designated to receive prize money. However, only 18 mushers finished the race. The money from the other two places was re-apportioned among the mushers who finished.

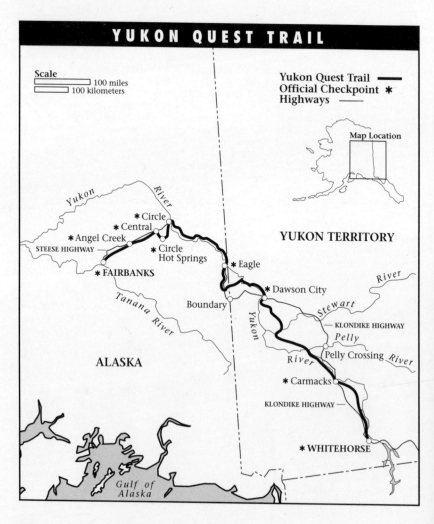

(Continued from page 191)
finish lines, there are nine official checkpoints. The shortest distance between checkpoints is 10 miles, from Central to Circle Hot Springs, and the longest distance between checkpoints is 290 miles, from Dawson City to Carmacks. The only checkpoint at which a musher may receive help of any kind is at Dawson City, where a 36-hour layover is mandatory. Rules allow for eight dogs minimum and 12 dogs maximum at the start. Five dogs are the minimum allowed at the finish, and only four dogs can be dropped during the course of the race. Each musher may use only one sled throughout the race, and mandatory equipment includes a sleeping bag, hand ax, snowshoes, promotional material and eight booties per dog.

Yearly Highlights, 1991 and 1992

The following is a collection of the more significant news events from mid-1991 to mid-1992 . . . the high spots for a record of the times. FACTS ABOUT ALASKA: THE ALASKA ALMANAC® wishes to credit the Anchorage Daily News, the Anchorage Times and the Fairbanks News–Miner as the primary sources of information for Yearly Highlights.

Iditarod Musher Saved From Life-Threatening Storm

A fierce storm along the Bering Sea coast in March 1992 trapped several mushers competing in the Iditarod Trail Sled Dog Race.

Bob Hickel, a musher racing in his second Iditarod, turned back to help fellow-musher and friend, Bob Ernisse, caught in the storm between White Mountain and Safety. Frostbite and hypothermia hit Ernisse quickly as he became trapped between checkpoints by heavy snows and high winds.

Hickel, son of Alaska Gov. Walter J. Hickel, and Robin Thomas, a resident of Nome, came to Ernisse's aid and carried him by sled to the Safety checkpoint.

Ernisse, the only one of the five mushers trapped in the storm that didn't finish the race, was taken to Nome's hospital. Ernisse vowed to try the competition again.

Kodiak School District Adds Alutiiq to Its Curriculum

This year Kodiak High School and the village schools in Akhiok and Old Harbor have added one of Alaska's Native languages—Alutiiq—to the district roster.

The language program, funded by an $80,000 federal grant, was obtained by the Kodiak Area Native Association. And learning Alutiiq will be like learning any other foreign language, such as French or Japanese, but with interactive videos and computers as study aids.

Junior High Tabloid Garners National Honors

The Falcon Flash, the school newspaper published by Clark Junior High School in Anchorage, won the honor as the most outstanding intermediate school newspaper for 1992 by the American Scholastic Press Association.

The newspaper's story on sexual harassment was heralded as an outstanding non-school story, and was selected from more than 1,000 entries from junior high schools, high schools and colleges across the country. Shana Price and Lamond Venning, both in eighth grade, wrote the story during Clarence Thomas's Supreme Court confirmation hearing.

Bride and Groom Celebrate Unusual Ceremony in Nome

Though it wasn't exactly the winter wedding in Nome the newlyweds had hoped for, it was special anyway. The couple had wanted to be married on a Bering Sea ice floe on the international dateline between the Diomede Islands, but the ice just wasn't thick enough.

So on Jan. 26, 1992, Takako Takano and Junichi Ohmae, of Japan, settled on the next best thing. They tied the knot bedecked in hiking boots, parkas and mukluks on the ice and snow behind Nome's Country Store. The officiator of the marriage wore a rainbow-colored caftan.

Takano and Ohmae have a history for loving the unusual. She's already parachuted over the North Pole, canoed along the Amazon River and joined a Soviet ski team that crossed the dateline. His job as bureau chief of a Japanese newspaper has already taken him to the South Pole.

What next? The wedding reception, of course. The couple invited their guests to don hiking gear and bring sleeping bags to celebrate at a reception in a camp near Mount Fujiyama in May 1992.

Aleuts Remember 50-Year-Anniversary of Internment

In June 1942, about 880 Aleuts from Alaska were taken from their villages and interned in Southeast Alaska. Unlike Japanese–Americans, the Aleuts were not interned because of their racial heritage, but rather because their homes on the Aleutian and Pribilof islands were in the World War II war zone.

Some villages planned to commemorate the 50-year anniversary of this little-known event in U.S. history with ceremonies, reported the director of the Aleutian–Pribilof Island Association, Dimitri Philemonof. The association is also in the process of raising money to film a documentary on the internment in hopes of getting this part of Alaskan and American history recorded.

Mudslides Wreak Havoc for Residents of Kodiak

Leave it to Mother Nature to choose Halloween to wreak havoc on Kodiak. More than 8 inches of rain was reported to have besieged Kodiak on Thursday, Oct. 30, 1991, causing flash floods, mudslides and the evacuation of about 150 residents from most of the 50 homes in the downtown hillside area. Mudslides ripped houses from foundations and sent them sliding downhill. Fortunately, no one was seriously injured.

The resilient residents of Kodiak were busily getting homes and lives back to normal within hours of the catastrophe. Borough and city officials reported initial property damage to be about $5 million. To help get funding to get Kodiak back together, Gov. Walter J. Hickel declared Kodiak a disaster area two days after the mudslides.

Two Sisters Remain Sole Speakers of Eyak Language

Sophie Borodkin, 80, and sister Marie Smith, 72, are the last remaining Natives who can speak the Eyak language.

Eyak is one of the 20 Native languages in Alaska, 16 of which risk extinction because the Native children are not learning the languages of their elders.

Michael Krauss, director of the Alaska Native Language Center at the University of Alaska Fairbanks, believes the fault lies with the public school system, English-language broadcasts on television and radio, as well as religious and secular notions that Native languages aren't important. Krauss and his team are working to preserve all 20 languages.

To aid the effort to preserve Alaska's Native languages, Sen. Frank Murkowski sponsored a bill in Congress that would provide $2.5 million annually for five years for grants to Native villages and Native regional corporations established by the 1971 Alaska Native Claims Settlement Act. The funds, to begin in 1992, would finance language centers, language training and media centers encouraging the use of Native languages.

Anchorage Police Shoot Grizzly Roaming Downtown

A grizzly bear, weighing about 500 pounds, was killed by Alaska Department of Fish and Game biologists as he wandered through parts of downtown Anchorage in October 1991.

The 3-year-old chocolate-brown grizzly attracted hundreds of interested bystanders. So many in fact, that wildlife officials said there was no safe avenue to steer the bear naturally out of the city. One radio station was giving up-to-the-minute reports on the bear's whereabouts, which seemed to increase the number of bear-watchers. Biologists were concerned about what the bear might do if it were cornered.

Biologists had hoped to tranquilize the bear, but the procedure was deemed too risky. According to biologist Dave Harkness, the tranquilizer darts don't always penetrate a bear's thick, winter coat, and even if one did, it may take up to 5 minutes for the tranquilizer to work.

Anchorage Physical Education Teacher Wins National Award

Bonnie Hooper, a physical education teacher at O'Malley Elementary School in Anchorage, won top honors as the National Physical Education Teacher of the Year for 1992.

Hooper, who uses everything from parachutes to hula hoops in her classes, not only took the award from the National Association of Sports and Physical Fitness, but she met Arnold Schwarzenegger. The actor, best known for his roles as the supremely fit "Terminator," is the head of the President's Council on Physical Fitness. He congratulated Hooper on her accomplishments and promised to visit her when he next travels to Anchorage. Schwarzenegger already visited Anchorage in October 1991.

Hooper is also a finalist for the Disney Salute to Teachers award, as one of the top five teachers in the physical education category.

The Disney Channel planned to film Hooper and her class for a show.

Open Season on Bears

It was not a good year for bears across Alaska, at least those who were caught rummaging through garbage or wandering within city limits in 1991.

In fact, several concerned citizens in Juneau formed "Save Our Bear" in early 1992, a group dedicated to help educate residents about garbage and litter regulations in the hope of preventing the slaughter of problem bears. The group also plans to hire personnel to tranquilize problem bears and fly the bears out of the city to more remote areas.

Last year, authorities were forced to kill 15 garbage-rummaging bears. Another 6 bears were killed by cars, and there were numerous reports of minor injuries from bear-people encounters as well as aggressive behavior by bears.

The Nuggets in Them Thar Hills Aren't Gold

Big business cashed in on yet another of Alaska's natural resources—moose nuggets. A *Wall Street Journal* article appearing in August 1991 touted this prevalent Alaskan commodity as a "hot" item to buy when visiting the Last Frontier.

Crafty entrepreneurs have taken the nuggets from forest trails to the assembly line. As soon as Kathy Parker copyrighted her moose nugget-topped swizzle sticks, others quickly began cashing in on this natural success.

These moose nuggets adorn tie tacks, swizzle sticks, lip balm, key chains, earrings and necklaces. Seasonal delights range from Mother's Day favorite Tundra No. 5 perfume, which is actually moose nuggets in a bag, to the Yuletide Moozletoe. And there are even some related delectible edibles.

Karen Underwood, who owns a candy shop called Tundra Chocolates in Eagle River, has created a chocolate moose nugget look-alike (made without any moose additives). Last August alone, Underwood reported that brisk sales of the all-natural nuggets topped 55 pounds.

Native Author Lauded for Newest Work

Peter Kalifornsky, a self-taught Dena'ina Athabascan author and ethnographer, drew rave reviews from anthropologists, Alaskans and scholars nationwide for his book, *A Dena'ina Legacy, K'tl'egh'i Sukdu.*

The book, published in 1992 by the Alaska Native Language Center at the University of Alaska Fairbanks, is a selection of 147 of the stories, poems and language lessons that Kalifornsky has been writing for 20 years.

Kalifornsky, born in 1911, received help compiling and editing the book from Jim Kari, associate professor of linguistics at the University of Alaska Fairbanks; and Alan Boraas, associate professor of anthropology at Kenai Peninsula College. To date, the book has been nominated for this year's American Book Award.

Tundra Times Closes Its Doors

The *Tundra Times*, Alaska's weekly

newspaper that became a unifying force in the Alaskan Native community and a Native voice to state and federal lawmakers for more than 20 years, published its last edition on Dec. 23, 1991.

With founder Howard Rock, the *Tundra Times* helped mold the Alaska Native Claims Settlement Act, as well as keeping a spotlight on Native interests in federal and state legislation over the years.

The demise of the newspaper is thought to be due, in part, to better overall communication and information systems that link rural Alaska and the rest of the world, and less dependence on the *Tundra Times* for information in the Bush.

At press time, however, Alaska Newspapers Inc. had entered into negotiations to buy and re-establish the *Tundra Times*.

Alaska Highway Rates Listing on Federal Travel Advisory

The U.S. State Department in February 1992 placed the Alaska Highway on the federal travel advisory, a listing that advises U.S. citizens of dangerous travel destinations. But it didn't take long for the State Department to revise the warning.

This emergency advisory, which was issued during the 50th anniversary year of the Alaska Highway, warned travelers about the "inhospitable" conditions along the length of the 1,520-mile highway. The Alaska Highway warning shared the same taped telephone hotline message as an outbreak of meningococcal disease in eastern Canada and the perils of war-torn Iraq and Yugoslavia.

Officials in Alaska and Canada, who had been preparing for the year-long celebrations in honor of the Alaska Highway, objected strongly to the advisory and demanded that the State Department's warning be changed, which it was just a short time later.

Villagers Vote to Move Entire Town of Kivalina

The townspeople of Kivalina, bordering the Chukchi Sea in northwestern Alaska, voted 74–7 in March 1992 to move their town.

The 140-year-old village of about 300 people lies on a narrow coastal spit. Not only has the town outgrown its small natural confines, but the arctic waters are eroding its shores at a rate of two feet each year.

Each spring, melting snow causes water levels to rise, cutting off the village from the mainland.

Kivalina, which began as a seasonal Native fishing and hunting camp, has homes, a school, a small airport, a Native food store, some electricity, no running water, and no sewage system. Most of the village's residents live by subsistence hunting and fishing.

The chief obstacle in actually moving the village is money. Officials report that a request of $250,000 has been made from the state capital budget to study the feasibility of such a move.

Anchorage Deemed Second-Most Livable City

Anchorage was listed in the No. 2 spot, behind Honolulu, HI, according to a new book touting the nation's 100 most livable cities.

Author John Tepper Marlin used life expectancy as the foremost indicator to rank the top 100 cities in his book, *The Livable Cities Almanac.*

Marlin rated the Northeast at the bottom, with New York City placing 89th and Buffalo, NY, last. Overall, the Northeast, says Marlin, has more people dying faster.

A healthier diet helped place Honolulu and Anchorage in the top two positions, the author said, citing the fact that people in both these cities eat more fish than does the rest of the nation.

The top 10 cities on Marlin's list were: Honolulu; Anchorage; Denver; Charlotte, NC; Bridgeport–Stamford, CT; Washington, D.C.; Salt Lake City, UT; Seattle; Miami, FL; Sacramento, CA.

Reindeer Falls in Love With Bulldozer

In the fall of 1991, a young reindeer, who had been separated from the rest of its herd outside Nome, fell head over hoof for a yellow bulldozer along the Nome–Council Highway.

The year-old reindeer didn't fall for just any old bulldozer. It was a 1969 D6

Caterpillar. For three weeks, the reindeer slept next to the bulldozer, crawled under it during the rain, and even licked some old mud off its shovel.

State biologist Bob Nelson is worried about the reindeer's survival. Reindeer, like caribou, are social creatures, reported Nelson, adding that it is very important that the animals stay in a group. But even he is stumped about the reindeer's infatuation with the bulldozer.

However, the romance was doomed from the start, since the state Department of Transportation retires the Caterpillar into storage each year at the end of the fall. Nelson expressed the hope that the reindeer would eventually return to its herd.

Alaskan Schusses to Silver Victory in the Winter Olympics

Hilary Lindh's Olympic victory brought cheers from Meribel, France, all the way to her hometown of Juneau in February 1992.

Lindh's silver-medal win in the women's Olympic downhill marked the first-ever medallion for an Alaskan at the Winter Games and the third Olympic medal earned by an Alaskan.

The 22-year-old Lindh, who had been disqualified after missing a gate in the 1988 Olympics in Calgary, continued to gain momentum toward victory, prior to her silver win at the 1992 Games. She had placed fifth in three training runs just days before her win, and she seemed to hold the winning edge as the only Alaskan who had Olympic experience at these Games.

Two other Alaskans have won medals in the Olympics for team sports—Kris Thorsness of Anchorage won a gold medal on the 8-person rowing team at the 1984 Olympics in Los Angeles, and Andrea Lloyd of Sitka won a gold medal on the women's basketball team at the 1986 Games in Seoul, Korea.

Two Rivers in Southeast Listed As Top 10 Most Endangered

The Alsek and Tatshenshini rivers coursing through parts of Alaska and Canada were listed as two of the top 10 most endangered and threatened rivers of 1991, according to a list published by the American Rivers Association.

Both the Alsek and Tatshenshini rivers, which are situated in one of the world's most pristine wilderness regions, are threatened by the possible startup of an open pit copper mine.

Taxpayer Gives Sum to IRS, Down to the Last Penny

Agents at the Internal Revenue Service in Anchorage had their hands full in April 1992, when one taxpayer decided to pay his 1991 federal taxes in pennies—26,596 of them.

It took IRS agents more than four hours to count, roll and package the thousands of pennies totaling $265.96 from Brother Tom Patmore, who is a minister of the Universal Life Church and a resident of Clam Gulch.

The coppers weren't intended to try the patience of IRS agents. The pennies are simply a byproduct of his search for the rare 1943 all-copper "wheat" penny, which depicts a field of grain instead of the Lincoln Memorial on the flip side of the coin.

This wasn't the first time Patmore used pennies to pay a bill. He said he's paid his property taxes with them for four years, but ran into problems when Homer Electric Association refused to accept his pennies and cut off his power.

Buyers Have New Dreams for Fairbanks' Newspaper

The owners of Media News Inc., a publishing firm that owns interest in more than 65 daily and weekly newspapers nationwide, purchased the 90-year-old *Fairbanks News–Miner* newspaper in February 1992 for an undisclosed amount.

President William Dean Singleton and Chairman Richard Scudder, both of Media News Inc., reported after the sale that the *News-Miner* would be owned by Scudder's grandchildren and Singleton's children in family trusts, rather than by Media News Inc. itself.

According to *Forbes* magazine, Media News Inc.'s holdings are valued at more than $550 million, a figure which Singleton admits is actually a bit low. Among the newspapers owned by Media News are the *Dallas Times Herald,* the *Denver Post* and the *Houston Post.*

Rocket Launch a "Success" at Poker Flat

"Spirit II," a military research rocket that became the first guided missile launched at the Poker Flat Research Range near Fairbanks, was a roaring success, reported scientists at the center in spring 1992.

The 47-foot rocket's nine-minute flight in March recorded roughly seven-and-one-half minutes of data, while observing the infrared light from the northern lights. The rocket then landed, with the aid of a parachute, near Beaver, about 10 miles away from the launch pad.

Data from the launch, funded by the Air Force, may be of use in programming Strategic Defense Initiative satellites. The study of atmospheric conditions, such as the northern lights, may be helpful in determining whether an SDI satellite can spot the difference between an incoming warhead and naturally occurring phenomenon.

The University of Alaska runs the 5,100-acre Poker Flat Research Center, northeast of Fairbanks. During its 23 years of operation, more than 1,500 meteorological rockets have been launched by the center. Poker Flat is the only research facility of its kind in the country that is not administered by the federal government.

Anchorage Artist Hits the Big Time

Annabelle, one of two elephants at the Alaska Zoo, has taken the Anchorage art world by storm. This painting pachyderm creates abstract art with bright acrylics and has sold 23 works in the first two days of her exclusive opening in June 1991.

Some of Annabelle's works, such as *Trunk's Up* and *My Right Foot,* aren't selling for peanuts, either. At the low end of the scale are works for $125, and a 3-painting series commanded a price tag of $1,050.

Proceeds from Annabelle's artwork will be used for improvements for the Alaska Zoo, which is privately funded. However, some of the money is still needed to purchase painting supplies for Annabelle, as well as enormous amounts of butterscotch candies to soothe and entice the artist while she works.

It took weeks of encouragement, coaxing and teaching her not to eat the paintbrush before Annabelle felt comfortable at the drawing board. Elephant keeper David Hall reported that some days Annabelle is reluctant to pick up a brush at all, and other days, there's just no stopping her.

Alaska's Still Booming

Growth seems to be the buzzword for Alaska these days. According to data from the U.S. Census Bureau, the state of Alaska joined Nevada and Idaho as the country's fastest-growing states between April 1990 and July 1991.

The trend of the population moving to the South and West that began about 30 years ago continues into the 1990s. Alaska's population rose from 550,000 in 1990 to 570,000 in 1991, an increase of 3.7 percent. The U.S. population overall increased 1.4 percent during the same period.

Southeast Sets New Record for Annual Rainfall

Though Juneau has a reputation as one of the rainiest cities in the nation, the state's capital broke an all-time record for drizzle in 1991. In fact, it hadn't rained this much in 30 years.

More than 68 inches of rain fell on Juneau in 1991. The city's average annual rainfall is 53.13, compared to Anchorage's 15 inches a year and Seattle's average of 39 inches.

The rain, which has descended in a slow drizzle on about 6 out of every 10 days rather than quick downpours, has caused a stir in Juneau. "It drives people crazy, kind of like cabin fever," reported Lt. Robin Lown of the Alaska State Troopers, who added that tempers are shorter and people quickly grow tired of being cooped up.

Bars are also reported to be doing a brisk business this year. Other businesses, such as construction, have slowed as the rains created scheduling problems and lengthy delays.

But Juneau residents didn't suffer the agony of inclement weather alone. Annette broke a 30-year record for rain in 1991 with 132.06 inches. Kodiak also broke its record of 91.09 inches established in 1943, as the rain levels in 1991 rose to 96.09 inches.

In water-logged Sitka, even the tourist industry has been hit. At least 10 cruise ships bypassed the Southeast port this summer. Rob Allen, vice president of Allen Marine, estimated that loss at about 10,000 visitors. If each visitor spent an average of $60 in Sitka, that translates to about $600,000 less for the local economy.

Tourists Want to Know Truth About Alaska

With an estimated 700,000 visitors roaming around the state of Alaska in the summer of 1991, the Alaska Convention and Visitors Bureau attests to fielding some unusual questions. Dispeling some of the myths visitors have about Alaska is almost a full-time job.

Donna Hyatt, who has worked at the Log Cabin Visitor's Center on Fourth Avenue in Anchorage for the past 10 years, has a book filled with notes from staff members and the favorite questions of the day. For instance, visitors have wanted to find out about whale-watching tours on glass-bottom submarines; which restaurant in town sells whale meat; directions to the local nude beach; where to catch a bus to Dutch Harbor; when do the northern lights turn on; and even what time the next chairlift leaves to go to the top of Mount McKinley.

And the crew at Denali National Park, and those working at nearby restaurants, lodges and information booths, have collected a few notable gems of their own. Visitors have boldly asked when the next caribou parade goes by; what time the bears are scheduled to be let out; how the tundra is mowed; and what time the glaciers slide by.

Far North Launches Girl Scout Program

The North Slope Borough Assembly approved a $75,000 grant to help launch a Girl Scout program in northern Alaska.

The grant received the nod from the assembly after local mothers of 75 girls held a hearing in favor of starting a Girl Scout group in Barrow. The village of Kaktovik also has about 18 girls who are interested.

Esther Jeffrey, a mom of two girls

from Barrow, reported that the Girl Scout program in the Far North will be customized to learn about local culture, land and peoples. Ready to volunteer her services for the Girl Scouts, Jeffrey is arranging programs for Scouts to share information with local elders on cooking Native foods and sewing furs. Not to mention the added benefit of Girl Scout cookies in the North Slope Borough.

The North Slope Borough Assembly subsidizes the Boy Scouts, which has been active in the North for several years.

Tragedies Befall Adventurers on Northern Trek

Extreme cold, misfortune and bad press overshadowed four adventurers who set off in late October 1991 on a 3,059-mile journey by dog sled along the Northwest Passage.

The estimated 5-month trek to retrace the 1923 route of Danish explorer Knud Rasmussen, was led by Lonnie Dupre of Minnesota. Also on the trek was Tom Viren, of Minnesota, and biologists Malcolm Vance and Jon Nierenberg.

By December 1991, the expedition had lost its corporate sponsors and two members of the expedition, Viren and Nierenberg, quit after 19 of the 36 sled dogs died. The death of the animals caused animal rights groups and well-known Alaskan mushers to rally against the expedition, calling for Dupre to stop.

Vance and Dupre finished the trek, and arrived in Churchill, Manitoba, on April 25, 1992, with 15 dogs. They reported actually traveling 185 days, 64 of which were spent in complete darkness. Severe sunburn plagued the mushers on the final leg of their journey to Churchill.

The purpose of the expedition was to travel by dog team along the Northwest Passage to study cultural changes in Inuit villages previously visited by explorer Rasmussen, and to study Arctic flora and fauna, and the effects of pollution in the Far North.

Gov. Hickel Dedicates Bradley Lake Hydroelectric Project

After years of construction, the

Bradley Lake hydroelectric power project began providing energy to almost 75 percent of Alaska's population in September 1991.

Gov. Walter J. Hickel announced that the state's largest hydroelectric generating project near Homer "is clean and nonpolluting." Construction was lauded by environmental groups for its responsibility and concern for local wildlife.

The $312.5 million price tag for building the project will be shared by six utilities—Chugach Electric, Matanuska Electric Association, Golden Valley Association, Anchorage's Municipal Light and Power, Homer Electric Association and the city of Seward. In addition, the state will contribute about half of the funds with oil-revenue dollars.

Alaska Reindeer Herders Celebrate Centennial

The year of 1991 marked 100 years of reindeer herding in Alaska.

In 1891, the Rev. Sheldon Jackson, who was the general agent for education in Alaska, raised private funds to bring 16 reindeer from Siberia to the Unalaska Islands in the Aleutians. In 1892, 171 more reindeer were brought to Alaska. Jackson believed that Alaska Natives were destined for starvation if they weren't given some options for livelihood when wild game was scarce.

Reindeer continued to be imported from Siberia until 1902. The Alaska Natives were coached by Siberian and Lapp herders in the business of reindeer herding. By 1905, there were about 10,000 reindeer in Alaska.

Until 1937, Alaska Natives shared management and ownership of the herds with the U.S. government, Laplanders, church missions and the Lomen Co. But Congress agreed in the Reindeer Act of 1937 to allow Alaska Natives sole control of reindeer on their lands.

Today, there are about 25,000 reindeer on the Seward Peninsula and about 12,000 on Nunivak, Umnak and Hagemeister islands.

Recent Gold Finds Near Fairbanks Entice Prospectors

The gold rush days may be returning to Fairbanks in the very near future, according to findings from mineral strikes in the area.

Ester Dome, northwest of Fairbanks, has deposits that hint at sizable finds below its surface, similar to the 3.2-million ounces of gold reserves at Fort Knox gold mine on Murphy Dome, according to Gary Anselmo, president of the Silverado Mines Ltd., based in Vancouver, Canada.

Ester Dome is just one of 15 deposits that Silverado, with American Copper and Nickel Co., is exploring in a neighboring 15-square-mile area. Nearby, the Fort Knox mine, purchased for $200 million by Colorado-based Amax Gold Inc. in 1991, is expected to open in 1995, and pump between $60 and $70 million into the local economy.

Ketchikan Snags Top Spot on Cost-of-Living Index

It may be expensive to live in Alaska, but Ketchikan takes the all-time prize this year.

Ketchikan was rated 150.1 for the second quarter of 1991, according to a report by the American Chamber of Commerce Researchers Association. This rating reports that costs in Ketchikan are 50 percent higher than the average living costs in 300 communities across the country.

Alaska's city of Kodiak previously held the top distinction, with Ketchikan in the No. 2 position.

In the study, costs are compared for 59 products, as well as housing, utilities, transportation and health care. Some economists criticized the report, saying that it includes one-shot expenditures, such as moving or buying a home.

Other Alaskan cities rated in the study included Kodiak, with 147.6; Juneau, 138.8; and Anchorage, 131.

Movie Filmed in Kotzebue Receives Honors

Salmonberries, a movie filmed partially in Kotzebue, won the best film award at the 1991 Montreal World Film Festival.

German director Percy Adlon's film weaves a love story into a woman's search for identity. Canadian country singer k.d. lang plays a 20-year-old woman who is half-Inuit, half-white. She befriends a middle-aged librarian who has been living in Kotzebue after escaping from East Germany.

Salmonberries was selected the top film out of 22 contenders. Richard Gay, a vice president of the film festival, called the shots of Kotzebue "stunning," and admitted that "it's surely one of the reasons we chose the film."

Rare Pod of Dolphins Entertains Southeast Watchers

Approximately 2,000 white-sided dolphins made a rare appearance in Ketchikan in winter 1992, as their pod made its way along the Inside Passage.

Unusually warm weather was probably the reason for the dolphins' arrival, according to wildlife biologists. Pilot Steve Shrum reportedly was the first person to see the pod near Ship Island in late February. He said the dolphins enjoyed the local fishing at first, but the tables turned when several killer whales came to dine on the dolphins.

The dolphins seemed to enjoy Shrum's attention, as he landed in the midst of the pod in his floatplane. The dolphins, which can grow up to 8 feet long and can complete aerial somersaults as part of their play, entertained Shrum until he began taxiing for take-off. At that point, the dolphins tried to keep pace with the plane.

Alaska Bar Donates Wall to Charity

Some of the more popular bars in the wilds of Alaska share their simple character. The Call of the Wild, an eating and drinking establishment in Big Lake, is one place that shares the typical qualifications—a log cabin with sawdust strewn on the floor and a wall that has become a community endeavor.

At some places, customers affix business cards to the community wall; at another, it's underwear. But at the Call of the Wild, customers have signed and taped up dollar bills to cover the wall.

Last winter in 1991, owner Buddy Ray took off 9 years of "wallpaper," with the help of friends and patrons. Ray ended up with more than $1,600, which he donated to the Hospice of Alaska, a program providing counseling and care for families with terminally ill relatives.

Before beginning on the wallpaper-stripping project, Ray expressed some concern. "I just hope the building doesn't fall down when we take off all the tape," he said.

National Park Service Rejects Guiding Company's Appeal

James Ridenour, the director for the National Park Service, rejected an appeal from Genet Expeditions to allow the firm to guide mountaineers on Mount McKinley.

The National Park Service revoked Genet Expeditions' guiding permit in January 1991 because of "a continued pattern of unsafe practices observed and documented since 1988."

Genet Expeditions, the largest and best-known outfitter operating on Mount McKinley in Denali National Park, was originally formed in 1968 by Ray Genet. Since 1984, the guiding service has been owned by Harry Johnson, an Anchorage businessman.

The firm's permit was revoked after receiving marginal ratings from the National Park Service in 1988 and 1989, and an unsatisfactory rating in 1991. Owner Johnson had previously contested the 1991 rating saying it was based on a series of "trivial" incidents that did not seriously jeopardize anyone.

John Morehead, Alaska regional director for the park service, reported that none of the incidents were sufficient to revoke the permit on their own, but said "if you look at the incidents cumulatively, there's a pattern of unsafe behavior."

Johnson brought suit against the National Park Service and the Department of the Interior to regain his permit. The future plans of dozens of climbers, Genet guides and an air-taxi firm were left in limbo because the permit had been revoked.

Search Called Off for Man Who Fell Into Crevasse

Alaskans face a special set of dangers in the Last Frontier, and tough decisions. The Alaska State Troopers halted rescue efforts for an Anchorage man who fell into a crevasse on Gakona

Glacier in April 1992.

Steven Keiner, 46, was reportedly riding on his snow machine when the edge of a crevasse broke and he fell in. Keiner's friends could not see or hear him, but sent for help from nearby Summit Lake.

Officials estimated that the crevasse was about 100 feet deep. However, rescuers descended about 140 feet before melting snow and falling ice hindered their attempts. Alaska State Troopers, the Alaska Air National Guard, Alaska Mountain Rescue and volunteers searched nearby crevasses before the rescue attempt was halted about a day later.

Basketball Teams Star in Cable TV Special

The Dillingham Wolverines boys basketball team challenged the Naknek Angels boys team in Bristol Bay in fall 1991, as the national cable sports network ESPN recorded the competition.

As part of a one-hour special for the weekly show Scholastic Sports America, the Alaska youth basketball represented the unique aspect of the state's athletes traveling by plane a distance as far as 500 miles to compete in state games, since they can't drive to the games.

The segment on Alaska included some of the state's treasured sights and sounds: the Seward Mountain Marathon, Anchorage athletics, as well as the aftermath of the *Exxon Valdez* oil spill in Prince William Sound.

Environmental Groups Fear Demise of Sea Ducks

The spectacled eiders and Steller's eiders are two varieties of sea ducks facing possible extinction in Alaska, according to several environmental groups.

The decline of spectacled eiders is most keenly seen on the Yukon–Kuskokwim delta. In recent years, the eiders roughly numbered between 48,000 and 70,000 pairs, according to estimates from the U.S. Fish and Wildlife Service. Today, however, the spectacled eiders are estimated at 2,700, which signifies a drop of more than 90 percent.

Environmental groups, including the Biodiversity Legal Foundation, the Wilderness Society and the Sierra Club, are pressing the U. S. Fish and Wildlife Service to find out why these sea duck populations are dwindling.

Steller's eiders face more optimistic odds, according to the Biodiversity Foundation's Jasper Carlton, who noted that the number of these ducks have dropped only about 50 percent to 70 percent in the past two decades.

Carlton reported that the drop in the number of ducks can be attributed to subsistence hunting or arctic pollution, but cautions the federal agency to investigate the reasons for the declines to prevent the extinction of the ducks.

Harvard University, Anyone?

Alaska Natives who have already earned an undergraduate degree are invited to attend the Harvard Graduate School of Arts and Sciences free of cost. The program offers a scholarship for Harvard's annual tuition of $15,050, as well as $10,500 for living expenses.

Among the Alaska Natives who have attended Harvard and returned to Alaska are: Elsie Itta, coordinator for Cultural Integration at the North Slope Borough School District; Claudette Bradley, coordinator of X-CED, a cross-cultural education program in rural Alaska; and William Demmert, previously the state commissioner of education and now an education professor at Stanford University.

Soviet Research Station Found, But Supplies Missing

Remnants of a Soviet research station aboard an ice floe off the Arctic Coast were recovered in October 1991, but hundreds of barrels of fuel and chemicals were missing.

A U.S. Coast Guard flight crew spotted the research station floating west of Barrow. The Soviets had reported that 500 drums of diesel fuel, 30 drums of aluminum powder, 10 drums of lubricating oil, four bags of caustic soda and 600 empty drums had remained at the station.

The Coast Guard expects minimal environmental impact because of the distance from any land mass. But North Slope and federal officials expressed concern about the dangers of floating fuel barrels during whaling season. The ice floe reportedly broke loose from the Soviet coast last July, and 23 people requested aid from the Coast Guard in escaping from the station. Usually ice, currents, sea-floor topography are studied by such research stations.

Hey, Where's the Real Prince William Sound?

The *Exxon Valdez* oil spill is the subject of a soon-to-be released docudrama produced by Home Box Office and British Broadcasting Co. But the filming will actually be done in British Columbia, according to HBO spokeswoman Nancy Lesser, who said, "You'll definitely think you are in Valdez when you see this. I promise you."

Lesser said that filming a movie in an area other than the actual location is quite a normal practice for moviemakers, and is usually done to save costs. To aid in authenticity, there will be some backup shots of Valdez and actual news footage used in the made-for-HBO movie.

Record Cold Snap Hits Fairbanks, Anchorage

Just when Alaskans think spring is just around the corner, Mother Nature plays a practical joke. Residents of Fairbanks awoke April 13, 1992, to a temperature of 23 below zero, which shattered the record set 78 years ago.

Likewise, low temperatures in Anchorage also broke a record cold as the mercury dipped to 9 degrees.

Meanwhile in Valdez, residents took shovels in hand again to move 33.3 inches of snow that fell during a 24-hour period. Valdez still needs 46 more inches to beat the record snowfall of 560.7 inches that descended in the winter of 1989.

Plans Tabled for Extracting Copper–Gold Ore

Cominco Alaska Exploration will likely postpone the company's project to excavate a sizable copper–gold deposit near Lake Iliamna.

Though estimates of the ore deposits have doubled to about 500 million tons, the remote location of the Pebble Beach deposit and the low grade of the ore have become reasons to table temporarily the development of the project.

Copper prices were running about $1 per pound at the time of the decision, a price too low to be cost-effective with any current development.

Oil Spill Blamed for Closure of Cutthroat Trout Fishing

The 1989 *Exxon Valdez* oil spill was partially responsible for the April 1992 closure of cutthroat trout sport fishing in the Prince William Sound, according to state Fish and Game biologists.

The emergency closure affected the west side of Prince William Sound at Eshamy Creek and Green Island Creek. Area biologist Kelly Hepler reported that mortality rates of the cutthroat trout were significantly higher in the oil spill area than in other areas of the sound, according to findings by state and federal scientists. Hepler also said that the high mortality rates were not solely blamed on the oil spill, but that the area of closure is a popular sport fishing location as well.

Barrow Celebrates Spring Amid Sub-Zero Temperatures

There was a chill in the air—50 below zero, to be exact—last April 1992 as residents of Barrow turned out for the annual Spring Festival.

The festival, which celebrates the sun's return to the Far North and the coming whaling season, was filled with events. Cross-country ski and skating races, sled dog races, a parade and the Top of the World Golf Classic played with bright-orange golf balls on the snow and ice.

In efforts to offset the cold, the Rotary Club of Barrow sold hand warmers along with everyone's favorite picnic food—hot dogs.

Orphaned Polar Bear Cub Dies at Alaska Zoo

A male polar bear cub, which had been brought to Anchorage's Alaska Zoo with his sister in March 1992 after being orphaned in the wild, died in April after falling off a three-foot-high platform in their cage.

Though the cage floor had been lined with straw, the playful cub had apparently fallen and was killed instantly, according to Sammye Seawell, director of the zoo.

Efforts were in the works to find a new home for the cubs, whose mother had been killed by a Native hunter near the village of Wainwright on the Chukchi Sea. The 4-month-old cubs were captured by U.S. Fish and Wildlife biologists and transported to the zoo in March 1992. At press time, the female cub was scheduled to find a new home at the Morelia Zoo in central Mexico.

Researchers Produce "Reinbou" and "Carideer"

Researchers at the University of Alaska Fairbanks have successfully produced a hybrid of the caribou and reindeer, with the catchy names of "reinbou" and "carideer."

Although the purebreds and the hybrids look almost identical, there are differences, according to researchers. Bob White, a professor of zoophysiology and nutrition at the University of Alaska Fairbanks, reported that interbreeding could produce an animal with leaner meat and larger antlers. This is part of a 5-year study that began in 1987. Scientists have already determined that the caribou–reindeer hybrid is fertile.

Reindeer and caribou are known to have a common ancestor, which lived in central Europe about 7,000 years ago. The animals that moved across the Bering land bridge in Alaska became caribou, gradually developing longer legs to move more easily through the snow. The ancestors that stayed in Europe eventually became domesticated reindeer.

Exxon, Alaska Settle Lawsuit Over Oil Royalties

Exxon Corp. and the state of Alaska agreed to an out-of-court settlement in April 1992 of $128 million, ending a 14-year-old lawsuit over oil royalties amounting to $170 million.

The settlement concludes one of the longest and most detailed lawsuits in Alaska. More than $500 million has been already received in total settlements from other firms cited in the lawsuit. Originally, the state of Alaska accused several oil companies of reportedly shortchanging the state treasury by $902 million.

In 1990, Atlantic Richfield Co. settled on $287 million of its $319 million claim. Likewise, Mobil Corp. settled on $10 million of its $20.4 million claim.

As background to the case, the state of Alaska leased land to the firm to explore and develop oil in the 1970s, in return for a one-eighth share of the oil. The oil companies were to pay a royalty to the state, as well as a per-barrel severance tax on production. The dispute arose in figuring the value of the royalty oil at the wellhead, less the costs of transportation.

To date, the state of Alaska has spent more than $68 million on the case, which includes $21 million in private attorney fees and $29 million in research, according to state figures.

Forest Service Quits Cleaning Up Salmon Habitat

The U.S. Forest Service is trying to break a 20-year habit of cleaning up streams for juvenile salmon fry.

The Forest Service once believed that removing fallen trees and other natural debris created a better environment for the fish, but the agency has revised its strategy. Now, the Forest Service is providing natural log structures in creeks and streams to improve the habitat and provide deep, safe pools where silver salmon fry and Dolly Varden trout can thrive before setting out for other waters. The Forest Service tested the waters for the experiment in Starrigavan Creek, near Sitka in southeast Alaska.

Terry Suminski, a biologist technician with the Forest Service, reported that the logs placed in streams have created calm pools, which protect fry from storms, spring flood waters and natural enemies.

Gender Influences Alaska's Pay Scale

Recent reports from the Alaska Department of Labor indicate that the gap in average incomes for women and men have widened between 1988 and 1990.

The average woman's income in 1988 was 61.7 percent of the average man's income. In monetary terms, that's $14,962 for women in contrast to $24,232 for men, according to

F. Terry Elder, an economist with the labor department's Research and Analysis Section in Juneau. He also reported that by 1990, the gap had widened. Though the average woman's salary had risen to $16,934, the salary for men also had jumped to $27,655, leaving the average woman's salary at 61.2 percent of the average man's salary. Elder noted that minor reporting errors may be the cause of the widened pay gap, but he also noted that he did not expect to see any significant changes in these figures for 1991.

Nationwide, the average woman's salary reflects a pay difference of about 70 cents for every dollar that a man earns.

Villagers Catch Spring Bowhead Whale

Whaling Capt. Harrison Miklahook, Sr., and his four-man crew caught a 27-foot bowhead whale off the shores of Savoonga on St. Lawrence Island in April 1992.

Members of other whaling crews and some of the 545 villagers of Savoonga helped butcher the whale, a task that took 12 hours to complete. Thin shore ice couldn't hold the entire whale carcass, so the whalers cut the whale into sections.

Miklahook's catch was the second whale caught during the spring whaling season. The first whale was caught in February near the village of Gambell, also on St. Lawrence Island.

Mushers Weather Tough Trail in Kobuk 440

The mushers competing in the Kobuk 440 sled dog race along a 440-mile stretch of the Kobuk River near Kotzebue admitted that the severe arctic weather made the 1992 race the toughest one yet.

Veteran French musher Jacques Phillipe grabbed the first-place prize of $8,500 for crossing the finish line in 77 hours, 47 minutes, 40 seconds. Ed Iten of Ambler, who won last year's race, finished about 20 minutes behind Phillipe. Third place went to Jim Wilson, also of Ambler, who arrived in Kotzebue two hours behind Iten. Two hours later, Lucy Nordlum arrived, followed by fifth-place finisher, Kathy Swenson.

Cleanup Crews Seek Compensation for Work on Oil Spill

Cleaning solutions and crude oil fumes were blamed as the cause of illnesses now being suffered by cleanup crews who worked on the 1989 *Exxon Valdez* oil spill. As a result, the members of the cleanup teams are filing suits in federal and state courts for millions of dollars in compensation against the Exxon Corp., Exxon Shipping Corp. and Exxon Pipeline Co., in addition to two local contractors providing cleanup crews to work on the spill.

In one lawsuit, David Driver is seeking compensation for lingering skin problems. He believes that the skin problems were a result of exposure to chemicals that were used, which violated rules established by the Occupational Safety and Health Administration. Driver names VECO International in his suit. VECO, an oilfield service company, was one of the contractors for Exxon.

Anchorage Times Is Sold, Shut Down

The *Anchorage Times*, Alaska's oldest newspaper, ceased publication with the June 3, 1992, edition, leaving the state's largest city with one newspaper.

The afternoon newspaper sold its publishing equipment, but not its downtown building and land, to the rival morning *Anchorage Daily News* under an agreement concluded June 1.

Until the sale, Anchorage had been the smallest city in the U.S. with two competing newspapers.

The victory of the *Daily News* marked one of the most abrupt reversals of fortune in modern daily journalism. The paper was near collapse when McClatchy Newspapers Inc., a Sacramento-based chain, bought it in 1979. Circulation was about 12,000 daily, compared with nearly 50,000 for the *Times*. The *Anchorage Daily News'* total paid circulation for the period ending March 31, 1992, was 60,874 daily and 82,641 Sunday. The *Anchorage Times'* circulation was 44,057 daily and 42,256 Sunday. McClatchy publishes 11 daily newspapers.

Volcanic Plume Misses Anchorage

Mount Spurr erupted Saturday, June 27, 1992, sending a rush of steam 8 miles high and showering ash over Mount McKinley and scattered settlements to the north.

The volcano, 80 miles due west of Anchorage, exploded at 7:04 A.M. with surprisingly little warning to scientists watching seismic monitors. The eruption subsided after four hours.

No damage or injuries due to the eruption were reported, and airlines suffered only minor disruptions. High-altitude winds blew the volcanic ash away from Anchorage toward the Brooks Range, missing McGrath to the west and Fairbanks to the east.

On Mount McKinley, climbers reported seeing a huge, dark cloud roll in around 10:30 A.M. Ashfall was very heavy on the north side of the mountain.

Savoonga Singers Entertain President Bush

The Savoonga Singers, from St. Lawrence Island, sang for the President's 40th Annual Prayer Breakfast in Washington, D.C. in February 1992.

Dressed in traditional mukluks and kuspuks, the eight women sang "How Great Thou Art" in English and Siberian Yup'ik for President Bush and the 4,000 guests attending the breakfast.

The President and Mrs. Bush greeted the women before the breakfast began. The singers were invited by Alaska Sen. Ted Stevens, who was this year's prayer breakfast committee chairman.

Anchorage Museum Receives $1 Million Gift

The Anchorage Museum of History and Art received a pledge of $1 million from the Kreielsheimer Foundation in Seattle in April 1992. The funding is the largest gift given to the museum foundation, according to museum director Patricia Wolf.

The Kreielsheimer Foundation, which solely supports the arts, gives funds to art organizations with long-term results.

The Kreielsheimer Foundation funds began with Leo Kreielsheimer's uncles and father who were innovators in the Seattle leather business, as well as in Pacific Coast salmon canneries.

The money for the Anchorage museum will be invested in the endowment fund and a portion of the interest from the account will be used for procuring major exhibits.

Mount Spurr Erupts, Dumps Ash on Anchorage

Mount Spurr erupted for the second time in 1992, sending an ash plume 60,000 feet into the air, halting air traffic out of Anchorage and raining ash from the Matanuska Valley to Yakutat in Southeast Alaska. The explosion, which occurred at 4:41 p.m. on Tuesday, August 18, came with almost no warning. Pilots flying over the volcano were reporting a plume with ash before scientists noticed the growing tremors on the peak. Mount Spurr's June 27th eruption also came with relatively little warming.

Anchorage received the brunt of the ash fallout, which darkened the sky and buried the city in up to 1/4-inch of the stuff. Residents with respiratory ailments were encouraged to stay indoors to avoid exposure to the ash. Air filters and surgical masks were out of supply in a matter of hours. Visibility during the ashfall was almost zero, hampering traffic. Many city and government offices operated on reduced schedules. Three thousand weary travelers were stranded at Anchorage International Airport. Normal air traffic did not resume until several days after the eruption.

A week after the explosion, cleanup crews were still trying to remove the ash.

Record Water Use in Anchorage

Anchorage set a record for water use on Wednesday, August 19, 1992, the day after the eruption of Mount Spurr. In an effort to wash ash from roads, driveways, sidewalks, cars and lawns, residents of the city used an estimated 60 million gallons of water, nearly double the average daily use for this time of year. The previous record of 47 million gallons was set in July 1989.

Obituaries

We recognize the significant contributions of just a few of the many Alaskans who died this year, from June 1991 through May 1992. Due to limited space, we are including some of the more prominent Alaskans who left a special mark on the state's history in business, politics and social development.

BAADE, Dixie, 80, died Sept. 21, 1991, in Seattle. She was a cofounder and board member of the Southeast Alaska Conservation Council and an environmentalist in Alaska.

In 1944, she first came to Ketchikan to work as a microbiologist for the Territorial Department of Health, and later founded and operated a health laboratory for 17 years. She moved to Kupreanof near Petersburg with her husband, Bob, and lived there for many years.

During the 1960s, Mrs. Baade became involved in efforts to prevent pulp mill pollution from the Ketchikan Spruce Mill. She served on the boards of the Petersburg Conservation Society, Alaska Center for the Environment, and Alaska Conservation Foundation. Her efforts to help the Alaskan environment won her the Alaska Conservation Foundation's Celia Hunter Award.

She also was active in the formation of the Alaska Sports and Wildlife Club, worked with the Territorial Sportsmen to help wilderness classification of the Tracy Arm–Fords Terror Wilderness Area. In addition, she was active in the Tongass Conservation Society in Ketchikan and helped establish the Misty Fjords National Monument. She is survived by two nieces.

CARTER, Thomas L., 77, died Dec. 24, 1991, in Wasilla. Born in Bowbells, ND, he had lived in Alaska for 51 years.

He served in the U.S. Army during World War II. He had worked in the Willow Creek mines, the Alaska Road Commission, Alaska Railroad, the Matanuska Electric Association and Teeland's Country Store. He was also active in the community, serving as director of the Wasilla Boys Youth Camp, which he founded. In addition, he was active in the Veterans of Foreign Wars Post 9365, the Sacred Heart Catholic Church, the Knights of Columbus, and the Wasilla City Council. He also was instrumental in helping develop the Wasilla Fire Department and the Wasilla Ambulance Association.

He is survived by his wife, three daughters, one son, several grandchildren and great-grandchildren.

CHAMBERLIN, William C., 67, died April 3, 1992, in Olympia, WA. He was a horse trainer and a retired contractor in Anchorage.

Mr. Chamberlin lived in Anchorage since he moved to Alaska with his family in 1937. He was a veteran of World War II, having been in the Marine Corps during assaults on Pelilu and Okinawa in the Pacific campaigns.

He retired after 24 years from the Defense Department as a civilian employee at Elmendorf Air Force Base, where he worked as an airfield foreman of asphalt paving operations. In 1990, he also retired from his contracting firm, Chamberlin Grating Co.

He was an active member and leader of the Anchorage Sled Dog and Racing Association, the Chugach Range Riders, Anchorage Ski Club, International Cessna 170 Association, Local 302 of the International Union of Operating Engineers, American Horse Shows Association Zone 12, and the Anchorage Horse Council Section 16 Equestrian Center. He also worked with the National Park Service in developing walking and hiking trails in the Anchorage area.

He is survived by his wife, two sons, his sister and several grandchildren.

EASTAUGH, Fredrick O., 78, died Feb. 18, 1992, in Auke Bay. A lifelong Alaskan, he served as a Republican representative in the territorial legislature from 1953 to 1955, and was active in Alaska's mining industry.

Born in Nome, Mr. Eastaugh moved to Juneau before attending the University of Washington. He returned to Juneau, where he became a partner in the law firm of Robertson, Monagle and Eastaugh.

In addition to his law practice, he remained an advocate of Alaska's mining industry, and was active in the Alaska Miners Association. He also served as city magistrate in Juneau. He is survived by his wife, a son and a daughter.

FEERO, William E., 68, died Oct. 15, 1991 in Kirkland, WA. A lifelong Alaskan, he was the mayor of Skagway for three terms and an avid tourism promoter.

When he was 13, he and his family moved to Skagway, a city where his father and grandfather ran pack trains to the Klondike gold rush fields through White Pass during the 1890s.

After serving in World War II, Mr. Feero returned to Skagway and worked for the White Pass & Yukon Railroad. He also bought the Broadway Theater with his wife, Beverly, and transformed it into the Sourdough Hotel. He was first elected mayor of Skagway in 1950, and continued to promote the local tourism industry. He also worked for Westours, ran a sightseeing bus, and reopened the Klondike Highway into the Yukon. In 1990, he was honored at the Southeast Alaska Tourism Conference in Skagway, winning an award for his contributions to the tourism industry.

He is survived by his wife, two sons and two daughters.

FENNIMORE, Nellie Reeve, 98, died June 15, 1991, in Anchorage.

Born in Colorado, she moved to Alaska after a journey aboard the steamship *Aleutian* in 1933, and lived in the Cache Creek area, McGrath and Anchorage. She married George Fennimore in 1944 and assisted him on mining and construction projects statewide.

She worked as a camp cook on several construction projects, a baker at Charley Odermat's Star Bakery during the 1930s, operator of Mrs. Kimuras Chop Suey House, and a cook at the USO during World War II.

She was active in a number of civic and social activities until her death. An avid rockhound, Mrs. Fennimore was 80 years old when she explored Australia's opal fields. She also received the Lady Milicent Medal for Service to others in 1958 from the Rebekah Lodge, the highest of honors.

She is survived by her husband, one daughter, several grandchildren, great-grandchildren, and great-great-grandchildren.

GAINES, Harry, 60, died July 31, 1991, in Soldotna. He was a well-known fishing guide along the Kenai River.

A native of Texas, he worked as a radio announcer, band manager, and police officer in New Mexico before coming to Alaska with his family in 1970. He began working for Value Mart, but soon started fishing full time and became a leading fishing guide on the Kenai River. Some of his clients included Tom Selleck, Kenny Rogers and Lloyd Bridges.

In addition to his guiding business, Mr. Gaines was involved in the local Kenai community as president of the chamber of commerce and was active in environmental issues, such as protecting the Kenai River's salmon runs.

He is survived by his wife, a son and stepson.

GOODFELLOW, James J., 65, died July 28, 1991. He was a retired Alaska State Trooper.

During World War II, he served with the U.S. Navy as a pharmacist's mate in the Pacific Theater, and earned several medals, including the Purple Heart. After the war, he attended the University of Nebraska at Lincoln, before moving to Alaska in 1951. He then joined the territorial police, now known as the Alaska State Troopers. He served with the Troopers in Fairbanks, Juneau and Anchorage, earning the rank of colonel. He also worked as a personnel officer, trainer at the Alaska State Trooper training center in Sitka, and as a fish and wildlife protection officer.

He had retired and had moved to Prairie Farm, WI, where he was living at the time of his death.

He is survived by his wife, a son, a stepson, sisters and grandchildren.

HALE, John Heald, 68, died June 26, 1991, in New York City. He became a homesteader after coming to Alaska from Canton, NY, in 1947.

He graduated from the U.S. Naval Academy, and served with the Navy for a short time before coming to Alaska. He returned to Alaska in 1967 after attending Columbia University.

Also known as the Commander, Mr. Hale worked as a manager of the Alaska State Fair, in the Matanuska-Susitna Borough and the town of Aniak. In addition, he founded KABN radio broadcast to listeners in the Mantanuska Valley.

He is survived by family and friends in Alaska.

HEINMILLER, Carl, 79, died June 10, 1992, in Seattle. A resident of Haines, he was the former state magistrate and civic leader, who helped revive Tlingit dance and art.

During World War II, he served in the U.S. Army in the South Pacific and was captured by the Japanese. After he retired from the Army in 1946, he and several other veterans bought and developed 400 acres at Fort Seward in Haines. The group renamed the area Port Chilkoot and developed the town. Mr. Heinmiller served as mayor, police chief and fire chief before the town became part of Haines. From 1968 to 1988, he served as the magistrate in Haines.

He also worked as a carver of traditional Tlingit designs and helped develop the Chilkat Dancers. He was adopted into the Raven Clan of the Chilkats in 1957. In addition, his lifelong contributions to the Boy Scouts were recognized in 1991, when he became the first Alaskan to receive Scouting's highest honor, the Distinguished Eagle Scout Award.

He is survived by family and friends in Alaska.

HILL, Donald, 62, died March 9, 1992, in Hawaii. He had been a lifelong Alaskan and businessman in Anchorage, chiefly developing movie theaters in the state.

Born in Fairbanks, he later moved to Anchorage, where he spent most of his life. He worked with the television and radio stations of Lathrop Co., served as manager of KENI radio, and was in charge of the Lathrop theater operations in Fairbanks, Anchorage and Cordova. He became executive vice president of the Lathrop Co. in 1979.

He also was active in city and local politics, and served on the Anchorage Planning Commission, the Greater Anchorage Platting Board and the Anchorage Miners Association.

Anchorage's Hill Building, now housing city hall, was named after Mr. Hill's father, Harry Hill.

He is survived by two daughters, a son, his mother and two grandchildren.

HILL, Mason, 88, died March 11, 1992, in Whittier, CA He was an innovator in the discovery of commerical oil in Alaska.

Born in California, Mr. Hill was a longtime resident of Alaska. In 1957, he was the chief geologist for the Richfield Oil Co., and helped discover oil at the Swanson River site on the Kenai Peninsula. He also assisted in the geological mapping of the North Slope and Atlantic Richfield's holdings at Prudhoe Bay.

He retired in 1969 as manager of international exploration for the Atlantic Richfield Co. Since then, he had been teaching at Whittier College, California State University at Los Angeles, Cal State Irvine and Pomona College. He was well-known for his work on earthquake plate tectonics.

He is survived by family and friends in California and Alaska.

JOHNSON, Robert, 58, died Nov. 21, 1991, in Seattle. He was a captain with the Alaska Marine Highway System ferries.

Before coming to Alaska in 1963, he had worked in the waters of the Great Lakes. He served as captain of the *Matanuska* for 21 years and became chief mate on the *Wickersham* on its first voyage from Norway. He retired in 1990 after 27 years of service.

He is survived by his wife, three sons, a daughter, four brothers, a sister and several grandchildren.

KING, Gloria J., 60, died Feb. 10, 1992, in Palmer. She was a longtime resident of Alaska and a local florist.

She came to Alaska with her parents in 1945 aboard the Alaska steamship *Yukon*. She lived in Anchorage and Kodiak until 1985, when she retired to Friday Harbor, WA, with her husband, William, who died April 2, 1991. During her years in Alaska, she owned and operated the Alaska Flower Shop, and Flowers by June in Anchorage.

She was a member of St. Bartholomew's Episcopal Church, Pioneers of Alaska Auxiliary No. 9 and the Junior Women's Club in Seward.

She is survived by her two daughters, two sisters and grandchildren.

KULL, Dove Montgomery, 94, died Dec. 8, 1991, in Juneau. She was an active social worker, who spent much of her life lobbying for human rights in Alaska.

Born in Oklahoma, she worked as a social worker in her home state, before moving to Alaska in 1959. In Alaska, she served as a social worker for homesteaders and Athabascan Natives in southcentral Alaska. She also worked with the Aleuts on the Pribilof Islands during the post-territorial period, organized children's programs in the state's welfare department, and helped develop federal funding for the state's first accredited child-care center.

Mrs. Kull also worked at the U.S. Public Health Service in Kotzebue, before returning to Juneau to help establish programs for the elderly. She received numerous awards for her many contributions to human rights. She is survived by her son.

LEISER, Mann, 70, died Jan. 9, 1992, in Anchorage. He was a noted horticulturist, author and founder of the Alaska Greenhouses.

He became Anchorage's first city horticulturist, and developed four local greenhouses in Russian Jack. He founded the Alaska Greenhouses Inc. in 1969. He also worked as a columnist for the *Anchorage Times*, and appeared in gardening shows on television and radio.

He is survived by his wife, two daughters and three sons, all of Anchorage; two brothers, a sister, grandchildren and great-grandchildren.

LINDAUER, Jacqueline, 54, died April 13, 1992, in Anchorage. She was the editor and publisher of the *Aleutian Eagle* and the *Alaska Commercial Fisherman*. With her husband, John, she also founded several weekly Alaska newspapers, including the *Barrow Sun*, the *Valdez Pioneer, Bethel Village Voice, Bristol Bay News, Borough Post* and the *East Aleutians Advocate*.

Before coming to Alaska in 1976, she had been a high school teacher and a college professor in California. In addition, she also had written several books about business communications. She is credited with adding many courses and student activities to the roster of the University of Alaska Anchorage during her employment there, including the Great Alaska Shootout basketball tournament.

Before launching her career in publishing, she had been special assistant to the general manager at the Alaska Railroad and helped manage the Alaska Radio Network. Her community efforts included working on the Anchorage Arts Council, the Anchorage Museum Association, and Common Sense for Alaska, in addition to assisting the Aleuts in reparations during their displacement in World War II.

She is survived by her husband, son and daughter, and her father.

McCARREY, J.L. Jr., 86, died Feb. 6, 1992, in Anchorage. He was the last federal territorial judge to serve in Alaska.

Born and raised in Utah, he graduated from the University of Utah in 1940, after which he and his wife Cora moved to Anchorage. During World War II, he was in the Signal Intelligence Corps of the U.S. Army at Anchorage.

He was appointed federal district judge for the territory of Alaska in 1952 by then-President Dwight D. Eisenhower. He served as judge until statehood in 1959, when he returned to private practice of law.

He was admitted to practice law before state and territorial courts, the Ninth U.S. Circuit Court of Appeals, U.S. Tax Court and U.S. Supreme Court. He also was a member of the Alaska, Anchorage and Federal Bar associations.

Mr. McCarrey was an active member of the Mormon Church, Anchorage Lions Club, Pioneers of Alaska and the Sons of the American Revolution.

He is survived by his wife, two sons, two daughters, two brothers, six sisters, grandchildren and great-grandchildren.

MERDES, Edward, 65, died Dec. 5, 1991, in Fairbanks. He was an attorney in Fairbanks and served as an assistant attorney general to the Territory of Alaska.

Before coming to Alaska, he graduated from law school at Cornell University in 1951. He also served as a brigadier general in the National Guard for a short time. During his 39 years in Alaska, he was an assistant attorney general to the Territory of Alaska and assisted in efforts toward statehood. He also served as state senator from 1969 to 1973, in addition to being an attorney in Fairbanks.

He was an active member of the Catholic Church, a founding member of the Jaycees of Alaska, and helped coach many sports activities for children, including the Little League, Babe Ruth baseball, and Little Dribblers basketball. He also was reportedly the oldest active member of the Alaska Bar Association.

He is survived by his wife, three sons, two daughters and grandchildren.

NERLAND, Arthur Leslie "Les," 89, died Feb. 18, 1992, in Issaquah, WA. He was a pioneer in Alaskan business, having owned and operated Nerland's Home Furnishings for more than 50 years.

He was born in Dawson, Yukon Territory, and grew up in Seattle before moving to Fairbanks in 1930. There, he and his wife, Mildred, founded Nerland's Home Furnishings before moving to Anchorage in 1988 and Issaquah in 1990.

Mr. Nerland served on the Fairbanks City Council and as mayor of Fairbanks from 1938 to 1940. He was chairman emeritus of the Nerland Corp., and was president of the Alaska National Bank and the Miner's and Merchant's Bank. He also was active in the Eastern Star, the Masons, the Board of Regents of the University of Alaska, and the Alaska Constitutional Convention. He was a member of the Alaska Pioneer Home, the Alaska Business Hall of Fame and Pioneers of Alaska, as well as helping as founder of the Rotary Club in Fairbanks.

He is preceded in death by his wife, Mildred. He is survived by two sons, a daughter, grandchildren and great-grandchildren.

NOLAN, James A., 90, died Oct. 24, 1991, in Wrangell. He served in the Alaska territorial House of Representatives and territorial Senate for more than 22 years.

He first came to Alaska in 1919 to work at a marble quarry on Prince of Wales Island, and later settled in Wrangell, where he owned and operated Wrangell Drugs and a soda fountain business with his wife, Elsie.

Mr. Nolan was elected to the Wrangell City Council in 1928, and worked as a U.S. deputy marshal from 1934 to 1945. He also served on the Wrangell Chamber of Commerce for many years.

He also served in the Alaska territor-ial House of Representatives from 1946 to 1950, and worked in the territorial Senate beginning in1950 until long after statehood in 1967. In addition, he was a University of Alaska regent, a director of the National Bank of Alaska, and a recipient of Alaska's Man of the Year Award in 1973.

He is survived by his sister and a nephew.

O'CONNOR, Lawrence, 43, died Feb. 8, 1992, in a traffic accident near Nome. He was the president and chief executive officer of the Bering Straits Regional Corp.

He worked as an air traffic controller before becoming the Native regional corporation's chairman in 1977, and later president and CEO of the corporation in 1990. He was active as a civic leader in Nome, working on the Chamber of Commerce and the Rotary Club. He also founded the Iditarod Basketball Classic almost 20 years ago.

He is survived by his wife, two daughters, two sons, and his mother, all of Nome; and several brothers and sisters.

OLANNA, Melvin Asitona, 50, died Aug. 31, 1991 in Seattle. An Alaskan Native, he was well-known as a print artist and sculptor.

He was born in Ikpik, and later attended school at the Institute of American Indian Arts in Santa Fe, NM, as well as the Alaska Native Arts Center in Fairbanks. His Native designs in print and sculptures in wood, bone and stone were recognized the world over. He also helped foster the careers of other Native artists. He is survived by his wife.

OSTROSKY, Kathryn L., 68, died April 5, 1992, in Anchorage. She was a former legislator and a longtime educator in Alaska.

Before moving to Alaska in 1954, Mrs. Ostrosky graduated from Heidelberg College in Ohio and worked as a congressional aide in Washington, DC. She then moved to North Carolina, where she taught school and continued to be an active member of the Congress of Racial Equality.

In Alaska, she taught school in Dillingham, Tanana and Naknek, where she lived with her husband, Hank, and their children for 14 years. During her years in Naknek, Mrs. Ostrosky was a member and president of the school board, as well as publisher of the *Bristol Bay News*.

In 1971, she moved with her family to Anchorage, where she was elected to the Alaska House of Representatives in 1974. She also was a member of the national Order of Women Legislators.

Mrs. Ostrosky worked for the University of Alaska Adult Basic Education Center in Anchorage for the past 15 years, in addition to running her own bed and breakfast business.

She is survived by her husband, two daughters, sisters, a brother and grandsons.

REED, Daniel Mike, 33, died Feb. 25, 1992, in Anchorage. A lifelong Alaskan, he had been an artist whose work was recognized statewide.

Born in Fairbanks, he worked on art projects throughout the state, including carvings for Totem Park in Ketchikan, murals for state institutions, artwork for Nikiski High School. He also received special recognition for his work with youth programs in the state.

He is survived by his parents, a brother, a sister, and several aunts, uncles and nieces.

SWANSON, Henry, 95, died Dec. 21, 1991, in Unalaska. He was a lifelong Alaskan who chronicled years of Aleutian Island history.

He was born in Unalaska in 1895 and lived there all his life, except the time he spent at an Indian boarding school in Oregon. After serving with the U.S. Navy during World War I, he returned to Unalaska and began farming blue fox. His extensive knowledge of the Aleutian Islands led the U.S. Army during World War II to consult Mr. Swanson to help mapmakers and transport supplies to island outposts.

He also held many public offices in Unalaska and Dutch Harbor over the years. He was instrumental in stopping the U.S. Navy from selling Dutch Harbor, which was eventually given to Native corporations instead. He testified that a life of moderation and an ability to change with the times was the key to his longevity.

TITUS, Charlie, Sr., 68, died April 10, 1992, in Fairbanks. Well-known as an Athabascan elder, he had been a teacher of Native culture in Fairbanks and a counselor at the Alcohol Recovery Camp in Old Minto.

He also worked as a village public safety officer in Minto, where he raised a family with his wife, Annie. He had worked on the steamer *Nenana,* the Alaska Railroad and the trans-Alaska pipeline.

His many contributions to the community included serving on the Denakkanaaga Board of Elders, Alaska Board of Game, the Fairbanks Native Association, the Cultural Heritage Board as well as the Minto Village Council.

Mr. Titus enjoyed the outdoors, actively participated in Native dance and song and competed in the 1948 North American Sled Dog Championship.

He is survived by his wife, four sons, nine daughters, a sister, a brother, and several grandchildren, great-grandchildren, nieces and nephews.

TWEEDY, Isabella, 76, died in July 1991, in Fairbanks. She was a longtime Alaskan and an alcoholism counselor who helped many people.

She began her career by working as a writer for television and radio, and was one of the first female disc jockeys west of the Mississippi River. She earned her high school degree at the age of 57, graduated from the University of Washington when she was 61, earned a master's degree in psychology when she was 65, and became a doctor of theology when she was 69.

Fifteen years ago, she moved to Sitka, where she worked as an alcoholism counselor. She moved to Fairbanks three years later, and began working at the Fairbanks Native Association. Her caseload sometimes included 180 clients. She also traveled to the Soviet Union to help teach the Soviets about alcohol-treatment techniques.

She is survived by two daughters, a son, grandchildren and great-grandchildren.

WALKER, Frances Park, 78, died April 11, 1992, in Reno, NV. A longtime resident of Alaska and journalist, she came to Alaska in 1943, as support personnel for the U.S. Army Corps of Engineers.

Mrs. Walker was the society page

editor for the *Fairbanks Daily-News Miner* from 1947 to 1952. She and her husband, Edgar, published the *Walker's Weekly* in Delta Junction for many years, before moving to Valdez in 1961. After the earthquake in 1964, she began publishing a daily newsletter for the community, as well as working for the Alaska Department of Highways as personnel manager. In 1969, the Walker family owned and operated the Village Inn motel in Valdez.

She was a member of the All America Cities Committee and the Pioneers of Alaska Auxiliary Igloo 2. She also helped establish the Delta Junction School and the Delta Junction Chamber of Commerce.

She is survived by her husband, two sons, two daughters, sisters and several grandchildren.

WESCHENFELDER, Ernest, 76, died July 7, 1991, in Anchorage. A lifelong Alaskan, he had worked with the Civil Aviation Administration during his early years.

Born in Douglas, he lived in Douglas, Juneau and Spuhn Island in Auke Bay, where his parents homesteaded the 160-acre island and commercially raised blue fox.

After graduating from the University of Washington, he worked as a forest ranger in Palmer, prior to joining the Civil Aviation Administration as a draftsman. During World War II, he was instrumental in designing militarily strategic runways in the state.

He moved to Washington, DC, with his wife, Florence, in 1950, to work for the CAA at the Pentagon. He also worked on the Titan missile program, and later helped develop the telescopic arm that was used to gather soil samples on Mars.

He chose early retirement, and joined the Peace Corps with his wife, where their assignment took them to Africa. He later returned to Anchorage with his wife in 1988.

He was active in the Pioneers of Alaska, Igloo 15, the Anchorage Lions Club, the Anchorage Elks Lodge No. 1351 and St. John's United Methodist Church.

He is survived by his wife, a son, four daughters and several grandchildren.

WOODS, Antoinette Mayo Roberts, 97, died Dec. 22, 1991, in Fairbanks. She was a well-known midwife who delivered many children in the Interior village of Rampart during her life in Alaska.

Born in the now-abandoned river settlement of Nuklukyet on the Yukon River, she spent most of her life in Rampart. She delivered her own baby in 1924, and helped deliver more than 100 babies, including 15 for one couple in Rampart. She is credited with saving many lives during the 1932 epidemics of whooping cough and measles, which ravaged the local villages. She practiced medical techniques that she learned from her mother, and was known not to charge for her services.

She is survived by five children, grandchildren and many great-grandchildren.

WOODS, Nellie, 83, died Sept. 7, 1991, in Noatak. She was a well-known Inupiaq elder.

During her younger years in 1929, she accompanied her husband, Peter, in a journey along the Arctic Coast of Alaska to Herschel Island in Canada to lead a herd of reindeer to starving Eskimos. The journey took almost three years to complete, during which time she gave birth to two children, one of whom died in infancy.

She is survived by three daughters.

ZIEGLER, Robert, 70, died Sept. 29, 1991, in Ketchikan. He had been a pioneer Alaska attorney and legislator.

He served in the Army Medical Corps during World War II, and later graduated from the University of Virginia with a law degree. He moved to Ketchikan to join his father's law firm of A.H. Ziegler in 1949, where he worked until his retirement in 1989.

He was the former president of the Alaska State Bar Association and was serving as president of the Ketchikan Bar Association.

He also was a member of the territorial House from 1957 to 1959. He served in the legislature after statehood, and from 1965 to 1987 for six terms in the state Senate. He also was the chairman of the Judiciary Committee for many years.

Among his survivors are a daughter and a son.

Suggested Reading

Beaman, Libby. *Libby, the Sketches, Letters and Journals of Libby Beaman, Recorded in the Pribilof Islands 1879-1880.* Tulsa: Council Oak Books.

Blackman, Margaret B. *Sadie Brower Neakok: An Inupiaq Woman.* Seattle: University of Washington Press, 1989.

Caras, Roger. *Monarch of Deadman Bay: The Life and Death of a Kodiak Bear.* Boston: Little Brown, 1969.

Davidson, Art (text); Art Wolfe (photography); Galen Rowell (foreword). *Alakshak: The Great Country.* San Francisco: Sierra Club, 1989.

Elliot, Nan. *I'd Swap My Old Skidoo for You.* Issaquah, Wash: Sammamish Press, 1989.

Greiner, James. *Wager With the Wind.* New York: St. Martin's Press, 1982.

Hirschmann, Fred, and Kim Heacox. *Bush Pilots of Alaska.* Portland: Graphic Arts Center Publishing Co., 1989.

London, Jack. *The Call of the Wild.* New York: Macmillan, 1904.

Lopez, Barry. *Of Wolves and Men.* New York: Scribner's, 1978.

McPhee, John. *Coming into the Country.* New York: Farrar, Straus & Giroux, 1977.

Muir, John. *Travels in Alaska.* Boston: Houghton Mifflin, 1915.

Murie, Adolph. *A Naturalist in Alaska.* Tucson: University of Arizona Press, 1990.

Murie, Olaus. *Journeys to the Far North.* Palo Alto: The Wilderness Society and American West Publishing, 1973.

Murray, John. *The Republic of Rivers.* New York: Oxford University Press, 1990.

Nelson, Richard. *The Island Within.* San Francisco: North Point Press, 1989.

Oswalt, Wendell. *Bashful No Longer.* Tulsa: University of Oklahoma Press, 1990.

Potter, Jean. *The Flying North.* Sausalito: Comstock Editions, 1986.

Stuck, Hudson. *The Ascent of Denali: A Narrative of the First Complete Ascent of the Highest Peak in North America.* Lincoln: University of Nebraska Press, 1989. (Originally published in 1914.)

Woolcock, Iris. *The Road North: One Woman's Adventure Driving the Alaska Highway.* Anchorage: Greatland Graphics, 1990.

Alaska Northwest Library

Many North Country books are suggested as related reading throughout *FACTS ABOUT ALASKA: THE ALASKA ALMANAC*®. Following is our Alaska Northwest Library. These books are available in bookstores or direct from Alaska Northwest Books™, 22026 20th Ave. S.E., Bothell, WA 98021, or call toll free, 1-800-343-4567. Write for our free book catalog. Mail orders require a postage and handling fee of $1.50 fourth class or $3.50 first class per book.

Alaska Bear Tales, by Larry Kaniut. Dramatic encounters between bears and humans. 324 pp., $12.95

Alaska Sourdough, by Ruth Allman. Handwritten recipes "by a real Alaskan." 198 pp., $9.95

Alaska Wild Berry Guide and Cookbook. How to find and identify edible wild berries, and how to cook them. Line drawings and color photos. 212 pp., $14.95

The ALASKA WILDERNESS MILEPOST®. Where the roads end, the real Alaska begins. A guide to 250 remote towns and villages. Fifth edition, 480 pp., $14.95

The Alaskan Bird Sketches of Olaus Murie. With excerpts from his field notes, compiled and edited by Margaret E. Murie. 64 pp., $11.95

Alaskan Igloo Tales, by Edward L. Keithahan. Arctic oral history written down in the early 20th century, with illustrations. 144 pp., $12.95

Alaska's Saltwater Fishes, by Doyne W. Kessler. A field guide designed for quick identification of 375 species of saltwater fishes. 384 pp., $19.95

Alaska's Wilderness Medicines, by Eleanor G. Viereck. Use of trees, flowers and shrubs for medicinal and other purposes. 116 pp., $9.95

The Alaska–Yukon Wild Flowers Guide. Large color photos and detailed drawings of 160 species. 227 pp., $16.95

Along the Alaska Highway. Photography by Alissa Crandall, text by Gloria J. Maschmeyer. Compelling color photographs and engaging text combine to reveal the people and landscape along this epic highway. 96 pp., $16.95

Artists at Work: 25 Northwest Glassmakers, Ceramists and Jewelers, by Susan Biskeborn. Photographic portraits by Kim Zumwalt. This book examines the lives and art of these nationally recognized regional artists. Black-and-white photographs bring the reader close to the creative process by capturing the subjects in their work environments, and color photographs display the beauty of the art they produce. 172 pp., $24.95

Baby Animals of the North, text and illustrations by Katy Main. A children's book about wildlife in the Last Frontier guaranteed to captivate the young and young at heart. Color illustrations. 36 pp., laminated board with dust jacket, $13.95

Baidarka, by George Dyson. The history, development and redevelopment of the Aleut kayak. Illustrations and photographs. 231 pp., $19.95

Building the Alaska Log Home, by Tom Walker. Comprehensive book for log home history and construction. 192 pp., $19.95

Caprial's Seasonal Kitchen: An Innovative Chef's Menus and Recipes for Easy Home Cooking, by Caprial Pence. One of America's brightest young chefs, Caprial Pence secured a four-star rating for Fullers restaurant in Seattle. In her first cookbook, Pence invites the home chef to discover the secrets of her innovative cooking style. 240 pp., hardbound, $19.95; softbound, $12.95

Capture of Attu. The Aleutian campaign of World War II, as told by the men who fought there. 80 pp., $6.95

Chilkoot Pass: The Most Famous Trail in the North, by Archie Satterfield. A guide for hikers and history buffs. 224 pp., $9.95

The Coast of British Columbia, by Rosemary Neering. Photographs by Bob Herger. Beautiful photographs reveal the scenic diversity of British Columbia's coastal region; insightful text explores its geological, natural and human history. 160 pp., hardbound, $34.95

Cooking Alaskan, by Alaskans. Hundreds of time-tested recipes, including a section on sourdough. 512 pp., $16.95

Dale De Armond: A First Book Collection of Her Prints. Special color sampler featuring 63 of the Juneau artist's works. 80 pp., $14.95

Destination Washington®. An insider's guide to the state of Washington. 196 pp., $4.95

Discover Alaska, foreword by Art Davidson. A comprehensive guide to America's Last Frontier and all its spectacular contrasts, including historical views and colorful photographs. 64 pp., $8.95

Discovering Wild Plants: Alaska, Western Canada, the Northwest, by Janice Schofield. Facts, pictures and illustrations detailing more than 130 plants. 368 pp., hardbound, $34.95; softbound, $26.95

Doris Dingle's Crafty Cat Activity Book, by Helen Levchuk, illustrated by John Bianchi. Doris Dingle, one of the world's great cat lovers, shares her years of feline know-how in this book of toys and games guaranteed to keep your cat entertained. 96 pp., $12.95.

Eye of the Changer, by Muriel Ringstad. This excellent children's book is a Northwest Indian tale. 96 pp., $9.95

Golf Courses of the Pacific Northwest, by Jeff Shelley. A comprehensive guide to year-round golfing at golf courses and driving ranges in Washington, Oregon, northern Idaho, the greater Sun Valley area, and north-western Montana. 344 pp., $19.95

The Great Bear, edited by John A. Murray. A collection of essays about the grizzly by such contemporary writers as John McPhee, Roger Caras and A.B. Guthrie. 248 pp., $14.95

The Great Northwest Nature Factbook, by Ann Saling. Hundreds of fascinating facts on the remarkable animals, plants and natural features in Washington, Oregon, Idaho and Montana. 200 pp., $9.95

The Great Southwest Nature Factbook: A Guide to the Region's Animals, Plants, and Natural Features, by Susan J. Tweit. For residents and visitors alike, *The Great Southwest Nature Factbook* is a take-along guide to the natural wonders of Arizona, New Mexico, southern Colorado, and Utah. 224 pp., $12.95

Grizzly Cub: Five Years in the Life of a Bear, by Rick McIntyre. A true story of a young bear's first five summers, as recorded in words and 56 color photographs by Denali National Park ranger Rick McIntyre. 104 pp., $14.95

Guardian of the Whales: The Quest to Study Whales in the Wild, by Bruce Obee. Photographs by Graeme Ellis. Before the 1970s, little was known about the life patterns and behavior of whales in the wild. But a few intrepid researchers took to the waters to photograph and study these creatures in their habitats. *Guardians of the Whales* weaves the most up-to-date research with stunning color photographs and tells the personal stories of the researchers who have begun to unfold the mysteries of gray, humpback, minke, and killer whales. 184 pp., hardbound, $34.95

Guide to the Birds of Alaska, by Robert H. Armstrong. Updated and expanded; the perfect guide to 437 species found in the 49th state. Revised edition, 349 pp., $19.95

A Guide to the Queen Charlotte Islands, by Neil G. Carey. This revised 10th edition provides all the maps and information needed when visiting these rugged islands. 104 pp., $10.95

Heroes and Heroines in Tlingit–Haida Legend, by Mary Beck. Nine Native legends from the Northwest Coast, with introductions that compare the characters in Tlingit and Haida tradition with classical mythology. Illustrated. 126 pp., $12.95

Heroes of the Horizon, by Gerry Bruder. Author Bruder relates the heroic adventures of 28 veteran bush pilots who flew in Alaska's golden age of aviation, from the 1930s through the 1950s. 280 pp., $12.95

Hibrow Cow: Even MORE Alaskan Recipes and Stories, by Gordon R. Nelson. The former Alaska State trapper's recipes and humorous tales in his fourth cookbook. 215 pp., $9.95

The Hidden Coast: Kayak Explorations from Alaska to Mexico, by Joel W. Rogers. Author Rogers provides an enticing introduction to the splendor of seldom-seen rugged coastal spaces accompanied by stunning color photographs. 168 pp., $19.95

I Am Eskimo: Aknik My Name, by Paul Green with Abbe Abbott. Documentary of Eskimo life at the turn of the century, with illustrations. 96 pp., $12.95

Iditarod: The Great Race to Nome. Photography by Jeff Schultz, text by Bill Sherwonit. Foreword by Joe Redington and preface by Susan Butcher. Powerful photographs provide a dramatic visual record of the courageous human and animal competitors; the text chronicles the origins of the trail and follows the racers on the world's longest sled dog race. 144 pp., $19.95

In the Shadow of Eagles, by Rudy Billberg, as told to Jim Rearden. A true aviation pioneer recounts the adventures of his flying days from a barnstormer to an Alaska bush pilot. 352 pp., $12.95

Journeys Through the Inside Passage, by Joe Upton. Writer and fisherman Joe Upton shares his seafaring adventures along the misty coves and rugged coast of British Columbia and Alaska. 192 pp., $12.95

Juneau: A Book of Woodcuts. Handsome prints by Dale De Armond; a whimsical history of Juneau. 50 pp., 10 x 8, slipcased, $12.95

Kendlers': The Story of a Pioneer Alaska Juneau Dairy, by Mathilde Kendler. A half-century of a young German girl's love affair with Alaska. 168 pp., $7.95

Kootenay Country: One Man's Life in the Canadian Rockies, by Ernest F. "Fee" Hellmen. A compelling account of the author's life fishing, hunting and guiding in the rugged Kootenays of British Columbia. With photographs and a map. 222 pp., $9.95

Living By Water, by Brenda Peterson. A collection of essays reflecting on the ways water shapes the lives and spirits of the inhabitants—animals and humans—near the shores of Puget Sound. 144 pp., hardbound, $15.95; softbound, $9.95

The Lost Patrol, by Dick North. First book to unravel the tragedy of the Mounted Police patrol that perished in the winter of 1910–11 in the Northwest Territories. 149 pp., $9.95

Lowbush Moose (And Other Alaskan Recipes), by Gordon R. Nelson. A former Alaska State trooper adds special flavor to mouthwatering family recipes by telling the stories behind them. 210 pp., $9.95

Martha Black, by Martha Black. The story of a pioneer woman from the Dawson goldfields to the halls of Parliament. 149 pp., $9.95

The MILEPOST® All-the-North Travel Guide®. 1992–93 edition. All travel routes in western Canada and Alaska, with photos and detailed maps. 640 pp., $16.95

More Alaska Bear Tales, by Larry Kaniut. A keen naturalist and seasoned storyteller, author Larry Kaniut in his second book recounts more true encounters between bears and humans. 296 pp., $12.95

The Nature of Southeast Alaska, text by Robert H. Armstrong, Richard Carstensen and Rita M. O'Clair; illustrations by Richard Carstensen; photographs by Robert H. Armstrong and Rita M. O'Clair. An intimate guide to southeastern Alaska's plants, animals and habitats by authors who know the area's most guarded secrets. 256 pp., softbound, $17.95

No Room for Bears, by Frank Dufresne, illustrated by Rachel S. Horne. The author, one of the country's most admired nature writers, weaves together personal adventure tales with bears, along with sketches of the evolution, varieties, and folklore of this extraordinary animal. An outdoor classic. 256 pp., $12.95

Northwest Landscaping, by Mike Munro. This practical guide helps you create the garden you've always wanted, with plenty of practical, hands-on advice. 192 pp., softbound, $16.95

Nome Nuggets, by L.H. French. A soldier of fortune's account of the 1900 Nome gold rush. 64 pp., $5.95

NORTHWEST MILEPOSTS®. A complete guide to Washington, Oregon, Idaho, western Montana and southwestern Canada. 328 pp., $14.95

Northwest Sportsman Almanac. Edited by Terry W. Sheely. Coffee-table beautiful, tackle-box informative guide to outdoor recreation. 304 pp., hardbound, $34.95; softbound, $19.95

Once Upon an Eskimo Time, by Edna Wilder. A one-year (1868) vignette in the 121-year life of an Eskimo woman. 204 pp., $12.95

Pacific Halibut: The Resource and The Fishery, by F. Heward Bell. An impressive book on the history of this fish and fishery. 279 pp., hardbound $24.95; softbound $19.95.

Raven: A Collection of Woodcuts. Dale De Armond woodcuts, Tlingit tales of Raven. Signed, numbered, limited edition. 115 pp., 12 x 12, $100

Raven. Small format edition of Dale De Armond's woodcuts. 80 pp., 8½ x 9, $13.95

Ray Troll's Shocking Fish Tales: Fish, Romance, and Death in Pictures, illustrations by Ray Troll, text by Brad Matsen. Alaskan artist Ray Troll presents the best of his T-shirt and fine art images with Matsen's fascinating mix of legend, natural history, and true stories to remind us that the sea is alive! 48 full-color images, 22 black-and-white drawings, 104 pp., $15.95

Rie Munoz, Alaskan Artist. An illustrated selection of her work. A high-quality collection of limited-edition prints from one of Alaska's foremost artists. 80 pp., $19.95

Ring of Tall Trees, by John Dowd. Dylan's family has just moved to the farm they've always wanted. But a logging company has plans to clear-cut the old-growth forest that surrounds their farm. Calling on Native ritual and myth for help, Dylan and his friends work to save the trees. *Ring of Tall Trees* presents this timely topic in a balanced and informative manner, making this story as appealing to adults as it is to children. For ages 7 to 12. 128 pp., hardbound, $14.95

Roots of Ticasuk: An Eskimo Woman's Family Story, by Emily Ivanoff Brown. Handed down from parent to child to grandchild, this story tells of Eskimo customs and taboos and of attempts to westernize a proud culture. 120 pp., $9.95

Seattle Brews: The Insider's Guide to Neighborhood Alehouses, Brewpubs, and Bars, by Bart Becker. Here at last is the definitive guide to fine, handcrafted beer in Seattle. Come on a guided tour of 100 Seattle area alehouses, brewpubs, and bars. Includes a brief history of local brewing, how to cook with beer, and brewpub listings from Alaska to California. 180 pp., $9.95

Seattle Emergency Espresso: The Insider's Guide to Neighborhood Coffee Spots, by Heather Doran Barbieri. Espresso cravers can now find more than 100 espresso carts, coffeehouses, and cafes. This definitive guide to the local espresso scene also includes profiles of the major roasters, recipes for coffeetime treats, and an introduction to espresso's unique language. 180 pp., $9.95

Seattle Picnics: Favorite Sites, Seasonal Menus, and 100 Recipes, by Barbara Holz Sullivan. Discover little-known gardens and stunning urban grottos around Seattle while enjoying unusual and easy-to-prepare picnic fare. 304 pp., $10.95

S'gana: The Black Whale, by Sue Stauffacher. *S'gana* is the story of a boy's struggle to save a dying killer whale. In the process, he makes discoveries about himself and his Haida Indian past. For ages 7 to 12. 224 pp., hardbound, $15.95

Shamans and Kushtakas, by Mary Giraudo Beck. Nine gripping tales of the battle between the forces of good and evil: a powerful mix of history and legend to dramatize the values and traditions of Tlingit and Haida societies in Southeast Alaska. 128 pp., $12.95

Skagway Story, by Howard Clifford. Skagway in the late 19th century. 180 pp., $9.95

Skystruck: True Tales of an Alaska Bush Pilot, by Herman Lerdahl with Cliff Cernick. From early bush pilot to major airline captain, the remembrances of a lifetime of adventures. 192 pp., $9.95

Smokehouse Bear, by Gordon R. Nelson. Great stories and recipes from Alaska. 180 pp., $9.95

To the Top of Denali: Climbing Adventures on North America's Highest Peak, by Bill Sherwonit. A comprehensive collection of Mount McKinley climbing stories, written for armchair adventurers and seasoned climbers alike. 368 pp., $10.95

Toklat: The Story of an Alaskan Grizzly Bear, by Elma and Alfred Milotte. A children's book about a grizzly and her three cubs. 124 pp., $9.95

Trapline Twins, by Miki and Julie Collins. Tales of the unique lifestyle of identical twin girls in Interior Alaska, trapping, dogsledding, canoeing and living off the land. 224 pp., $12.95

Travelers of the Cold: Sled Dogs of the Far North, by Dominique Cellura. The author traces the history of man and sled dog beginning with Eskimo legend, to the growing interest in the sport of sled dog racing. The strength and character of these animals are captured in beautiful color photographs. 172 pp., hardbound, $32.95

Two in the Far North. Margaret Murie's classic adventure about life on the Alaska frontier. In this edition, Murie extends her story to today's Alaska wilderness and parks issues. 396 pp., $12.95

The War Canoe, by Jamie S. Bryson. A compelling novel about a young Tlingit's coming of age in an Alaska that is enriching its present by recapturing the wisdom of its Native past. 198 pp., $9.95

A Whaler and Trader in the Arctic, by Arthur James Allen. True adventure at the turn of the century. 224 pp., $9.95

Where the Sea Breaks Its Back, by Corey Ford; illustrated by Lois Darling. Walk with early naturalist Georg W. Steller in an epic story of exploration during the days of Russian Alaska. 224 pp., softbound, $12.95

Wild Echoes: Encounters with the Most Endangered Animals in North America, by Charles Bergman. Author Bergman's powerful encounters with endangered species, together with his interviews with experts in the field, bring the reader closer to understanding our role in their survival. 336 pp., $12.95

Winging It!, by Jack Jefford. Pioneer Alaska aviator Jack Jefford was a "pilot's pilot," one who daily faced the dangers of bush flying, helped settle a frontier, and who now tells his own story. 320 pp., $12.95

Winter Watch, by James Ramsey. For 266 days, the author tested himself against the solitude and isolation of an Arctic winter while living in an old log cabin. 154 pp., $9.95

Index

FACTS ABOUT ALASKA: THE ALASKA ALMANAC® has subject categories organized alphabetically for easy reference. Following is an index to the many topics discussed.

Many other fascinating books are available from
Alaska Northwest Books™.
Ask for them at your favorite bookstore,
or write us for a complete free catalog.

Alaska Northwest Books™
A division of GTE Discovery Publications, Inc.
P.O. Box 3007
Bothell, WA 98041-3007
1-800-331-3510